Publishing the Family

 New Americanists *A Series Edited by Donald E. Pease*

THE WHOLE FAMILY

A NOVEL BY
TWELVE AUTHORS

━❧ June Howard ❧━

Publishing the Family

Duke University Press   Durham & London 2001

© 2001 Duke University Press   All rights reserved
Printed in the United States of America on acid-free paper ♾
Designed by C. H. Westmoreland
Typeset in Janson by Tseng Information Systems, Inc.
Library of Congress Cataloging-in-Publication Data
appear on the last printed page of this book.

This publication is made possible in part by an award from
the University of Michigan Publication Subvention Program, funded
by the Office of the Vice President for Research, the College of Literature,
Science and the Arts, the International Institute, the English Department,
and the Program in American Culture.

For Jim, Nick, and Alex

❧ Contents ❧

List of Illustrations   ix | *Acknowledgments   xiii*

Introduction   1

1. "A Strangely Exciting Story"   13
*How It Began / Authorship and Collaboration / Scenes of Reading
and Writing*

2. The Hearthstone at Harper's   58
*Harper's and Antebellum Print Culture: A House Undivided / Harper's
and Postbellum Print Culture: "A Climb up the Spiral Staircase" /
Harper's in the New Century: "Everybody's Busy Day" / A Family
Performance: The Composite Novel as Vaudeville*

3. Making the Family Whole   106
*What Is a Family? / The Father's Family / The Female Counter-family /
Intimacy and Publicity*

4. The Sometimes-New Woman   158
*Sex and Education / The Subtle Syncretism of Mary Wilkins Freeman /
The Extraordinary Miss Jordan / Female Modernity and the Magazine*

5. What Is Sentimentality?   213
*Embodied Thoughts / Feeling Right / Home Sweet Home / Feeling and
Form / Sentimentality in Circulation, circa 1908*

6. Closing the Book   257
Culture and Commerce / Perfect Felicity (with Professional Help)

Appendix 1. Contents and Characters of The Whole Family   *283*
Appendix 2. The Generations of the "Family"   284
Notes   285 | References   305 | Index   331

❧ Illustrations ❧

1. Advertising section, *Harper's Bazar*, December 1906   16
2. Illustration for *The Whole Family*, ch. 2, "The Old-Maid Aunt," *Harper's Bazar*, January 1908   18
3. Table of contents, *Harper's Bazar*, December 1907   39
4. Marie Olivier, "Latest Hints from Paris," *Harper's Bazar*, September 1908   40
5. "Economy in Dress," *Harper's Bazar*, October 1908   41
6. "For Older Women," *Harper's Bazar*, April 1908   42
7. "In the Public Eye," *Harper's Bazar*, January 1908   43
8. "The Housemother's Problems," *Harper's Bazar*, December 1907   44
9. Mary Heaton Vorse, "Some Experiences of a Mother," *Harper's Bazar*, June 1908   45
10. Charles William Eliot, "The Higher Education for Women," *Harper's Bazar*, June 1908   46
11. John Kendrick Bangs, "Miss de Billion in Paris," *Harper's Bazar*, June 1906   47
12. Lilian Whiting, "A Magic Moment," *Harper's Bazar*, August 1908   48
13. W. G. Fitz-Gerald, "Women in the High Alps," *Harper's Bazar*, June 1908   49
14. Josephine Grenier, "Veranda Meals," *Harper's Bazar*, July 1908   50
15. "Crochet Insertions and Medallions," *Harper's Bazar*, July 1908   51
16. Advertisements, *Harper's Bazar*, December 1908   52
17. "Twelve Popular Authors Join in Writing a Splendid Novel," *Harper's Bazar*, December 1908   56
18. Harper's Franklin Square building, with the Cliff Street building visible in the rear, from Eugene Exman, *The House of Harper*   61
19. "Sectional view of the Cliff Street building," from Jacob Abbott, *The Harper Establishment*   62

20. "The Power-Press," from Jacob Abbott, *The Harper Establishment* 63

21. Thomas Nast, "The Universal Cry," from *Thomas Nast's Almanac, 1872* 65

22. Undated photograph of Fletcher, James, John, and J. Wesley Harper by Matthew Brady 67

23. Cover used for Harper's catalogs, 1847 and 1848 74

24. Colophon from title page of Mary Wilkins Freeman's *Six Trees* (1903) 75

25. "The Counting-Room," from Jacob Abbott, *The Harper Establishment* 76

26. Floor plan, from Jacob Abbott, *The Harper Establishment* 76

27. Photograph of Colonel Harvey's office at Franklin Square, from Eugene Exman, *The House of Harper* 91

28. At Colonel Harvey's home, December 1907, from Eugene Exman, *The House of Harper* 92

29. Illustration for *The Whole Family*, ch. 5, "The School-Girl," *Harper's Bazar*, April 1908 119

30. Line drawing of mansard roof, from Virginia McAlester and Lee McAlester, *A Field Guide to American Houses* 126

31. Illustration for *The Whole Family*, ch. 3, "The Grandmother," *Harper's Bazar*, February 1908 137

32. Sideboard, unknown (American), 1855–65 142

33. Illustration for *The Whole Family*, ch. 4, "The Daughter-in-law," *Harper's Bazar*, March 1908 145

34. Detail from "In Jocund Vein," *Harper's Bazar*, December 1907 154

35. Detail from "In Jocund Vein," *Harper's Bazar*, January 1908 154

36. Illustration for *The Whole Family*, ch. 1, "The Father," *Harper's Bazar*, December 1907 167

37. Photograph of Mary Wilkins Freeman by Floride Green, 1900 174

38. Illustration for Mary Wilkins Freeman, "Billy and Susy," *Harper's Bazar*, November 1907 176

39. Illustration for Mary Wilkins Freeman, "Billy and Susy," *Harper's Bazar*, November 1907 178

40. Elizabeth Jordan at seventeen, from *Three Rousing Cheers* 181

41. Elizabeth Jordan at thirty, from *Three Rousing Cheers* 184

42. Illustration for *The Whole Family*, ch. 5, "The School-Girl," *Harper's Bazar*, April 1908 196

43. Illustration for Mary Stewart Cutting, "Oil of Gladness," *Harper's Bazar*, December 1907 197

44. Title decoration for "The Confessions of a Professional Woman," by Anne O'Hagan, *Harper's Bazar*, September 1907 200

45. Title decoration for "The Married Woman and the Spinster," by Anne O'Hagan, *Harper's Bazar*, July 1907 200

46. Ed Frascino, cartoon, "Diary of a Traditional Woman/Diary of a New Woman," *New Woman*, June 1971   208

47. Advertisement, *New Woman*, June 1971   209

48. Cover, *New Woman*, January 1999   210

49. Advertisement, *New Woman*, January 1999   210

50. Illustration for *The Whole Family*, ch. 10, "The School-Boy," *Harper's Bazar*, September 1908   252

51. Frontispiece and title page from *The Very Little Person*, by Mary Heaton Vorse (1911)   255

52. End decoration for *The Whole Family*, ch. 12, "The Friend of the Family," *Harper's Bazar*, November 1908   258

53. Oak and mahogany sideboard with iron hardware, 1912–16   264

54. Photograph of Henry James by Alice Broughton, *Harper's Bazar*, July 1907   267

Color Plates *(between pages 114 and 115)*

Plate 1. Edward Hopper, "The Mansard Roof," 1923

Plate 2. Cover, *Harper's Bazar* December 1907

Plate 3. Cover, *Harper's Bazar* April 1905

Plate 4. Cover, *Harper's Bazar* August 1906

Plate 5. Cover, *Harper's Bazar* July 1906

Plate 6. Cover, *Harper's Bazar* May 1907

Plate 7. Cover, *Harper's Bazar* September 1908

Plate 8. Cover, *Harper's Bazar* July 1908

Plate 9. Illustration for *The Whole Family*, ch. 12, "The Friend of the Family," *Harper's Bazar*, November 1908

⟡ Acknowledgments ⟡

It has been my good fortune, during the years in which I intermittently researched and composed this book, to be part of an extraordinary intellectual community at the University of Michigan. I have had wonderful partners in inquiry outside Ann Arbor as well. Public thanking is a sentimental practice I have come to understand and appreciate in the course of this project; and this is my chance to express my gratitude to those who have been—in the most utopian sense of the word—my colleagues. I mean most of all those named below, but also many other people who have contributed to the spirit of interdisciplinary adventure and principled critique that has made my work possible: especially locally, in the Programs in American Culture and Women's Studies and the English Department, and nationally, in the American Studies Association. Those who have sustained and helped me range from students who were not concerned with the book I was writing but with whom I had lively dialogues about issues and authors to scholars I have never met but whose writing transformed my thinking. I hope that this study in some measure reflects the exhilaration I have felt in conversations over the past decade and more.

I am profoundly grateful to the colleagues who commented on the manuscript and strengthened it by their suggestions. Sandra Zagarell read every chapter at least once, and some chapters in several drafts—often taking time she could not easily spare from her own work and always offering encouragement and insightful suggestions in perfectly balanced proportions. David Scobey and Jonathan Freedman were indispensable interlocutors, and my conversations with them constantly influenced me. I thank Rebecca Zurier and Abby Stewart for their generosity in supporting my efforts in their fields of expert knowledge, in chapters 4 and 5, respectively. At a crucial moment, Sidonie Smith helped me to conceptualize the whole. I greatly benefited from comments on portions of the manuscript by Lauren Berlant, Sara Blair, Julie Ellison, Gordon Hutner, Anita Norich, Adela Pinch, and Priscilla Wald. Gina Hausknecht, Kate Masur, and Grace Wang, who assisted me with the project, made important contributions of several sorts. I thank Michael McCullough, who years ago as an undergraduate student first got me interested in *The Whole Family*. I would also like to thank the anonymous readers who gave their time and counsel, and my editors at Duke University Press: Katie Courtland and Ken Wissoker; their patient, thoughtful work with my manuscript has made the book much stronger.

I also thank the University of Michigan's Humanities Institute, and the College of Literature, Science and the Arts for leaves that allowed me to concentrate on this project for several semesters. I want especially to thank Earl Lewis, Dean of the Horace H. Rackham School of Graduate Studies, for support that enabled me to finish the manuscript.

These acknowledgments so far have recognized the professional conditions of possibility for my writing. The dedication recognizes a different horizon—the companions of my everyday and happiest life, my partner, Jim Dean, and my sons, Nicholas and Alexander Dean. I am fortunate indeed to have them conjure with me something that goes by the name of the family—incorporating the thick connectedness of kinship, the friction and delight of living under one roof, and the intricate immersions of intimacy. Their conversation and their love have informed this work at every moment. I thank them for making everything possible, and also for leaving me alone in my study now and then.

An abridged version of chapter 5 appeared in *American Literary History;* my thanks to that journal for allowing the material to appear both there and here. Finally, let me thank the institutions and individuals who allowed me to include some images among all these words. The University of Michigan's Office of the Vice-President for Research, Department of English, and American Culture Program subsidized the inclusion of color plates. I am grateful for permissions from the New York Public Library, the Library of Congress, the Brooklyn Museum, Alfred A. Knopf and Random House, the Yale University Art Gallery, the University of Virginia Library, cartoonbank.com (for the *New Yorker*), Max Palevsky and the Los Angeles County Museum of Art, and the Special Collections Department of the University of Michigan Library.

❧ Introduction ❧

Each month from December 1907 through November 1908, one chapter of a novel titled *The Whole Family* appeared in *Harper's Bazar*,* accompanied by a list of its twelve authors and an invitation to readers to guess which one was responsible for that month's contribution. Book publication by Harper & Brothers followed immediately after the final chapter appeared. The idea for this composite novel originated with William Dean Howells, who established its opening scenario in a chapter focusing on the father of the family; the project was coordinated by Elizabeth Jordan, editor of *Harper's Bazar*, who wrote a chapter as well. Other contributors included Henry James, Mary Wilkins Freeman, Elizabeth Stuart Phelps, Mary Heaton Vorse, and writers widely known at the time but rarely remembered today, such as the prolific humorist John Kendrick Bangs and Mary Stewart Cutting, author of *Little Stories of Married Life, Little Stories of Courtship*, and *The Suburban Whirl*. Jordan devotes an entire chapter of her autobiography to an entertaining account of this collaboration; Alfred Bendixen corrects and publicizes the story in his introduction to a 1986 reprinting of the novel. Both Jordan and subsequent commentators write of the contributors as themselves constituting a sort of literary family—an extremely quarrelsome one.

Each author was asked to contribute a chapter from the point of view of a particular member of the family. Building on but contesting the characterizations Howells had sketched out, each wrote as an advocate

---

*The Harpers originally named the magazine after the German fashion magazine *Der Bazar*, and its title was not spelled with two *a*'s until 1929.

for the virtues and views of that individual—and therefore frequently countered the claims of earlier chapters. Is the unmarried aunt (the role assigned to Freeman) a pathetic, man-hungry spinster or a charming modern woman? Is the "artistic" son (played, unsurprisingly, by James) an ineffectual dilettante or the book's true center of consciousness? The reader begins to wonder—will one of the daughter's suitors be capable of sustaining the role of hero, and can the multiplying tensions of the novel be contained by the narrative resolution of a marriage?

More questions arise for the literary critic and historian. How do we interpret a text that does not have a single author? Why would workers in the culture industry undertake such a collaboration, and does this assemblage of writers usually sorted into very different categories change our view of the relation between "high" and "low" culture in early twentieth-century America? What can we learn about the gender-inflected nature of writing and reading from a project in which eight female and four male writers worked together to produce a text for a women's magazine? What about this historical moment led the contributors to try to define the American family, and what do their pitched battles over gender roles and family values tell us about contemporary attitudes? Why did the project become so contentious and charged, and why does it engage the imagination with such persistence?

The story of *The Whole Family*—by which I mean both the series of events through which the novel was created and the tale it conveys—affords an extraordinary point of entry for an examination of print culture and social life in the early twentieth century. My approach may be described as "microhistory"—a term borrowed from European historians who use it not simply for any small-scale investigation, but specifically for those that begin with the particular in order to enter into the interconnections of things. Giovanni Levi suggests that to understand the simple act of buying a loaf of bread one must study the world's grain markets. Similarly, to read this composite fiction I reconstruct a complex landscape of literary institutions and ongoing struggles over meanings and values. Thus this is not a book "about" *The Whole Family*. (I hope that my work will prompt some readers to turn to the novel to assess my claims and reach their own conclusions about its significance, but I provide enough information in my exposition to make it unnecessary to know that book in order to read this one.) Neither is it about the stack of magazines containing the novel's separate chapters, or the authors who contributed to it, or even the response of its readers. My object of study is a historical process refracted through an episode.

Another name for my approach—centered in literary scholarship and history but drawing on other disciplines as well—is American studies. Conversations in that broad field have been central to my intellectual life during the years in which this book was researched and composed, and it may be considered a contribution to the famously frustrated "search for a method." In my view, that search need not be imagined as a quest motivated by yearning for a permanent procedure—for some sort of methodological grail that would end doubt and struggle by providing infallible access to knowledge. Rather, the value of American studies is precisely that it is such a well-established site for relentlessly experimental and self-reflective dialogue. Continuing the conversation, this volume suggests an alternative to the strategy of many influential American studies books—from Henry Nash Smith's *Virgin Land* through Eric Lott's *Love and Theft* and Lisa Lowe's *Immigrant Acts*—that track one complex and consequential idea through many sites. I greatly admire those works and recognize that they find different things in different places; but an increasing wariness of sweeping narratives has led me to choose a more stubbornly empirical approach. I examine one complex site traversed by many ideas and forces.

My strategy does not eliminate such narratives, of course; I could not eschew them even if I wanted to, for any powerful category that purports to describe social life at any level—from "author" and "literature" to "public" or "private" to "American" and "modern"—implies at least one immense system. Each of the chapters that follow takes a distinctive shape in response to its topic; yet each undertakes some common tasks. Each at some point examines the conceptual categories that define its object of study, self-reflectively investigating the social maps and narrative traces embedded in its vocabulary. Each also selectively surveys relevant scholarship in several fields, sketching the intellectual landscape that is the condition of possibility for my work. Each offers thick description of some aspect of the historical period. Each puts the story of *The Whole Family* and materials associated with it, such as the lives and works of its authors, articles that appeared with it in *Harper's*

Bazar, and other closely contemporary publications and events, into dialogue with those discussions. The separation of these tasks from one another is only heuristic; each involves the others in a thoroughly recursive process. Nevertheless, if I interrogated all of these elements all the time, it would become impossible to write comprehensible sentences; I have tried to be rigorous without becoming overly involuted. Similarly, writing for an interdisciplinary audience entails explaining matters well known in one field but not in others; I have done my best to provide expositions that are at once thought-provoking and accessible.

Another crucial reference point for my approach is the tradition of Western Marxist cultural criticism. Here too, even more urgently, I am engaged with—that is, I both draw on and resist—powerful, sweeping narratives. I take for granted not only the possibility but the vitality of a nonreductionist, nondeterminist historical materialism that attends seriously to culture and agency, in which no outcomes are known and an ethical commitment to social transformation has been separated from any putative science of society. I think this is best called, in Stuart Hall's expressive phrase, "a marxism without guarantees." Marxist thought, whether upper- or lowercased, has constantly offered an important alternative to the disciplines, providing an impetus and framework for integrative thought that is one of the wellsprings of the current efflorescence of interdisciplinary scholarship.

Because this book generates its critical space by moving between close study of a moment and narratives of historical change, periodization emerges as an especially salient methodological problem. The story of *The Whole Family* demonstrates that ideas and habits usually depicted as following one another in sequence actually coexist. Historical actors circulate through a variety of unevenly developed institutions; and they think syncretically, creating constellations of attitudes that enable them to live through changes without starting over. A microhistorical approach allows me to treat this single episode as an untidy conglomeration of practices, each showing the traces of many past moments. Periodization represents diachronic process by a synchronic figure; its basic gesture is to create a time line divided into labeled sections (with more or less prominent acknowledgments of blurring at their boundaries). I visualize what I do instead as unraveling and following threads of disparate materials and varied lengths braided into a

particular historical "moment." In some sense, then, what I offer is a *refine*
diachronic account of the synchronic.

This effort to capture the irregular complexity of historical process
follows a multitude of others, of course. It especially shows the influence of Raymond Williams's argument in *Marxism and Literature* that
cultures include dominant, residual, and emergent elements. A history
braided of those three strands still seems to me too regular, and the
narrative of a fixed sequence of modes of production lingers in the off-
ing. Yet Williams makes it clear that residual practices not only per-
sist but are remade for current situations, that the dominant is always
a partial system, that not all innovations are oppositional—and so on,
until the relations of the elements are satisfyingly tangled. Also, *emergent* avoids the teleological term *progressive* (found so often in Marxist
and other committed criticisms), which with its embedded notion of
progress toward a better future strongly implies the racialized story of
advancing "civilization" that is a recurring topic in the chapters that
follow.

Challenges to "master" narratives have arisen both as methodological resistances and through the recognition that they are inadequate
to the perspective of subordinated groups. The story of civilization is
not just changed but invalidated by the counternarrative of the color
line, and by asking if women had a Renaissance. Feminist scholarship—
another indispensable interdisciplinary reference point for my work—
has been particularly rich in critiques of periodization (see J. Kelly;
Warren and Dickie). I have generally reacted skeptically to the assertion that "the master's tools will never dismantle the master's house"
—not so much to Audre Lorde's original and devastating critique of
academic feminism as to the way the phrase has been taken to mean
that existing approaches are hopelessly contaminated—because I believe that the engaged critic cannot afford to discard levers like logic.
The ensuing twenty years have perhaps sublated that disagreement, as
the basic conceptual constructs of intellectual work—the tools of the
trade—have been transformed in our hands. The far-reaching, ongoing
recovery of the history and culture of communities of color has fundamentally changed what scholars mean by "American." In a postcolonial
and globalizing world, the institution of national literature has become
the object of our study rather than its assumed grounding. Masculinity,

whiteness, the nation appear not as obvious facts but as hegemonizing maneuvers in complex systems. This book is a contribution to metropolitan literary history focused through a publication of the New York-based house of Harper's, one of the most powerful commercial cultural institutions of the Empire City, and it depends at every point on a broader—even less easily plotted and periodized—understanding of cultural history in which official "America" is no longer the center. It is a feminist literary history that contests both canonical ignorance of women's work and the claim that there is a separate women's tradition. I first became interested in *The Whole Family* years ago because it shows the literary marketplace as gender-inflected but not segregated. Again, it no longer seems necessary to argue this question; both the gendering of authorship and female authors' engagement in mixed discourses are well established.

Let me say clearly that I am not opposing periodization. Again, a retreat from historical argument only mires one in unexamined narratives: apparently arbitrary divisions using round numbers and the assumption that materials with the same date are connected are underpinned by a notion of empty, abstract time that is itself distinctively modern. What I am doing is taking periodization very seriously—as a cognitive enterprise difficult enough, and consequential enough, that we should consistently question not only its claims but also its categories. Like genre criticism, it realizes its power as a practice of interpretation and explanation, not classification. I would argue that this is so across the historical disciplines, but most confidently that it is an indispensable recognition for literary history. The claim that language and literature not only reflect but also shape experience and events—implicit in everything I have said so far, and fundamental to what follows—scarcely needs to be argued these days; yet it is more often asserted as a principle, or assumed as a truism, than demonstrated in detail. I use the method of microhistory because I have found both the precision of a close focus and the breadth of a long perspective necessary for making rigorous arguments about that impress of culture on history. The social agency of the literary is not exerted within any single instant or on an era in general; yet it can be pressed into visibility by constructing a dialogue between historical particulars and periodizations of various kinds.

6   *Publishing the Family*

micro history

My sources and my methods are eclectic, within the broad and contested field of historicism. My effort to write criticism that neither reduces history to a setting nor reduces literature to an effect follows Roy Harvey Pearce's affirmation, in his 1958 defense of historicism against the dominance of formalism, that "[l]iterature is not an expression of (or above) history, but rather an expression *in* history" (35). I have been influenced by Fredric Jameson's injunction in *The Political Unconscious* to "Always historicize!" (9), and by his compelling accounts of the relations of cultural forms and modes of production; but most important for my topic here is his magisterial "Marxism and Historicism." That essay frames the philosophical problems of identity and historical otherness, the possible connections and estrangements of past and present, as I will not begin to do here; it has made historicism thinkable again after the poststructuralist assaults on it. The "new historicism" has also, in a very different way, demonstrated that criticism can be both historically oriented and informed by poststructuralism. In many versions it shifts attention from artifacts to practices and posits the discursive and material as reciprocal; in Louis Montrose's account, its concern with the relation of synchrony and diachrony, with "the historicity of texts and the textuality of histories" (410), is congruent with my own.

I am, of course, emphasizing the common ground rather than the ample disagreements of these approaches. What I seek on that terrain is the ability to apprehend both the past-ness and the present-ness of the past. The fundamental contention of historicism is that no human phenomenon can be adequately understood apart from its place in history; the people of even such a recent past as the early twentieth century were *different* from us, and a concerted effort is required to imagine them and their world. Yet historicism in the sense in which I mean it is not antiquarianism, collecting obsolete otherness for its own sake. Nor can it be merely empirical—history as the proverbial "one damned thing after another." When we study the past we recursively double and redouble our involvement in it; for we too can be understood only in history, yet we exercise agency within it. It is not—precisely not—that we recognize ourselves in the past, but that we learn to tell a story that links past and present and shapes our future.

In some sense these are the same goals I have pursued in all my published work; I have written before about the irrevocable openness of the historical moment, about the challenges of periodization and our own placement in the narratives we create. I have become more skeptical of grand narratives, replacing History with histories, but also more confident of our ability to achieve a more limited knowledge. These problems of historical alterity now seem to me continuous with those of particularism and universalism, cultural relativism and ethical commitment, community and cosmopolitanism—oppositions that occupy the foreground of American intellectual debate at the turns into both the twentieth and the twentieth-first centuries and which I will pursue elsewhere. In *The Whole Family* (I have realized somewhat belatedly) I have chosen a topic that foregrounds precisely such questions of the relation between the part and the (possibly) whole—between the chapter and the novel, the moment and the story.

In the early twentieth century, the gesture of equating a publishing enterprise and a family evoked powerful fantasies of wholeness and fears of fragmentation. These fabulations both turn on the most basic dilemmas of modern identity and social organization, and depend on particular historical circumstances such as the workplace culture at Harper's. Sometimes tensions are explicitly thematized. Howells specified the conflict between individuality and family life as the novel's theme and wanted to engage the controversy over coeducation then current in the periodicals—thus doubly invoking changes in the position of women, although he was dismayed when the "New Woman" entered the scene as the independent spinster rather than the college girl. Sometimes tensions are played out at the level of form— Howells probably envisioned the novel as realistic, but the chapters deploy wildly various literary conventions. Henry James was so distressed by what he called the sentimentality of the chapters following his that he wrote to Jordan wishing he could have "saved" the novel by finishing it single-handed. One reviewer observed at the time that as one "turn" followed another, "characteristic and amusing" but disconnected, *The Whole Family* became a kind of literary vaudeville performance. Yet in the first decade of the twentieth century vaudeville itself conjured a potent solidarity, forging a national audience by appealing to highly diverse and dispersed audiences through a booking system centralized in New York. The composite novel too embodies a deeper dynamic of unity and disunity.

The early twentieth-century writers and readers of *Harper's Bazar* would have taken it for granted that a family consisted of blood relations residing together. Although cross-cultural observation shows clearly that kinship and household are not necessarily combined, vernacular and much expert discourse of the present day makes the same conflation. Similarly, the fact that the English royals and the family farm continue (however tenuously) to exist somehow fails to remind us that the separation of kinship from state, and household from economy, is a relatively recent historical phenomenon. Such forgetfulness itself entails the naturalization of the family, as an apparently inevitable yet perpetually endangered institution that provides both the forum of politics and the economic marketplace with "individuals" as participants. The progressive concentration of emotional bonds into the home and the loss of other identifications amalgamates intimacy as a third element in the deceptively self-evident, self-sufficient wholeness of the family—and all this common sense requires a great deal of storytelling.

The cultural work that creates the image of the family as a haven in a heartless world is powerfully aligned with that which, as the reach of the culture industry expands, figures art as a realm of value above commerce. Works of cultural studies have argued that the novel serves as a school for selves, occupying a privileged position in the formation of modern interiority and gender identity. Other works have shown that those reading experiences are incorporated into racialized narratives of the nation. Yet others have asserted that the very concept of the aesthetic is made possible by the detachment of expressive culture from concrete social relations in a world of commodity production. Both the family and literature are imagined as realms that form subjectivities and provide arenas for a satisfying affective life—and in both cases the very gesture that forms a protected enclave also surrounds it with forces that constantly threaten invasion. It is perhaps still useful, but certainly not sufficient, to observe that the home is no haven, and art no ivory tower; we need to go on to investigate the nature of these institutions' permeability, the significance of their imputed isolation, the puzzle of their profound affinity. Lines drawn between private and public, between culture and commerce, are—like racial categories and national borders—divisions that can never divide. That does not stop them from having effects. They project bounded entities, set the terms of connectedness, and are woven together in circuits of reciprocally stabilized instabilities with real consequences. It is this process that I examine in the pages that follow.

The chapters of this work are organized topically. Each frames broad conceptual questions and offers a historical and interpretive argument that can be read independently, while meshing with the other chapters to develop an expansive reading of *The Whole Family*.

The first chapter lays the groundwork by telling the story of the novel's production and reception, and considering the nature of the "composite novel" and its challenge to commonsensical understandings of authorship. Chapter 2 takes the publishing house as its unit of literary-historical analysis. It demonstrates what a powerful and pervasive presence Harper & Brothers was in American cultural life of the nineteenth century and reexamines the striking story of the house's modernization in the early twentieth century. I conclude that the family business Harper & Brothers in a real sense "authored" *The Whole Family,* and that close attention to its history requires us to revise our understanding of the literary marketplace at the turn of the century, balancing the current emphasis on "culture" as the site of distinctions between popular and elite with more attention to mixed and middling readerships.

Chapter 3 turns directly to the topic of the family, offering a critical account of the category and sketching the invention, in the early twentieth century, of the family as an object of sociological study and the location of a crisis. Howells mingles perceived problems and proposed solutions into his chapter's apparently celebratory portrait of middle-class domestic life, and subsequent chapters mount emphatic critiques of the institution. This concern with changing gender roles continues in chapter 4, which reconstructs the renewed controversy over coeducation during the first decade of the twentieth century and considers the versions of female modernity mapped out in the life and works of Mary Wilkins Freeman and Elizabeth Jordan. Those instances, some examples drawn from Jordan's *Bazar,* and a few drawn from the late twentieth-century magazine *New Woman* demonstrate how persistently women reinvent themselves by synthesizing tradition and innovation.

Chapter 5 takes up a question that arises from the controversies of the contributors to *The Whole Family* and has also been much debated in American literary history. It places the concept of "sentiment" in terms of recent work on emotion in the social and biological sciences, and argues for reclaiming the category's link to eighteenth-century "sympathy" and against the conflation of domestic ideology and literary sentimentality. This chapter makes a long circuit away from and back to the composite novel itself, yet the issues it engages refract, in terms of form, those that concern the others: the relation of art and commerce, the individual and the social, the private and the public. Its perspective on sentimentality allows us to appreciate both the literary-historical ironies and the cultural purchase of some of the latter chapters of the novel. Throughout, but here especially, the story of the heterosocial undertaking of *The Whole Family* demonstrates that notions of "separate spheres" are forces within social life, not descriptions, and certainly not analyses.

The final chapter considers how the collaborators' disparate understandings of the relation of culture and commerce, and their affiliations with disparate genres, are played out in the latter part of the novel. Its last two chapters mobilize not only the marriage plot but the power of professionalism and nationalism to achieve narrative closure.

Taken in its entirety, this volume calls on a wide range of scholarship in literary, cultural, and social history and theory. Assuming an interdisciplinary audience unevenly familiar with those knowledges, I provide conceptual maps of issues and thick descriptions of the period that often synthesize what is known, and sometimes innovate. Such investigations are of interest in themselves, and—as is no doubt clear already—they frequently lead me far from *The Whole Family.* Yet the microhistorical perspective counters any temptation to find at the local level only the working out of a general narrative known in advance (whether of possessive individualism, consumer culture, or another of the marvelously powerful paradigms of contemporary scholarship). I return regularly to the novel, and I do not take it as an allegory of the dialogic nature of the text or of any set of social contradictions, any more than spots are a metaphor for measles. It is, rather, an index—a sign that is an integral part of the formations to which it points. My goal is to apprehend both the detail and the horizon, and to contribute both to the understanding of a particular moment in American history and to the development of our frameworks for critical analysis of culture and social life.

Both particular moment
&
Develop methods

1

The whole family --
Novel creation.

❧ "A Strangely Exciting Story" ❧

How It Began

In the spring of 1906 William Dean Howells suggested an unusual idea for a serial to Elizabeth Jordan, the editor of *Harper's Bazar.* "He thought it might be interesting," Jordan wrote many years later, "to publish a novel of twelve chapters, to be written by twelve authors, under the title *The Whole Family.* Of these, eleven would write their chapters as supposed members of that family, while a twelfth, the Friend of the Family, would 'sum up' in the final chapter." [1] Howells disclaimed any intention of asking the contributors to conform to his conception of the characters, writing to Jordan that they "must be left in entire freedom." But he worked out the plan of the book in some detail, specifying that the family should consist of a grandmother, who would "open the affair," a father, mother, son and daughter-in-law, daughter and son-in-law, a little girl and boy, a maiden aunt on either the father's or mother's side, a young girl, and the female friend who was to sum up. He also suggested eight writers (including himself, Samuel Clemens, Mary Wilkins Freeman, and Jordan) and proposed that "[t]he family might be in some such moment of vital agitation as that attending the Young Girl's engagement, or pending engagement, and each witness could treat of it in character. There could be fun enough, but each should try seriously to put himself or herself really into the personage's place. I think the more seriously the business was treated, the better." [2]

Howells clearly understood the impossibility of retaining control over such a collaboration but could not resist the temptation to try. He closed his letter with "Excuse the meddling," only to add after his signature, "P.S. The note of the whole might be confidential, but kindly criticism, reciprocal, among all the characters, but especially leaving open the Young Girl and her betrothed." He seems to have envisioned *The Whole Family* as an amusing, circulation-building novelty for the *Bazar*, yet also to have cherished the hope that it would be a substantial work of literature. It would provide a forum for discussing issues of the day—Howells specifically mentioned coeducation—and presumably model the sort of literary realism he had long advocated; he envisioned a family "in middling circumstances, of average culture and experiences," and wrote when he sent his chapter to Jordan that he had been "feeling for the great American average in the situation." He took the project "seriously" enough to be dismayed when other members of the fictional family actually took liberties with his design.

Jordan was enthusiastic about the idea of producing what she calls in her autobiography a "composite novel," and set to work lining up contributors at once. She had high aspirations: "[W]ith Mr. Howells making the first drive from the literary tee, and the cooperation of Henry James and Mark Twain practically assured, my ambition was to bring together what P. T. Barnum would have called the greatest, grandest, most gorgeous group of authors ever collaborating on a literary production" (258). Those invited to participate were linked to Harper & Brothers Publishers by varied avenues: several were closely associated with the house as editors and authors, several were linked to those by friendship, some regularly published books with the firm, some published elsewhere but contributed to Harper's periodicals, especially the *Bazar*. Alfred Bendixen writes in his introduction to the 1986 reprinting of the novel that the project was "designed to be a showplace for Harper's family of authors" (xiii), which describes Jordan's desire although it exaggerates the coherence of the final list (see appendix 1). As Bendixen points out, only an enormous and prestigious publishing company like Harper's, with the aid of an influential writer and critic like Howells, could possibly have succeeded in mounting such a collaboration.

Indications of the difficulties ahead appeared immediately when some of Howells's and Jordan's first choices declined to participate and the planned order of the contributions had to be altered to accommodate the schedules of those who agreed. Jordan takes, throughout the chapter of her autobiography she devotes to *The Whole Family*, a comically rueful tone. "Several authors were tied up and could not write a chapter till their contracts had been carried out. Others could not begin the work for two years. My daily mail was made up of large problems. Many authors preferred to write chapters other than those assigned to them—often chapters already assigned to some one else. The mother selected yearned to contribute the chapter of the married daughter; the selected son-in-law passionately preferred to be the friend of the family. Every author except Mr. Howells desired to write a final chapter" (261). Nevertheless, by December 1906 *The Whole Family* was being advertised as forthcoming in *Harper's Bazar* (see fig. 1), with Mark Twain, who eventually declined, listed among the contributors.

The troubles of this early period were a mere intimation of what was to follow. In the event, Howells opened the novel with a chapter on the father of the family. Jordan sent proofs to all the contributors, who read it, she reports, "with the interest and respect due to the work of the Dean of American Literature." Among the other contributors only Mary Wilkins Freeman, who was to represent the maiden aunt, was free to write her chapter immediately, and it was when Jordan sent out the proofs of the second chapter that "the epoch-making row of *The Whole Family* began!" (263). The authors speedily constituted themselves as advocates for the characters they represented and began to engage in "reciprocal" criticism notably lacking in the "kindly" tone Howells had suggested.

Freeman did not think Howells had treated her character very well; Jordan, concurring, writes that he "had relegated Elizabeth to the chimney corner. He was not interested in her" (263). Freeman makes her single by choice, "as pretty and as up-to-date" (in Jordan 266) as a young girl, and deposits her squarely in the middle of the action by revealing that the young man to whom her niece Peggy has just become engaged is actually in love with Elizabeth (see fig. 2). "This wholly unexpected twist of the tale proved to be the explosion of a bomb-shell on our literary hearthstone," Jordan writes. "Every author on the list dropped all other interests to write me about it. They all knew me well, and many of them were my friends. They wrote intimately and in a state of high excitement" (264). Some approved, feeling that the first chapter had been slow moving and that the second offered more possibilities for

HARPER'S BAZAR
FOR 1907

N 1907 **HARPER'S BAZAR** will enter upon the fortieth year of its long and honorable career. It will also enter upon a new era, upon an even broader, greater field than the one it has filled so admirably in the past.

HARPER'S BAZAR will continue to be the magazine of the up-to-date woman. It will still be the court of final appeal in all questions of fashion, entertainment, household decoration, and good form But it will be more than this. It will be "guide, philosopher, and friend" to countless women of less experience, less opportunity, narrower environment, simpler ideals.

Many thousands of women living in the small towns of the South and West are now among the readers of the **BAZAR.** To be a practical help to all our readers, and to follow more and more the trend of the time which, among the best people, is away from ostentation toward simplicity, the **BAZAR** will preach rational economy. Its fashions will still be the most beautiful published, but there will also be page after page of eminently practical designs for women of simple tastes and small incomes.

Among our strongest departments will be one containing **FRENCH LESSONS ON ECONOMY IN DRESS,** by Flora McDonald Thompson. Mrs. Thompson will tell **BAZAR** readers from month to month the secrets of the perfectly dressed French women, women who dress better, at less cost, than any other women in the world.

IN ITS DOMESTIC DEPARTMENTS, long famous, every reader of **HARPER'S BAZAR** will find something *for her*. There will be elaborate menus and simpler menus, suggestions for the most novel, up-to-date luncheons and dinners, and for the plainest home repasts. This magazine will live strictly up to its motto:

"If you want to *know*, ask the BAZAR."

Among the strong literary features planned for 1907, **HARPER'S BAZAR** will publish

Elizabeth Stuart Phelps's Great Novel **WALLED IN** *With illustrations by Clarence F. Underwood*

WOMEN AND SOCIETY
By Right Reverend Henry C. Potter, Bishop of New York.
A series of papers turning upon the various questions of to-day as they affect American women.

HENRY JAMES ON THE MANNERS OF AMERICAN WOMEN. A brilliant series of papers following his articles now appearing in HARPER'S BAZAR, "The Speech of American Women."

1. Advertising section. *Harper's Bazar* 40.12
(December 1906): 10–11.

THE LIFE BEYOND THIS. Three contributions of extraordinary interest by Elizabeth Stuart Phelps.

AND

THE WHOLE FAMILY

A novel of twelve chapters—each chapter to be written by a different American author. Thus the list reads:

The Father: William Dean Howells.
The Mother: Edith Wyatt.
The Grandmother: Mary Heaton Vorse.
The Small Boy: Mark Twain.
The Daughter-in-law: Mary Stewart Cutting.
The Son-in-law: John Kendrick Bangs.
The Married Son:
The Married Daughter:
The School Girl: Elizabeth Jordan.
The Young Girl (engaged): Alice Brown.
The Maiden Aunt: Mary E. Wilkins Freeman.
The Friend of the Family: Dr. Henry Van Dyke.

OUR PRACTICAL FEATURES.

Among the **BAZAR'S** 1907 list of pre-eminently practical features by experts on the different domestic lines, are the following:

MARIANNA WHEELER'S TALKS TO MOTHERS. By the ex-Superintendent of the Babies' Hospital of New York City.

MISS MARTHA CUTLER'S PAPERS ON HOMES AND HOME DECORATION. Illustrated by herself.

JOSEPHINE GRENIER'S NEW AND EXCLUSIVE RECIPES. Illustrated with photographs.

MARION FOSTER WASHBURNE'S ARTICLES ON THE TRAINING OF CHILDREN.

HARPER'S BAZAR PAPER PATTERNS—some at 25 cents, others at 15 cents each—prices which bring them within the reach of all women.

HARPER'S BAZAR for 1907 will be bigger, better, more interesting, more helpful than ever before. The price of single copies is fifteen cents each. The subscription price is only one dollar a year. *Send in your subscription now.*

| "If you want to *know,* ask the Bazar." | MAKE YOUR FRIENDS HAPPY by sending them HARPER'S BAZAR as a CHRISTMAS GIFT | "Harper's Bazar Sets the Fashion." |

HARPER & BROTHERS, PUBLISHERS

2. Illustration for *The Whole Family*,
ch. 2, "The Old-Maid Aunt": "Elizabeth."
Harper's Bazar 42.1 (January 1908): 2.
By Alice Barber Stephens.

action. Others, particularly Howells and Henry Van Dyke, were horrified—Howells, in a letter that "almost scorched the paper it was written on," actually asked Jordan not to publish Freeman's contribution. Jordan's own opinion of the chapter and the necessity of avoiding offense to any of Harper's family of authors prohibited that: "I had to remember that, like Mr. Howells, Miss Wilkins was one of Harper's most valued and successful authors. To reject her chapter was impossible" (264).[3] In her perplexity Jordan turned to Henry Mills Alden, editor of *Harper's Monthly*, for guidance and mediation. Indeed, the authors' discussions "grew so fiery" (267) that she eventually also sought the support of both Frederick Duneka, the general manager of Harper's, and Col. George Harvey, its president.

The battle over Aunt Elizabeth (or "Lily" [34], or "the deadly Eliza" [176], as she is variously called) continued, both in letters and in the text of the story, through the entire collaboration; the different authors interpret her character and behavior quite differently. A second explosion took place over Edith Wyatt's chapter on "The Mother," which caused Duneka to "break into the discussion" with a letter that calls the chapter "confused, dull, stupid, vapid, meaningless, halting, lame . . . cruelly incompetent drivel" (Jordan 273). Henry James called that chapter "a positive small convulsion of debility" and lamented: "Does your public *want* that so completely lack-lustre domestic sentimentality?" (Edel and Powers 52). Virtually every chapter occasioned discussions, debates, and discontent. Jordan wrote later, "If I had realized the possibilities of the situation I would not have sent to any one of those twelve authors any part of that novel until the time came for him or her to write a chapter. Then I would have sent all the preceding chapters together, and the waiting author would have had the cumulative effect of them. He would also have had the inevitable literary spasm caused by the collaboration to date—but it would have been only one spasm instead of eleven—and his mind would have been promptly diverted by the need of writing his own chapter at once" (263). As it was, the correspondence was voluminous, and gossip about *The Whole Family*'s problems spread quickly; according to Jordan, at least, "all literary New York discussed it" (268).

The range and urgency of these disputes, coupled with the narrative creativity required to adjudicate them through the story line, are

what make *The Whole Family* so interesting. It seems appropriate to turn
Ronald Dworkin's analogy between case law and the "chain novel" back
on this fiction: "[E]very novelist but the first has the dual responsibilities of interpreting and creating. . . . This must be interpretation
in a non-intention-bound style because, at least for all novelists after
the second, there is no single author whose intentions any interpreter
can, by the rules of the project, regard as decisive." A judge writing an
opinion, Dworkin suggests, is similarly "a partner in a complex chain
enterprise . . . [who] must determine, according to his own judgment,
what the earlier decisions come to, what the point or theme of the practice so far, taken as a whole, really is" (192–94). (Or what it ought to
be; some of the contributors to *The Whole Family* turned out to be judi-
cial activists.) Cutting into this product of mingled interpretation and
creation at any point reveals traces of a complex negotiation. Unraveling those traces sometimes entails a considerable work of historical
reconstruction, and the artifact is revealing for that very reason.

    The topics over which the battles were fought were important ones.
To claim, as the *Bazar* "Books & Writers" department did in reporting the book publication of *The Whole Family*, that "[n]ever before
has the American family, as an institution, been so subtly discussed"
certainly overstates the case. Yet the urgent concerns managed in *The
Whole Family* do consistently arrange themselves around and through
the complex category invoked in its title. The early twentieth century was a period, like our own, of profound change and perceived
crisis in the family. The novel rapidly becomes a debate over diverg-
ing models; what some writers consider domestic bliss, others see as
claustrophobic misery. Both Peggy's coeducation and Elizabeth's unconventional spinsterhood involve the contributors with the controversial figure of the "New Woman." Would women willingly, could
they legitimately, choose lives outside the marriage relation—and in
doing so were they rejecting the family or redefining it? I will show that
the very forms through which the contributors narrate their claims,
sentimentality and realism, embed them in a gender-inflected literary history that constructs the social location of reading in relation
to the family. And Harper & Brothers was a family business, publishing
the works of its family of authors for readers in family circles all over
the country.

The way these topics are worked out depends crucially on two aspects of the novel that I explore in the rest of this chapter: it was produced collaboratively, and its production was arranged through Harper & Brothers for *Harper's Bazar*. I offer an initial account (to be developed in later chapters) of what this particular site in the magazine world implies about the novel's place in the early twentieth-century's cultures of letters—that is, in Richard Brodhead's indispensable formulation, the "scenes of reading and writing" in which the project takes shape.

Authorship and Collaboration

The powerful notion of the "social text" as a site of struggle over meanings applies fully to singly-authored works and guides my readings of the separate chapters of the composite novel. But one advantage of studying a composite novel is that it dramatizes that notion—indeed, *The Whole Family* almost literalizes it; the title proclaims a unity, yet both the contentious process of its writing and the novel itself persistently betray conflict and fragmentation. Despite contemporary reviewers' exclamations over the book's consistent style, the narrative is, in the strict sense, incoherent: it veers among different designs that cannot be contained within a single frame. This is not only a matter of the incompatible versions of Aunt Elizabeth. Toward the end of the novel, for instance, Alice Brown actually treats the chapter that immediately preceded hers as a hoax, so that none of the events recounted in it "really" happened. For the historicizing critic, such disjunctures are intriguing openings for analysis, and I make use of them in subsequent chapters; for the contributors, they constituted failures of craft. Elizabeth Jordan's final words on the subject in her autobiography— voiced, she writes, with the "accumulated zest" of many years of discretion—are: "*The Whole Family* was a mess!" (280). The last chapter of this study will consider the shape of the novel as a whole and ask where and on what terms it succeeds or fails. The questions that concern me here point rather toward the conditions of literary production: *Whose* craft are we talking about? What is the significance of this collaborative form for the institution of authorship?

From the perspective of the social text, individuals are as much written *by* discourse as writers *of* it. And from that perspective, the commonsense view of the author as the origin and owner of words is inextricably part of modern individualism. Foucault's "What Is an Author?"—asserting the category's historicity and showing how it works as "the principle of thrift in the proliferation of meaning" (159)—is a familiar and necessary reference point here. Authorship was not, of course, invented at some abrupt, identifiable moment; Roger Chartier finds an "author-function" assigning texts to proper names already at work in some manuscript books of the Middle Ages. He points out, however, with Foucault, that in the early years of printing, such attributions had less to do with property rights than with accountability, and also that the author of a book was no more responsible for it than "the printer who published it, the bookseller or the pedlar who sold it, or the reader who possessed it"—each "could be led to the stake if they were convicted of having proffered or diffused heretical opinions" (50). Peter Stallybrass, in his intertwined accounts of "Shakespeare, the Individual, and the Text," gives a profoundly defamiliarizing picture of Renaissance dramatic texts as produced in "a network of collaborative relations, normally between two or more writers, between writers and acting companies, between acting companies and printers, between compositors and proofreaders, between printers and censors," and portrays the author we call Shakespeare as the creation of eighteenth-century editing (601). With similarly startling effect, Martha Woodmansee shows us Samuel Johnson simultaneously contributing to the development of literary biography and a canon of English authors (in, for example, *Lives of the Poets*) and participating in far more corporate and collective forms of composition. Theoretical insight and empirical inquiry work fruitfully together in the current historicizing of authorship.

The most commonly cited source for the notion of the author as a solitary creator, often virtually a demiurge, is Romanticism. Woodmansee quotes Wordsworth: "Of genius the only proof is, the act of doing well what is worthy to be done, and what was never done before: Of genius in the fine arts, the only infallible sign is the widening the sphere of human sensibility, for the delight, honor, and benefit of human nature. Genius is the introduction of a new element into the intellectual universe" (16). The heroic individualism of the early nineteenth century was still visibly at work in aesthetic ideologies of the late nineteenth and early twentieth centuries, on both continents. Howells, for example, was hostile to the notion of "genius," arguing that art derived from "powers and diligence" that anyone could exercise. Yet he visualized the "true realist" as an innovator with privileged perceptions: "He feels in every nerve the equality of things and the unity of men; his soul is exalted, not by vain shows and shadows and ideals, but by realities, in which alone the truth lives."[4] Indeed, anyone who teaches high school or college students will not need to be persuaded that the belief that an artistic work is first and foremost an expression of its creator and the conviction that originality is a self-evident value still prevail at the turn into the twenty-first century. And originality not only makes an author's work artistically his or her own but also constitutes a claim to ownership. Accountability, aesthetic identity, and intellectual property develop as distinctive but interdependent institutions (see R. Griffin).

One of the most elaborated consequences of the Romantic and Romantic-influenced notion of expressive authorship has been the valorizing of authorial intention in modern textual criticism. Jerome McGann, editor of Byron and a prominent theorist of editing, writes:

> As the very term "authority" suggests, the author is taken to be — for editorial and critical purposes — the ultimate locus of a text's authority, and literary works are consequently viewed in the most personal and individual way. Furthermore, just as literary works are narrowly identified with an author, the identity of the author with respect to the work is critically simplified through this process of individualization. The result is that the dynamic social relations which always exist in literary production — the dialectic between the historically located individual author and the historically developing institutions of literary production — tends to become obscured in criticism. (81)

Increasingly McGann's view prevails; the 1992 version of the policy statement by the Modern Language Association's Committee on Scholarly Editions, in fact, abandons the doctrine of copy-text and final intentions in favor of a more institutional and collaborative understanding of literary production (in which, of course, the author necessarily still figures).[5] Another important editor of the Romantics, Jack

Stillinger, also argues for a recognition of the social nature of literary production in *Multiple Authorship and the Myth of Solitary Genius.* These perspectives do not tell us what the significance of composite novels is, yet they do remove substantial obstacles to thinking about them.

Accounts of authorship attend, of course, not just to an aesthetic ideology such as Romanticism but to broader transformations—to, for example, the emergence of what Habermas has named the public sphere, which both literature and literary criticism inhabit. Stallybrass and Allon White describe the coffeehouses of eighteenth-century England that have served as the classic location for discussions of that moment as "an idealized space of consciousness which is being systematically *scoured,*" defined against the disorders of the marketplace, alehouse, street, and fairground as well as against the domains of the state (93). For them any understanding of culture as refinement depends on, and can never escape, its "low Other": culture as commerce. For a later period Mary Poovey points to the "mixed lineage of the Victorian image of the writer," identifying a tension between "leisured men of letters, those medieval court scribes and Renaissance intellectuals whose education marked them as privileged men, even if their daily meat came from patrons," and "the professional writer . . . descended from the early and mid-eighteenth-century hacks who sold ideas by the word and fought off competitors for every scrap of work" (102–3). Romanticism reanimated the prestige of the man of letters by finding a new source for it. But Grub Street was an equally crucial site for defining the role of the writer. Poovey like other scholars puts in evidence what the unitary notion of authorship conceals: focusing particularly on serial publication, she shows that the transformation of English literary production during the nineteenth century generated constantly more complex arrangements of editing and recompense, manufacturing and distribution, and observes that given "the range of jobs involved in producing a physical book, and the various claims that could be made on its ownership, it was no means inevitable that authorship would be conceptualized as an individualistic activity" (106). Such a conceptualization focused attention on contradictions in the role of the writer rather than the social order.

In America neither the patronage nor the commercial system was well developed through the mid-nineteenth century. Howells writes in

"The Man of Letters as a Man of Business" that before the Civil War no author "lived by literature"—except perhaps Poe, "and we all know how he lived; it was largely upon loans" (*Literature and Life* 7). Richard Brodhead supports the point, noting too the consequence that "American writing of the earlier nineteenth century is a virtually *undistributed* literature" in which the writer is never quite certain of an audience.[6] Howells was, of course, himself a successful businessman of letters, indeed a powerful cultural broker and an active participant in the fight for the International Copyright Law (1891). His remarkable essay vacillates painfully and perceptively through an analysis of the mixed institution of authorship at the end of the nineteenth century. It opens with the assertion that everyone ought to work and no one ought to "live by art": "A man's art should be his privilege, when he has proven his fitness to exercise it, and has otherwise earned his daily bread; and its results should be free to all." In fact, he suggests that people (above all, artists themselves) recognize something "profane, something impious, in taking money for a picture, or a poem, or a statue" (1). Yet the essay goes into intimate detail, for many subsequent pages, on the specific arrangements that make literature a sometimes profitable but more often unprofitable business.

Howells's ambivalence about commerce and culture is evident in the way he almost seems proud of writers' general fecklessness in dealing with money, even as he apologizes for it. He also wavers on the nature of his relation to the commodity he produces—for most of the essay he presents the author as an entrepreneur, but he reverses himself in the conclusion to suggest that this is accurate only for the rare case in which the writer is also a publisher. Ordinarily "the author is, in the last analysis, merely a working-man" dependent from day to day on his wage, and "if he is sick or sad, and cannot work, if he is lazy or tipsy, and will not, then he earns nothing" (33–34). Thus he is "really of the masses" and only "apparently of the classes," but fits with neither—so that "in the social world, as well as in the business world, the artist is anomalous . . . [and] perhaps a little ridiculous" (35). Again, the contradictory role of the writer occupies the foreground of an account that could also imply a critique of commodified cultural production (see M. Westbrook). Both Howells and his close friend Samuel Clemens understood authorship as profoundly social, and throughout their fictions, essays, and autobiographical writings they puzzle over what sustains cultural authority and what it achieves (see Lowry *"Littery Man"*). *The Whole Family*, as we will see, contributes to that conversation.

A number of critics engaged in historicizing authorship and understanding collaboration hope to escape the contradictions of modern, individualist authorship by, in Woodmansee's phrase, "recovering collectivity." She and Peter Jaszi are thoroughly convincing in their advocacy for reconstructing intellectual property law and policy to recognize, for example, the collective rights of indigenous peoples in folklore. I am somewhat more skeptical when they celebrate the collaborative possibilities of hypertext and the Internet.[7] Similarly, Wayne Koestenbaum achieves a complex, appreciative view of the erotics of male literary collaboration in his *Double Talk*, one of the few full-length studies of collaboration; but what interests him most is "how authors affectionately combine identities" (ix). Such slides into the utopian are less historically rigorous than the projects in which they are embedded. There is, of course, no such dissolving of individual point of view in *The Whole Family*—postmodern, erotic, or otherwise; each of its multiple subjectivities is vehemently entrenched. One of the few scholars to write about it finds it wanting for precisely that reason. Laura Brady treats the novel in a diagnostic and judgmental mode, identifying the reasons for the novel's failure: "The project was a series of individual works tacked together, rather than a process of integrated writing. . . . Without dialogue or shared goals, successful collaboration is not viable—as *The Whole Family* illustrates" (188). This, I would suggest, is another kind of romanticizing. In contrast, Dale Bauer also writes about "The Politics of Collaboration in *The Whole Family*" as characterized by competition rather than cooperation, but finds the struggle for control over the narrative fascinating and revealing—as I do—and suggests that its form reflects the competitive nature of the publishing industry.

Just what *is* a "composite novel"? Elizabeth Jordan seems to have been the first to have used the term in print, in her description of *The Whole Family* in her *Bazar* editor's column for December 1907. She consistently used it to designate a book-length fiction with a continuing plot composed serially by several authors. In following her, I am not so much relying on a stable usage as attempting to create one (the term has also been used for groupings of pieces by a single author, more commonly called short story cycles or sequences). It is difficult to know just how rare such collaborations are, for no one indexes them as such. They are virtually invisible in standard publishing and literary history, and mostly ignored or deplored in criticism of the authors who contributed to them.[8] Before 1907 the most famous participant in such a collaborative scheme seems to have been Harriet Beecher Stowe; several readers who wrote to *Harper's Bazar* about *The Whole Family* mentioned *Six of One by Half a Dozen of the Other* (1872), although it has now virtually disappeared from view. This too was a project developed for and serialized in a magazine, but the plot and many key points were agreed on in advance and individual contributions are not identified. *Six of One*, like *The Whole Family*, relies on courtship as its organizing principle (six young men and women are maneuvered through many possible heterosexual pairings, in the end finding their true partners through the crisis of the Chicago Fire) and presents itself as a dialogue between the sexes (three of the six authors were men, three women).

The production of collaborative fictions was more common in the late nineteenth and early twentieth centuries than at any time before or since, but few of those works had much success or enlisted writers who are remembered today.[9] *A House Party* (1901), a collection of stories with a frame narrative rather than a novel, features distinguished contributors such as George Washington Cable and Sarah Orne Jewett as well as one writer, John Kendrick Bangs, who also collaborated on *The Whole Family*; and its publisher not only, like the *Bazar*, organized a guessing game as to who had written each chapter, but offered one thousand dollars for the correct answer. When she declined her invitation to join the Family, Elizabeth Jordan's close friend Kate Douglas Wiggin (best remembered as the author of *Rebecca of Sunnybrook Farm*) had already contributed to a smaller-scale epistolary romance by four hands, *The Affair at the Inn* (1904); she did another with the same collaborators published in 1911. Jordan herself organized another composite novel, published in 1917, whose fourteen contributors include another veteran of the Family, Mary Heaton Vorse (as well as Fannie Hurst and Mary Austin); the profits from *The Sturdy Oak* were devoted to the suffrage movement, which also supplied the topic of the novel. After *Bobbed Hair* (1925)—whose twenty authors include

Dorothy Parker—even playful participation in such projects by even marginally prestigious writers seems to have ended.

In detective fiction, on the other hand, the composite novel became an at least tenuously established form. The Detection Club, established in Great Britain in 1930 "chiefly for the purpose of eating dinners together at suitable intervals and of talking illimitable shop" (Christie 2), published several different sorts of collaboration commercially appealing enough to be reprinted recently. The way an author's signature serves as a kind of brand name, promising a particular reading experience, is clearly at work here. The fact that the first full-length novel, *The Floating Admiral* (1931), includes contributions by Agatha Christie, Dorothy Sayers, and G. K. Chesterton is prominently featured on the cover of the current paperback reprint edition. This volume treats collaboration as a game, explaining the ground rules contributors were asked to abide by (such as the requirement that their design explain all the information given in previous installments) and printing each author's separate solution to the mystery. Intention-bound interpretation is indeed at a loss confronting such a text. The Detection Club has a contemporary successor in the Adams Round Table, founded in 1982 in New York (although the front matter of one of its collaborative publications, *Missing in Manhattan*, compares it to the Algonquin Round Table, instead).

Composite fictions have become uniquely prominent in the field of science fiction in the form of the "shared-world" anthology. Such works are often too loosely unified to be read as novels, but the specification of a set of planetary conditions connects their parts more strongly than a setting might in another genre. *Cosmos*, published serially in 1933 and 1934, is (like many of the composite novels I have mentioned) a playful narrative that originated in the magazine world; its contributors (like the members of the Detection Club) include the most prominent writers in a disparaged field. Some subsequent shared-world projects, such as *Medea* (1985), organized by Harlan Ellison and in preparation for ten years, and *Murasaki* (1992), by six Nebula Award winners, are quite serious in tone and enlist critically admired participants. Others are more formulaic or lighthearted. Successful series like Thieves' World and the Wild Card "mosaic novels" now run to many volumes and are a well-established feature of the science fiction marketplace.[10] Some shared-world series demonstrate the blurring of the line between production and consumption in science fiction, for fan communities have produced not only self-published "zines" but also commercial volumes; Marion Zimmer Bradley, in fact, has edited and "authorized" volumes of fan fiction set in her Darkover universe, sometimes including her own work as well.[11]

Some of the best-known shared-world series originated in television or film rather than print science fiction. Star Trek was the first and probably remains the most extensive of these enterprises; it now includes not only television programs and movies, fiction by many hands, and comic books, but also action figures, trading cards, T-shirts, key chains, coffee mugs, and so on. The Star Trek universe is both a thoroughly commodified branch of the culture industry and a site where the line between production and consumption blurs. The authors in the Pocket Book series must adhere to a strict "bible" of official Federation history and character biographies, and generally they produce a franchised fiction without much distinction. But thousands of pages of self-published fan fiction explode plotlines in all directions (a widely noted example: in the K/S, or "slash," zines, Kirk and Spock are lovers). Whether from a commitment to sharing his world or because the Star Trek fan community kept it alive after the original series was canceled in 1969, Gene Roddenberry made no attempt to assert authorial control over this proliferation and reportedly discouraged Paramount from interfering to protect its copyright (see Van Hise). (The corporation has taken a different attitude toward Internet "publication" and seems to be moving toward restricting print materials as well; see Holloway). The zines continue to flourish, although now that commercial culture producers (some of them former fans) have reappropriated the project, they control a smaller percentage of an expanded universe. Visualizing Star Trek—or Star Wars, or Dr. Who—as a sort of multimedia composite fiction reminds us that Hollywood's division of labor can be understood as collaboration; and that literary production too has an industrial dimension effaced by the privileging of authorship.

Many of the works I have cited, from *The Whole Family* to the Star Trek series, are not only collaborative but *serial* productions. As Jennifer Hayward has shown, serialized narratives ranging from Dickens's novels to comic strips to soap operas share formal features inseparable from the material circumstances under which they are created and circulated. Their deferral of closure, their incorporation of contemporary issues, and their acknowledgment of audience response all work to enlist continuing engagement from a mass audience. Hayward's demonstration that serials constitutively make a place for the participation of readers or viewers is a salutary rebuke to the tradition that treats mass culture as sheer manipulation, and its audience as passive. It also casts light on Jordan's decision to run the entire list of contributors to *The Whole Family* with each chapter and ask readers to guess who had written this installment, and on the novel's frequent moments of metacommentary—gestures that invite readers into the collaboration. Although Hayward does not treat composite novels, her work shows the late nineteenth and early twentieth centuries as the era of the magazine serial—following one in which individual writers' novels were published in parts, and preceding one in which visual media with highly developed divisions of labor came to dominate serial forms. The composite novel retains a relation to individualized authorship because each chapter is "by" someone; yet the chapters, taken not so much together as in succession, compose a common creation. The presence of the literary serial in the periodical workplace enabled the dispersed collaboration of the composite novel; thus it is not surprising that examples cluster at the turn of the century.

In the latter twentieth century composite novels do occasionally appear outside the niches of mystery and science fiction, although no author with the stature of Stowe or Howells has contributed to one. The most notorious example is certainly *Naked Came the Stranger* (1969), a parody of sexy best-sellers published as a singly authored novel under the pseudonym Penelope Ashe but soon revealed to be the work of twenty-four journalists. It differed from other composite novels by concealing its process of production rather than using it as a selling point (as well as by the fact that the authors deliberately set out to write the worst book they could) but became a media sensation only when the collaboration was revealed.[12] The title of *Naked Came the Manatee*, a recent suspense thriller by thirteen Florida authors, positively reviewed as "a wacky romp of a novel," alludes to the earlier collaboration. Its commercial possibilities derive not only from the oddity of the form and the best-seller status of contributors such as Dave Barry and

Elmore Leonard, but also from its regional interest; the volume had its origins in a serial published in the *Miami Herald*'s *Tropic* magazine (see Gambone). The collaborative novel *Caverns* (1990), on the other hand, emerged out of the academic creative writing establishment—it was written in a class taught by Ken Kesey at the University of Oregon.

Other recent examples can be found in innovative media. In 1990 the independent comics magazine *Raw* initiated a project in which each of a long list of cartoonists drew three panels with a simple stick figure as the protagonist and mailed them on; the results were eventually edited and published as *The Narrative Corpse*, with contributions from sixty-nine artists. The artists were allowed to see only the three panels directly preceding their own; the inspiration cited was a surrealist parlor game in which people added sentences or drawings to a sheet of paper whose successive folds prevented them from seeing what went before. In 1997, John Updike organized a composite-fiction extravaganza on the Internet. He wrote an opening, and one of the newest institutions of literary culture took it from there. "In a contest that is part lottery, part chain letter," the *New York Times* reported, "Amazon.com, the on-line bookseller, is asking imitation Updikes to continue the story with one or more sentences, with the conclusion to be written by the eminent novelist, himself. Every day a winner will be chosen and awarded $1,000. At the end of the competition . . . a Grand Prize of $100,000 will be given to one of the contestants, in a random drawing from all eligible entrants. Unabashedly, Amazon calls the multiplex mystery 'The Greatest Tale Ever Told' " (Gussow, "John Updike" and "Now the Plot Quickens"). The tale's setting in the offices of a magazine is appropriate to a work whose very mode of existence reflects transformations in the culture industry. In these varied examples, the disparity of motives for and sites of collaboration is perhaps most apparent. Yet not only do all remind us in one way or another that narrative making is a business, most retain some sort of connection to serial publication, and two originated, as *The Whole Family* did, through the brokering of magazine editors.

All these collaborations invite us to question individualist assumptions about originality, the ownership of cultural artifacts, and interpretation. Taking up that invitation does not prevent us from talking about authors, of course; I will still say different sorts of things when examining two stories by Henry James and when juxtaposing one by James with one by Alice Brown. Yet it enables us to resist the common-sense and critical traditions that disparage composite novels like *The Whole Family* as anomalous. A historical perspective on authorship lets us both understand and distance ourselves from the assumption that fiction succeeds by intensely expressing individual vision. Sergio Perosa concludes his study of James's chapter by quoting from the last line of the novel, "we don't want the whole family," and adding, "we want the lonely author" (130). Collaborative and composite works may be unsuccessful by any or all standards—and I must admit that few of the works I have just surveyed seem to me likely to sustain the sort of extended attention I have given *The Whole Family*—but they are not automatically misguided. At minimum, each one deforms the dominant arrangements of literary production and directs our attention to grounds of coherence other than authorship.

The Whole Family seems shapeless and baffling if we try to read it as we would the work of a single author. The grounds on which it makes sense are collaborative ones: it was a forum for dialogue over the family and a range of associated issues, and it was an expression of the corporate entity Harper & Brothers. The remainder of this chapter sketches the print culture that was the site of that dialogue, examining where each of the contributors fit into it and showing how it received *The Whole Family*. Then Chapter Two follows out the consequences of revisionary accounts of authorship, by narrating literary history with a publishing house—rather than a person, or a personified genre or national tradition—as the protagonist.

Scenes of Reading and Writing

The members of the "Family" are very unevenly remembered today. The late twentieth-century critic's attention is most likely to be caught by the participation of Henry James. (His name is cannily listed first on the spine of the 1986 reprint of the novel, even though his contribution comes seventh, and even though both Howells as the originator of the idea and the author of the first chapter and Jordan as the editor have stronger claims to that position). Howells is also a familiar figure, at least to specialists in American literature; critical estimates of the value of his work have varied, but his place in literary history is not disputed. Mary Wilkins Freeman has consistently held a small place in the canon; at present, under the influence of feminist criticism, her work may well be read more frequently than Howells's. The recovery of women writers has also brought Elizabeth Stuart Phelps back into print and a certain amount of attention to Alice Brown. Vorse is remembered as a radical journalist and novelist, although not for the sort of fiction she contributed to *The Whole Family*. The rest of the contributors are virtually forgotten.

However, when Jordan's column asserts that *The Whole Family* "is a book of distinction, written by authors of distinction" ("With the Editor" 1248), this is not—or rather not only—an example of her promotional hyperbole, but an accurate description of the status of the contributors. William Dean Howells and Henry James were the most eminent living American authors. Henry Van Dyke was both a minister and a professor at Princeton, as well as a widely respected and popular writer of books of many different sorts: moral essays, fiction, meditations on outdoor life, poetry, literary criticism, travel sketches. John Kendrick Bangs was a less solemn but equally prominent figure, known both for the pages of jokes and cartoons he edited for the Harper's periodicals and for his own volumes of amusing tales (*A Houseboat on the Styx* was an 1896 best-seller, for example). He had edited *Harper's Weekly* for two years at the turn of the century. Mary Wilkins Freeman was a leading local color writer, both widely read and critically respected throughout her long career. Elizabeth Jordan was included in a 1901 *Bookman* article profiling American magazine editors (three out of fifteen were women, all placed at the end of the group). An April 1908 *Bookman* article titled "Some Recent Women Short Story Writers" suggests the female contributors' standing. It mentions eight writers who established the tradition of female excellence in short story writing in America, among them Elizabeth Stuart Phelps and Alice Brown; discusses the work of eight writers, among them Edith Wyatt, Mary Stewart Cutting, and Mary Shipman Andrews; and mentions in conclusion eight more writers whose work was worthy of note, among them Mary Heaton Vorse and Elizabeth Jordan. Its roster of twenty-four notable women writers thus includes seven of the eight women writers in *The Whole Family*, omitting only Freeman, whose prominence hardly requires confirmation. (Given the promotional practices described below and in the next chapter, I should probably note here that the *Bookman* had no special connection with Harper's.)[13]

The illustrator chosen for *The Whole Family* was also distinguished. Alice Barber Stephens was a formally trained artist whose studies included work abroad and at the Pennsylvania Academy of the Fine Arts during the period when it was directed by Thomas Eakins. (The work of hers most often seen today is the 1879 painting *Female Life Class*, set at the Academy, in which a nude woman model is juxtaposed with elegantly dressed women art students at their easels.) Stephens had been well established for many years at the time and had won awards for both her oil painting and her illustration. She had been invited to return to the Pennsylvania Academy to teach (although she was unable to do so because of poor health), taught at the Philadelphia School of Design for women, and served on the fine arts jury for the 1904 St. Louis Exposition. Stephens's style is simple and realistic yet full of feeling, and she was known particularly, but not exclusively, for her portrayals of children.[14] Stephens was, in other words, someone Jordan would have chosen to indicate both the domestic theme and the seriousness of the novel.

The fact that the contributors were writers, and an illustrator, of note does not mean that all of them were identified with high culture, or that any of them inhabited that realm exclusively. Certainly there were no positions in American literary culture more prestigious than Howells's and James's, although as subsequent chapters will show, they often hoped they were writing for the general populace as well as the elite. Bangs and Van Dyke were gentlemen who used their cultural authority as a platform from which to address a broad middle-class audience. Local color writers like Freeman and Brown crossed between elite and popular markets with relative freedom. Wyatt attracted Howells's attention in that genre with stories of ethnic Chicago and was also a progressive journalist. Jordan was not only a journalist and editor but also wrote light fiction. So did Cutting and Vorse, mainly for the women's magazines. Andrews's popular fiction focused on boys and the outdoors, although a sentimental *Scribner's* story about Lincoln had recently made a hit. Phelps was a didactic domestic fictionist whose work frequently appeared both in magazines and between hard covers for decades after the mid-nineteenth-century period with which that formation is usually associated. Their literary culture was mixed in another sense too; as *The Whole Family* so clearly demonstrates, it was heterosocial—gender-inflected but not divided into separate spheres.[15]

It was Harper's that brought these authors together, and the next chapter examines in more detail the question of what the history of the house can teach us about the various cultures of letters. But only Howells, Jordan, and Bangs "belonged to the shop" (as Harvey put it to Howells).[16] Among the others, only Freeman really "was" a Harper's author. Stephens might be thought of as a house artist; her work could be seen in many places but it appeared (in the words of a contemporary) "almost without interruption in 'Harper's Magazine'" (North 273). Many of the contributors, in fact, had long-term connections with other publishers—Cutting with Doubleday, the Chicagoan Wyatt with McClure, Van Dyke with Scribner's, and the New Englanders Phelps and Brown with Houghton Mifflin. (In 1906 Phelps accused Houghton Mifflin of "forcing" her, by paying her so little themselves, to place a serial with Harper's and let them publish the book; see Coultrap-McQuin 190–91.) James was remarkably sophisticated in his negotiations with publishers and placed works with a great many; in the ten years between 1895 and 1905 he published seventeen books under ten different imprints: five in England and five in America (Harper's, Scribner's, Macmillan, Houghton Mifflin, and the avant-garde press of Herbert Stone; see Anesko, *Friction*). In short, the image of the Harper's "family" should not lead us to overestimate the solidarity produced by Franklin Square.

It is not surprising that almost all the contributors to the composite novel already published their work in Harper's periodicals; most notable writers of the period did so. What seemed unusual to contemporaries—and has surprised later critics as well—was finding the revered Henry James publishing in a women's magazine. His friend Howells did not, in fact, originally think of him in connection with the project; the invitation was no doubt suggested by Jordan, who had been introduced to James in London and had helped to arrange lectures during his visit to the United States in 1904 and 1905. Around the time of *The Whole Family* he published essays on his recent trip in the *Monthly* and two long series of articles in the *Bazar* on the speech and the manners of American women. (I discuss his attempt to appeal to this audience more fully in the last chapter.) Jordan barely appears in studies of James's life, yet their relationship occupies many pages of her autobiography. In fact, she reports that they enjoyed each other's conversation so much during the season she spent in London that gossip linked them romantically (209, 216). She gives detailed impressions of his manner and affectionate descriptions of small incidents, capping her account with a joke Duneka played on them after James's visit. He circulated a story that "swept through the Harper offices and soon was joyously quoted throughout literary circles. Briefly, it recited that just before sailing Mr. James had sent me a written proposal of marriage which, owing to his new and highly involved literary style, I was unable to comprehend. I at once replied, however, asking Mr. James what his letter was about; but owing to my illegible handwriting the Master was unable to read my reply, and received the impression that I had refused him. Mr. Duneka asked the cooperation of the staff in straightening out this tragic tangle" (220). Whether or not one fully credits Jordan's stories, this is an irreverently admiring perspective that helps us understand how "the Master" was integrated into the early twentieth-century literary marketplace.

Harper's Bazar was better able to accommodate James's work than other women's magazines because although it shared their domestic orientation and intimate, helpful tone, it was a *fashion* magazine with a metropolitan sophistication. A monthly "Letter from Paris" and articles on the home lives of European royalty mingled with short stories about mischievous children and recipes for spring salads, attempting to appeal both to privileged urban women and to those interested in reading about the lives of the privileged and in finding practical domestic counsel. The gowns most prominently pictured were elegant and expensive; yet the cover price of an issue of the *Bazar* in this period was a reasonable fifteen cents, and articles on "economical dressing" were included as well. The December 1906 issue's prospectus for the next year, its fortieth, states the magazine's mission:

> HARPER'S BAZAR will continue to be the magazine of the up-to-date woman. It will still be the court of final appeal in all questions of fashion,

entertainment, household decoration, and good form. But it will be more than this. It will be "guide, philosopher and friend" to countless women of less experience, less opportunity, simpler ideals.

Many thousands of women living in the small towns of the South and West are now among the readers of the BAZAR. To be a practical help to all our readers, and to follow more and more the trend of the time which, among the best people, is away from ostentation toward simplicity, the BAZAR will preach rational economy. Its fashions will still be the most beautiful published, but there will also be page after page of eminently practical designs for women of simple tastes and small incomes. ("Harper's Bazar for 1907" 10)

Among the prominently advertised features that Jordan hoped would appeal to both the best people and the simple people was, of course, *The Whole Family*.

The composite novel's authors were, in fact, much more consistently *Bazar* contributors than Harper's authors in any general sense. One exception was Edith Wyatt, who was invited to participate because of Howells's admiration for her work; this was only one of his efforts to bring her to Harper's.[17] (Her experience as a member of the Family may well have ensured their failure.) Another was Mary Raymond Shipman Andrews; she was solicited to contribute the sort of writing she was known for elsewhere, but her *Whole Family* chapter seems to have been her only contribution to Jordan's *Bazar*. Otherwise, Henry Van Dyke had published several essays between 1902 and 1905 but was the least strongly affiliated contributor. Phelps's work appeared in the *Bazar* regularly; her serial *Walled In* concluded in the December 1907 issue in which Howells's opening chapter on the father appeared, and a series of meditations on the afterlife began almost immediately.[18] Sections of what became Vorse's *Autobiography of an Elderly Woman* appeared anonymously during 1906 and the attributed series "Experiences of a Mother" ran at the same time as *The Whole Family*. Cutting published a long series of "Talks to Wives" during 1906 and two short stories in issues that also contained installments of the composite novel. Freeman was a constant contributor; she bracketed the composite novel with a Thanksgiving story in November 1907 and a Christmas story in December 1908. Brown published stories in 1906 and 1908.

Howells was powerfully identified with Harper's and published occasional pieces in the *Bazar*. Jordan's editorial and Bangs's humor departments ran every month, of course, but she also contributed short stories and he contributed poems; his satiric verses on the doings of Miss Follette de Billion were a regular feature. Not only *The Whole Family*, in fact, but the *Bazar* as a whole demonstrates its editor's impulse to juxtapose practitioners of very different kinds of writing.

Magazines in general are characterized by variety, of course, and women's magazines from *Godey's* to *Sassy* have mixed articles ranging from literature to personal grooming, celebrity coverage to decorating advice. One point to be registered here is the massive continuity of the female culture industry (see ch. 5). Even now the tone of intrusive intimacy protested by an anonymous contributor to the *Atlantic Monthly* in 1906 remains pervasive:

> There are recipes for everything, from domestic bliss to cleansing compounds. . . . My good is sought in a thousand ways; in gentle exhortations to be up and doing in every possible direction; in succinct columns of Don'ts; in pithy paragraphs of Useful Information; in exploitations of the fashions; in Health Talks and Beauty Hints. My good, I say, for there is in it all something so pointedly personal, it is so obviously addressed to my wants and my interests as a woman, that it is not to be evaded or put by. . . . [T]he Woman's Page . . . pursues me, weighs me, and finds me wanting, without my invitation,—with a concurrence upon my part merely forced and reluctant. Quite against my will, I am spurred to the performance of imperative duties galore unmentioned in the Decalogue, duties of physical culture and hygiene, of charmcraft and economy. (Anon., "The Melancholy of Women's Pages")

Close examination of Jordan's *Bazar* also, however, demonstrates the specificity of the long, ambitious stretch it attempted, ranging from elite culture and high fashion to marital advice and homely detail. (Figures 3–16 illustrate this range.) As befit a Harper's publication, it engaged with serious issues and demonstrated a fundamentally moral perspective even as it offered the tutelage in conspicuous consumption to be expected of a sophisticated guide to style. These tensions were reduced when William Randolph Hearst purchased the magazine in 1913;

HARPER'S BAZAR, DECEMBER, 1907

"HARPER'S BAZAR Sets the Fashion"

CONTENTS

		PAGE
In the Intimacy of Kimonos and Undressing	*Frontispiece*	1142
The Gift and the Giver	ANNE O'HAGAN	1143
Illustrated by Rose O'Neill		
Oil of Gladness. A Story	MARY STEWART CUTTING	1150
Illustrated by The Kinneys		
The Ballad of the Mothers. A Poem	THEODOSIA GARRISON	1158
Illustrated by Ellen Macauley		
The Whole Family. Part I. The Father	By ????	1161
A Novel by Twelve Authors		
Joe's Side of It	A MERE MAN	1171
Illustrated by The Kinneys		
Walled In. A Novel. Chapter XVI	ELIZABETH STUART PHELPS	1177
Illustrated by Clarence F. Underwood		
With the Majority. A Poem	PRISCILLA LEONARD	1188
Yule-tide Fashions		1189
Outdoor Costumes	MARIE OLIVIER	1194
Miscellaneous Fashions	Illustrated by Ethel Rose, Guy Rose, and A. M. Cooper	1198
Lessons in Economical Dressing		1202
Decorating the Christmas Tree	MARTHA CUTLER	1206
Illustrated by the Author		
The Housemother's Problems	"BAZAR" READERS	1209
The Christmas Dinner	JOSEPHINE GRENIER	1216
Illustrated with Photographs		
The Selection of Christmas Gifts	CHRISTINE TERHUNE HERRICK	1220
Illustrated with Photographs		
Diet for Young Children. Part V	MARIANNA WHEELER	1226
	(Ex-Supt. of the Babies' Hospital, New York)	
How to Train the Speaking Voice. Part I	KATHERINE JEWELL EVERTS	1228
The Importance of Good Manners	MAUD HOWE	1233
Simple Book-shelves	MARTHA CUTLER	1236
Illustrated by the Author		
English Recipes	E. V. MILLETT	1239
Ajour or Toledo Embroidery	BESSIE B. GRABOWSKII	1241
Illustrated with Diagrams		
Our Girls	ANNA OGDEN	1244
For the Children. Illustrated		1246
With the Editor		1248
In Jocund Vein		1250
Illustrated by A. B. Walker, T. S. Allen, W. L. Jacobs, and J. Nuttall		
Reflections Concerning Women	GEORGE HARVEY	1252

Regular Departments: Questions of Household Decoration, Questions of Good Form and Entertainment, With the Corresponding Editor, Advice to Mothers, The New Christmas Toys, and Cut Paper Patterns.

Vol. 41, No. 12. Subscription Price, $1.00 a Year *(Published Monthly)*: Single Number, 15 Cents. Postage free to all Subscribers in the United States, Mexico, Cuba, Porto Rico, and Philippines. To Canada, 35 cents extra. Foreign Postage, 72 cents a year.

HARPER & BROTHERS, PUBLISHERS

NEW YORK: Franklin Square   LONDON: 45 Albemarle Street, W.
Also for sale at Brentano's, 37 Avenue de l'Opéra, Paris

3. Table of contents.
Harper's Bazar 41.12 (December 1907): n.p. (end of issue).

LATEST HINTS FROM PARIS

BY MARIE OLIVIER

SOME very dainty linen and muslin and shantung one-piece dresses are still being developed and shown in the custom workshops to tempt the lover of pretty apparel to late summer purchasing. Most of them continue along conservative lines, and in no way hint of the surprises in store for the seekers after the novel in dress in the near future.

Yet the producers and importers are already inviting the critical to view the daring garments which they plan to lay before us within the coming month. Literally nothing else is talked of but the radical changes which will positively appear in women's dress. Everywhere the word in dressmaking and manufacturing circles is, "Have you seen the new Empire dress? What do you think of it? How do you

SMART COSTUME of plain and embroidered brown filet over Nattier-blue silk, which also is used for bands.

think it will take?" Probably not one woman in ten thousand, without having seen the new gowns, can even fancy their utter impossibility. Not only are they impossible on the score of modesty and reprehensible on the ground of taste. They are entirely impractical for the ordinary purposes of life, and could not, even with modifications, serve for anything but display purposes. They are a revival, not of the most artistic Empire period, as their name would imply, but of the period ten years before the Empire, when profligacy flourished in France. They were an expression of the lawlessness of those times, and were promptly banished in favor of the really graceful Empire gowns, when France regained her moral sanity and health.

I can almost hear some one ask, "What! Are

4. Marie Olivier, "Latest Hints from Paris."
Harper's Bazar 42.9 (September 1908): 855.

Economy in Dress

A FUTURE MODEL AFTERNOON SKIRT in cloth; it fastens under one side of back panel.

because discriminating buyers will not pay for wearing-apparel a season old; and, third, hasty buying of the very new in fabric, color, or shape. New shades of standard colors are especially dangerous, unless the person selecting them is a prophet. Not very many are, and even astute tailors go slowly in purchasing, until this or that dress form or color has "made good."

THERE are three dangerous rocks in the beginning of a season on which a woman who must practise economy is likely to founder: the first, cheap novelties; the second, advertised bargains which are sold cheap

COAT with soutached revers and cuffs; folded satin waistcoat; shows front panel of skirt.

5. "Economy in Dress."
Harper's Bazar 42.10
(October 1908): 964.

FOR OLDER WOMEN

THERE are especially appropriate materials just now for older women to whom a touch of violet, a gown of mauve, of garnet, rich blue, or deep green, is often so becoming. It is a season for black and white, and violet and gray, combinations; and for grays, which are particularly distinguished for the really silver haired woman. Among the ash, smoke, and elephant grays, the silvers, and that gray which is just off the mole tone, there is an endless variety to select from according to the complexion of the wearer. That is a particularly smart costume which you will see pictured on the next page. It is modelled in black and white faille, with black satin stripe. Practically the same effect may be had this year in foulard and other thin silks, in organdies, lawns, and zephyrs, so that the costume may readily be realized with even simple materials. The model dress here

MODEL STREET GOWN for an elderly woman; blue cloth trimmed with braiding.

shown is given a vest of white mousseline, and lower "mitt" sleeves of white lace appliqué with black Chantilly motifs. A vest of black filet over white would be effective. This is a costume especially fitted for afternoon wear at weddings or receptions.

Among the pretty adjuncts for old ladies' dresses are the lingerie cape collars, and the berthas of lace or net or silk, richly embroidered. Some of the capes have stole front ends, which come almost to the foot of the dress. Berthas and capes of this sort are made of silk, cashmere, and other soft materials, some of the cashmere capes being patterned all over with soutache, like the wrap shown on page 334. These are for outdoor wear, and are given a soft rolling collar that meets below a shallow V opening in the front. A soft collar and short jabot will finish such capes at the throat. The collars, in batiste or other lingerie form, are usually about fifteen inches deep from

6. "For Older Women."

Harper's Bazar 42.4

(April 1908): 340.

IN THE PUBLIC EYE

THE Empress of Germany, a recent photograph of whom we reproduce here, during the twenty-seven years of her married life has helped and guided her husband through her influence. She has, however, never shown the slightest wish to play a part in politics. She is content to be a model wife and mother, and a silent doer of pious and charitable work. To sum up an appreciation of her character and usefulness, the following words, spoken by the German

THE BARONESS VON STERNBURG.

German ambassador to the United States, holds an enviable position in diplomatic and social Washington. She has beauty and charm—the native charm and cleverness of the American woman, with the added polish of travel and European court experience.

THE LATEST PORTRAIT OF THE GERMAN EMPRESS.

Emperor with great feeling at a banquet given in the province of Schleswig-Holstein, her native state, at the time of their silver-wedding celebration, are all that is necessary. He said: "Sprung from this soil is she who to me is the embodiment of all womanly virtues and who through all the difficult and arduous duties of my position has been a most helpful and congenial mate."

The Baroness von Sternburg, wife of the

THE LITTLE CROWN PRINCE OF ITALY.

THE HOUSEMOTHER'S PROBLEMS

READERS of HARPER'S BAZAR are invited to contribute to this department, which will contain, from month to month, the most helpful and practical suggestions received. All contributions should be very short—none exceeding 250 words—and each paper should contain *the solution of some problem which has confronted the writer in her domestic experience.*

Contributions accepted will be paid for at regular rates. Articles should be written on one side of the paper, sent in an envelope and not rolled, and signed in full, with the writer's address. The signature will not be used in printing the article. Contributions should be addressed to the Editor of HARPER'S BAZAR, Housemother's Department, care of Harper & Brothers, Franklin Square, New York.

Contributions found unavailable for this department cannot be returned. Authors of manuscripts which are available will be promptly notified of the acceptance of their contributions—if possible within a month of the date of their receipt. After six weeks any MS. not accepted may be offered elsewhere.

Systematizing the Household Spending

DURING the first year of my married life our bills were paid in a "go as you please" way—too much money being spent for some things, and not enough left for others. I was in despair, when a solution of the problem occurred to me.

I purchased six large, oblong envelopes, and marked them as follows:

1. Rent, gas, and electric light.
2. Food and household incidentals.
3. Husband's money.
4. Wife and children's money.
5. Servant.
6. Savings.

In discussing the matter with my husband —who is too busy a man to attend to household details—he decided to give me each month his entire salary, as my "envelope system" would take care of everything, including his allowance. He made an estimate of what he needed for car fares, lunches, cigars, an occasional dinner down-town with friends, and his clothing. That amount is put each month in his envelope.

I pay cash for everything, for I know exactly how much money is to be spent in each department, and I see to it that the amount is not exceeded. Expenses must necessarily fluctuate, and if at any time a larger sum than it contains is needed from a particular envelope, the amount is borrowed temporarily from the envelope marked "Savings." A slip of paper containing this memorandum is placed therein, and the amount borrowed is returned from the funds of the following month—greater economy being practised to cover the deficiency.

My envelopes are a decided success, and of great assistance to me.

L. M. W.

NEW YORK, N. Y.

The Care of Flannels

EVERY housekeeper will admit that the care of our flannels is very important.

First, they should be soaked overnight in soft water. If the water is hard, add a teaspoonful of borax to each gallon. Then make a suds of mild soap with a little ammonia added, and wash at once.

The water in which woollens are washed should never be hot. Contact with hot water makes them hard and shrinks them. The rinsing water should be of the same temperature—lukewarm.

Never wring flannels, but press out the superfluous moisture between the hands. Hang them in the sun when possible.

If flannels are washed according to these

8. "The Housemother's Problems."

Harper's Bazar 41.12 (December 1907):

1209.

Some Experiences of a Mother

By Mary Heaton Vorse

II

ILLUSTRATED BY HARRY LINNELL

IT was all very well for Helena to declare that theories were fallible; it was very salutary for her to admit humbly that she knew very little about being a mother. Yet when it is a matter of education, one has to have some theories, hasn't one? If one had no theories, where would education be? There wouldn't be any, of the definite school kind. And education is a theory which confronts a mother so quickly. It seems only about three weeks after a child is born that it comes time for him to learn his letters and to begin to gather facts about the world in which he lives.

Helena and Gifford had discussed all Philip's career from the moment there was any Philip. They began high up in the scale, giving him the choice among several professions. Next they decided to what college Philip— Gifford's college, naturally. When they came to the matter of preparatory schools they travelled a less sure path. Helena was for having Philip's name registered right away in one of the big schools. Gifford was more conservative. He pointed out that in sixteen years the nature of a school may change; and when Helena to that replied, "Harrow" and "Eton," he objected that the great public schools of England are a more stable matter than our large private schools in this country. So they left that weighty question unsettled, and continued to shilly-shally with it, even though Philip went from long clothes into short dresses, and again into little tunics, and even, at the time of which I am writing—when Philip has occasional real trousers, not the baggy kind, but real ones, such as boys wear—they have, I'm sorry to say, not yet decided to what preparatory school he shall go. Helena still urges that his name be entered at a big school.

They haven't even decided the subject of public school or private school, although they talk about it late into the night.

Meantime, Helena had been teaching Philip to read. She even sent him to the kindergarten, but he set about catching things so industriously that she took him out again.

"If he can get chicken-pox and measles," she wisely argued, "he can get scarlet fever and diphtheria, and the baby will have them, too. I've only one son and one daughter."

So here was Philip at six and a half, a little "ahead" of the children of his age in public school, but with education not dealt out with any systematic hand. Still, Helena had nibbled around the edges of the problem. Children ought to be taught to have a natural interest in animals. There would be less unkindness in the world if they were systematically taught to love every living thing. She came to this conclusion before the period of which I speak. To be accurate, it was upon the day that she found Philip smashing caterpillars between two stones. He had collected quite a lot of them.

"What are you doing?" she asked him. It was no idle question. She didn't know.

"Makin' deaders of caterpillars," he replied, "good an' deaders. Look!" And with pride he lifted one stone from the other. There was no doubt that they were good and

9. Mary Heaton Vorse,
"Some Experiences of a Mother."
Harper's Bazar 42.6
(June 1908): 523.

HARPER'S BAZAR

VOL. XLII
No. 6
JUNE, 1908

THE HIGHER EDUCATION FOR WOMEN

BY CHARLES WILLIAM ELIOT, LL.D.
PRESIDENT OF HARVARD UNIVERSITY.

THE future of the higher education for women seems likely to be somewhat different from its past. The quality of the resort to the separate colleges for women has changed, and the policies of those colleges are not what they were twenty-five years ago, while education has plainly declined.

We cannot tell much about the future, except as we study the past and the present; and therefore the first thing I want to do is to state as clearly as I can what seems to me to have been demonstrated during the last thirty-five years concerning the higher education of women in our country.

I remember very well the beginnings. I remember the doubts which accompanied those beginnings; doubts in some of which I shared. Three doubts at least—doubts in their nature important with regard to the immediate success of the higher education of women, and important, certainly, with regard to its future—seem to me to have been resolved; three distinct apprehensions concerning the effect of the higher education on women seem to me to have been removed.

In the first place, there was perfectly sincere doubt (because there was little experience to go upon) whether young women were so capable as young men of receiving what was then called the higher education; or, in other words, whether young women had the capacity to master by study the traditional subjects of the higher education. That doubt has been completely removed. We have proved by actual trial that young women can learn all the more difficult subjects of education just as well as young men; and there is some

10. Charles William Eliot,

"The Higher Education for Women."

Harper's Bazar 42.6 (June 1908): 519.

Miss de Billion in Paris

BY JOHN KENDRICK BANGS | **PICTURES BY GEO F. KERR**

WHEN Follette returned from old Paris last year
I ventured to call on her, hoping to hear
Of wonderful things she had seen on the jaunt,
Of Châteaux, and homes of the Ancient Romaunt;
Of scenes that in history blazon the page,
When Knights were chivalrous—O dead and gone age!—
When tourneys were held and the troubadours sang,
And Palaces rang
With the racket and clang
Of Princes and Nobles returning from war
For God and for Country and King of Navarre!
I longed for a hint of some wonderful scene
Where strong hearts were pinned to the sleeve of a
Queen;
Where life was worth living, but never so dear
But men gave it up for a chance to appear
As Lord of a Joust where a glove was the prize,
A kerchief, a glance of a pair of blue eyes,
A smile from a fair demoiselle of the Court,
Or some other gift of a similar sort.
I longed for a glimpse of the grim castle wall,
The dungeon, the drawbridge, the terrible fall
Of deep oubliette.
Dark, danksome and wet;
The dread prison-house of Marie Antoinette.
I longed for a hint of those heroes of old,
With hearts overbold,
Who did without question just what they were told:
Moved mountains, razed hills—
Tho' pestered by bills—
Swam streams that were swollen and waded through
gore
To rescue some maid on some opposite shore.
I wanted to see no more from afar
Those haunts of Dumas!
The scenes that e'er bring to my heart such a thrill
I dream of them still,
Though years have passed by since I read of the clan
Of Athos and Aramis, brave d'Artagnan,
Of Porthos and all of that wonderful crew
Who, 'twixt me and you.
Never could do
The deeds that they did in those Days of Romance
Had they like ourselves dwelt in Days of Finance.
I wanted to hear of that beautiful spot
Where Abelard lies, not wholly forgot,
With fair Héloïse planted there alongside,

11. John Kendrick Bangs,
"Miss de Billion in Paris."
Harper's Bazar 40.6
(June 1906): 499.

A Magic Moment

J. VERRIER

BY LILIAN WHITING

I love you, love you! only this
     I have to say;
All other visions, hopes, and dreams
     Must go their way.

Your lightest word outweighs for me
     The universe beside;
My thought responds to all your own
     As ocean's tide

Unfailingly leaps up to meet
     The moon's sure call;
Or as the stars in evening skies
     Must shine for all.

Life is no longer drift and dream,
     But vivified:
And all its radiance, all its faiths,
     Are multiplied.

Music and magic lay their spell
     Upon the days
That dawn in rose and wane in gold
     And purple haze.

O wondrous spirit-call that came
     From out the air!
To make all life forevermore
     Divinely fair.

12. Lilian Whiting,
"A Magic Moment." *Harper's Bazar*
42.8 (August 1908): 728.

WOMEN IN THE HIGH ALPS

BY W.G.FITZ-GERALD

IT seems strange that among the many thousand fatalities in the Alps, there is little or no record of women having come to grief. I think it is not so much because they are less adventurous as that they are more prudent and far-sighted. The number of women Alpinists increases every year; and an American woman, Mrs. Fanny Bullock Workman, F.R.G.S., herself disputes with Sir Martin Conway the honor of having climbed highest in the tremendous Himalayas.

In August, 1906, the Alpine honors of the Swiss valleys—at any rate as regards women—lay with Miss Alma Brownlee of Chicago, who all but conquered one of the most difficult aiguilles of Mont Blanc, and only gave up in a blinding snowstorm and hurricane. Miss Brownlee's hands were badly frozen; but her greatest trial was to turn her back on the aiguille itself, whose spotless purity shimmered against the sky, and from whose summit the treacherous gusts trailed the snow in spectral streamers for thousands of feet into the wooded valleys below.

A woman whose Alpine feats are respected by members of every Alpine club is Mrs. Aubrey Le Blond; for there is hardly a peak in the entire Alpine chain which she has not conquered, with her famous guide, Joseph Imboden of Zermatt. Not only does Mrs. Le Blond hold many important records, even from men, but her feet have known many a virgin peak in Tyrol and Norway, the Engadine and Valais; the High Savoy, the Pyre-

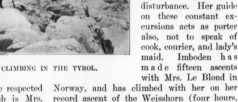

CLIMBING IN THE TYROL.

nees, and the Alps of Dauphigny. Strange to say, Mrs. Le Blond was a dying woman when she took to mountaineering.

"You are consumptive," the doctors told her. "Go to Cairo, or Mentone, or Algiers." She did, and grew worse. Then she thought a little for herself, went off to Chamonix and began upon that well-known training-peak, the Breithorn, and forthwith found life, and a life so well worth living that she would exchange it for none other. While her doctors were still aghast at her supposed madness, the provoking invalid began work on the Grandes Jorasses—a grim name to veteran Alpinists—and in two days of long, laborious step-cutting in the solid ice the 14,000-foot summit was reached.

She climbs only in autumn, for, quaintly enough, she fears the thunderstorms and the curious hissing of the ice axe during electrical disturbance. Her guide on these constant excursions acts as porter also, not to speak of cook, courier, and lady's maid. Imboden has made fifteen ascents with Mrs. Le Blond in Norway, and has climbed with her on her record ascent of the Weisshorn (four hours, exclusive of halts) and the Piz Bernina (four hours, forty minutes).

Often enough the cold has been so piercing that wine, poured into a glass, has frozen instantly on the sides.

"I was taking the thermometer once," Mrs. Le Blond told me, "when I saw it sink as low as it would go—thirteen degrees be-

VERANDA MEALS

BY JOSEPHINE GRENIER

ANY ONE who has not formed the habit of eating on the porch in summer has not yet fathomed the delights of warm weather. Whether the porch is large or small, beautiful or ugly, does not really matter, so long as there is room for a table and chairs, and there are vines or awnings, or both, to screen it from passers.

It is necessary that hot food should be served on hot dishes out of doors, and, of course, it is a simple matter to heat the platters and plates; but it is better yet to have a cover for the platters and to keep the vegetables in hot covered dishes on the sideboard. There are very nice hot-water dishes in heavy blue-and-white china in the Japanese shops which, with covers, make perfect dishes for hot food; still, by utilizing a chafing-dish with a hot-water pan, an excellent substitute can be made for using for many things—luncheon dishes especially.

RASPBERRY SHERBET IN LEMON CUPS.

A coffee machine is helpful at breakfast, and a tea urn at luncheon; either can have a folding pasteboard screen made at home to keep off draughts.

Of course, fruit is the usual thing at breakfast in summer, and much more can be done to make this attractive than many housekeepers think. Try serving freshly gathered strawberries on a flat dish with strawberry leaves under the fruit. Have raspberries arranged in the same way, but in pyramid shape. Plums should lie on a bed of moss with a narrow edge of leaves; peaches and pears should be wiped off and the two mixed with their heavy green foliage; grapes should be alternated on a flat dish, purple mixed with green, or green with brown, with tendrils and small grape leaves. A little trouble pays wonderfully with fruit.

When cereal and fruit are served together it is essential that the cereal should be very well cooked and seasoned; then pour it into a mould and let it get firm; put it on an ice-cold platter, and surround with red raspberries or cut-up peaches; these are the best two fruits to use. When one tires of oatmeal and other similar things with fruit, a good change is boiled rice; this is very nice with raspberries and plenty of thick cream.

Eggs are, of course, the staple for summer breakfasts. A variation from the tiresomely plain omelette is made by folding in creamed hard-boiled eggs, or mushrooms, or chopped olives, or pease, all cooked in a thick white sauce. Or use a mixture of chicken livers and kidneys cooked in brown sauce, with parsley, olives, and plenty of seasoning. Tomato omelette makes a nice breakfast dish, too, either with or without the addition of chopped green peppers and onion.

Corn fritters, fried eggplant, fried and creamed tomatoes, are all good, and mushrooms are delicious for breakfast, broiled on toast, or fried with bacon, or mixed with scrambled eggs. To broil these in the best way they should be peeled, the inside rubbed with butter, and turned first toward the fire; when this is done, turn them over and drop a bit of butter into the cup; butter the other side, and broil that last. Another way of cooking them is to peel them, fill the deep

14. Josephine Grenier,

"Veranda Meals." *Harper's Bazar*

42.7 (July 1908): 684.

CROCHET INSERTIONS AND MEDALLIONS

THE use of hand-crocheted laces for the adornment of lingerie gowns and blouses and for joining the seams of these is more than ever before considered the final touch of smartness in a summer outfit. Yards and yards of the lace may be used in any width from an inch down to a tiny beading. The effect is much prettier than can be given by the use of any machine-made finish, and the crocheted laces are practically everlasting. They are made in set patterns and also in the more elaborate designs with many little picots.

These laces may be put on the blouse front in all sorts of dainty ways. Perhaps the prettiest method is to baste the lace in place as you want it and then to hem the edges securely in place with a firm thread (about No. 70 sewing thread

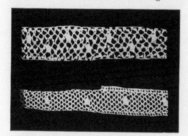

IRISH LACE INSERTIONS.
Nos. 203 and 204. Price, 50 cents a yard each.

is right) on the right side. After this has been done the material may be cut away from the under side, leaving margin enough to turn in at each side. This may be caught back by feather-stitching on each side in the crochet cotton or a rather firm and well-twisted mercerized embroidery cotton. A clever woman who did not know how to make a blouse for herself and had never learned to embroider, bought ready-

SIMPLE CROCHET BEADINGS.
Nos. 205 and 206. Price, 30 cents a yard each.

made a fine batiste blouse with the front tucked to make a broad yoke. On this she basted some of this crocheted Irish insertion, forming a crossed network of squares over the tucks, and when

her lace had been hemmed in place she feather-stitched the edges as described and set a little Irish lace medallion in each square. The edge of this medallion was hemmed and when the material had been cut away on the under side the raw edges were neatly whipped down. The result was a blouse which looked like the most expensive of hand-made imported gowns. The machine stitching of the tucks did not seem in

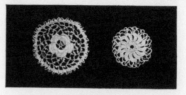

IRISH CROCHET MEDALLIONS.
No 207. Price, 30 cents each or $1.50 for six.
No. 208. Price, 15 cents each or 75 cents for six.

keeping with the rest, so she ripped out the machine work, and in holes left by the needle she ran the tucks by hand.

The crochet insertions are admirably adapted for use in petticoats because of their durability. The cost is more than for ordinary machine-made laces, but when one takes into account the fact that the lace and embroidery are the parts of a petticoat that wear out, the comfort of having something that survives much wear will reconcile many women to the added original expense.

The two laces in the first illustration measure

NARROW IRISH INSERTION.
No. 209. Price, 40 cents a yard.

about one inch wide each. The edge may be finished with the extra beaded edge, or not. The next two patterns are about three-fourths of an inch wide, and the fifth insertion measures three quarters of an inch in width.

The medallions speak for themselves. The one with the rose centre is a little over two inches across, and the wheel one and a half inches. They are suitable for decorating waists, whole gowns, and summer neckwear.

The little medallions are used, also to adorn the stiff linen collars that every one is wearing with shirtwaists. A circle is cut out at each end of the finished collar, and the raw edge is buttonholed or crocheted, and one of these crocheted medallions set in. This harmonizes most effectively with the bow or jabot of Irish crochet that is so often seen.

15. "Crochet Insertions and Medallions."
Harper's Bazar 42.7 (July 1908):
n.p. (end of issue).

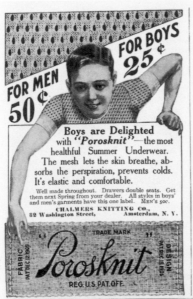

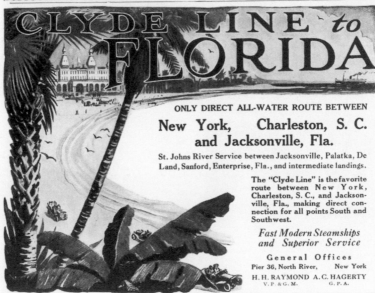
16. Advertisements.

Harper's Bazar 42.12 (December 1908):

n.p. (end of issue).

Frank Luther Mott notes that it immediately became more directly and visibly oriented to the "gay, and 'smart'" (3: 390). (The anomaly of the title's spelling was also rectified.) The magazine continued to publish distinguished authors—Jane Trahey's coffee-table book of selections from the *Bazaar*'s first hundred years includes stories by Flannery O'Connor, Colette, Eudora Welty, and Isak Dineson.

The Whole Family was an unusual undertaking, yet one that could easily be accommodated within the *Bazar*'s usual range of discourses. (I show in chapter 3 that this was true not only for its variety of contributors but also for the topics it treated.) The guessing game foregrounded the element of "fun," to use Howells's term, but the way was open for the project to be taken "seriously," as he wished. Alfred Bendixen implies that it was, writing in his introduction to the 1986 reprint that when the novel was published in book form, "it met with good sales and polite reviews" (xxxv). However, the reception of the novel seems to me at once less respectful and more revealing than that description suggests. We need not remain within any interpretive bounds set by contemporary reactions, yet they offer some clues for efforts to reconstruct the discourses that intersect in this narrative and to understand its significance. Reviews of *The Whole Family* do invariably note the contributors' distinction, but in reporting the unusual nature of the project what they mostly emphasize is its strangeness.

Bendixen treats the *Bookman*'s comment that the work is "a monument to its anonymous projector and editor," for example, as an unambiguous compliment. Yet what follows makes this tribute to the organizer's ingenuity emphatically tongue-in-cheek: "The man—or woman—who could draw Mr. Howells, and Mr. James, and Mrs. Phelps Ward, and Dr. Van Dyke into such a scheme, and hold them to playing the game with straight faces in public, possesses qualities worthy of this record. His name deserves to be written on brass—than which, in spite of Horace, there is nothing more perdurable" ("Chronicle and Comment" 423). The anonymous author compares the collaborative process to the children's game in which a whispered sentence is passed on from one person to another (what we now call "Telephone"), commenting: "This sort of thing has more than once been the amusement of hilarious house-parties and circles of giggling boarding-school girls; never before, we believe, has it enlisted the co-operation of a group of authors every one of whom is known to the public that reads" (423). He (or she) goes on to propose that a strict set of rules for such sport be set up, with penalties for authors who snarl the plot or exceed their allotted number of words. The *Bookman* certainly took note of the publication of *The Whole Family*—but more as an oddity, and an occasion for facetious comment, than as a serious work of literature.

The *Nation*'s brief comment on *The Whole Family* is also humorous. Like all the reviews it begins with a comment on the collaboration: "This must have been good fun for everybody involved, though how it all came about is a question for the curious. We know, in a general way, who got together this company of strange bedfellows. Their joint performance was, we believe, the subject of a guessing-contest. But on what principle were they chosen? . . . One fancies Mr. James hypnotically persuaded to take his place in the circle between facetious Mr. Bangs and soulful Elizabeth Stuart Phelps, and caused to produce an excellent parody of himself" ("Current Fiction" 552). Its praise is mild ("The result is sufficiently amusing"), and the anonymous author emphasizes not the novel's unity but the vivid individuality of each "monologue." "It is pure vaudeville, but many of the 'turns' are characteristic and amusing; none more so than that of Mr. James, who holds the stage (if not the house) twice as long as most of the others, and, as he would say, gets beautifully nowhere" (553). In comparing the composite novel to a variety-based form like vaudeville, the *Nation*'s anonymous reviewer concisely captures the distinctive quality of the novel; I return to this image at the conclusion of the next chapter.

The *New York Times* review by Florence Finch Kelly, which Bendixen does not mention, treats the novel seriously but as a failure. Its subtitle mentions that the book was written by "Twelve Leading Literary Lights" but calls it a "Comedy of Confusion." Kelly finds some chapters skillful but is not so impressed by the status of the contributors that she fails to observe that the narrative becomes incoherent. She also does not hesitate to comment on James's involved style: "Charles Edward's shades of thought and feeling are pursued to the very last and finest nuance, and then nailed down with an 'exactly,' and his ruminating train of thought pursues its determined way, regardless of erupting parentheses, until it finds a period at a dignified remoteness from the starting point. It is quite possible to determine what the young man is talking about by reading each sentence over twice." Kelly considers the sole unifying element of *The Whole Family* to be the chapters' consistent cynicism—although she finds a way to treat this un-Harperish quality as genuinely literary, suggesting that the novel's focus on the Talberts' "foibles" is true to the tradition of comedy.

Only the *North American Review* gave the novel a long, unequivocally positive notice, calling it "continually amusing, often hilariously funny," and asserting that despite its "composite workmanship" the narrative has a "fundamental unity" of atmosphere, style, and spirit—the authors are "fundamentally in earnest, and all have proved faithful to certain homely yet spiritual ideals that lie at the base of American life." Clarence Gaines finds both "genuine sentiment" from "the old elemental sources" (929) and the "up-to-date" quality that the *Bazar* strove for: "'The Whole Family' seems very typical of the 'new literature' in this country. It illustrates in a novel, attractive and not too serious form both sides of our modern fiction and our modern life—the sensitiveness to ideas, the sane, matter-of-fact recognition of things as they are" (930). As Bendixen notes, this review is almost "reverent" (xxxvi)—but one must wonder if that has something to do with a fact he does not mention: the *Review* was owned by George Harvey, the president of Harper's.

Harper's Bazar itself offered some testimony about contemporary reactions to *The Whole Family*. Judging by correspondence that was printed in June, November, and December 1908, it was well liked by readers, and they were deeply interested in guessing the authors of the chapters (and usually guessed wrong). The novel reminded at least one reader of *Six of One by Half a Dozen of the Other*, and a reminiscence about the earlier collaboration was printed.[19] Of course, we cannot take this as anything but partial—in both senses of the word—evidence of readers' response; not only is the material fragmentary, but editorial selection and presentation of such materials was completely continuous with the promotional process. So, for that matter, was the review of *The Whole Family* that appeared in the *Bazar* the month after the serial's conclusion, marking its publication as a book. Such notices were not unusual—puffing Harper books in Harper periodicals was an old family-business tradition. Every month the *Bazar* "Books and Writers" department featured books published by the house; those reviewed in

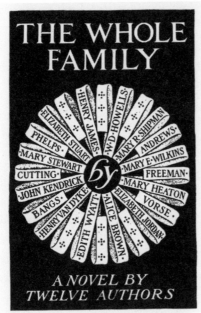

17. "Twelve Popular Authors
Join in Writing a Splendid Novel."
Harper's Bazar 42.12 (December 1908):
advertising supplement, 2.

the same issue as *The Whole Family* were by Elizabeth Jordan and by *Monthly* editor Henry Mills Alden.

What the *Bazar* review and the advertisements for the novel, taken together, mainly tell us is how the Harper's establishment hoped to sell *The Whole Family.* The review asserts that the serial attracted an extraordinary amount of attention: "Letters have poured in from all over the country. . . . Women's clubs have discussed the situations of *The Whole Family* and the problem of the authorship of the various chapters." The distinction of the contributors is cited, and the book itself is praised: "It is, as a novel, absorbingly interesting, and its environment and plot are those which should appeal to all American readers. Never before has the American family, as an institution, been so subtly discussed; rarely have twelve characters in a book been put before the public with such peculiar vividness and charm. . . . The book may be *bought* because twelve distinguished authors have written it. It will be *read* because it is well worth reading." The fact that the novel was advertised not only in the *Bazar* (see fig. 17) but concurrently in *Harper's Monthly* and *Harper's Weekly* shows that it was being marketed as a serious novel, and to male as well as female readers.

The advertisement's text actually gives a more candid account of the character of the novel than the *Bazar*'s review. "This is a strangely exciting story which rather runs away with one. . . . The curious thing is that while twelve distinguished authors have written it, it reads straightaway with breathless galloping." *The Whole Family* is not a neglected masterpiece, nor even a respectable minor work by some major authors, but it is "strangely exciting." Its very eccentricity—so clear to reviewers at the time—now directs our attention to the complex array of choices and forces that shape the episode and the text. A literary history that turns around such a runaway narrative cannot remain within any familiar orbit.

Harper's -- Institution

❧ The Hearthstone at Harper's ❧

elite /Highbrow

Today, the identification of a book as published by Harper & Brothers is
likely to be an inert bibliographic reference. For most of the nineteenth
century, and still in 1908, however, it was much more than that. The
imprint assured a certain prestige; it did not so much guarantee a book's
quality as mark it as part of a powerful, extended cultural apparatus.
Particular aspects of *The Whole Family* become more intelligible when
this institutional framework is reconstructed—and that reconstruction
also brings into focus the importance of Harper's itself, something that
has been better appreciated in publishing than in literary history. John
Tebbel writes that "[t]he story of the Harper brothers and the house
they founded is certainly the most remarkable in the history of American publishing. As a family history alone, it is a fascinating record of
nineteenth-century social, cultural and even political life, while as publishing history the long narrative of the house which functions today as
Harper & Row, still one of the two or three leaders, is a classic study."[1]
(The house's later metamorphosis into the international firm Harper-
Collins is also revealing.) Current cultural history has revived familiarity with *Harper's Monthly* as a "quality magazine," a pillar of genteel
culture. Yet the *Monthly* was only part of the Harper's establishment,
and by taking a longer and wider look we can both enlarge and compli-
cate our understanding of the social relations of literary production.

My research on Harper's began in my effort to understand *The Whole
Family*, and the collaboration that produced it remains a reference point
here—but one I will range well beyond, for my topic in this chapter is
not a text, not only an episode, but an institution. Harper's played an
important role in the development of a national print culture, and its

history refracts the struggles of successive generations over the relations of culture, class, and commerce.

Harper's and Antebellum Print Culture

A HOUSE UNDIVIDED

The development of print culture in America is an extraordinary story. One is tempted to hyperbole by the transformations of the antebellum period, which encompass not only tremendous technological innovations in paper making, printing, and related technologies such as lighting and corrective eyeglasses; but also improvements on a vast scale in transportation and thus in the distribution of newspapers, books, and magazines; and an enormous expansion of schooling and libraries. It is not hard to understand why nineteenth-century publishers and twentieth-century historians of publishing alike often sound as though they are chronicling a triumphal progress. George Palmer Putnam, at a banquet held in 1855 by the Association of New York Publishers, cited statistics showing that eight times as many original American works were published in the United States in 1853 as had been published in each of the years between 1830 and 1842. Comparing that increase of 800 percent with the population increase of 80 percent, he asserted that "literature and the bulk of the book trade advanced ten times faster than the population. If we compare the numbers printed of each edition, the growth is still greater; for 20 years ago who *imagined* editions of 100,000 or 75,000, or 30,000, or even the now common number of 10,000" (Zboray 3). This remarkable period of growth in publishing and the reading public, sometimes called "the great revolution," was characterized by intense competition and great instability in the industry. Harper & Brothers emerged from it as the largest publisher in the world.[2]

The firm was founded as J. & J. Harper in New York in 1817.[3] The young brothers James and John Harper combined savings from the wages they earned as skilled printers with a few hundred dollars borrowed from their father, a Long Island farmer and carpenter, to buy two presses, some fonts of type, and binding equipment. Their printing, according to tradition, quickly became known for its excellent quality.

The Harpers undertook some jobs on commission—their first complete book was a translation of *Seneca's Morals* for the bookseller Evert Duyckinck—but soon ventured into independent publishing with an edition of Locke's *Essay on Human Understanding.* Their younger brother Joseph Wesley Harper joined the business in 1823, Fletcher Harper came in 1825, and the name Harper & Brothers was adopted in 1833. By 1830 the Harpers claimed they were publishing a book a week. In the years leading up to the Civil War the firm was known not only for its fine printing and its size, but also for the wide range of material it published, from inexpensive novels through biography, travel, and history to a sumptuous illustrated Bible. Their successes included Scott's *Waverley* novels, Dana's *Two Years before the Mast*, and an abridged edition of *Webster's Dictionary; Moby-Dick* was a notable failure. The inexpensive Family Library and School District series both swelled sales and made some people (most famously Thoreau) worry that Harper's was selecting what Americans read. The firm was remarkable and remarked as well for its rapid adoption of innovations in production such as stereotyping, electrotyping, and steam-driven presses. And the brothers were equally inventive and energetic in their pursuit of new methods of distribution and marketing—according to Tebbel, they "laid the groundwork for modern publicity practices" (1: 276).

The dramatic story of the complete destruction of the Harper's plant by fire in 1853, the brothers' decision not to retire with their fortunes but to rebuild, and the construction of their famous fireproof offices and printing plant on Cliff Street and Franklin Square is recounted by virtually every chronicler of publishing from that era to our own.[4] The new Harper establishment covered half an acre, its two blocks of buildings linked by a series of iron bridges and served by a common staircase and hoist in the courtyard (see fig. 18). The whole was a model of rationalized production housing every operation of publishing—each in its separate space, following the strict division of labor that had come to characterize the industry since the Harpers' early days (see fig. 19). From the first, Franklin Square was seen as the embodiment of the brothers' determination and the company's consequence. An 1855 addition to Jacob Abbott's Harper's Story Books series called *The Harper Establishment; or, How the Story Books Are Made* describes it in extraordinary detail. A very small portion of Abbott's descrip-

18. Harper's Franklin Square building, with the Cliff Street building visible in the rear. Uncredited illustration from Eugene Exman, *The House of Harper* 42.

tion of the presses explains the engraving I include as figure 20: "The feeder has just placed a sheet to be printed on the inclined table before her. This table is called the *apron*. In a moment a set of iron fingers will come up from below, and, taking hold of the lower edge of the paper, will draw it in under the platen, between the platen and the form" (119, 121). Abbott took it for granted that the engineering marvel of Franklin Square, with its enormous productive capacity devoted to serving the American reader, commanded public attention and admiration. Increasingly, Harper & Brothers was not only celebrated but was celebrated for being celebrated.

The powerful presence of Harper's in American cultural life during the second half of the nineteenth century had as much to do with the magazines the firm published as with the books, something that the separation of the various media in standard histories tends to obscure.[5] In 1850 the first issue of *Harper's Monthly Magazine* proclaimed its design "to place within the reach of the great mass of the Ameri-

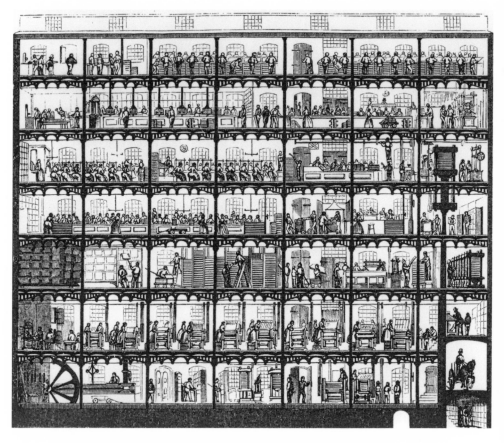

19. "Sectional view of the Cliff Street building." From Jacob Abbott, *The Harper Establishment* 42.

can people the unbounded treasures of the Periodical Literature of the present day" ("A Word at the Start" 1). The *Monthly* relied—like the brothers' book business—on English fiction and reprinted essays on biography, travel, and science. The magazine gradually came to include more original and American material and a very large number of illustrations; the two most famous departments—the "Editor's Easy Chair" and the humor department, the "Editor's Drawer"—were established early, although others came and went. Frank Luther Mott calls the response to the *Monthly* during the 1850s "phenomenal": it was "the greatest success in magazine history up to that time" (2: 390). Abbott's *Harper Establishment* makes a rare break from its cool, documentary description to try to convey the sheer size of the magazine's circulation, at that time 140,000 a month: "Few persons have any idea how large a number this is as applied to the edition of a book. If magazines were to *rain down*, and a man had only to pick them up like chips, it would take him a fortnight to pick up the copies of one single number, supposing him to pick up one every three seconds, and to work ten hours a day" (158). The image of magazines pouring from the sky captures the tone of contemporary accounts of Harper's success.

The *Monthly* eschewed the controversial. Henry Mills Alden, its editor for fully fifty years, from 1869 to 1919 (and one of those to whom Jordan turned in her difficulties over *The Whole Family*), wrote in 1902 that from the beginning it "excluded partisan politics and all subjects upon which readers were divided on sectarian lines in religious thought and feeling," and came to exclude the "timely" as well ("Editor's Study" 646–47). In 1857 the Harpers began the more topical *Harper's Weekly*, which had short, readable articles on politics and current events as its mainstay although it also included English fiction. From early on

20. "The Power-Press." From Abbott, *The Harper Establishment* 120.

The Hearthstone at Harper's 63

the *Weekly* was distinguished for its illustrations; Mott calls its thousands of pictures "a vital illustrated history of the years from 1857 to 1916" (2: 469). Historians remember particularly the work of cartoonist Thomas Nast (including his contribution to the campaign against Tammany Hall, which was fought in the pages of the *Weekly*). The magazine operation was further expanded in 1867 with the founding of *Harper's Bazar,* which began as a weekly fashion magazine modeled on, and reprinting plates from, *Der Bazar* of Berlin (its German origin explains the unusual spelling of the magazine's title, which was not changed until 1929). Mott calls the *Bazar* "a ladies' *Harper's Weekly,* with the same type of English serials, double-page pictures, miscellany, and humor, and with fashions and patterns taking the place of politics and public affairs. The art work was excellent, with cartoons by Nast and engravings by the great *Weekly* group" (3: 389). The Harper's magazines aspired to address the full range of interests that the American middle class cultivated in public. (In figure 21 Nast claims an even broader audience.)

J. Henry Harper's bulky official history of the firm, *The House of Harper: A Century of Publishing in Franklin Square,* was published in 1912 (by Harper's, of course). Its anecdotes of the brothers' humble but virtuous and industrious family and their early days as working printers are complemented by a description of the daily operations of the firm as characterized by perfect fraternal harmony and complementarity:

> From the beginning the affairs of the firm were conducted on the basis of absolute trust and confidence. The brothers had a tacit understanding that each had a veto power, and that nothing should be undertaken in the administration of the business if one of them disapproved. In consequence of the adoption of this principle, the House was never divided, while at the same time, it has probably been saved from many doubtful enterprises. There was a sort of implied division of labor, but it was a matter of implication only, not of expressed agreement. They were all four hard-working men, working in perfect harmony, and each one naturally fell into the groove to which he was best adapted. . . . How singularly free the firm was from all individual selfishness, and how thoroughly fraternal, is indicated by the fact that for a long time no separate accounts were kept between the brothers, but each one took from the cashier's drawer what

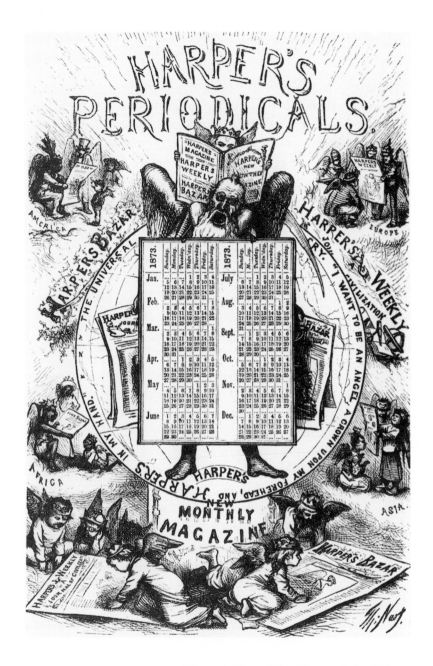

21. Thomas Nast, "The Universal Cry." From
Thomas Nast's Almanac, 1872, published
by Harper & Brothers.
The New York Public Library.

he required for his own needs, and the rest remained a common fund.[6] (22–23)

The reference to a "House divided" here works by double-talk; weighty biblical and national rhetoric can be invoked because it is used lightly. Yet the passage and the book as a whole do indeed imply that the national order is sustained by such men as the Harper brothers, implicitly relying on a more widespread conviction—evidenced, for example, in Matthew Brady making their collective portrait part of his cumulative gallery of distinguished Americans (for the significance of the gallery, see Panzer; for the image, see fig. 22). Yet, the assertion of seamless family solidarity coexists with somewhat contradictory evidence in stories of the Harpers' sharp business sense; J. Henry not only praises the brothers' generous refusal to keep accounts among themselves but also solemnly tells the story of how Wesley's father charged him for his board, then returned the money to him so he could buy into his brothers' firm (21–22). It seems that the family did not always rely on the invisible hand to do their arithmetic.

The Harpers' reluctance to institute separate accounts and double-entry bookkeeping is treated by their chroniclers as an archaism that demonstrates their personal integrity; character, that is, not a system of scrutiny, guarantees their honesty.[7] Thus their resistance manifests their link to an older system of production; as Leonore Davidoff and Catherine Hall demonstrate in their study of the formation of the English middle class during the latter eighteenth century and the first half of the nineteenth, the form of most business and professional enterprises developed directly from the family household and relied on the sort of trustworthiness evoked in Harper's anecdotes about the brothers. Such enterprises expanded by taking partners who functioned like family members: "[E]very partner could act as an agent for the other but was also liable for all debts. 'Partnerships were in some senses *brothers* who represented each other.' . . . The whole thrust of the partnership was active participation. Its essence was the personal nature of the relationship for no stranger could be substituted. . . . [F]irms tended to be judged on the quality of their partners, a judgement frequently given moral, even religious overtones" (200–201).[8] The gradual acceptance of more accurate and impersonal ac-

22. Undated photograph of
Fletcher, James, John, and J. Wesley Harper
by Matthew Brady. Prints and Photographs
Division, *Library of Congress.*

counting was essential to the development of modern business organizations with limited liability. Yet even as Harper's was on its way to becoming a joint-stock corporation (in 1896), rationalization was counterbalanced by the reiteration and reworking of its image as a family enterprise. My purpose here is not to retell a story of changes in business practices and the consequences of incorporation that has been amply told elsewhere. I want rather to underscore the way each trace of the past exists in the present and has consequences that proliferate into the future. The family business enters the historical stage not once, with the end of its era clearly marked, but over and over, at many levels and in many ways.

Thus, while J. Henry's description of the founders contributes to our long view of Harper's and its importance in American cultural history, *The House of Harper* interests me still more as a document of its own moment; this most developed example of what we might call a house ideology dates from only a few years after *The Whole Family*. The process of enhancing the myth of origin continues into the modern period, as one can see by examining versions of a story that must have had a strong oral tradition in Franklin Square—it is told in J. C. Derby's 1884 memoir *Fifty Years among Authors, Books and Publishers*, by J. Henry Harper in *The House of Harper* and again in a 1934 memoir, in Eugene Exman's subsequent official house history of 1967, and in Tebbel's and Madison's scholarly histories. J. Henry wrote in 1912: "A gentleman once asked James the natural question: 'Which of you is the Harper and which are the Brothers?' 'Either one is the Harper,' was the reply, 'the rest are the Brothers'" (22). Later the story was—let us call it—simplified: "[A]nyone who asked which was the Mr. Harper and which were the brothers got the same pat answer: 'Any one of us is Mr. Harper, and all the rest are brothers'" (14).[9] In each case fraternal equality and solidarity are affirmed; but Exman's version both removes any possible implication that the two elder brothers had a different status from the younger and turns a single exchange into a habitual posture. I am telling the story of Harper's in roughly chronological order, but a piece of evidence like Exman's description of the middle of the nineteenth century, published in 1967 but produced out of an affiliation with Harper's that began in the 1920s, distributes the weight of its evidence more intricately across time.

Accounts from inside Franklin Square acknowledge—and those originating elsewhere feature more prominently—the fact that the absence of an international copyright agreement was the key to Harper's success in the antebellum period and beyond. As Mott puts it in his account of the founding of *Harper's Monthly:* "[T]he Harpers, honorable men and good Methodists as they were, meant to take these 'unbounded treasures' from the British periodicals without so much as a thank-you, precisely as they had pirated hundreds of novels for their various Libraries" (2: 385). Such reprinting was legal and routine, but English authors and publishers still denounced it as dishonest, and American writers who found themselves disadvantaged in the marketplace resented it as unpatriotic. There was a particularly loud outcry over the Harpers' piracies, presumably because they were so successful, perhaps also because the brothers' sterling morality was so publicly praised. Another anecdote that has become (in Tebbel's phrase) "part of publishing lore" (308) describes a visit to the Harper offices in 1849 by George Palmer Putnam—a devoted advocate of international copyright who scrupulously tendered royalties to foreign authors—and Swedish author Frederika Bremer, in hope of dissuading the brothers from printing a pirated edition of her novels that would reduce sales of Putnam's authorized one.

> Miss Bremer was received courteously by Fletcher Harper, given a grand tour of the plant, and while she was being taken down to her carriage, Putnam had a quiet word with Harper.
>
> "Do you not think, Mr. Harper," Putnam said, as his son recalled, "bearing in mind that the little lady's sojourn in this country is dependent upon the receipts from her books, and that she has come over here trusting to American hospitality and to American good faith, that it might be in order for you to withdraw your announcement of those competing editions?"
>
> Fletcher Harper, "the good Methodist," as Putnam refers to him sarcastically, replied, "Mr. Putnam, courtesy is courtesy and business is business." (1: 308–9)

The Harpers did frequently pay for early proofs of works they wished to be the first to print in America, and also made voluntary payments to English authors, so they had defenders as well as detractors. But the association of the Harpers with piracy was strong enough, and was remembered long enough, for Algernon Tassin to title a chapter of his 1916 book on American magazines "Harper's—The Converted Corsair."

Publishing historians present the Harpers' treatment of Putnam and Bremer as a violation of "courtesy of the trade"—customs, initially worked out in the 1830s in correspondence between Fletcher Harper and Henry Carey, by which publishers established claims to books by announcing planned editions (ostensibly *after* making arrangements with foreign authors or publishers). This was called—again indexing Harper's leadership in the industry—"the Harper rule" (Tebbel 1: 274). (Of course, trade courtesy did not necessarily benefit authors; it managed competition among publishers.) Such violations were frequent, but Tebbel calls this "one of the more cold-blooded examples" (1: 309). In fact, however, Exman shows that the story as told in the younger Putnam's 1912 memoir cannot be accurate. News of Harper's cheap reprints is said to have appeared in *Harper's Monthly*, which did not exist in 1849; and in any case the firm had been printing Bremer's novels since 1843, and would have had to actually withdraw books in print to avoid competing with Putnam's edition.[10] But the story indicates how Harper's evoked from observers not only admiration but also anxiety over the relation between the profit motive and moral and aesthetic values. Tebbel suggests in reporting as early an episode as the brothers' increased financial conservatism in reaction to the panic of 1837 that "[i]t may well be that Harper's was the first house to be regarded as being commercial and thinking more of business than of literature" (1: 276). In 1840 Richard Dana Sr. wrote while negotiating the sale of his son's book that the brothers were "sharp and vulgar men to all appearance" (cited in Madison, *Irving* 26)—and in fact the Harpers, having bought the copyright of *Two Years before the Mast*, declined to share its unexpectedly large profits with the author and were criticized for their decision to abide by the contract. The frequency with which Fletcher Harper's remark about the origins of the *Monthly Magazine*—"If we were asked why we first started a monthly magazine we would have to say frankly that it was as a tender to our business, though it has grown into something quite beyond that" (*House* 84–

85)—is quoted provides another example of widespread ambivalence toward the Harpers' blending of commerce and culture.

There is no evidence that the Harpers themselves saw a contradiction between the two.[11] Certainly they did not consider their dissemination of English writers unpatriotic; the constant increase in the number of pages rolling off their presses was good for Harper's, but was it not also good for America? The development of the national literature was important, and the first number of the *Monthly* reprinted a brief contribution to the debate over the conditions for an American literature from *Dublin University Magazine*. Yet informing and educating the citizenry was at least equally important, for, in Robert Wiebe's words, "[w]here European cultures invoked ancient traditions and folk spirits to unite their nations, American culture called on democracy, which occupied the heart of America's romantic nationalism. By midcentury, popular understanding made America and democracy synonymous" (83). So *Harper's Monthly* was serving the nation while tending the firm's business; publishing historian Charles Madison quotes them as asserting: "Literature has gone in pursuit of the million, penetrated highways and hedges, pressed its way into cottages, factories, omnibuses, and railroad cars" (*Book Publishing* 24).[12] The scholarship documenting the difficulties of distribution in the relatively undeveloped transportation system of the mid-nineteenth century shows that this was no empty rhetoric; the Harpers worked hard to get their publications into the hands of the people. And indeed it seems likely that American cultures of letters grew up more rapidly and widely than they would have without the reduced prices made possible by free access to English books; in the short run authors on both sides of the Atlantic were shortchanged, but in the long run the market expanded.

The progressive interpretation of the expansion of print culture as inherently democratic depends on the figure of an apparently undifferentiated "people," already invoked above. Ronald Zboray argues against it, pointing out that for most of the antebellum period books were simply too expensive for working-class people; that when cheap paperbacks did become available in the 1840s they were sold in urban "periodical depots" to which rural Americans had no access; that country booksellers could never offer more than a small selection of books; and that distribution followed the rail lines and left whole regions outside the mainstream. "Even," he writes, "within the highly cultivated markets of the Northeast, the reading public became fragmented by sex, class, and religion in the face of the onslaught of new titles. In short, if the democratization of literature means the equal participation of all in a unified print culture, the antebellum years witnessed a distinctly undemocratic trend" (*A Fictive People* 15). Yet more people were indeed reading more books, and Zboray's alternative terms are themselves also value laden—the fragmentation he describes might be thought of as diversity, and the cohesive print culture he imagines, as uniformity. Each binary proves too simple to capture the changes; the reading public is not only both more and less democratic, by different definitions, but dispersal (also known as diversity) and standardization (also known as cohesion) are increasing at the same time. Thus Carl Kaestle writes: "An expansion of literacy can draw more people into reading the same things (for example, McGuffey's *Readers* or syndicated newspaper columns) but at the same time encourage the development of distinctive reading materials that serve different groups" (55). And—despite both progressive common sense and Habermasian images of the public sphere—there seems to be no direct, necessary correlation between literacy and political participation; Robert Wiebe argues in *Self-Rule*, his cultural history of U.S. democracy, that although the nineteenth-century populace was poorer and less formally educated than that of the twentieth, it produced a more assertive and self-confident electorate (6–7).

The "great mass of the American people" invoked in the first issue of *Harper's Monthly* had important, implicit exclusions—certainly all non-whites, more ambiguously wage-earners; unlike the political public, it included white women. It is uncontroversial to suggest that the readership's center was the emerging middle class, although the contours of "middle class" are themselves controversial. But studies so often mention *Harper's* in the same sentence with *Atlantic Monthly* (founded 1857) as a genteel, "quality," or even highbrow magazine that it is worth emphasizing that its project was originally framed in terms of inclusion, not distinction. Harper & Brothers also produced many books cheaply enough to compete with pulp fiction, and started *Harper's Young People* in 1879 with the declared purpose of providing an alternative to dime novels. This completed the Harper's family of magazines: the "family newspaper" *Harper's Weekly* directed to a masculine interest in current events (although no doubt read by women as well); the *Monthly* addressing the cultural interests of both sexes (although the feminization of culture worried some people); the "family paper for women" *Bazar* devoted to fashion, housekeeping, and female-centered fiction and essays; and *Harper's Young People* for boys and girls (during the brief — for Harper's — twenty years of its existence).[13]

The extended Harper's magazine apparatus seems to have projected a fantasy of the "whole family" onto its readership, soliciting the interest and purchasing power of men, women, and children separately, yet uniting them through their complementary participation in cultural consumption. *E pluribus unum*: the family, like "the people," did not abolish differences among individuals — but it consolidated them into a single figure. Exman comments explicitly on how frequently the image of the family is invoked in the discourses of the firm: "The title page used in Harper catalogues for 1847 and 1848 is dominated by a drawing of a family gathered around a library table. [see fig. 23.] This family motif runs throughout Harper publishing in the nineteenth century, from the beginning of the Family Library in 1830 to their admonition to Thomas Hardy in 1894 that *Harper's Magazine* must contain nothing which could not be read aloud in a family circle" (Exman, *House* 31). The still-familiar Harper's colophon of one hand passing a torch to another first appeared in the first book of the Family Library, and evidently refers both to the transmission of cultural tradition and to the anticipated passing on of the business from one generation to the next (Tebbel 1: 278; see fig. 24). (The fact that they had sons to provide for is always cited in discussions of the brothers' decision to rebuild after the 1853 fire.) Harper's, a family business, published for families. Such images reinforce the link between Harper's and the middle class; as Richard Brodhead so powerfully argues in *Cultures of Letters*, that domestically defined group made "a newly central place *for* literature among its organizing habits and concerns," and made reading one of the defining activities of the home (44). However, we should not therefore disregard other characteristic sites of reading, such as railway journeys (see Zboray 72–75). Harper books were there too, competing with Putnam's Railway classics in pursuing the million.

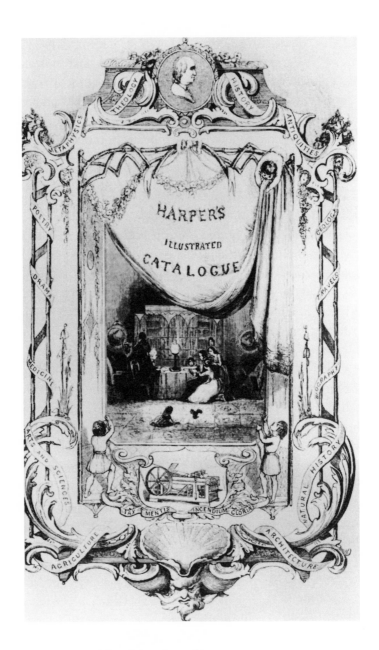

23. Cover used for Harper's catalogs, 1847 and 1848. *The New York Public Library.*

24. Colophon from title page
of Mary Wilkins Freeman's
Six Trees (1903).

The brothers' artisan origins also lent them a certain republican aura; James in particular was said to have chosen printing as his trade after reading Benjamin Franklin's *Autobiography*.[14] And although some anecdotes portray the Harpers as grasping businessmen, others stress their loyalty to their employees and their approachability. J. C. Derby writes of his first meeting with the Harpers in 1838: "I shall never forget the feeling of awe with which I entered their door and presented my letter [of introduction], nor the kindness and cordiality with which they welcomed the youngster on his first visit to the great city, put him at his ease, and made him feel at home" (86). The brothers' solid virtue did not, according to legend, make them grim—there are many stories of James's bluff good humor, John's formidable but friendly imperturbability, Wesley's graciousness, and Fletcher's charm; their collective nickname was "the Brothers Cheeryble." Indeed, as described by J. Henry Harper the central open office of the Franklin Square building seems an extension of their brotherliness: all four were "always ready to meet any one who had business to transact, no matter who he was. It might be that a clerk wanted instruction, a foreman had a sheet just off the press to submit for color, imposition, etc., a compositor with proof for inspection, an author with a manuscript, a dealer wishing to leave an

25. "The Counting-Room." From Abbott, *The Harper Establishment* 16.

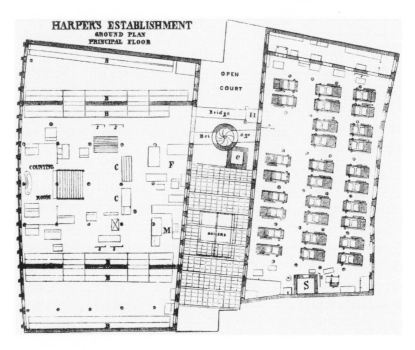

26. Floor plan. From Abbott, *The Harper Establishment* 21.

order for books, a paper-maker with samples, an old friend who wanted a few minutes' social chat, or a distinguished visitor who had just come to town. All these had free access to the counting-room, and were received with equal courtesy" (*House* 120; see figs. 25 and 26). The interest in the interior arrangements at Franklin Square demonstrated in many such accounts—to say nothing of magazine departments titled "The Editor's Study" and "The Editor's Easy Chair"—again direct our attention to the relentlessly domestic imagery of the House of Harper.

It did not stop the criticism of Harper's piracies, but the Franklin Square building, with a full-length statue of Benjamin Franklin over the entrance and smaller statues of Washington, Franklin, and Jefferson above, gave the firm a patriotic face (see fig. 18). (Franklin also appears on the catalog cover in figure 23, and Abbott managed to include two additional engravings of him in *The Harper Establishment*—as a boy carrying forms and as an old man amusing himself by setting type.) The prominence of Franklin at Harper's led to the widespread belief that the square was named after him (a claim that has been repeated in scholarship as recently as 1988). Actually, according to J. Henry Harper, the name derives from a Walter Franklin who lived there before the Revolutionary War and was, appropriately, a merchant.[15] Again, an apocryphal story is full of historical meaning, as the House of Harper becomes an icon of the nation-building power of (in Benedict Anderson's memorable phrase) "print capitalism."

Harper's and Postbellum Print Culture

"A CLIMB UP THE SPIRAL STAIRCASE"

Harper's continued to dominate book publishing after the Civil War. Its volume of publications was huge, its prestige enormous. J. C. Derby's 1884 memoir demonstrates both the prominence of Harper's in the latter nineteenth century and how powerful the image of the founders remained when he writes: "It is a singular fact that the *American Cyclopaedia*, which contains more than twenty-three thousand titles of subjects, gives but one title of a business firm, and that reads 'Harper & Brothers.' The reason for this exception is probably the fact that the four brothers acted as a unit in all their business transactions. They were known, individually, as exemplary Christian gentlemen; but, collectively, the brothers were inseparable. Their firm name was probably more widely known among English-speaking people than that of any other business house" (106). Again the Harpers represent not only good business, not only estimable culture, but a united family—a band of brothers joined by the business of culture, succeeding because of their solid values and family solidarity. Even given the changes in literary culture and the firm itself between this comment and 1907, it makes a great deal of sense that the House of Harper should generate a project called *The Whole Family* that aspired to produce good literature in order to sell magazines and books.

By the time Derby's memoir appeared, of course, a new generation of Harpers had been in control of the firm for some time. Three of the four founding brothers died in 1869 and 1870, Fletcher in 1877. The nominal head of the house after 1877 was James's son Philip; the effective editor in chief was Joseph W. Harper Jr. The latter, widely regarded as the ablest of the five sons who had joined the firm, is often called, even in publishing histories, "Brooklyn Joe"; the wide use of such distinguishing nicknames for the Harpers of the second and third generations marks both how many entered the business and how faithfully and frequently family names were repeated. (The Harpers themselves seem to have rather enjoyed the confusion.) Any male member of the family was welcome, and something like twelve were active in the firm at the end of the century.[16] Although Joseph Harper Jr. is generally depicted as a brilliant publisher and a formidable character, he and his cousins play a much smaller role in the Harper's legend than the founders do. For this period historians tend to focus less on individual personalities or fraternal relationships than on the general family solidarity of the inheritors (see, for example, Madison, *Book Publishing* 65–70). Tebbel writes, "Under the influence of this strong tribe of men, bound together by familial ties of affection, trust, blood and the sense of continuity that had distinguished the house from the beginning, Harper reached a peak of size and influence in the eighties" (2: 192).

The expectation of continuity embodied in the Harper colophon was in some measure fulfilled. All accounts represent the new generation of Harpers as loyal to the traditions of the firm and having excellent relations among themselves. The inevitable anecdotes about conversations between the brothers and their sons or grandsons about what hour they arrived at the office are good-humored ones. According to J. Henry Harper, every member of the second generation and many of the third learned typesetting before moving on to other roles in the business because "it was a matter of family pride that they should be practical printers as the four brothers had been before them."[17] Nevertheless, the younger Harpers had been raised in very different circumstances from the founders—with more social privilege and more formal education, with manual labor a family tradition rather than a necessity. Joseph Harper Jr. was a graduate of Columbia (the first member of the family to earn a college degree) when he began his publishing career in the composing room at Franklin Square.

Exman avers that the second generation brought a new "spirit of liveliness and fun" (the word *horseplay* is even used) to Franklin Square in the 1850s, and that, taking the prestige of their name for granted, they approached business with confidence (Exman, *Brothers* 345). Charles Madison reflects the sense that the young Harpers were well suited to their station in life when he writes: "From a public standpoint 'Brooklyn Joe' was ethically a cut above his father and uncles. He was aggressive yet affable, at once subtle and simple in manner" (Madison, *Book Publishing* 65). This new Mr. Harper made one important public change immediately: he reversed the firm's stand on international copyright. An Englishman working on that issue, C. E. Appleton, provided another testimonial to the consequence of Harper & Brothers when he wrote in 1877, after a visit to the United States, "it must be remembered that so far as any influence upon Congress is concerned, the little finger of Mr. Harper is thicker than the loins of all the literary and scientific men in the United States put together" (239). A collaborative American proposal for an agreement—inevitably called the Harper Treaty—revived the issue, although there was a long struggle before the legislation was finally passed in 1891. The undoubted social standing of the Harpers and the prestige of the house did not end public discussion of their commercialism, however. In James L. Ford's popular satire *The Literary Shop* (1894), for example, the heads of the firm must deal with a poets' strike, which they resolve by agreeing to install "emery wheels in the dialect shop instead of the old-fashioned cross-cut files and sandpaper that now take up so much of the men's time" and to require only one rhyme to the quatrain at the "metrical benches" (192)—thus restoring order at the "Franklin Square Prose and Verse Foundry." [18]

As Ford's images remind us, the period after the torch was passed at Harper's was one of increasingly sharp class divisions in America. By the 1890s many people saw social distances within the nation as vast beyond bridging. Populists' fierce advocacy of "the people," for example, invoked the long-standing power of that figure in order to resist an increased acceptance of hierarchy. The hard times, labor struggles, and heterogeneous immigration of the last third of the nineteenth century are historical commonplaces, and increasingly it is also recognized as a period of consolidation and institution building among the property-owning classes. Since 1980 a rich body of historical work has delineated the postbellum development of elaborated, stratified distinctions among cultural practices, a hierarchy closely imbricated with the social order. So effectively has the system put in place then done its work, so natural has it become to think in terms of high and low culture, that (just as it is unsettling to be asked to think of Shakespeare's works as collaboratively authored) it came as a surprise to many of us to learn from Lawrence Levine that "Shakespeare *was* popular entertainment in nineteenth-century America" (21). As we have come to see the relations of discourses and social structure as genuinely reciprocal, such reconstructions have seemed more and more important. When we acknowledge that class is both a postulate and a demonstrable social fact, that "the history of class is inseparable from the history of that category," [19] we have made a consequential place for intellectual and cultural history in any analysis of social transformation.

The various scholarly accounts of the development of cultural hierarchy can be assembled into a roughly periodized narrative. The 1849 Astor Place Riot, in which at least twenty-two people were actually killed in a clash over competing interpretations of Shakespeare, seems necessarily a key reference point, but the bulk of Levine's evidence comes from considerably later. Paul DiMaggio has concentrated on the urban upper class's development of institutions of sacralized high culture such as art museums and symphony orchestras—absent before 1850, emerging by 1870, and fully developed by the end of the century (and beginning to change again after 1910). John Kasson too finds both popular and elite cultural institutions taking their shape from just

after the end of the Civil War to the early twentieth century, arguing that "the specialization of artistic activities, their cultivation of authority, their injunctions to disciplined passivity, their emphasis upon
spectacle, and the kinds of audiences they helped create all marked a
move toward a more segmented, privatized society in which divisions
of 'taste' and deportment masked and reinforced divisions of class"
(216). Richard Brodhead, looking closely at literature, delineates three
"cultures of letters": a "low" one developing in the 1840s and organized
in the 1850s by the "story papers," the roughly contemporary "domestic or middlebrow world," and a literary high culture represented—and
created—most conspicuously by the *Atlantic Monthly* (*Cultures of Letters* 79). Brodhead is precise about dating, identifying "a palpable stiff-
ening of [the *Atlantic*'s] selection criteria in the mid-1860's" (87), and
explicit about the importance of studying literary cultures as a system
rather than separately, although he is less concerned with how print is
to be linked to other forms of expressive culture.

Alan Trachtenberg, on the other hand, foregrounds the ambivalence
toward democracy in "Gilded Age" understandings of culture. The
uplifting educational enterprises of the Chautauqua (founded by Methodists in 1874), for example, were both elevated and expansive: "a deliberate and conscious alternative to two extremes, the lavish and conspicuous squandering of wealth among the very rich, and the squalor
of the very poor. . . . Culture would offer a middle ground, and . . . a
democratizing influence, accessible to all those willing to raise themselves to the status of American" (143). Yet the linkage of refinement
and citizenship itself ratified the exclusion of the "other half." DiMaggio's account of Boston, where many of the distinctive techniques of
American hegemony were developed, anatomizes this tension from a
different perspective: "The Brahmin class . . . was neither large enough
to constitute a public for large-scale arts organizations, nor was it content to keep its cultural achievements solely to itself. Alongside of, and
complicating, the Brahmins' drive toward exclusivity was a conflicting
desire, as they saw it, to educate the community. The growth of the
middle class during this period—a class that was economically and socially closer to the working class and thus in greater need of differentiating itself . . . culturally—provided a natural clientele for Boston's
inchoate high culture" ("Cultural Entrepreneurship" 383). The civiliz-

ing, Americanizing role assigned to American literature in the public schools provides another example of this impulse. In fact, such ambivalence is intrinsic to the correlation of cultural and social authority at this historical moment; as DiMaggio puts it, "a secret or thoroughly esoteric culture could not have served to legitimate the status of American elites; it would be necessary to share it, at least partially. The tension between monopolization and hegemony, between exclusivity and legitimation, was a constant counterpoint to the efforts at classification of American urban elites" ("Cultural Entrepreneurship" 393).

Looking through the lens provided by a particular publishing house allows us to see this emerging story from an unusual perspective. Harper's is generally treated as part of elite culture; the *Monthly* in particular is mentioned as one of the "quality" journals by every commentator, and Brodhead considers it one of three that "produced the same high or distinguished zone in the literary realm that the classical museum or symphony orchestra produced in art or music, a strongly demarcated high-status arena for high-artistic practice" (*Cultures of Letters* 124). Indeed, J. Henry Harper makes it clear, in a memoir written many years after *The House of Harper*, that the firm functioned as a sort of secular cathedral of American literature. Fletcher Harper persuaded this favorite grandson, born like the *Monthly* in June 1850, to forgo college and enter the business very young, so J. Henry—"Harry"— Harper was already a partner in the mid-1880s period he evokes in the quotation below. The prose itself, however, is one of many long passages he quotes from manuscripts by Rev. van Tassel Sutphen, a reader for Harper's for many years and the second Joseph Harper's brother-in-law.

Fifty years ago the House of Harper was one of the regulation metropolitan sights; no out-of-town stranger failed to include it in his itinerary. Visitors were always welcome, and never a day passed that parties of countrymen were not on tour through the establishment under the personal conduct of a preternaturally sharp-faced office boy. A hurried peek through the leather-bound swinging doors which veiled the glories of the private office, a climb up the spiral staircase to gaze upon the humming activities of the composing-room, a trip through the factory with its intricate processes of assembling, stitching, binding, gilding, and lettering;

finally a breathless glance at the clanking presses, devouring with insatiable maw huge stacks of print paper, and giving birth to incredible piles of book signatures, a miracle at which Father Gutenberg himself might have marveled. Then out into the street, each yokel firmly clutching an illustrated pamphlet entitled, "My Visit to Harper & Brothers," a brochure descriptive of his breath-taking experience, a diploma of romantic adventures to be carried back in triumph to Yaphank or Lonelyville for exhibition to envious stay-at-homes, mental provender to be chewed over again and again during the long evenings of a North American winter. A visit to the House of Harper; why it was equivalent to a pious Mohammedan's journey to Mecca; one felt entitled to assume the dignity of a Hadji; even to contemplate the propriety of purchasing a green turban. (*I Remember* 25–26)

Both distinction and the vocabulary of sacralized culture are prominently in evidence here, in burlesque tones that reflect both the class-specific audience Harper's memoir addresses and the lost world this was by 1934.

Immediately following this passage Sutphen himself makes an imaginary "pious pilgrimage" (27) through the Franklin Square establishment (no longer standing in 1934) in a lovingly detailed tour of the premises that goes on for pages. He concludes it with reverence and without irony, reflecting that for generations the House of Harper

stood there in Franklin Square, a beacon light of intellectual thought and literary progress, an island of spiritual forces surrounded by an ocean of material brick and mortar. No one knows how many thousands of MSS. passed through the editorial mill during those fruitful years, a small percentage to be placed in permanent form through the mechanical energies of composing and press rooms, bindery, and shipping department; no one can form even a wild guess as to how many millions of copies of the best literature of the English-speaking world were trundled out through the Cliff Street archway to spread the gospel of sweetness and light, of truth and beauty to mankind. But through all these years the fountain head remained clear and unpolluted, sending forth its crystal streams for the refreshment of a thirsty universe. Happy is the man who can claim to have had even a humble share in creating and distributing that beneficent flood. (47)

This is easily recognizable as the vocabulary of the "apostle of culture," Matthew Arnold (although it does not, of course, come close to capturing the actual complexity of his thought). As Levine suggests, citing an essay that appeared in *Harper's Monthly* two years before *Culture and Anarchy*, Arnold's writings and lectures were received so enthusiastically in America precisely because they articulated and refined views already circulating (223). The Harpers themselves helped to forge this sacralizing view of literature.

These passages, taken together, imply the tension between privilege and democracy that so often characterizes the contested category "culture." On the one hand, Harry Harper clearly sees culture as the monopoly of an elite; the country folk who visit Franklin Square do not genuinely possess it. This view of high culture as distinction is the one that has become pervasive in current criticism. On the other hand, he also visualizes books and magazines flooding out to foster the self-cultivation of humankind. Culture goes "in search of the million" (as the first generation at Harper's wrote)—and finds it. After all, if those visitors from the country were utterly uncultivated, why would they bother to turn up in Franklin Square? The desire to reach more and more Americans also indistinguishably combined the wish to uplift the populace and unify the nation, and the desire to increase sales. Looking through the lens of publishing house history foregrounds the commercial considerations in this dynamic relation between exclusive and inclusive conceptions of culture. Richard Brodhead has shown how James Fields in mid-century developed ways to mark some literature as distinguished and market it on that basis (*School* 55). The contrary movement in the industry is at least as powerful; DiMaggio takes from Max Weber the point that "the market declassifies culture: presenters of cultural events mix genres and cross boundaries to reach out to larger audiences" ("Cultural Entrepreneurship" 378). Harper's constantly used both strategies.

In the 1890s, the Harper magazines were faced with unprecedented competition in their search for the ever-expanding million from inexpensive monthlies such as *McClure's* (discussed in the next section). In *Selling Culture*, Richard Ohmann develops an examination of this transformation of the magazine world at the turn of the century into a powerful account of the linked emergence of the professional-managerial class and a national mass culture. That group "between labor and capital" established a culture between low and high quite different from the intermediate formations discussed so far. Harper's figures in this story almost entirely as the *Monthly*, which is itself understood as a stodgy, uniformly elite journal. Ohmann even cites Alden's allegiance to the "great middle class" as "the main audience for the best literature" as evidence that editors did not know who their readers were.[20] I would argue instead that the quotation points, first, to the complexity of the "middle"—a category as polyvalent as any in American discourse, even its constant companion "culture"—and, second, to the misplacement of Harper's and the way the microhistorical perspective can refine our understanding of cultural hierarchy.

We have already seen how central Harper publications were to the American middle class through the nineteenth century—and how many that "middle," although claimed as a national common ground, excluded. There is no exact, inevitable relation between social position and morality or taste, but the middle class brings itself into being partly through a set of elaborated explanations of how position is deserved. The domestic culture of letters is one of the central elements of that system. (These are matters I discuss in more detail in chapter 5.) I would, however, reserve the term *middlebrow* for a later moment when the relation to high culture has become more defining, and more vexed. There is a trace of that unease in Sutphen and Harry Harper's image of the country visitors to Franklin Square, suggesting that Jonathan Freedman is right to find it at the very end of the nineteenth century, although the fully developed cultural formation analyzed by Joan Shelley Rubin and Janice Radway occurs considerably later.

The complexity of the "middle," and of the relation of middling and elite, is perhaps most visible, however, in the fact that the memoirist's—and very likely the office boy's—amusement at the provincial's naiveté does not so much divide an upper class from a lower as the New Yorker from the yokel. One can debate whether or not the turn-of-the-century magazine world Ohmann delineates is truly a mass culture, but it is clearly a *national* culture. And New York is not just a sophisticated city—it is the capital of that national culture. Robert Wiebe's argument that after about 1890 the United States had shifted from a two-class to a "three-class system . . . : one class geared to national institutions and policies, one dominating local affairs, and one sunk beneath both of these in the least rewarding jobs and least stable environments" (115) explains a great deal, although it is periodized too starkly. Differentiation between what Wiebe calls the "new national class" and the "reconstituted local middle class" is both a gradual and a constantly dynamic process; the two cannot necessarily be distinguished at any given moment by criteria such as wealth, political power, or education. Harper's was a metropolitan and national institution—but it was not associated only with the national class, for its publications were very dear to the hearts of the mostly local middle classes for a very long time.

The professional-managerial groups cross-cut these categories as well, with a constitutive and constantly increasing orientation to the national; as Ohmann notes, for them "[c]losely monitored circles of local acquaintance had given way to metropolitan and national affinities, to a greatly extended axis of respectability" (159). And as DiMaggio makes clear, high culture always included a national dimension —cultural capital relies on credentialing at that level, on university-accredited expertise, for example—yet tightly knit urban upper classes were gradually replaced by a national elite far less invested in the maintenance of cultural boundaries. Thinking about the role of region helps guard against any temptation to see cultural hierarchy as a single, vertical ladder paralleling a class hierarchy.

The powerful institution of Harper & Brothers sat squarely in the midst of the tension between inclusion and exclusivity that is constitutive for American cultural politics over a very long period. Certainly there were lines it did not cross. The color line was one; and white Americans without any aspirations to respectability were also not addressed. But even those without much money were invited, by good books with low prices, to do some improving reading. (Children in school, of course, were rather more firmly pressed.) And no doubt African Americans aspiring to culture bought those books, despite the fact that Harper's own horizon was bounded by whiteness. The house had a wide reach because it addressed not a single audience but a range of ambiguously demarcated groups with allegiances to "culture." Thus, although the ubiquitous references to the *Monthly* as an exemplar of genteel culture are not wrong, they mislead by obscuring differences among the "quality journals." Harper's literary journal never became so strictly highbrow as the *Atlantic;* it included the same prestigious writers but put them in a more mixed setting. The often-cited contrast between Boston and New York is part of the difference, although it allegorizes more than determines it.[21] The traces of their different origins and the continuing effect of their daily embedding in different publishing houses mattered at least as much, especially the fact that the *Monthly* was always—certainly in the eyes of those producing it, and probably for many readers as well—part of the Harper family of magazines.

It is enormously helpful to distinguish among "cultures of letters"; but those categories—very much like genres—must be understood as structuring forces within practices that are traceable in texts, not as separate institutions that *contain* authors and artists, books and paintings, or magazines. Different elements of the system depend on each other at a larger scale as well, and not only for contrast; the most sacralized art exhibit was publicized in newspapers. "Literature" in particular, I would argue, was composed of an enormous palimpsest of diffused cultural practices, including a powerful association with democracy, and was a product difficult to insulate from the market; it constantly oscillated across the boundaries established by cultural hierarchy. Approaching literary history through the story of Harper's unsettles familiar units of analysis, and thus helps prevent classification from substituting itself for the untidy specificity of historical events. In 1890 the editors of the house chose to publish Howells's *A Hazard of New Fortunes*—topical but certainly also literary and itself concerned with the institutions of culture—in the *Weekly.* In 1891 Hardy's *Tess of the d'Urbervilles*, a daring novel by an unquestionably distinguished author, ran in *Harper's Bazar.* In 1894 the quintessentially middlebrow *Trilby* bolstered the circulation of the *Monthly.*[22] One of the most intriguing things about *The Whole Family* is the appearance of (for example) Henry James, Elizabeth Stuart Phelps, and Mary Heaton Vorse, ordinarily thought of as inhabiting very different cultures of letters, not only together, but together in the pages of *Harper's Bazar.* But before we can ask what solidarity was being conjured in that particular project, from 1906 through 1908, we must follow Harper's through a period of rapid and radical change.

Harper's in the New Century

Harper & Brothers entered the twentieth century with something of a bang: on December 4, 1899, the firm went into receivership.

For William Dean Howells, "It was as if I had read that the government of the United States had failed." The firm's collapse shocked the literary and publishing worlds. Their books were ubiquitous as ever; when the *Bookman* printed the first best-seller list in 1895, Harper's had published four out of the ten books on it (Exman, *House* 178). The entire country had been in a severe depression since 1893, of course. Competition from the new inexpensive monthlies was hurting periodical profits, and the loss of income from the 1890 sale of the textbook division was being felt. But the obituaries and editorials published in 1896 on the deaths of the firm's second-generation leaders, Philip and Joseph Harper, tended to assume its finances were (in Exman's word) "impregnable" (*House* 173). Howells continues: "It appeared not only incredible, but impossible; it was, as Mr. J. Pierpont Morgan said, a misfortune of the measure of a national disaster. . . . I had heard some intimation that things were not well with them, but I had not been uneasy, for the simple reason that what could not happen would not. Yet it had." [23]

In the aftermath of the event some observers asserted that Harper's administrative practices were too conservative, even obsolete, and generally inefficient. Tebbel quotes an article in *Publisher's Weekly* ("which would not have thought of criticizing the Harpers in the days of their glory") deploring their failure to keep the business "abreast of the times" and reporting that "for years it was said that the Harper establishment and the Department of State were the only institutions in America which did not use the typewriter" (2: 198–99). Both *Publisher's Weekly* and J. Henry Harper's house history point to the high pay and casual attitude of many of the younger Harpers (650). But chroniclers agree that the crucial factor was the withdrawal of assets as partners died or retired, without arrangements being made to replace the capital. (Indeed, it had been the need to amortize Fletcher Jr.'s equity when he died leaving no son in the firm that had led to the sale of the textbook division.) In 1896 the combination of declining income and drains on capital meant that the Harpers had to borrow money to carry on. They turned to J. P. Morgan, the leading financier of the day, and that was the end of the family business; the firm was reorganized as a stock company heavily indebted to Morgan. The crisis came in 1899, when the Harpers were unable to make their interest payments and lost control of the company. The subsequent reorganization of Harper's was so abrupt and thorough that it serves as a case study in modernization. In his study of the emergence of progressive publishing, Christopher Wilson not only so uses it but also notes that at the time, with the trade "rendered acutely self-conscious not only by the depression but by the copyright campaign," the transformations of Harper's and Appleton's were taken as "object lessons" (75).

Book publishing had been the sector of the industry slowest to change. Wilson dates professionalized reporting and rationalized management in newspapers from the late 1880s (64), and the transformation in magazines is usually dated from the 1893 "revolution." Although they were using strategies developed gradually, often by publications directed at women, youth, or the working class, it was certainly a watershed moment when (in the midst of a financial panic) the entrepreneurial editor S. S. McClure brought out a monthly magazine for fifteen cents and John Brisben Walker and Frank Munsey quickly cut the prices of *Cosmopolitan* and *Munsey's* below that—selling their magazines below the cost of production and relying on advertising income to turn a profit. Richard Ohmann summarizes: "They took from the weeklies the idea of a lively pictorial appearance, from these and a few of the monthlies a willingness to hustle ads and let them be splashy, from the women's magazines and the mail order journals the idea of a very low price that would attract a large audience of people with only a little extra money to spend" (29). These mass-market monthlies borrowed from the quality journals, too, in offering carefully calibrated combinations of improving and interesting articles (fiction, accounts of exotic places and famous people, reviews) and a distinctively national perspective.

Wilson and subsequent commentators consistently define the new magazines *against* the monthlies like *Harper's* and the *Atlantic*, which were associated with established book-publishing houses and equally slow to change; genteel culture becomes the thesis required by the antithesis of progressive publishing. Wilson emphasizes the quality editors' commitment to taste, morality, and "culture as a 'civilizing' force," and characterizes the pace of work in their offices as calm and reflective, "modulated by the process of editorial work as it was originally conceived: receiving a daily batch of contributions, wading through manuscripts scrupulously, penning letters of guidance." The atmosphere at the new magazines, in contrast, was full of "push and pep" (43–44). Wilson shows the magazine revolution as not only a matter of circulation, financing, and layout, but also "a major transition in editorial attitudes towards the manuscript, the text, the labor of words" (53). The progressive editors scorned literary style, valuing instead energy and inventiveness; they not only printed articles on the topical and timely, but commissioned them and virtually collaborated with their authors—playing a role that was perhaps less conspicuously authoritative than that of the previous generation, but that gave them even more power over the creative process and the final product.

S. S. McClure himself was briefly in charge at Harper's during the financial maneuverings of 1899—he was called in by J. P. Morgan to try to turn the business around but was unable to command enough capital to take over. Instead, with Morgan's approval, the Harpers invited George S. Harvey, who had been editor of the *New York World* under Joseph Pulitzer and had recently purchased the distinguished *North American Review*, to assume leadership of the firm. Harvey, after reviewing the firm's accounts, saw no way out but a complete reorganization. The directors consented, and—amidst assurances that Harvey as agent for the State Trust Company would look after both the interests of the creditors and the honor of the house—Harper's went into receivership. And William Dean Howells, on his way home from a lecture tour, read the news in the *New York Herald*.[24]

Colonel Harvey (as he was called) brought with him to Harper's a number of former colleagues from the *World*, a conspicuously modern newspaper in an already modernized sector of the industry: Frederick Duneka became general manager, Elizabeth Jordan editor of *Harper's Bazar*, and Arthur Chandler head of advertising and promotion. (He introduced other new staff as well, but Jordan calls these four "in the vernacular of the day, 'a close corporation' " [173].) He instituted severe economies, selling the reference department and cutting labor costs

27. Photograph of Colonel Harvey's office at Franklin Square. Uncredited illustration from Exman, *The House of Harper* 186.

by leasing linotype machines. He had the desks of the Harpers themselves, except for J. Henry Harper's, moved to the top floor—where the typesetters had worked—and most of the family soon resigned. (The other exception was one of Wesley's grandsons, "Joe Madison," who remained until 1927 when he retired as head of the purchasing department.)[25] Exman reports that after Harvey had moved into the mahogany-paneled private office formerly occupied by "Brooklyn Joe" and hung a portrait of J. P. Morgan on the wall, few but his close associates "dared to venture into [his] sanctum" (189). Yet he also says that those who did became devoted to him—as J. Henry Harper clearly did (see figure 27 for one side of this story, and figure 28 for the other). Harper wrote in 1912: "The present House of Harper is a monument to Harvey's uncommon gifts of reorganization and re-establishment. . . . I have never met a man more liberally endowed with the qualifications of a publisher than Harvey. Journalist, editor, and author, he is alert, genial, conscientious, and diplomatic" (*House* 651). His later

28. At Colonel Harvey's home, December 1907. From left to right: W. D. Howells, Mark Twain, Harvey, H. M. Alden, David A. Munro, and M. W. Hazeltine. Uncredited illustration from Exman, *The House of Harper* 193.

memoir manifests the same devotion to Harvey (less solemnly—he is "the gay, sardonic, autocratic, inscrutable 'Colonel,' with the eternal cigar cocked at a jaunty angle between his close-pursed lips" [93]) but gives a more memorable and ambivalent account of the change in style. The large, open "counting-room" had (he writes) been "crowded with office furniture of all sorts—roll-tops, handsome old-fashioned secretaries, and even one or two high book-keepers' desks. When the Harvey administration came in these nondescripts were replaced by flat-topped desks all of the same pattern and coloring, with the general manager's big table in the centre, directly under the clock. Now it was no longer possible to indulge in a post-prandial nip under the friendly cover of a massively-topped secretary, and all was fair and above-board; this was a real office establishment and it was everybody's busy day" (27–28).

Elizabeth Jordan gives a vivid account of the change in pace, from the opposite perspective. She had been a reporter and editor on the *World* for ten years, and when she departed for Harper's was in charge of what she considered the two most important departments in the

Sunday paper, although they made an odd pair: the Comic Supplement (home of the "Yellow Kid") and the "high brow" Editorial Forum (165). Jordan's autobiography (like those of many in her generation of journalists, editors, and publishers) shows her working incessantly, thoroughly in her element in the "frantic rush of the *World* offices" (173). Becoming editor of the *Bazar* fulfilled a youthful ambition, but, she writes, "I had been living in an atmosphere where the news of the world broke over me like pounding breakers. The contrast of the academic calm of Harper's sometimes depressed me" (171). In the passage below Jordan describes setting to work on the issue of the magazine in preparation when she took over as editor on the first working day of 1900:

> I tore it to pieces and started out to make it over, with about two days before me for the job. . . . I hastened to the downstairs office of a young Mr. Demorest, then the head of the mechanical end of the art work, with hands full of illustrations I wanted processed immediately.
>
> "What's the quickest time you can make on these pictures?" I asked him. . . . What I really wanted was to make up the new pages late that afternoon. The feat might have been possible on the *World*.
>
> Mr. Demorest looked at the pictures, then at me, and made a calculation. His brow was corrugated by the violence of his mental efforts. It was subsequently corrugated every time we met.
>
> "Lem' me see," he brought out thoughtfully. "This is Tuesday, ain't it? You can have these a week from tomorrow!"
>
> It was at this moment I fully realized I was in a new atmosphere—a literary atmosphere, given up to quiet living and high thinking. Mr. Demorest did rather better than he had promised; but the strain on him was so great that he offered me a confidence which became part of the annals of Franklin Square.
>
> "Miss Jordan," he said on this second occasion, "I ain't makin' no excuses for bein' late with me work, for I know they don't go. But I give you me word I got so much to do that they's times when I leaves this place feelin' noivous!" (172)

I quote at length here partly to begin to sketch a portrait of Jordan— little-known now, yet fascinating, and vital to my story. But this light-hearted anecdote also richly evokes the clash of work habits between Harvey's group and the old Harper's, suggests the class dimensions of

workplace authority, and even alludes to a much-discussed psychological consequence of modernization: nervousness.

Harvey's reorganization stressed not only office efficiency but also
aggressive marketing. Harper's had always, as we have seen, gone
"in pursuit of the million"; under the new regime, and increasingly
throughout the industry, there was increased competition for popular
authors and more stimulation of demand through advertising (Wilson 74–75). (The International Copyright Law had not been intended
to encourage such measures, but by offering improved security for ex-
ploiting literary properties it did. Investing money in promoting an
author or book was better business when increased sales were certain
to benefit the investor, not someone with a competing edition.) What
Wilson calls the "principle of anticipation" (75) extended beyond advance contracts and advance publicity, into the creative process itself;
not only magazine but book editors as well could invent potentially
profitable projects, solicit salable authors to write them, and supervise
their composition with an eye on the market from beginning to end.

The Whole Family, of course, was the product of exactly that process.
It was conceived and planned at Harper's; commissions were given to
authors who were, for the most part, already associated with the house;
and advance publicity in the *Bazar* was designed to stir up interest in
the novel and the collaboration. The serial was also promoted by being
made into a guessing game—the full list of contributors was printed
each month, and readers were invited to guess which author was responsible for each chapter. During its run, Jordan printed letters from
readers offering comments on the novel and speculations about who
had written what. Its appearance in book form was immediately noted
in the *Bazar*'s "Books and Writers" department: "Letters have poured
in from all over the country earnestly asking the authorship of the various chapters. . . . Altogether the interest in *The Whole Family* has been
unique, and it is especially gratifying to notice that the circle of interest has widened to a degree which takes in the whole country and is
beginning to be felt on the other side of the ocean" (Review n.p.). The
collaboration attracted notice, certainly, but there is no evidence that it
was on the *Trilby*-like scale implied here; this is the hyperbolic language
of "aggressive marketing."

It is worth stopping for a moment to reflect on the fact that the inspiration for this manufactured literary event came from none other than the Dean of American Letters, William Dean Howells. After Harper's failed he had considered connections with other publishers, but Harvey and Duneka persuaded him to enter instead into closer relations with Harper's. He not only published with them but also drew a salary, functioned as a literary adviser, and even had an office in Franklin Square for a time. (He wrote to Samuel Clemens a month after the failure: "They have a very active man at the head of affairs, and there is a prospect of things being better managed than under the old régime, where no one was head" [*Life* 120–21].) Howells's promotional practices come in for considerable notice in the 1903 satire *The Literary Guillotine* (written by William Wallace Whitelock but published anonymously), in which various authors are put on trial for crimes against literature. He is shown declining to defend Richard Harding Davis — " 'Tut, tut!' cried Howells, impatiently, 'Davis is of no importance to literature, he doesn't publish with Harper's any longer' " (248); and proposing to release John Kendrick Bangs from prison and substitute Brander Matthews — "The Professor's books don't sell, anyhow" (249). To the remark "Certainly no one can accuse you of not taking a practical view of literature" he replies: "No one, sir. That's what my boss always says to me. 'Mr. Howells,' he said only the other day, 'the Easy Chair is the best advertising medium Harper's possesses. The way you manage to ring in our books while apparently writing on matters literary, is a subject for constant wonder' " (249–50). Any promotion of Harper's books in a Harper's periodical was certainly faithful to the spirit of the brothers who started the *Monthly* "as a tender to our business." But for Howells in 1906 to propose a collaborative novel to the editor of the *Bazar* also certainly marks an innovation, showing his concern with the business of the whole house and also that he had enlisted in the anticipatory practices of the new order.

Both Howells and Henry Mills Alden, also strongly identified with the old Harper's and old-fashioned genteel culture, not only worked closely with Harvey but stayed with the firm longer than he did; Alden edited the *Monthly* until 1919, and Howells occupied its Easy Chair until his death in 1921. (The magazine itself went substantially unchanged until 1925.[26]) As Wilson points out, many of the editors of the quality journals continued on into the new century; and I would argue that when he calls Alden and his cohort "flickering candles in a world gone neon" (41), he accepts too teleological a view. Contemporary accounts testify amply to the perception that the quality journals were obsolete and progressive publishing the wave of the future. (Whitelock has Alden reply to a request for a definition of literature by saying that he formulated one as a boy in Vermont and wrote it down: "Unfortunately it's at the office of the magazine, or I should read it to you. I always read it every morning, so as to keep it fresh in mind. For the moment I can't recall it, but of one thing you may rest assured: I haven't changed it one iota from that day to this" [258].) Yet they also show that people constantly synthesize, creating constellations of attitudes that let them live through changes without clearing the slate and beginning again. Jordan reports that "Colonel Harvey was like a son to Mr. Alden, and the older man repaid him with an affection and loyalty very beautiful to see" (174). Our own scholarly desire to periodize, to create tidily dramatic narratives, can lead us to emphasize the former over the latter; the microhistorical approach provides a corrective. One of the clear consequences of reading literary history through Harper's is to show that attitudes and practices thought of as following one another in a historical sequence in fact coexist, both among groups of people and within individuals.

In her memoir Elizabeth Jordan confesses that she and the other Harvey recruits probably "made the whole Harper staff feel 'noivous' in those first days of reorganization" and indeed "became prominent features in [their] worst dreams," and that she herself felt "especially 'noivous'" (172–73). Yet eventually, she reports, they "struck a happy medium of pace . . . , and everybody was happier. . . . I was doing work I loved, in an atmosphere of harmony; and I was meeting frequently and intimately many of America's most luminous literary figures" (173). Everything she writes about *The Whole Family* makes it clear that for Jordan, promotion and distinction meshed seamlessly. Similarly, she saw no conflict between her "immense admiration" for her predecessor at *Harper's Bazar*, the "mature, motherly, very gentle, and very sweet" Margaret Sangster (128), and her "whole-hearted admiration" (107) for the brilliant modernizer Harvey. Neither was she troubled by any incompatibility between her New Woman habits such as going home alone from the *World* offices at 3:00 or 4:00 A.M. and her habit of rhetorically subsuming all human connection into the family. Indeed, Jordan epitomizes the early twentieth-century blending of old and new, without visible strain combining loyalty to tradition and enthusiasm for innovation. She seems never to have met a contradiction she could not subdue (or at least blithely disregard).

It is not surprising that the Harper staff at every level was anxious, faced as they were with firings, pressure to produce, and a distant, intimidating chief. The story of Harvey's best-known innovation vividly evokes the contrast in management styles, revealing it as part of the broader shift in attitudes toward hierarchy. The old Harper's had sponsored an annual excursion for its employees; as described by Sutphen and quoted by J. Henry Harper in *I Remember*,

> on some pleasant Saturday morning in June of each succeeding year, the "Happy Little Harpers" would be loaded on a tug, and transported to City Island or somebody's amusement park. The supreme event was the baseball game, and great was the joy of the factory contingent when some gangling office boy or husky "comp" succeeded in striking out Dick Davis [Richard Harding Davis] or tagging J. Henry at third base. Then came the dinner—clam chowder, gargantuan plates of corned beef and cabbage and potatoes boiled in their jackets, pies of every known variety of digestive deadliness, and all washed down by copious draughts of able-bodied beer. . . . The "Colonel" attended one of these hick-minded, ostentatiously democratic affairs—and just one; this sort of thing was not calculated to put Harper & Brothers back on the map. And so he proceeded to invent and execute his own series of publicity stunts. (102–3)

Both in its scornful tone and in its portrait of such "ostentatiously democratic" events as a thing of the past, this account encapsulates what Robert Wiebe calls the early twentieth century's "demolition of the People" (11).

For the outing Harvey substituted his famous series of literary banquets. The first was a dinner at Delmonico's for 150 distinguished representatives of the house; others followed, in honor of visiting luminaries and the birthdays of celebrated authors, at elegant restaurants and hotels, and once in the counting-room at Franklin Square (for Alden's seventieth birthday). Four hundred, including President Taft, attended the celebration at Sherry's of Howells's seventy-fifth birthday. These occasions did indeed generate publicity and create the sense that Harvey was putting Harper's "back on the map." Perhaps because they evoke the earlier dinners organized for *Atlantic Monthly* contributors (quietly in the magazine's early days, but formally and publicly for about a decade beginning in 1874), and certainly because of who participated, they have been taken as representing the genteel establishment. That association is not wrong, and in any case the assertion of cultural distinction had always had a promotional element; but it misses their implication in the marketing strategies of progressive publishing.[27] The dinners were also events manufactured by the very man of whom Josephine Bacon, disgruntled over the rate of compensation she was being offered for a magazine piece, wrote to her friend Elizabeth Jordan: "Mr. Harvey should be managing a breakfast food" (Jordan Papers). They represent an innovation that calls on familiar gestures, a continuation that changes things.

Harvey's fifteen-year reign at Harper's was generally viewed by his contemporaries as a successful adaptation of the house's tradition. It was not, however, a success from the perspective of the Morgan Company. The partner in charge of the account was less impressed by the conspicuous consumption of the banquets, Harvey's political influence, or his claim to have increased the firm's assets in "Copyrights and Goodwill" than he would have been by progress in liquidating its debt—virtually all income seems to have gone into interest payments, and in fact Morgan made some further loans to Harper's and personal loans to Harvey. In 1913, under pressure from Wall Street, Harvey sold the *Weekly* to the McClure Company and the *Bazar* to William Randolph Hearst. (Both periodicals were losing money, although Jordan claims in her autobiography that the *Bazar* would have shown a profit if it had not been required to carry a quarter of the Harper's overhead [306].) In 1915 the board of directors' view of Harvey's management had grown so negative that the loyal J. Henry Harper resigned from it; a few months later Harvey himself resigned and the board was reorganized under more resolutely prudent leadership.[28]

In assessing Harvey's reorganization of the firm, Tebbel writes that he took steps "which the Harper brothers would have thought inhuman, like firing most of the old compositors, many of whom had spent their lives with the firm" (2: 200). On the other hand, J. Henry

Harper asserts that "there has not been a move made by him that would not have received the hearty indorsement of the original founders of the House" (*House* 651). Any claim of radical discontinuity of course depends on a radical simplification of the house's past. Images of the dignified pace of editorial work occlude the way Harper's early success depended on winning races to get early proofs from England and be the first to get books printed and in the hands of booksellers (Exman 5–6); images of the founders' humane care for their employees ignore their eager adoptions of new technology and concern for the bottom line. What would James, John, Wesley, and Fletcher have thought of the early twentieth-century Harper's? The question is unanswerable—what is interesting is the fact that it gets asked. The brothers persistently compel the imaginations of people in publishing, and particularly those in Franklin Square; and assertions of continuity are persistently cast in the language of the family. We see, in the repetition of these gestures, traces of the fiction through which the corporate entity Harper & Brothers sustained itself. J. Henry Harper tells us not only that the founders would have approved of Harvey, but that Harvey understands himself as their inheritor, which seems to qualify him to inherit: "I believe he has always had these four brothers in mind, and if he had been a son or grandson he could not have carried out their aims more loyally" (*House* 651). In effect, Harper makes Harvey one of the family.

People who became connected with Harper's later in the century often understood themselves to be enlisting in a long tradition. Willie Morris remembers the look of the envelopes he received as a contributor to *Harper's Magazine*—"the impressive old *Harper's* crest with the lighted torch above the '1817,' a sight which never failed to thrill me" (15). Appointed as the eighth editor in 1967—the 150th anniversary of the founding of Harper & Brothers, he points out—he writes feelingly about the pioneers carrying bound volumes of the magazine "across the continent in their covered wagons" (20), the portrait of William Dean Howells hanging on the office wall (7), the huge oak catalog file listing each article, story, and poem published since 1850 (22–23). "The editorship of this venerable national institution mattered to me greatly," Morris meditates; "I . . . felt in my deepest heart the sweeping efficacy of its lineage and its possibilities" (6). There are some uncanny echoes as one reads his memoir: he thought the country needed "a truly *national* magazine" (9), and he found the pace of work at *Harper's* "languid" (32) compared with his previous jobs. Most strikingly for my purposes, Morris writes of his staff that "as our lives converged, . . . we would become a close group, singular as a family" (82); and, later, "we were a band of brothers" (363). The generalized usage of the family as an image of intimacy is certainly enough to explain these references; it is impossible to know—but irresistible to speculate—that they reflect a workplace in which the vocabulary of the family business continues to circulate.

My direct concern with the history of Harper's ends with the period of *The Whole Family*. But the saga of Harper's can be continued up to the present day. (I say "saga" deliberately, to acknowledge that here my own imagination is bolstering the strength of the connections.) The firm merged with Row, Peterson in 1962 to become Harper & Row (Exman 299); its owner since 1987 has been the Australian entrepreneur Rupert Murdoch. He merged the firm with the English publisher William Collins (referred to by *Publishers Weekly* as "something of a household name" and known especially for its religious list) to create HarperCollins. It seems appropriate that Murdoch was able to undertake his hostile takeover of Collins because Sir William Collins's widow and son, angry because the son "had been relegated to a nonexecutive role," sold their shares to him.[29] The *Economist* of London reported the distress of the Collins authors in an article titled, usefully for me, "The Brave New World of Publishing: Fathers and Sons," noting the "deep emotional bond of an author to his publishing house" and suggesting that "Britain's literary and cultural standards will probably survive Mr. Murdoch; what authors fear may not survive is the publisher as fond father" (83–84). The tension between publishing and modernization is itself virtually a tradition.

The extraordinary growth of Murdoch's global media empire (which includes movies, television, and newspapers as well as book and magazine publishing), with his aggressive style and lack of visible concern for any but financial considerations, has alarmed not only his competitors but custodians of culture as well. HarperCollins and Murdoch are frequently in the news. In 1990 the publishing world was astounded by reports that HarperCollins had carried the anticipatory principle to new extremes by paying $20 million for three works, two as yet unwritten, by thriller author Jeffrey Archer, buying movie, television, and audio rights as well for exploitation by the parent News Corporation (McDowell). The figure was considered outrageously high by publishers already deploring the level of advances, as they have periodically since the emergence of "progressive publishing" (HarperCollins refused to confirm it). In 1997 HarperCollins made front-page news by canceling books in order to cut costs in a slow market; one person in the industry "compared the elimination of accepted manuscripts to being jilted at a formal wedding," and the *New York Times* subtitled the article: "A Once-Genteel Industry Feels a Bare-Knuckle Corporate Blow" ("HarperCollins Cancels Books" A1). In 1998 Murdoch personally intervened in the publishing company to cancel a book by the last British governor of Hong Kong, reportedly to protect his business interests in China; the ensuing scandal eventually forced him to publicly apologize (see Hoge; Lyall). Amazingly, these dramas of class, commerce, and culture are still being played out by a family corporation—one so closely controlled that the *New York Times Magazine* reports that it almost appears to be "like a mom-and-pop business" (G. Brooks, 22). Journalists seem fascinated by the next generation's careers in the family business and the drama of succession—as of 1998, primogeniture seems to have triumphed, but Lachlan Murdoch's older sisters and younger brother reportedly still have hopes (see Hirsch; Fabrikant; G. Brooks). The saga continues.

A Family Performance

THE COMPOSITE NOVEL AS VAUDEVILLE

My claims about Harper's can be formulated simply. First, it matters. Literary history was once concerned either with authors and national traditions or with texts and forms; the now well-established turn toward institutions and discourses makes the publishing house an important object of study. Harper & Brothers has an important place in any narrative of cultural life in the United States in the nineteenth century, and a lesser but still significant place in narratives about the twentieth. Second, to understand the cultural practices and politics of the latter nineteenth and early twentieth centuries, we must recognize not only the force of distinctions between high and low but also the presence of mixed and middling discourses. The history of Harper's demonstrates the constant entanglement of gestures of inclusion and exclusion and the close embrace of commerce and culture. Third, its modernization constitutes a genuine break but also thoroughly and complexly incorporates people and attitudes already in place at Franklin Square, including the figure of the family business. Finally, family solidarity is so persistently invoked to enable investment in the firm as to suggest that *The Whole Family* is, in an important sense, *authored* by Harper's.

Among the individuals engaged on the project, Elizabeth Jordan most consistently calls on the vocabulary of the family. She uses the figure to talk about all aspects of her work at Franklin Square—for example, introducing the story of her "biggest catch" for Harper's, the signing of Sinclair Lewis, by writing: "I was immensely interested in my efforts to draw new writers of promise into the Harper book family" (339)—but it is remarkably pervasive when she writes about *The Whole Family*, in both her correspondence and her autobiography. She says that Howells suggested the project because of his "fatherly feeling" (258) for the *Bazar,* and that Freeman's chapter was "the explosion of a bomb-shell on our literary hearthstone" (264). She consulted Alden about the conflict between Howells and Freeman because the former was his friend and the latter "his beloved literary daughter" (265). She constantly refers to the authors involved simply as "the Family," and when she writes of widespread gossip about the controversial collaboration puts it in these terms: "I, of course, regarded everything concerning *The Whole Family* as highly confidential, to be confined to that Family and to the heart of the family in Franklin Square. Many of the other authors had no such inhibitions. . . . Intriguing gossip about the upheaval in *The Whole Family* spread, and all literary New York discussed it" (268). Other participants also make the link occasionally. Alice Brown wrote to Jordan, for example, that "we have all, unconsciously, become a 'family.' We have our general loyalty and particular preferences. We preserve the tone of 'affection mingled with contempt' so beautifully defined by Mr. Lear." [30] Here as elsewhere, Brown is considerably more willing than Jordan to think of the family as a mixed blessing.

The notion of the collaborators as a family creeps into the public presentation of the serial as well. Jordan writes in her "With the Editor" column for the December 1907 issue of the *Bazar*, which includes the first installment of *The Whole Family*: "In the writing of the novel the authors themselves experienced a deep sense of family association, and frequently expressed it. One of them wrote to the editor: 'We have actually *become* "a whole family" ourselves, with our individual likes and dislikes, and our frank domestic criticism. If —— brings about any more complications, *I* shall complain to father!'" (1248). Jordan's monthly column included both comments on the magazine's contents and other, often disconnected, thoughts on topics that occurred to her. But it can hardly be a coincidence that the next item is a few paragraphs on "The Family and the Quarrel," which opens: "In any family, anywhere, any day, there exists the making of a family quarrel," and ends by recommending the "rule of giving up whenever giving up is not wrong or cowardly," because "perfection in family life must be aimed for, or even a tolerable home atmosphere will not be attained" (1249). (Jordan did not make public the irritation the collaboration caused her until her autobiography was published in 1938, but she certainly gives a hint here.) The theme even appears in the novel itself by the sixth contribution. John Kendrick Bangs begins the sixth chapter, the son-in-law's: "On the whole I am glad our family is no larger than it is. It is a very excellent family as families go, but the infinite capacity of each individual in it for making trouble, and adding to complications already sufficiently complex, surpasses anything that has ever before come into my personal or professional experience" (124). It seems clear that, as Alfred Bendixen suggests, this is as much a comment on the authors as on the characters. *Yeah, yeah.*

Whether affirming or ironizing family solidarity at Harper's, these images remain, of course, metaphors. Chapter 3 examines the category of the family more directly, and it is good preparation to notice that people constantly invoke the family as a figure for intimacy in all sorts of groups, because fantasy and metaphor pervade every practice associated with the family and every discussion of the topic. But I want to note in closing another revealing metaphor applied to this troupe of literary performers. The *Nation*'s anonymous reviewer of *The Whole Family* describes the novel as "pure vaudeville," and observes that "many of the 'turns' are characteristic and amusing." As I suggested in chapter 1, this image captures a distinctive quality of the composite novel. *The Whole Family* certainly resembles vaudeville in being a series of disconnected acts that aspire to combine into a whole that satisfies an audience. More speculatively, we might compare Jordan's troubles in assembling the Family and mediating their quarrels to the notorious difficulties vaudeville managers faced in booking, transporting, and managing the rivalries and temperaments of performers.

There is also, I think, a deeper connection. The distinctive aspect of vaudeville, according to its historian Robert Snyder, is the way it appealed directly and intimately to highly diverse and dispersed audiences through a centralized national system. Vaudeville acts were highly improvisational, with performers inserting local references and adapting to the taste of the house wherever they played. Yet the Keith booking circuit, incorporated in 1906, managed the whole process from New York. Vaudeville was one of the variety-based cultural institutions that knit together a modern national audience. (Another, of course, was magazines.) And it was a form of commercial culture designed to appeal to families as the world of commercial leisure became increasingly heterosocial and respectable.

There is no record of what Howells thought of this description of the collaboration he initiated. He had not, as Jordan feared, "refused to have anything more to do with our unfortunate Family" after he failed to prevent the publication of Freeman's chapter; he continued to comment (sometimes severely) on the contributions, but by the time the book appeared he must have been happy to put the episode behind him. J. Henry Harper tells us that Howells did not "disdain good vaudeville, and as I am partial to it myself, I have frequently met him and his attractive daughter before the vaudeville curtain" (*House* 327). Thinking of *The Whole Family* in terms of this mixed form might have comforted Howells, for the novel is above all a mixed performance. It juxtaposes diverse genres, differently gendered cultural practices, the old-fashioned and the up-to-date, the elite and the popular. Its coherence and significance cannot be seen from the perspective of author-centered analysis, but they appear when the episode is narrated as part of the story of the House of Harper.

3

❧ Making the Family Whole ❧

When William Dean Howells proposed the creation of a composite novel to be published as a serial in *Harper's Bazar*, he also proposed a theme. He explained his idea for the fiction that became *The Whole Family* in a letter to Elizabeth Jordan: "What I wish to imply is that an engagement or a marriage is much more a family affair, and much less a personal affair than Americans usually suppose. As we live on, we find that family ties, which held us very loosely in youth, or after we ceased to be children, are really almost the strongest things in life. A marriage cannot possibly concern the married pair alone; but it is in the notion that it can that most of our marriages are made. It is also in this notion that most of them are unmade" (*Life* 223). He proposed co-education as a topic as well, writing that he would advocate it as a way of achieving better understanding between the sexes. From the beginning, then, Howells manifested a certain anxiety about the state of the family: about the current emphasis on individual choice rather than the welfare of the whole family, about tensions between men and women, about the failure of marriages and the unmaking of families—perhaps even the unmaking of "the family" as an institution.

Such misgivings were widespread in the first decade of the twentieth century, as indeed they are in its last and in the opening years of the twenty-first. Then and now, statements about the family—vernacular, expert, and fictional ones alike—conflate positions on a wide range of urgent social issues. My first task in this chapter is to analyze the concept itself, disentangling and reframing its elements to render it usable for critical analysis. Next I will show that Howells's opening chapter from the father's perspective is deeply informed by the early twentieth-century alarm over the family, mingling perceived problems and proposed solutions into its apparently celebratory portrait of middle-class domestic life.

His fears were fulfilled in the chapters that followed, as the next three contributors showed the Talbert household as miserably ill-adapted to the needs of its members. Howells's chapter "The Father," Mary Wilkins Freeman's "The Old-Maid Aunt," Mary Heaton Vorse's "The Grandmother," and Mary Stewart Cutting's "The Daughter-in-Law" constitute a fairly focused dialogue on family relations. This chapter focuses on the first third of the novel, only occasionally drawing in material from later contributions. (These do, of course, address the ongoing dialogue about the family, but in a less concentrated way as each author brings new subjects into play.) I reconstruct a discourse of the family around *The Whole Family*, reading it with other documents of the period, from early sociology to articles running alongside the novel in *Harper's Bazar*, and with social and cultural histories. Those documents include the accumulated fictions of these four chapters' authors; Mary Stewart Cutting especially deserves our attention here, as an unsung ideologue of the companionate family. Finally, I discuss how the novel and surrounding discourses narrate the paradoxical relation of print culture and domestic privacy. For common sense, "publishing," and "the family" are distant and incommensurate categories. One reason the story of *The Whole Family* engages the imagination is that as the fictional Talberts and the metaphorical family at Franklin Square are written into existence, they remind us that the modern family form comes into being on social grounds partially constituted and ceaselessly traversed by print. Interiority and publication are inseparable—never identical, never distinct, always intertwined.

What Is a Family?

The family is often simultaneously affirmed as inevitable and proclaimed as endangered. This position is not argued in so many words— if it were, its logical contradiction could scarcely be avoided—yet it underlies the sense of crisis characterizing so many discussions of the institution. At least some of its elements, such as the relation between mother and infant, seem untouchable to almost everyone. Two of the institution's most trenchant and uncompromising critics, Michèle Barrett and Mary McIntosh, speculate in *The Anti-social Family* that "nature is invoked . . . because the family is so closely allied to the undeniably natural process of biological reproduction. Yet eating is just as undeniably natural and no one would think of assigning restaurants or groceries to this category" (35). Indeed, one of first things one observes in studying the family is what an enormous amount of cultural work is expended to make the family seem so obvious (as great as, and complementary to although not necessarily consistent with, that devoted to heterosexual romance). Meanwhile, the frequent problems of particular families seem to add up to a crisis in the family, and the institution's imminent breakdown is regularly deplored.

The commonsensical assumption that a family simply, naturally "is" a group of blood relations residing together is easy to refute. Cross-cultural and historical comparisons show immediately that kinship and household are by no means invariably combined. The very notion of "family" is a positive hindrance in grasping the immensely diverse arrangements through which (for example) early Native American societies organized marriage, genealogy, and residence. And we must hold the word's current meaning in abeyance when reading early English sources, which use *family* to refer to everyone in an aristocratic household, including servants and other nonkin residents; or (in a usage that survives today) to an extended, often geographically scattered lineage. The image of a family as a father, mother, and children—with other relations possibly but not certainly included—in a single household corresponds to the bourgeois family form that emerged around the middle of the eighteenth century and did not seem self-evident in either England or the United States until the middle of the nineteenth. (Probably. The timing is, and is likely to remain, a topic much disputed in the scholarship.)[1] From (probably) the latter nineteenth century, emotional bonds were progressively concentrated in the home, and by the mid-twentieth other identifications were much diminished; the dimension of *intimacy* was incorporated into the family's self-evident wholeness. This amalgamation becomes common sense—so obvious that even a profound challenge to the institution such as gay and lesbian activists' effort to claim its privileges tends to rely on demonstrations that same-sex partnerships establish publicly acknowledged bonds embodied in stable private homes.

Disaggregating the elements of kinship, household, and intimacy defamiliarizes the family and lets us see it more clearly. So does feminist analysis that has drawn "attention to the violence and degradation hidden within the walls of the nuclear household, and to the broader social and economic inequalities connected with it" (Barrett and McIntosh 19). The widely advertised view of the family as a haven in a heartless world is necessarily challenged by recognizing the frequency of domestic violence and sexual abuse of children by family members, and by noting how unequally domestic labor and resources are divided among family members. Pieties about the central role of the family in the American way of life may also be challenged by recognition of the central role of the family in reproducing social class (or not, depending on one's politics). Barrett and McIntosh argue that "the family embodies the principle of selfishness, exclusion and pursuit of private interest and contravenes those of altruism, community and pursuit of the public good. Society is *divided into* families and the divisions are deep" (47). They follow in the tradition of Charlotte Perkins Gilman, who wrote in 1898: "We may preach to our children as we will of the great duty of loving and serving one's neighbor; but what the baby is born into, what the child grows up to see and feel, is the concentration of one entire life—his mother's—upon the personal aggrandizement of one family, and the human service of another life—his father's—so warped and trained by the necessity of 'supporting his family' that treason to society is the common price of comfort in the home" (*Women and Economics* 278). Of course, none of this negates the fact that families frequently satisfy real needs and offer real satisfaction. It does mean that there are aspects of the family as an institution that are not remembered—that are specifically repressed—when one pays a compliment to the reliable, supportive affection of a group of friends or coworkers by saying they are "like a family."

In their synthesis of family history, Steven Mintz and Susan Kellogg show Americans worrying about the state of the family "over three centuries. . . . Puritan jeremiads were already decrying the increasing fragility of marriage, the growing selfishness and irresponsibility of parents, and the increasing rebelliousness of children" (xx). The continuity conceals a difference, however, for in colonial society family households were not imagined as havens, but rather were (accurately) understood as continuous with the economy, the church, and the state. They were the site of production and education, of social services and social order; in the often-quoted words of English Puritan William Gouge, a family was "a little Commonwealth" (Coontz, *Social Origins* 83). Twentieth-century Americans find it relatively easy to project themselves back into a world of household production, which evokes appealing visions of economic self-sufficiency; explicit deference to paternal authority also remains an available image. But the utter lack of personal privacy, the detailed regulation of behavior by religious and civic authorities, the fluidity of household composition as relatives (including children) and servants came and went, the dense webs of obligation and deference that linked both individuals and neighboring households are deeply unfamiliar. As Stephanie Coontz puts it, "we need to distinguish the importance of *families* in colonial life from the importance of *the* family. The biological family, in fact, was less sacrosanct and less central to people's lives than it was to become during the nineteenth century" (*Social Origins* 83–84).

The ideal of family and community to which colonial Americans aspired was in fact already passing in Europe. They invested their hopes for social order in the creation of unchanging, harmonious communities—under constantly unprecedented circumstances. I am, of course, sketching family history in extremely broad strokes, neglecting enormous and important differences among regions and classes, to say nothing of the profoundly differing experiences of different races.[2] But for European Americans generally, consensus and community were not only difficult to achieve, they were gradually replaced by commerce and complexity. Hence the sense of endangerment that produced jeremiads; hence the creativity devoted to rethinking the family form. Linda Kerber comments that "[o]ne plausible way to read nineteenth-century defenses of separate spheres . . . is to single out the theme of breakdown; the noise we hear about separate spheres may be the shattering of an old order and the realignment of its fragments" (22). The fact that the old order often failed to be orderly does not prevent it from appearing as that elusive moment of the family's wholeness, a moment that is always receding into the past.

As we look back from the perspective of the twentieth century, it is separate spheres domesticity that appears as the stable, "traditional" home. The bewhiskered Victorian father surrounded by wife, sons, and daughters stands in the popular—and too often the scholarly—imagination as a sort of daguerrotype of the patriarch. Yet in the nineteenth-century middle-class family ideal, relations were already less formal and hierarchical than in the colonial family, more emphasis was placed on romantic love and personal affection, and children stayed at home longer and received more attention (Mintz and Kellogg xv). Household had already been divided from the official economy, and kinship officially divided from the state (although the separation is not yet and may never be complete, as I noted in the introduction, the family farm and the English royals continue to exist, although they are certainly not thriving, today). Male dominance and a gendered division of labor remained, but this family was no longer patriarchal in the strict sense. A man's home was his castle not because he was the king in miniature but because it was private.

Privacy is itself a social construct, of course, and in its strong sense must always be a paradox. Beyond that generality, the modern family is established, regulated, and often subsidized by the state. The population is the nation's—marriages and births, once licensed and recorded by families and churches, are now documented by government agencies, and appropriate procreation (whether that means producing one child or producing many) may be a patriotic duty (see Balibar and Wallerstein 100–103). In the United States, certainly, the health of the family and the proper state policies for supporting it—including protecting its "privacy"—are favorite concerns of politicians. I turn in chapter 5 to a more theoretical discussion of the modern division of social life into distinct spheres and how modern selves are shaped by these landscapes of detachment and connection. Here let me simply note that public and private, and men's and women's realms, are always intricately intertwined; to speak of them as separate is to cite a force in social life, not to analyze it.

However, the unreconstructed image of Victorian "separate spheres" points usefully to a daily life spent largely in the company of one's own sex; another element often forgotten in popular images of this family form is its homosociality. Gender segregation, of course, characterized not only homes but also schools, workplaces, political life, and so on. The third form that emerged in (probably) the early twentieth century, the "companionate family," placed greater emphasis on conjugal intimacy and formed part of an increasingly heterosocial world. What was at stake was no longer complementarity but compatibility. Here we enter the moment, and encounter the topic, of *The Whole Family*.

I should note that the term *companionate marriage* actually came into use in the 1920s, and that the ideal of the companionate family was (probably) not fully developed and dominant until the 1950s. My parenthetical qualifications are meant to acknowledge that periodization is always interpretation, and always debatable. I would not make this family form as old as Carl Degler does: he controversially dates the "modern" family from the early nineteenth century, emphasizing the "affection and mutual respect between the partners" rather than the separation of spheres, and the increasing power of women at home rather than their public disabilities (8). Yet my readings of *The Whole Family*, *Harper's Bazar*, and related documents do show substantial changes in attitude during the early twentieth century. Well before the vocabulary we use now began to circulate, educators, psychologists, social workers, legal scholars, and sociologists—and, I would add, journalists and fiction writers—were elaborating a new vision of family happiness. They saw the home as the site of emotional fulfillment and sociability, constructing it in terms that feel quite familiar to the late twentieth-century reader. (The sexual satisfaction of the married couple, on the other hand, did not emerge as a value until the 1920s.) The discourses of the first decade of the century sometimes echo Victorian paeans to the holiness of the home, but they have more in common with the ubiquitous advice on communication and images of family fun proffered by the newspapers and magazines of today.

The early twentieth century was another period in which the family seemed urgently in need of healing. Mintz and Kellogg describe widespread, acute apprehension: "The turn-of-the-century family was clearly an institution in flux, buffeted by stresses and pressures that have continued to confront twentieth-century families to this day. A rapidly rising divorce rate, an alarming fall in the birthrate [among the upper classes], a sexual revolution, and a sharp increase in the numbers of women continuing their educations, joining women's organizations, and finding employment—each of these worked to transform the middle-class family. Many Americans believed that the family was being destroyed" (108–9). A steady stream of publications discussed the state of the family with varying degrees of alarm, from *A History of Matrimonial Institutions* to *The Divorce Problem* to *Will the Home Survive*.[3] The family became an object of study in a new way in the emerging discourses of the professions, especially the professionalizing social sciences.

In December 1908, just as the book version of *The Whole Family* appeared, members of the new American Sociological Society were in Atlantic City for its third annual meeting, on the topic "The Family." The discussion began with the long history of institutions—William Sumner's presidential address begins with the position of women in "savage" societies and works its way through evidence from the Bible and Roman historians to the present—but it also included the synchronic view of the Pittsburgh survey of family life. Attitudes ranged from the arguments of Charlotte Perkins Gilman for the socialization of domestic labor and women's equality to a doctor's startlingly explicit paper on husbands infecting their wives with syphilis to denunciations of divorce by a minister and a rabbi.

The speakers did agree, however, that the family was in trouble—a consensus registered most compactly in Albion Small's protest against it: "As I review my own impressions from the discussions thus far, it seems to me that a stenographic report of everything that has been said would give the city editor of a yellow journal all the excuse such an imaginative gentleman usually requires . . . for asserting that this Society regarded the American family as on trial, with the presumption rather strongly against it" (190). Small finds the family to be the victim, not the cause, of the evils described; and considers in any case that problems exist primarily among the rich and poor, where "pretty much everything else is out of gear too," while among the "industrious middle stratum" the family works "at least as well" as other institutions (192). Those voicing alarm about the state of the institution must have wondered if his references to "invidious inferences," "smart flings at the family" based on "manipulations of the evidence that are either ignorant or disingenuous," and "hysterical . . . innuendo" were meant for them. But they would have agreed with Small's assertion that what was *really* on trial were the conditions that interfered with family life; even Gilman frames her radical proposals as a call for "a home that is no one's workshop" (29). And most would have found it difficult to dissent from Small's patriotic assertion that "with our human nature as it is, there is no conceivable form of association in which men and women could be more helpful to each other and better placed to do their best for society, than in the form frankly filled by the spirit of the typical American family" (194). From this early moment, to name the deficiencies of the family is immediately to produce its defense.

These papers, as well as the dominant popular discourses of their moment and our own, convey above all else the desirability of domestic life. The family remains the unquestioned unit of household organization, thus apparently inevitable; but it also becomes something people *choose* and in which people's choices matter. James Hagerty posed the problem of the modern family to the American Sociological Society in a paper titled "How Far Should Members of the Family be Individualized?" Before the industrial era, he asserts, the family "was organized to perpetuate the family name and unity, and no rights of individual members were recognized which compromised this purpose. This ideal has been changed to one where social welfare is sought in the recognition of the rights of individual members of the family to the greatest possible latitude of their capacities and power" (181). But the proponents of conjugal intimacy neatly transform the demand for individual rights into an argument on behalf of the endangered family. The home turns out to be the place where individual emotional needs can best be met and individual personalities can best be developed, the place where one can be most whole and happy. Provided, of course, that family members have the right attitudes and possess the right skills—the companionate family is one of those modern institutions constitutionally dependent on expert assistance.

Harper's Bazar, as a magazine for the "up-to-date" woman, kept readers informed about expert opinion on such topics as the state of the family and the changing roles of women, and provided them with authoritative guidance about how to create a happy, healthy home. During the period of *The Whole Family* Charlotte Perkins Gilman contributed several articles, including "The Passing of Matrimony" for the June 1906 issue; in January 1907 Jordan reprinted a *North American*

Plate 1.
The Mansard Roof, by Edward Hopper, 1923.
Watercolor over graphite on paper.
Reproduced by permission of
the Brooklyn Museum.

Plate 2.
Cover. *Harper's Bazar* 41.12
(December 1907).

Plate 3.
Cover. *Harper's Bazar* 39.4
(April 1905).

Plate 4.
Cover. *Harper's Bazar* 40.8
(August 1906).

Plate 5.
Cover. *Harper's Bazar* 40.7
(July 1906).

Plate 6.
Cover. *Harper's Bazar* 41.5
(May 1907).

Plate 7.
Cover. *Harper's Bazar* 42.9
(September 1908).

Plate 8.
Cover. *Harper's Bazar* 42.7
(July 1908).

Plate 9.

Illustration for *The Whole Family*, ch. 12,
"The Friend of the Family": "That brave little girl,
waving her flag of victory and peace." *Harper's
Bazar* 42.11 (November 1908): 1040.

Review editorial in which Harvey states his support for woman suffrage; Rev. Henry Potter (the bishop of New York) wrote "The Modern Home" for March 1907; and Charles William Eliot (the president of Harvard) contributed "Higher Education for Women" for the June 1908 issue. Essays by prominent figures complemented articles by more regular contributors, which tended to be oriented toward capturing subjective experience or offering specific advice. In 1906 and 1907 Jordan ran a series by Mary Heaton Vorse on the experiences of the young mother, another by Anne O'Hagan from the spinster's perspective, and six "Talks to Wives" by Mary Stewart Cutting—one directed to "the Wife Who Is in Danger of Losing Her Husband's Affection," another to "the Wife Who Suffers from Incompatibility." The *Bazar*'s fiction concerned itself with the same range of topics. In context, *The Whole Family* is revealed as a rather brilliant variation on the *Bazar* formula of combining distinguished visitors with familiar voices to provide authoritative and vivid accounts of home life.

Howells, characteristically perceptive, framed his proposal for *The Whole Family* precisely in terms of the tension between individualism and the family. How, he asked, can we think of the selection of a spouse as a personal matter but still remember its corporate consequences? The novel does in fact succeed in being about the "whole family"; in her study of turn-of-the-century "problem novels" Phyllis Steele notes it as a rarity because it includes three generations rather than focusing on the problems of a married couple (401). Jordan picked up the theme of individualism as a threat to the family in her editorial column for the December 1907 issue, in which Howells's opening chapter appears. Her explicit comment on the serial, as we have seen, confines itself to promotion, trying to intrigue the reader by mentioning the "very candid brotherly and sisterly comment in 'the family's' distinguished literary circle" (1248) without revealing the scope or depth of the controversy. But the collaborators' antagonisms are displaced only as far as the next page, where Jordan gives her thoughts on "The Family and the Quarrel." As I have said, her columns were collections of diverse thoughts not necessarily linked by any thread, but the connection to *The Whole Family* is obvious when Jordan writes: "In any family, anywhere, any day, there exists the making of a family quarrel. For a family presupposes at least two opinions and sets of tastes, and perhaps six. To be in a family at all is to meet opposition to the full individuality of the individual, as exemplified in oneself. The great value of the true family relation is that it teaches an individual to be a social unit and not a free lance" (1249). That, at any rate, was the hope expressed by Howells and Jordan, salaried employees of the House of Harper. But the free-lance contributors made achieving family solidarity a considerable challenge.

Women's individualism was (and is) far more disruptive than men's, for women's deference and the deferral of their needs are frequently the unspoken basis of family peace. As William Jay Youmans wrote in 1891, "when the importance of individuality has been insisted on, the individuality in view is that of man. It is he who has been exhorted to assert himself, to be true to his opinions, to live his own life; the exhortation has not been to any great extent addressed to his wife or his sisters. Enough for them if they can be so fortunate as to minister not unworthily to some grand male individuality. Women, however, though not particularly invited to the lecture, have been listening to it" (305). The characters created by the female contributors to *The Whole Family* press their claims in, and sometimes against, the family. They are ready for a reckoning with the institution. But inducing men to choose the family was (and is) an equally urgent matter. Howells's subtle and ambivalent opening chapter begins there, locating "The Father" in a form of masculine domesticity quite specific to the early twentieth century.

The Father's Family

Howells had personal reasons for having engagements and their consequences for families on his mind. No one knows why his daughter Mildred's engagement was broken in 1904, but biographers agree that the episode made him and his wife, Elinor, unhappy (see Anesko, *Letters* 381 n. 8). In any case Howells, who was entering his seventies during the period of *The Whole Family*, had already spent decades writing fiction in which marriage and the family are central concerns, including one of the earliest novels dealing with divorce—*A Modern Instance*, published in 1882. And as a critic of American literature and commentator on the life of the middle class, he was well aware that since that time a whole literature had proliferated around the "crisis" of the family. During the first decade of the twentieth century Howells was carefully reading and considering the work of Robert Herrick, for example. He even wrote to the author to ask if he had intended to endorse the adultery committed by one of the characters in his 1908 "Colossus of Matrimony," *Together*. Reassured, in 1909 he published a long appreciation of Herrick's work in the *North American Review*. In it he finds Herrick's criticisms of modern life and modern women accurate and important, although he criticizes *Together*'s ambiguity on that one point of sexual morality and suggests that the "new ferment of the old wine of individualism in women's character" is "observable" but less pervasive than the novelist thought.[4] The topics Howells proposed for *The Whole Family* were not spur-of-the-moment thoughts about what might interest the audience of a women's magazine; rather, they emerged out of his hopes and fears for social order. For him and for his contemporaries, they were matters of deep and continuing concern.

Howells opens "The Father" with a sentence that undermines its own optimism: "As soon as we heard the pleasant news—I suppose the news of an engagement ought always to be called pleasant—it was decided that I ought to speak first about it, and speak to the father" (3). The prospect that the news may turn out to be unpleasant after all, and the implication that there is a disparity between emotional truth and verbal convention, appear immediately. Howells makes the father of the family an old-fashioned patriarch—Cyrus Talbert is the leading man of Eastridge, "Blackstone's ideal of the head of a state, a good despot" (12). Yet the descriptions of his power proceed mostly by negation: he had been manager of the mill and now owns it, but "[n]obody ever said that Talbert had come unfairly into that, or that he had misused his money." He had been president of the village for two terms and still "was felt in a great many ways," but he "made something of a point of not being prominent in politics"; he "took a great interest in school matters" but "had a fight to keep himself off the board of education" (11). He "guarded his own interests, and held the leading law firm in the hollow of his hand, [but] he was not oppressive, to the general knowledge" (11–12). The text does not imply that Talbert is secretly dishonest or oppressive, but it makes that rejected image more vivid than any alternative. The description of his "family relations"—he is "of the exemplary perfection which most other men attain only on their tomb-stones" (12)—similarly fails to convey assurance while refusing to convey doubt.

The speaker here is Ned Temple, the Talbert family's new next-door neighbor and (we learn later in the chapter) the owner and editor of the local newspaper, the *Eastridge Banner*. Howells's plan had not actually specified first-person narration, but he had asked that each author "try seriously to put himself or herself into the personage's place" (*Life* 2; 225); Jordan's editorial commentary in this very issue of the *Bazar* asserts that the contributors write "in the first person and as the mouth-piece, so to speak, of a member of the family" (1248). And everyone but Howells does. He chooses to develop his character through a dia-logue between Temple and Talbert, and through an intricate web of in-direct perceptions woven around that conversation. Temple describes the father of the family and records his speech, but also reports what his wife and the Talbert ladies said during their visits back and forth, explains what she thought of them, mentions speculations he and his wife have engaged in about various members of the family, and even passes on Eastridge's "friendly gossip" (17) about them. The chapter is characteristic, as contemporary reviewers observed. Like the rest of Howells's fiction, it implies that no point of view is adequate in isola-tion, that both characters and readers can approach (without ever ar-riving at) an understanding of "reality" only by accumulating partial perspectives and simultaneously entertaining multiple interpretations.

Howells's contribution thus lacks the tone of intimate address to the reader, the element of self-justification that so strongly marks the others. (Of course, as the author of the first chapter he did not yet have any aspersions to defend his character against.) The mode, as well as the placement, of the chapter explains why the father seems to fade from the action as the novel progresses. Howells gives Talbert a formi-dable physical presence—he is a large man, whose "manly frame" sways "amply outward, but not too amply, at the girth," with graying red hair, "blue, kind eyes and a face fully freckled" (5)—and "intellectual force" (11), yet he seems oddly thin and pale once the other characters have made their entrances. He is missing from the family tableaux Alice Bar-ber Stephens created illustrating crisis points in the novel (see fig. 29); in fact, he is the one character she never drew. Occasionally he is shown

29. Illustration for *The Whole Family*,
ch. 5, "The School-Girl": "Wouldn't it be
safer, wiser, for me to open it?"
Harper's Bazar 42.4 (April 1908): 363.
By Alice Barber Stephens.

trying to rule—Mary Stewart Cutting makes him a tyrant about punctuality—but Henry James's constant references to "poor Father" and Elizabeth Stuart Phelps's passing remark that he "sleeps like a bag of corn-meal" (186) are more representative. The final chapter's search for closure brings Talbert back onstage to put his foot down; but Henry Van Dyke's friend of the family praises Talbert's good sense and paternal devotion—then pulls the wool over his eyes and undermines his authority by conniving at Peggy's elopement. The *Nation* reviewer considers him "domestically inert and helpless in the hands of his womenfolk" (553). In fact, the father's intentions and acts have little effect on the outcome of events; the good despot may, it seems, be an ineffectual one.

Talbert may not be in charge of the family, but he is very much *in* it. The neighbors' early-evening chat over the backyard fence exemplifies—in minute detail—the early twentieth-century ideal that historian Margaret Marsh has called "masculine domesticity." Temple has just finished "rasping my lawn with the new mower," and Temple (in keeping with his greater affluence) is "making his man pour a pail of water on the earth round a freshly planted tree" (4). Both evince strong, minute interest in the day-to-day running of their households and especially in their children. They joke about their mutual preference for a midday dinner and a substantial late tea rather than a fashionably late dinner, for example, even mentioning specific dishes they like to see served; they talk about family resemblances and how to educate girls. And they constantly refer to and quote their wives. Temple repeats a well-turned compliment his wife has paid Peggy, and Talbert says, "I shall have to tell my wife, that" (7). The two neighbors are model companion-husbands.

Masculine domesticity does not, as Marsh carefully establishes, imply equal sharing of household responsibilities, or equality between men and women in any larger sense. It does entail husbands and fathers paying precisely this sort of attention to domestic life and entering into this sort of communication with their wives. "Fathers agreed to take on increased responsibility for some of the day-to-day tasks of bringing up children. . . . A domestic man also made his wife, rather than his male associates, his regular companion on evenings out. And while he might not dust the mantel or make the bed except in special circumstances, he would take a significantly greater interest in the details of running the household and caring for the children than his father had been expected to take" (Marsh 76). In one sense this model returns the father to the central role in the home characteristic of earlier family forms, before "separate spheres"; but he also returns to a position in which his authority is qualified by expectations of partnership between husband and wife, and of "disciplinary intimacy" rather than coercive control between parent and child.[5] The model is also premised on a relationship between work and home—specifically, Marsh proposes (67–89), on middle-class job security and fixed hours of employment and the heterosocial organization of suburban spaces that constituted the realm of leisure that was now to be devoted to family life.

During the first decade of the twentieth century *Harper's Bazar* frequently recommended masculine domesticity. Elizabeth Jordan's editorial column for August 1906, for example, takes up the conflict between a woman's duties to her husband and to her children: "She cannot put the baby to sleep nights, and at the same time go out to the theatre with her husband. She cannot help the boys with their lessons in the evening and at the same time be down-stairs entertaining her husband's friends at dinner." The solution? "*She may succeed in being both wife and mother by converting her husband to a sense of the possibilities of fatherhood*" (762, emphasis in original). Mary Heaton Vorse's fictional "Confessions" of a young wife and mother published during 1907 recount the subjective complexities of companionate marriage, and on one occasion readers were even given a response—"Joe's Side of It, by a Mere Man" (December 1907). In another women's magazine, Vorse's *Very Little Person* gave a more optimistic picture of a father's intense involvement in his daughter's first year of life.[6]

In these forums masculine domesticity was being advocated to women, not directly to men, and its appeal—indeed its benefit—for middle-class wives and mothers is clear. Yet, as Marsh points out, it could also serve as "a male reply to the feminists' insistence that women had as much right to seek individual achievement as men. . . . Husbands and wives would be companions, not rivals, and the specter of individualist demands would retreat in the face of family togetherness" ("Suburban Men" 181). The many, varied calls for men to choose the family mingled appeals to and on behalf of men, women, children, and society at large, and mingled complexly with other contemporary notions. James Hagerty too thinks that family solidarity might be preserved amid the rising tide of individualism by fathers' commitment to their children, but he seems to imply at the same time that it is particularly important for sons to be taken partly out of the hands of women and servants: "A very busy college man once told me that he had a schedule of one hour a day with his two boys which he always kept. 'I want a chance at them' was his statement" (American Sociological Society 190). Jordan's column moves from contemporary-sounding images of women faced with too many responsibilities, and men awakening to the pleasures of parenting, to a specter drawn from the discourse of eugenics: "To win a man from exclusive attention to the sordid concerns of business, the dissipations of pleasure-seeking, and apply him to the infinitely profitable, infinitely enjoyable work of participating in the care, the physical, mental, moral development of his children, that is a cure which American women are everywhere, under all circumstances, able to apply to the root of the evil of race suicide said to be seriously menacing our nation" (763). Clearly the American women being addressed are white and at least middle class; we are reminded that the family defended here is understood as a fundamental component of the racialized nation.

Domestic men did run the risk of appearing feminized. This was a period in which middle-class men were, as Gail Bederman puts it, "unusually interested in—even obsessed with—manhood"; "masculinity" and such stigmatizing slang terms as "sissy" and "pussy-foot" came into use in the late nineteenth century as gender roles and sexual identities were remade (10-11, 17). *Whole Family* contributor Mary Raymond Shipman Andrews shows Peggy's school-boy brother scorning her fiancé because he is cultured rather than athletic: "[T]he minute I inspected him over I knew he was a sissy. If you'll believe me, that grown-up man can't chin himself. He sings and paints apple-blossoms, but he fell three-cornered over a fence that I vaulted" (252). Masculine domesticity could, however, be combined with the ideal of strenuous virility. One of the supporters Marsh cites is proselytizer for muscularity Bernarr Macfadden, who believed that women as well as men should be fit, and men as well as women should be family-oriented. Senator Alfred Beveridge, Marsh writes, advised fathers to spend time with their sons explicitly to ensure that they would grow up to be manly (80–82). And in Andrews's "boy" fiction, sport and outdoor life are sites of tender masculine emotion as well as a vitality that guards against overcivilization. Fabulations of many sorts reconcile potentially contradictory elements of the discourses that construct Anglo-Saxon manhood as the ultimate achievement of "civilization."

The classic site of family togetherness is the suburb (to which we will turn in examining the work of contributor Mary Stewart Cutting). The Talberts, however, are placed in Eastridge, a small city in central New York that shares some ideological advantages with the suburb—it is pastoral without being rural, within easy reach of the metropolis (as evidenced by the characters' train journeys back and forth) yet removed from its dangerous diversity. It does not share the suburb's explicit modernity, however; Eastridge evokes a traditional America dominated by Small's "industrious middle stratum." And Howells's portrait of the Talbert household blends emerging ideas of men's active participation with longer-established images of family life. Here, as throughout *The Whole Family*, the narrative undertakes to demonstrate that old and new can be successfully synthesized.

The Talberts' house is the most visible expression of their traditionalism. Ned Temple tells Cyrus, and the reader, in so many words, that it "expresses something characteristic" (9). Again Howells is working in a familiar mode—in more than a third of his novels, residences express characters' "social stations and spiritual conditions . . . so that the places help convey what the people have been, what they are, what they aspire to become, what they turn out to be" (Frazier 277). Such spatialization is a literary device, but not only that. Howells's work over the course of his long career relied on, indeed arguably helped to shape, an understanding of the built world as dense with social meaning and itself an active force in social life. Gwendolyn Wright has shown that in the four decades between 1873 and 1913, it was widely believed that the home environment shaped its inhabitants and even "passersby," and that proper home design could promote "social welfare and family stability" (*Moralism* 1). Reading Howells's description of the Talbert home alongside such scholarly readings of architecture as social history demonstrates how precisely he is rendering the Victorian domestic ideal.

The Talberts live in "a vast, gray-green wooden edifice, with a mansard-roof cut up into many angles, tipped at the gables with rockets and finials, and with a square tower in front, ending in a sort of look-out at the top, with a fence of iron filigree round it. The taste of 1875 could not go further; it must have cost a heap of money in the depreciated paper of the day" (9). The house concisely embodies (although it certainly does not exhaust) the iconography of the two major themes Wright finds in late nineteenth-century writers on the home: "closeness to nature" (26) and "the independence and protective quality of each home" (31). Its complex asymmetry, for example, exemplifies both: "The irregular shape of each house was intended as a sign of natural complexity, as well as an expression of the particular family's daily domestic activities" (26–27). According to Wright, the use of wood, "natural" colors like gray and green (produced by paints or stains or by allowing wood to weather), ornamental details, and spaces for viewing the out-of-doors also represent the integration of the home and the natural world.

The size of the house is significant in two ways. Wright links the large and complex array of rooms in the Victorian house to the increasingly widespread view that a specific array of specialized activities ought to be taking place in them, arguing that by the 1870s most middle-class houses in the United States distinguished three kinds of rooms: "spaces for presenting the home ideal to guests and to the family, spaces for the production of domestic goods, and spaces for privacy" (*Moralism* 34). Talbert's description mentions all three—the house was built according to his wife's idea, he says, with "plenty of chambers and plenty of room in them, and two big parlors one side of the front door, and a library and dining-room on the other; kitchen in the L part, and girl's room over that; wide front hall, and black-walnut finish all through the first floor" (10). Talbert also explicitly acknowledges that the size of the house reflects his importance in Eastridge—it is "the early monument of his success": "My wife used to say we wanted a large house so as to have it big enough to hold *me*, when I was feeling my best, and we built the largest we could for all the money we had" (9–10). Wright describes wealthy families in Chicago at just this moment commissioning "celebrated East Coast architects to design mansarded mansions along Michigan Avenue and then Prairie Avenue, hoping to be able to assure themselves of a solid image of taste, propriety and fortune" (16). Such display is not confined to this period, of course. But the level of detail Howells includes and the precise fit between his details and Wright's confirm the indexical function of his architectural imagery.

It is also a significant detail that the Talberts did *not* use an architect. Talbert says: "[My wife] had a plan of her own, which she took partly from the house of a girl friend of hers where she had been visiting, and we got a builder to carry out her idea. We did have some talk about an architect, but the builder said he didn't want any architect bothering around *him*, and I don't know as *she* did, either" (10). Builders, as Wright shows, accused trained architects of being "bound to the traditions of Europe and the beck-and-call of the wealthy" (25), and argued that their own designs were more distinctively American, more democratic, more inventive. While architects and builders drew on common sources (Ruskin, for example) and developed styles in closer parallelism than they might have liked to admit (see *Moralism* 56, 79), the kind of exuberant domestic iconography that characterizes the Talbert home was associated with the builders and what Wright calls this "populist" strain in domestic architecture. Just as Talbert is the leading man of the town without ceasing to be *of* the town, the house is huge and ostentatious without ceasing to be down-to-earth. Each is the best of its kind, not a different kind from the others in Eastridge. In the Talberts, Howells evokes precisely the middling America that (I argued in chapter 2) was the audience most consistently addressed by Harper & Brothers.

The mansard roof, especially, evokes this paradoxical combination of distinction and democracy. Mansard roofs are steeply pitched for ten to fifteen feet, then flat on top, with (generally) windows in the steep lower slope and ornamentation under the eaves (see fig. 30 and pl. 1). The style is named after François Mansard, a French architect of the seventeenth century who was the first to use it extensively; it was revived in French cities during the Second Empire, partly because the design allows the full top story to be used as an integral part of the house, and in mid-nineteenth-century France rooms under the roof were not taxed as another floor. This was not an advantage in the United States, of course, where the mansard roof primarily conveyed an impression of European elegance. Many houses in the Second Empire style were built

Making the Family Whole 125

mansard (dual-
pitched hipped)
roof, with dormer
windows on steep
lower slope

molded cornices
bound lower roof
slope above and below

eaves normally
with decorative
brackets below

30. Line drawing of a mansard roof. From Virginia and Lee McAlester, *A Field Guide to American Houses* 241. Copyright 1984 by Virginia Savage and Lee McAlester. *Reprinted by permission of Alfred A. Knopf, a division of Random House, Inc.*

in the Northeast and Midwest in the 1860s and 1870s, and the mansard roof was used in about 20 percent of them (Wright, *Building* 136). In 1886 an architecture critic writing in *Century* magazine disparaged such "untutored" borrowings by carpenters, calling the use of massive mansard roofs on square wooden houses "a peculiarly bold and naif act of appropriation. . . . It was supremely ludicrous and supremely ugly, yet no feature we have ever made our own has been more universally beloved" (van Rensselaer 8). Howells captures the amalgam of populism and pomp associated with the mansard roof quite exactly when Temple calls the house "simple-hearted in its out-dated pretentiousness" (10).

Mansard roofs went out of fashion quickly after the panic of 1873. So if the Talberts' house was built in 1875, it evidenced their lack of sophistication even when it was new.[7] But Cyrus and his wife are satisfied with the way the house expresses and establishes their domestic ideal and their local eminence, and indifferent to fast-changing metropolitan taste. Again, Cyrus says in so many words that the house is emblematic: "I don't say but what it's old-fashioned. I have to own up to that with the girls, but I tell them so are we, and that seems to make it all right for a while. I guess we sha'n't change" (10). The younger generation not only has different tastes (something that as inheritors of the taste for newness we perhaps take too much for granted) but is oriented less to local, and more to national, standards. Again Howells takes the trouble to give specific architectural details—Talbert says, "I guess if my girls, counting my daughter-in-law, had their way, they would have that French roof off, and something Georgian—that's what they call it—on, about as quick as the carpenter could do it. They want a kind of classic front, with pillars and a pediment, or more the Mount Vernon style, body yellow, with white trim" (8–9). And again we encounter the paradoxical unity of distinction and democracy. Gwendolyn Wright points out that "Joy Wheeler Dow's articles on American architecture, collected as *American Renaissance* in 1904, documented the resurgence of neo-Georgian classicism all over the country. He stated emphatically that this kind of architecture was more conducive to social order than any other style. It restrained the vulgarity of popular display which had characterized the 'rabid democracy' of Andrew Jackson's presidency and the nineteenth-century builders' houses." Yet other writers presented the enthusiasm for the colonial as "part of the entire country's common heritage of democratic good sense and egalitarianism" (*Moralism* 252). Temple and Talbert amuse themselves with exactly this question of just how American the style is: " 'They call it Georgian after Washington?' This was obviously a joke. 'No, I believe it was another George, or four others' " (9).

As this passage shows, the two men quickly establish camaraderie through humor—Temple notes two-thirds of the way through the chapter that they "had formed the habit already of laughing at any appearance of joke in each other" (21).[8] The chapter has opened with a punctilious consideration of how the Temples can convey congratulations on Peggy's engagement without seeming to "bid for the familiar acquaintance of people living on a larger scale than ourselves" or giving an opening for intimacy before knowing that the upwardly mobile Talberts are as "desirable in other ways as they were in the worldly way" (1). Temple reports in oddly impersonal terms that "it was decided" it would be less "committing" for him to speak than the ladies. His role in the family council is unclear; his attitude toward this elaborate etiquette is noncommittal, almost but not quite ironic. Although his own habits are clearly different, he responds warmly to Talbert's informality, and when the older and wealthier man makes "unexpected confidences" about his family affairs says that he "liked him the better for them" (26). Similarly, Talbert's joking comments on the dishes he likes served at tea include "self-satire"—he says, "My wife thinks cake is light, but I think meat is"—but also place him at a certain distance from feminine social maneuverings: "In the place where my wife lived, a woman's social standing was measured by the number of kinds of cakes she had" (8–9). They are enmeshed in what Marsh would call masculine domesticity, minutely involved in the doings of their households—yet they are not wholly reconciled to it.

In fact, although the two men's conversation ranges over a wide, seemingly random array of topics, it returns again and again to differences and disputes between the sexes. Their jokes especially target women's foibles. They begin with the fact that Peggy has become engaged to another student at her coeducational college; Talbert mentions family controversies over Peggy's enrolling there, referring in passing to the views of "my wife, who's more anxious than I am about most things—women are, I guess" (6). When they return to the topic of women's education later he asks why, by the time a man is ready to change his mind about a situation, "a woman has got set in it like the everlasting hills? Is it because she feels the need of holding fast for both, or is it because she knows she hasn't the strength to keep to her conclusion, if she wavers at all, while a man can let himself play back and forth, and still stay put." Temple replies, " 'Well, in a question like that,' . . . and I won my neighbor's easy laugh, 'I always like to give my own sex the benefit of the doubt, and I haven't any question but man's inconsistency is always attributable to his magnanimity' " (27). Their enjoyment of each other's company is a thoroughly gendered solidarity.

Talbert's report of disagreements with his "girls" over modernizing the house forms part of this pattern of reference to tensions within the family. If anything, the jokes become slightly more edged as the chapter and the conversation progress. To Talbert's recommendation that the Temples rely on the local practitioner Dr. Denbigh, Temple replies: "You're quite right, I think, but that's a matter I should have to leave two-thirds to my wife: women are two-thirds of the patients in every healthy family, and they ought to have the ruling voice about the doctor" (21). Toward the end Talbert says about the family discussions of coeducation and Peggy's engagement, " '[A] woman likes to feel that she's a prophetess at any time of her life. That's about all that seems to keep some of them going when they get old.' I [Temple] knew that here he had his mother-in-law rather than his daughter in mind, and I didn't interrupt the sarcastic silence into which he fell" (26). Conflict between family members is a humorously treated undertone—but it is constantly there.

This opening chapter establishes a clear and detailed framework for what follows. Jordan and subsequent commentators have tended to emphasize Mary Wilkins Freeman's departure from Howells's plan on one key point—the age and appearance of the spinster aunt—and to write as if his influence on the book disappears when his chapter ends. Howells himself may have thought so; Jordan writes that he let her "see that he thought the novel was wrecked and that he himself lay buried among the ruins" (*Three* 267). But in truth the other contributors take the task of following the Dean of American Letters very seriously. They base their characters directly on the sketches Howells provides in the first chapter, incorporating virtually every detail, from the daughter-in-law's training at the Art Students' League to the schoolboy's attitudes toward girls. Each of them uses first-person narration, and each gives as sympathetic a portrait as possible within the lines that Howells has drawn—so they become advocates for the virtues and views of their characters, immersing us in a series of intense subjectivities. (The friend of the family comments in the last chapter that Talbert's "late-Victorian theory" of encouraging children's individuality had produced "a collection of early-Rooseveltian personalities around him" [296].) They show over and over that each member of the family feels misunderstood by the others. Thus the format of the novel turns out to lend itself to exactly the sort of fragmentation that Howells feared. He had represented gendered tensions within the family—but humorously, indirectly. The women writers who followed him shifted the prospect of the family's unmaking from the background to the foreground.

The Female Counter-family

Elizabeth Talbert, the narrator of the second chapter of *The Whole Family*, finds her family's image of her as "The Old-Maid Aunt" completely at odds with her image of herself as a fashionable, independent woman. The rest of the Talberts even get her name wrong—everywhere but Eastridge she is not Elizabeth but "Lily." She considers the whole notion of the "old maid" obsolete, in fact; and Freeman's correspondence with Jordan shows that on this point she speaks for her creator. I take up the controversial status of unmarried women in the next chapter. What concerns me here is the critique of the family that emerges from Elizabeth/Lily's position as a kind of cuckoo in the nest, a misrecognized and hostile stranger. Freeman gives a more disparaging account of the Talberts than any other contributor, but her portrait of the family as inimical to her character's emotional needs gets considerable support from the authors of the third and fourth chapters. Mary Heaton Vorse and Mary Stewart Cutting write from the perspectives of "The Grandmother" and "The Daughter-in-Law," thus extending the critique of the family to include voices from three generations of characters. These three women writers were themselves of different generations and held widely different views on social and political issues, including what would soon be called feminism; yet, they found themselves united in advocating for their female characters, against the family's father.

Freeman, like the other contributors, draws in detail on the information about her character supplied by Howells (that Elizabeth spends most of her time making long visits to friends, that she values taste and beauty, and that she has had a romantic disappointment are all points suggested in the first chapter and developed in the second). And when she challenges his family values, she cannily puts pressure on the very fault line he embedded in the text. Howells had imagined Elizabeth as herself an antiquity and had not included her in the group of "girls" pressing Cyrus to modernize the house; but she turns his mild acknowledgment of its unattractive obsolescence into an indictment.

> I sometimes wonder why it is that all my brother's family are so singularly unsophisticated. . . . Sometimes I speculate as to whether it can be due to

the mansard-roof of their house. I have always had a theory that inanimate things exerted more of an influence over people than they dreamed, and a mansard-roof, to my mind, belongs to a period which was most unsophisticated and fatuous, not merely concerning aesthetics, but simple comfort. Those bedrooms under the mansard-roof are miracles not only of ugliness, but discomfort. . . . [None of them knows] that today an old-maid aunt is as much of an anomaly as a spinning-wheel, that she has ceased to exist, that she is prehistoric, that even grandmothers have almost disappeared off the face of the earth. In short, they do not know that I am not an old-maid aunt except under this blessed mansard-roof, and some other roofs of Eastridge, many of which are also mansard, where the influence of their fixed belief prevails. (31–33)

Elizabeth suggests, that is, that the house may be not only expressive but constitutive of her relations' attitudes, virtually parodying the notion of home design as a moral force.

Freeman was thoroughly attuned to Howells's indexical use of architecture. Her father had been an architect and builder, she and her husband had built a new house in 1906, and in her fictions she too pays substantial attention to houses.[9] Her attitude toward the model of domesticity embodied in the Talbert home was in the current of contemporary opinion, which by 1908 overwhelmingly considered the Victorian home too formal and too cluttered.[10] In her chapter she extends her criticism to include Eastridge's bourgeois style in general, pressing Howells's domestic details into service as evidence. For example, Lily pities Ned Temple (now revealed as a former lover) for his wife's bad taste and absorption in the trivialities of housekeeping: "Fancy the books on the table being all arranged with the large ones under the small ones in perfectly even piles! I am sure that he has his meals on time, and I am equally sure that the principal dishes are preserves and hot biscuits and cake. That sort of diet simply shows forth in Mrs. Temple and her children. I am sure that his socks are always mended, but I know that he always wipes his feet before he enters the house, that it has become a matter of conscience with him; and those exactions seem to me pathetic" (35).

This tone of angry condescension characterizes much of the chapter. Lily skewers some of her relatives in passing and dissects others' flaws at length; few escape. Grandmother Evarts "would patronize the prophets of old" (31). Maria "repeats Grandmother Evarts, which is a pity, because there are types not worth repeating" (32). Peggy has no brains; Charles Edward has no resolution; and his wife, Lorraine, has bad posture and no style. When Lily tells her sister-in-law Ada about Harry Goward's infatuation, she "might as well have told the flour-barrel," for Ada placidly continues darning stockings "the same way that a cow chews her cud" (39). This calm, according to Elizabeth, is based on an utterly false security. Ada thinks that Harry is like Cyrus, and she believes that her husband has never thought of another woman—but Elizabeth knows that he "had been simply mad over another girl, and only married her [Ada] because he could not get the other girl, and when the other died, five years after he was married to Ada, he sent flowers, and I should not to this day venture to speak that girl's name to the man" (40). Ada is not just dull; she is also blind to her own husband's true feelings and willfully oblivious to her daughter's danger. Mrs. Temple is more volatile and becomes frantically jealous when Lily walks with her husband. Such constant revelations of deep emotions under the surface of daily life, combined with Lily's busy efforts to remedy the consequences of her fatal attractiveness, make the chapter almost melodramatic (as Freeman obliquely acknowledges at its end).[11] It cumulatively argues that Ada's world—which is Howells's—is not just superficial but delusory. Through Elizabeth, Freeman takes apart an image of the family she considers false and destructive, and which indeed—the chapter irresistibly suggests—provokes her to anger.

No wonder Howells was dismayed by what his collaborator had done with his characters. Freeman must have *chosen* to enter into this conflict with the Dean of American Letters—although when speaking in her own voice rather than Lily's she did not choose to acknowledge it directly. Her letters seem to shift the responsibility for her characterization to the situation Howells set up; she writes, for example, that in creating Elizabeth he was "thinking of the time when women of thirty put on caps, and renounced the world. . . . Peggy was twenty, and her aunt thirty-four. It is obvious nonsense to make it impossible that a man should fall in love with Elizabeth" (Kendrick 313). This convinced Jordan, who recounts in *Three Rousing Cheers* that "Miss Wilkins discovered from Mr. Howell's passing mention of Peggy's aunt . . . that the 'old maid' was about thirty-four" (263). But in fact the first chapter offers no specific information about Elizabeth's age. Given what Temple reports she could easily be older than her brother Cyrus, who has grown children, and she certainly need not be fifteen years younger.[12] Freeman was not forced into this "innovation in the shape of a maiden aunt" (Jordan 265), but rather made Elizabeth young in order to strengthen her case against the stereotype. Freeman also defended herself by pointing out that she had to do *something* to start some action. On this point most of the other authors sympathized, and subsequent readers have agreed. It is entirely unclear at the end of Howells's chapter what the plot of the novel, if any, is to be. The "shadows of diffidence" between the Temple and Talbert ladies (12) or the shades of opinion about female education might sustain one of Howells's own late fictions, but the other contributors felt the need of some explicit conflict between the characters. Freeman's "facer" (as Alice Brown called it [Jordan 275]) provided plenty of conflict.

The task of following Freeman fell to Mary Heaton Vorse. At this period Vorse was not the political radical she later became (and is remembered as being), but she was already something of a Bohemian. She and her husband were living at the A Club in Greenwich Village, in the center of a network of rebellious intellectuals and artists. She was also rapidly establishing herself as a successful magazine writer. Among her many contributions to the *Bazar* was a series called "In the Land of Old Age" (duplicitously attributed to "an Elderly Woman"), which is undoubtedly why Jordan invited her—at thirty-two, the youngest contributor—to write "The Grandmother."

Vorse is remarkably resourceful in constructing understandable, even sympathetic, motives for the unattractive behavior already ascribed to her character. Howells had represented Cyrus's mother-in-law (through the multiply distanced medium of Ned Temple's report of his wife's report) as an officious and trivial woman: "Mrs. Talbert's mother inquired, as delicately as possible, what denominations, religious and medical, we were of, how many children we had, and whether mostly boys or girls, and where and how long we had been married. She was glad, she said, that we had taken the place next them, . . . and said that there was only one objection to the locality, which was the prevalence of moths; they obliged you to put away your things in naptha-balls al-most the moment the spring opened" (16). (The text continues in this vein through a long paragraph that occupies most of two pages.) Vorse does not attempt to counter the portrait, but here, for example, is her interior view of the grandmother's interference in details of household management: "I do my best to prevent the awful waste of soap that goes on, and there are a great many little ways Ada could let me save for her if she would. When I suggest this to her she laughs and says, 'Wait till we need to save as badly as that, mother,' which doesn't seem to me good reasoning at all. 'Waste not, want not,' say I, and when it comes to throwing out perfectly good glass jars, as the girls would do if I didn't see to it they saved them, why, I put my foot down. If Ada doesn't want them herself to put things up in, why, some poor woman will" (61–62). The obsessive focus on details, the obstinacy, remain; but her concern is genuine and her thrift real and respectable (indeed, at the beginning of the twenty-first century Mrs. Evarts's position on recycling glass jars seems far from foolish). Unlike Howells and Freeman, Vorse makes it obvious that her first-person narrator is not wholly reliable. When the grandmother says something like, "Maria . . . had so much to say to Ada that I interfered, though it is contrary to my custom" (66), the point is precisely that she is deceiving herself about her customary behavior.

Vorse also makes it clear, however, that Mrs. Evarts loves her daughter and her grandchildren, and, as the chapter progresses, that her posi-tion in the family is difficult. The grandmother feels misunderstood by those around her, trapped in a role that does not accommodate her indi-viduality or meet her needs—she feels, in other words, just as Elizabeth does. This chapter, like the *Bazar* sketches that became *The Autobiog-raphy of an Elderly Woman* (1911), is about how an aging woman feels as her children kindly but firmly push her out of the center of the family, depriving her not only of power over domestic decisions but of partici-pation in their emotional lives. The *Autobiography* is eloquent on this experience of marginalization:

[T]here is a conspiracy of silence against me in my household. "We mustn't worry mother" is the watchword of my dear children, and the result of their great care is that I am on the outside of their lives.

Shadows come and go among them; they talk about them; I feel the chill of their trouble, but I'm never told what it's about. Before me they keep cheerful; when I come, the shadow passes from their faces and they talk with me about all the things that they think will interest me. I move in a little artificial, smiling world away from all the big interests of life.... So the great silence enfolds me more and more. I live more alone and solitary among those I love, groping in the silence, watching the faces of my children to find what is passing in their lives. (10–11)

Similarly, Grandmother Evarts says, "All at once you are aware something is wrong. You can't tell why you feel this; you only know that you are living in the cold shadow of some invisible unhappiness. You see no tears in the eyes of the people you love, but tears have been shed just the same. Why? You don't know, and no one thinks of telling you. It is like seeing life from so far off that you cannot make out what has happened" (70). She does not yet seem to feel that she must maneuver like a child to have her own way about her own comings and goings, as the narrator of the *Autobiography* does, but she too finds her own family unwittingly unkind.

The illustration by Alice Barber Stephens that ran with this chapter, as frontispiece for the February 1908 issue of *Harper's Bazar,* captures the themes and emotional tone of "The Grandmother" very effectively. Vorse writes of how intensely Mrs. Evarts participates in her daughter's life, yet how powerless she feels: "I can no longer protect her from anything—not even from myself, my illnesses and weaknesses. I sometimes seem to me, so eagerly do I follow the lights and shadows of my daughter's life, as if I were living a second existence together with my own" (60). Stephens's image shows Ada seated at a window lost in thought, her sewing forgotten in her lap; Grandmother Evarts, also seated, leans from behind her daughter, one hand on Ada's arm (see fig. 31). Her features are an older version of Ada's, and her expression and pose also echo her daughter's in their quiet sadness but express, in the slight downward turn of her mouth and the inclination of her body, a more open anxiety and a clear solicitude for Ada. Her dark gown contrasted with Ada's light one, her positioning against the dark wall and Ada's against the bright window, show the mother as, quite precisely, the shadow of her daughter. Vorse's emphasis on empathy not only enlists Stephens's collaboration but also carries out Howells's desire to show the family as a connected, indivisible entity. Mrs. Evarts tells the doctor: "It seems absurd, I know, for an old woman like me to get upset just because her grandchild does not get letters from her sweetheart, . . . [but] no one suffers alone in a family like ours. An event like this is like a wave that disturbs the whole surface of the water. Every one of us feels anything that happens, each in his separate way. Why, I can't be sick without its causing inconvenience to Billy" (77). Here Vorse directly alludes to Howells's suggestion that the novel treat engagement and marriage as a "family affair"; her whole chapter and Stephens's illustration indirectly convey the same point.

Vorse's writing about elderly women is driven by her sympathy for their disenfranchisement; thus it links quite directly with her later more explicitly political journalism and fiction. Articulating subjective experience, particularly the sensations of those without a public voice, was also a task the *Bazar* consistently took on in this period. Vorse's own other series during 1907 and 1908 were "Confessions of a Young Wife" and "Some Experiences of a Mother"; the former engendered equally intimate, anonymous rejoinders titled "Joe's Side of It" and "Confessions of an Older Wife." We also find in this period "A Plea for the Small Boy" and "The Teacher's Side of It." Many stories take a child's point of view, asking readers to consider the feelings of a small child faced with a new baby sister or a boy at the "awkward age" of thirteen.[13] Among the contributors to *The Whole Family* Elizabeth Stuart Phelps, in particular, shared this orientation. Her chapter (the eighth) gives the perspective of Maria "the manager," endeavoring to enlist sympathy for the dilemma of an older sister who has "the intelligence and forethought of a mother without a mother's authority or privilege" (186). Other works take on similar tasks; for example Phelps's novel *Walled In*, serialized in the *Bazar* throughout 1907, is an intimate account of an invalid's life. The magazine regularly offered its readers education in empathy, thus presumably better fitting them for life in the companionate family.

Vorse had already written about the unnecessary restrictions on older women's dress in one of her "Land of Old Age" sketches—the narrator says, "*I* would not have the courage to blossom out in so much as one daring pink ribbon" (41: 367). Wearing a pink gown with a pink hat was, of course, one of Lily Talbert's offenses against propriety (compare

31. Illustration for *The Whole Family*,
ch. 3, "The Grandmother": " 'Tell Mother
what's worrying you, dear,' I said, gently."
Harper's Bazar 42.2 (February 1908):
102.

her portrait [fig. 2] with the street dress considered appropriate "For Older Women" [fig. 6]). One also sees her remembered in Vorse's later appeal, in the *Autobiography*, to young people to feel sorry for women who try to preserve the illusion of youth, rather than ridiculing them: "You may be sure that almost all older women who refuse to grow old gracefully reveal some tragedy in these mistaken efforts" (266). However, within the chapter she firmly puts the old-maid aunt in her place. Elizabeth, in Mrs. Evarts's account, has reacted to her tragedy—the failure of her romance with Lyman Wilde—by refusing to grow into adult womanhood, becoming so vain and self-absorbed that she is willing to sacrifice her niece's happiness to her own hunger for attention from men.

The authors who followed Freeman, in fact, could treat Elizabeth as a reliable narrator only if they were willing to confine themselves to illustrating an already defined character and advancing the plot. (Jordan does essentially that in the fifth chapter.) To make the meaning of events swerve from the significance Freeman had given them and contribute to the thematic development of the novel entailed asserting some cognitive advantage over Elizabeth. Vorse has the grandmother diagnose her as "a case of arrested development" (68). In the fourth chapter, Mary Stewart Cutting gives the daughter-in-law much more information than Elizabeth suspects she has: "Miss Elizabeth Talbert is a howling swell. . . . I've heard lots of things about her from Bell Pickering, who knows the Munroes—Lily Talbert, they call her there. She thinks she's fond of Art, but she really doesn't know the first thing about it—she doesn't like anything that isn't expensive and elegant and *à la mode*" (92–93). Cutting strikes a careful balance, allowing Elizabeth her fashionable beauty but making her vain and self-absorbed (thus explaining why she fails to appreciate her nephew's wife), and asserting Lorraine's superior taste.

Cutting does enthusiastically enlist in the ongoing critique of the Talberts—Lorraine's opening line is: "I have never identified myself with my husband's family" (80). The married son and daughter-in-law are as thoroughly misunderstood by their relations as Aunt Elizabeth and Grandmother Evarts are. No one realizes that they are merely "existing" in Eastridge until they can get away to Paris and begin their real lives as artists; no one is even capable of understanding what it means to be an artist. Cutting ignores Freeman's aspersions against Cyrus and Ada's marriage (as do all the other contributors), but she portrays their relationship, and their whole domestic life, as conducted on terms so alien to the young people that it scarcely matters. The elder Talberts are not just benignly old-fashioned, as Howells had it. They are not only behind the times and unsophisticated, as Freeman suggested. According to Cutting, they are virtually fossilized.

Like Freeman, Cutting supports her reinterpretation of the family by renaming—Lorraine hates Charles Edward's "long-winded Walter-Scotty name," doesn't care "how many grandfathers it's descended from," and chooses to call him Peter. Her reaction to the family's hurt feelings over the matter reveals the individualism that is at the core of their differences: "[A]s long as *I* don't object to their calling him what *they* like, I don't see why they mind" (83). Lorraine feels constant pressure to reshape herself to fill a particular role in the family, and her characteristic mode of resistance is to assert that their motives are incomprehensible. When the Talberts are unhappy that she and her husband refuse to participate in their formal welcome to Peggy's fiancé, she "cannot see why people *will* want you to do things that they *know* you don't care to!" (90). When her mother-in-law is horrified by her slack housekeeping, she protests, "What difference it can make to *anybody* what time you make your *own* bed I can't see!" (98). Cutting creates a character to whom it is obvious that these are not family matters but personal choices, a character to whom self-expression and self-fulfillment seem self-evident goods. Lorraine acknowledges no system of values in which her husband's responsibilities in Eastridge might matter more than his artistic aspirations—her father went into business to support his family, but "*I* couldn't give up being an artist for anybody, no matter *who* starved, and Peter feels that way, too" (85). She can understand the family's attitude toward the conflict only as hypocrisy: "If I were to tell them that Charles Edward perfectly detests the business, and will *never* be interested in it and never make anything out of it, they'd all go straight off the handle; yet they all know it as well as I do. That's the trouble—you simply can't tell them the truth about anything; they don't want to hear it" (89). Lorraine refuses to accept the subordination of the individual to the family; she is, in Jordan's phrase, "a free lance."

Most emphatically, Lorraine rejects the Talberts' Victorian notions about her relationship with her husband. "The family are always harping on 'Lorraine's influence'" (83), for example, but she does not see why it should be up to her to persuade Charles Edward to smoke less, spend less, and pay more attention to the family business. Nor will she try to convince him to write to Harry Goward to learn his intentions toward Peggy; to her the request demonstrates that her mother-in-law is "the survival of a period when a woman always expected some man to face any crisis for her" (97). She does not care that the other members of the family look "pained" when Cyrus kisses Ada goodbye as he leaves the dinner table for the factory but she and Charles Edward merely nod at each other—she "cannot be affectionate to him before them" (89). Lorraine considers Charles Edward "the best sort ever" (80), and Cutting in fact shows her as a devoted wife. But these are individuals who have chosen each other; their companionate marriage does not divide duties or entail ceremonial gestures on Cyrus and Ada's Victorian model. Lorraine does not criticize the older Talberts' formal kiss, considering it animated by real feeling (Ada "always blushes so prettily" [89]). But she will not make kissing Charles Edward a ritual, and to reveal their improvisational intimacy would embarrass her. Their marriage is fundamentally *private*.

It is a fine irony that marries the slangy, emphatic Lorraine to a character created by Henry James, whose series "The Speech of American Women" ran in the *Bazar* during 1906 and 1907.[14] He alludes to his dismay on the topic within *The Whole Family* when Charles Edward reports warning his mother that a coeducational college will teach Peggy "to roar and snarl with the other animals. Think of the vocal sounds with which she may come back to us!" (162). James allows Ada to reply that his wife, and his marriage, are products of coeducation, and gives his character no good answer, although he makes no explicit comment on Lorraine's tendency to say things like "you're a Jim Dandy" (97). (He does have Charles Edward apologize for his wife's name, which Cutting chose.) But James's chapter, the seventh, in general sustains Cutting's portrait of Charles Edward and Lorraine's affection and their "exquisite and intimate combined effort of resistance" (148) to the rest of the family and the values they represent. He qualifies and complicates many issues and condescends to the "charming, absurd" (151)

Lorraine. But he also takes on, and develops, the contrast between their companionship and other ways of being married.

Charles Edward's narration makes much of the fact that Lorraine walks to the "Works" with him in the morning and meets him there in the afternoon for the walk home. A courting couple would be allowed to experiment with intimacy in public, but Eastridge finds it disturbing that a wife "should come forth with me at those hours, that she should hang about with me, and that we should have last (and, when she meets me again, first) small sweet things to say to each other. . . . They can't conceive how Lorraine gets out, or should wish to, at such hours; there's a feeling that she must violate every domestic duty to do it; yes, at bottom, really, the act wears for them, I discern, an insidious immorality, and it wouldn't take much to bring 'public opinion' down on us in some scandalized way" (170). James shows the spouses refusing to be divided into separate spheres—Charles Edward neglects his work, Lorraine her housekeeping, in order to pursue their absorbing conversation. And they refuse to confine their intercourse to the place provided for it, thus dividing themselves from the community. "What is it we *can* have to say to each other, in that exclusive manner, so particularly, so frequently, so flagrantly, and as if we hadn't chances enough at home? I see it's a thing Mother might accidentally do with Father, or Maria with Tom Price; but I can imagine the shouts of hilarity, the resounding public comedy, with which Tom and Maria would separate; and also how scantly poor little Mother would permit herself with poor big Father any appearance of a grave leave-taking" (170–71). James enters into collaboration with Cutting, extending her image of the couple violating old-fashioned expectations about leave-taking: both their refusal to exchange a ritualized kiss and their failure to adopt the daily routine appropriate for a husband and wife convey not the emptiness of their marriage but its fullness. Indeed, so long as we recognize the interpenetration of high culture and popular discourses we will not be surprised to find that the author of *The Golden Bowl* (1904) is deeply interested in the workings of companionate marriage.[15]

Cutting follows Howells and Freeman in using domestic design as an index to contrasting styles of family life. Howells had provided Lorraine with an opinion on the mansard roof; Cutting concentrates on another emblematic element of the Victorian home—the dining

32. Sideboard, unknown (American),
1855–65. Yale University Art Gallery, bequest
of Joseph Earl Sheffield.

room. Lorraine endures family dinners in silence: "I never pretend to talk at meals; I just sit and try to make my mind a blank until it's over. You *have* to make your mind a blank if you don't want to be driven raving crazy by that dining-room. It has a hideous black-walnut sideboard, an 'oil-painting' of pale, bloated fruit on one side, and pale, bloated fish on the other" (89). Her reaction seems exaggerated until it is juxtaposed with "Death in the Dining Room," Kenneth Ames's analysis of the material culture of middle-class dining in the mid-nineteenth century. Ames vividly evokes such "massive and aggressive" (58) sideboards, with their elaborate carvings of foods of all sorts but especially dead game animals, flanked by still lifes repeating the images of bounty and predation (see fig. 32). His description of twentieth-century viewers' reactions suggests that he might sympathize with Lorraine: "Surviving examples allow us to experience their powerful presence. While they induce in us a certain degree of awe, we tend to see them as alien, foreign, decidedly odd. On one level, they are fascinating; on another, slightly repulsive. Today it is difficult for many of us to believe that normal, well-socialized people in Victorian America voluntarily put these boldly expressive objects in their dining rooms and ate daily in their presence" (67). Ames's analysis underscores Cutting's prescience in making the family dinner represent what disturbs her about the Talbert household: "As they dined, they sat in the presence of a rich and intricate nonverbal text that spoke of the struggle for existence and the subordination of groups to other groups; of the interrelatedness of all living things; of order, hierarchy, domination, and survival; of history and progress; power and gender; of the inescapable truth that some must die for others to live" (76–77). Taking her seat in the dining room, Lorraine is compelled to occupy her subaltern place in the Victorian scheme of things; her silence embodies her resistance.

The sideboard was a conspicuous reminder of the specialization of spaces in affluent Victorian homes, invariably occupying a room devoted exclusively to formal dining. Lorraine locates it in a household regime as well—she and Peter hate the Talberts'

> little, petty cast-iron rules and regulations. . . . My father-in-law pulls out his chair at the dinner-table exactly as the clock is striking one, and if any member of the family is a fraction late all the rest are solemn and

strained and nervous until the culprit appears. . . . The menu for each day of the week is as fixed as fate, no matter what the season of the year: hot roast beef, Sunday; cold roast beef, Monday; beef-steak, Tuesday; roast mutton, Wednesday; mutton pot-pie, Thursday; corned beef, Friday; and beef-steak again on Saturday. My father-in-law never eats fish or poultry, so they only have either if there is state company. There's one sacred apple pudding that's been made every Wednesday for nineteen years. (87)

Lorraine mocks the equation of domestic regularity with the ceremonies of the state and the sacred, but again, her powerful reaction reflects the fact that visions of social and moral order are at stake. Her own house is "all at sixes and sevens" (86), with jelly on the sofa and paintbrushes everywhere, yet she is innately hospitable. After dinner at the Talberts', Lorraine and Peter annex Harry Goward (who has now become a youth with "artistic temperament" [89]), and they "all talked until three o-clock in the morning. We simply ate all over the house— goodness! how hungry we were! At Peter's home it's an unheard-of thing to eat anything after half-past six—almost a crime, unless it's a wedding or state reception. We began now with coffee in the dining-room, and jam and cheese, and ended by gradual stages at hot lobster in the chafing-dish in the studio" (91–92; see fig. 33).[16] Nothing is in its place, and lobster even evokes the image of metropolitan night life, yet Lorraine's household is the one that is genuinely nourishing.

Here, as in other chapters of this book, the recognition that attitudes identified with different eras coexist helps us to sort out what we see in *The Whole Family*. The development of an informal middle-class culture from the 1890s through the 1920s is well documented.[17] Howells clearly delineates a generational contrast, with visibly Victorian attitudes still flourishing but youth leading the way toward change. Subsequent chapters heighten the contrast, as successive contributors make Cyrus and Ada's style more dated, and as Cutting faithfully follows up Howells's references to the daughter-in-law's "easy-going" nature and artistic inclinations (13). Bohemians are by no means a staple in her fiction—Cutting's home ground is the suburb, and her youthful housekeepers more commonly try to keep up appearances on slender resources. Informality is frequently an index of sincerity, however, and she always values warmhearted hospitality over social display.

33. Illustration for *The Whole Family*, ch. 4,
"The Daughter-in-Law": "We ended at hot lobster in
the chafing-dish in the studio." *Harper's Bazar*
42.3 (March 1908): 202.

Maria and Tom Price (the married daughter and the son-in-law) are locally identified and relatively conservative in these early chapters, and in all accounts less cosmopolitan and closer to their parents than the other couple; thus the novel signals the complexity of the moment. Yet Charles Edward and Lorraine, for all their self-declared marginality, give the distinct impression that they represent the future. As Henry James observes in the seventh chapter (in Charles Edward's voice), classifying the earlier generations as traditional allows them to embrace a self-authenticating "modernity" (157–58).

Cutting's chapter makes it clear that the younger Talberts' informality is an innovation within a class culture, not the collapse of social distinctions. From the beginning, in which Lorraine explains her difference from her husband's family by phenotype—they "are all blue-eyed, fair-haired, and rosy, and I'm dark, thin, and pale" (80)—she locates people by race and ethnicity. The other narrators assume whiteness and navigate inside it without mentioning it; Lorraine marks its boundaries. The ethnic, exotic other provides her with raw material for her art: she is painting a portrait of an Armenian peddler (93). She asks her cook, Sally, for a minstrel performance when she is feeling sad (94); and she remarks in passing that "the darky was out all night, as usual" (92)—her casual racism throwing the *Bazar*'s assumptions about its readership into sharp relief. Lorraine does not want a black walnut pageant of the food chain looming over her as she eats, but Cutting identifies her as a civilized and cultured being: what those attributes signify is that she is located in the upper reaches of a class-inflected, racialized hierarchy.

Mary Stewart Cutting's fiction offers a detailed phenomenology of life in the suburbs of New York during the first two decades of the twentieth century and can help us reconstruct the discourses among which *The Whole Family* circulated. It deserves more attention than it has so far received from either literary critics or cultural historians. Her topics and publication venues, as well as the fact that she worked primarily although not entirely in the short story rather than the novel form, have prevented her from being noticed, let alone taken seriously. Volumes such as *Little Stories of Married Life* and *The Suburban Whirl* approximate what Sandra Zagarell has called "narratives of community," as characters living in the same neighborhoods repeat from one tale to another, sometimes in leading and sometimes in secondary roles, providing multiple, complementary perspectives on the "continuous small-scale negotiations and daily procedures" that structure local connectedness ("Narrative" 503). Yet each story is most crucially a portrait of a single family. Almost every plot somehow renews the intimacy of a husband and wife. It is, as Alfred Bendixen observes in his biographical sketch of Cutting for the reprint of *The Whole Family*, easy to understand why Jordan chose her to write the daughter-in-law's chapter; she specialized in writing about marriage. The foundation of this community is the companionate family—Cutting's stories prove over and over, and never finish proving, that choosing it makes people happy.

Masculine domesticity as Marsh describes it is often on view in Cutting's stories—husbands are minutely involved in their families and households. Just as often, a wife tries to persuade her husband to take more interest in domestic affairs. The resolution is usually an adjustment in her attitude rather than his, but the endings are always happy. Many stories portray a domestic mishap or social quandary; again, things invariably work out for the best. Others portray a serious struggle to make ends meet or a reexamination of values. The image of the daily exodus of husbands to their work in the city—leaving their wives to balance the demands of housekeeping, child rearing, and social engagements (occasionally, to follow on later trains for shopping and more socializing)—is the leitmotif of her work. This is a world in which production, and consumption and leisure, are deeply divided and immensely elaborated. When Cutting ventures outside her ordinary territory, as to a New England village in "Wings" (*Little Stories of Married Life*), it is to explore other sorts of separation: the situation of an engaged couple when the man goes to Australia to make his fortune, of married couples who live together but are emotionally estranged, and the permanent but perhaps illusory parting of death. Whatever else the stories are about, her protagonists confront the dilemma that a wife must be "her husband's comrade" (as Cutting puts it in one of her "Talks to Wives" [2: 729]) although she is constantly divided from him by the circumstances of their lives.

In one unusual story Cutting suggests that the success of companionate marriage can itself become a problem. In "Fairy Gold," the Beldens are claustrophobically wrapped up in domestic life: "There was in this household a god who ruled everything in it, to whom all pleasures were offered up, all individual desires sacrificed, and whose Best Good was the greedy and unappreciative Juggernaut before whom Mr. Belden and his wife prostrated themselves daily. This idol was called The Children. . . . He loved his wife and children dearly, but he remembered a time when his ambition had not thought of being satisfied with the daily grind for a living and a dreamless sleep at night" (*Little Stories of Married Life* 162–64). Belden leaves his house one evening on a trivial errand—his wife needs a pound of butter. By chance he ends up at a "Reform meeting" attended not only by local people but by family connections from a neighboring town and extemporizes a successful speech; he impresses everyone, receiving several invitations that will clearly lead to other invitations and to business and political opportunities. As so often in Cutting's work, a small cloud like running out of butter proves to have a silver lining. In this case, the quest for butter produces "fairy gold," as both husband and wife are awakened to their need for wider horizons.

The stories also bear traces of the old-fashioned sort of marital problems. In "A Little Surprise," when Mrs. Gibbons misses a rendezvous with her husband and must search for him, the people she asks for help consistently assume that he is delinquent in some way. " 'Aa—h!' said the head waiter. 'Monsieur was with another lady!' " (12). "The policeman's face changed from solicitude to the cheerful acceptance of a familiar situation. 'Give ye the slip, did he? A lady like you, too! Sure he's the bad lot, and not wort' your lookin' for' " (*More Stories of Married Life* 23). She knows they are wrong, but the experience (she winds up marooned in front of a "gin-mill" in the middle of the night) reminds her vividly how dependent she is. The nonfiction Cutting wrote for the *Bazar* confronts women's vulnerability more directly and gives a much bleaker picture. For example, the story "Mrs. Atwood's Outer Raiment" and the first of Cutting's "Talks to Wives" include very similar scenes of a conversation between a wife and a husband with a wallet in his hand. Mrs. Atwood is reluctantly discussing how much the new clothes she needs will cost—she dislikes asking her husband for money and is more concerned with the bills for coal and her daughter's music and dancing lessons. Cutting writes that Mr. Atwood's well-worn wallet "represented in its way the heart of a kind and generous man, always ready to do his utmost in help of family needs, without complaint or caviling. His wife always experienced mingled feelings when that leather receptacle appeared—a quick and blessed relief and a sharp wince, as if it really were his heart's blood that she was taking" (*Little Stories of Married Life* 142). Compare this dramatization from "To the Wives of 'Close' Men":

> *She.* "I'll *have* to ask you for a little money before you go, dear. There are some things I've got to buy to-day."
>
> *He.* "Why didn't you speak about it before? You know I'm always short at the end of the month."
>
> *She (tearfully).* "I put off asking you just as long as I could, Henry, but now I really *can't* wait any longer."
>
> *He (looking at the clock and pulling out his pocketbook).* "How much do you want?"
>
> *She (nervously).* "I—I don't exactly know. I *have* to get a pair of shoes—my feet are on the *ground*—and a hat for Mary, and a tooth-brush, and—"
>
> *He (on edge).* "I've got to work. *How much do you want?* Five dollars?"
>
> *She (hastily).* "Oh, more than that."
>
> *He (savagely).* "Fifty?"
>
> *She (flushing and confused).* "Oh no, *no!*"
>
> *He (taking a bill from his pocketbook).* "Well, here's ten; you'll have to make that do this time." ("Talks, I" 658–59)

On the other hand, when Mrs. Atwood spends her clothing money on other people, she finds that her family has secretly ordered what she needs—arraying her (Cutting observes) not only in "silk and wool" but in "honor" (158). In fiction, at least, we find a husband attuned to domestic detail and loving his wife for her self-abnegation—so she need not suffer its consequences.

Cutting, extraordinarily, considered women themselves responsible for their disadvantaged position in the economics of marriage. The scene above, for example, demonstrates that when a wife asks for money diffidently and emotionally, as if giving it were a favor, the husband "accepts her view" (658).[18] Women are also responsible for men's selfishness because they fail to teach their sons consideration and fuss over their brothers and husbands. (Thus Lorraine blames her mother-in-law

Making the Family Whole 149

for Peter's stubbornness—he has "had his own way ever since he was born" [83].) It is not hard to understand why a reader wrote to Cutting to ask why she and others "always write as if poor women were to blame for everything? Why don't you write up the other side of it? Why don't you 'pitch into' men?" Cutting's answer—that she is talking to wives, not husbands, and therefore is concerned with "what a woman may remedy in herself or may contribute to the happiness of a home" ("Talks, VI" 1173)—reminds us how consistently she avoided issues of power, how resolutely she demonstrated that there are no genuine conflicts of interest between men and women. Negotiations within the home are always informed by what alternatives women have outside it (the topic of my next chapter). Cutting occasionally touches on those prospects, invariably portraying independent women as engaged in a gallant struggle—and usually rewarding them with marriages of affection. But because she imagines life outside the family solely in terms of deprivation, she cannot seriously consider breaking the marriage contract. She can only endlessly renegotiate its terms.

For all her opposition to the form in which Howells embodied his understanding of the family, Cutting fundamentally agreed with him that an engagement is "a family affair." Indeed, in a story published a few years before *The Whole Family* she tells of a courtship from the perspective of the young man's mother, and has her observe, "When you read love stories they always make it seem as if there were only the two young people in the world—I dare say they think so themselves—but they're very much mistaken. I think the family has a great deal to go through" (*Little Stories of Courtship* 130). One of her pieces for the *Bazar* specifically deplores the erosion of family happiness when everyone resists being "merged in any life that is not of their own individual choosing" ("Social Life in the Home III" 707). Freeman too wove the family into her multiple imaginings of human connectedness; although she spoke for women's fulfilment within, and without, marriage as their needs and situations required. Vorse, belonging to a different generation, was never able to find a way to meld her profound knowledge of family life and her radical politics, but she eventually became as worried as Howells had been about the unmaking of the family. In a story she published in 1929, a veteran of the suffrage movement watches the casual romances of young people on an Atlantic crossing and realizes with a sensation of panic that what she is seeing is "a pretty portentous thing": "the Death of the Family" (515). The cacophony of these early chapters of *The Whole Family* demonstrates that "the family" is central to so many urgent programs that it is inevitably a matter and a site of contention. And such debate, of course, is precisely what the harmony of the home is supposed to exclude.

Intimacy and Publicity

At the end of Ned Temple and Cyrus Talbert's conversation over the fence, the newspaper editor asks if he may announce Peggy's engagement in the *Eastridge Banner.* Talbert hesitates but then agrees. Temple has this exchange with his wife, who is shocked by the request and its success:

> "What is the matter?" I demanded. "It's a public affair, isn't it?"
> "It's a family affair—"
> "Well, I consider the readers of the *Banner* a part of the family." (29)

At one level this is a comment on the rise of "society" journalism. Once again, Howells makes his characters old-fashioned—they are still not quite comfortable with an institution that dated from the 1880s.[19] At another level it plays on the extension of the family metaphor into the realm of publishing that (as we saw in the previous chapter) characterizes the discourses that circulated through Harper & Brothers, including *The Whole Family.* Howells affirms writers' and editors' commitment to those who consume their productions—in effect, paying a compliment to the readers of the *Bazar.* At yet another level, however, Temple's remark invokes the instability of the division between private and public. The circuits of print culture may gain legitimacy from their proclaimed continuity with family connections, but what are the consequences for the realm of intimacy? The fear that the home is being invaded by publication, that it is somehow threatened or diminished by links with a larger world, is not far below the surface.

Howells includes one sentence that invites readers to be wary of Temple. When he asks Talbert if he may print the announcement, he says, "I only suggest it—or chiefly, or partly—because you can have it reach our public in just the form you want" (28). The editor first asserts that his only wish is to serve his neighbor; but his successive self-corrections mark that as disingenuous and reveal that his own self-interest is involved. James takes up the hint, and Charles Edward writes of "the odd fellow Temple, who, for reasons mysterious and which his ostensible undertaking of the native newspaper don't at all make plausible, has elected, as they say, fondly to sojourn among us. A journalist, a rolling stone, a man who has seen other life, how can one not suspect him of some deeper game than he avows—some such studious, surreptitious, 'sociological' intent as alone, it would seem, could sustain him through the practice of leaning on his fence at eventide to converse for long periods with poor Father?" (171–72). Charles Edward discusses the Temples with Lorraine—their sophistication seems to mark them out as friends for the younger couple, yet they remain strangers. As he puzzles over Temple's motives he is seized with a sort of vertigo in which intimacy and publicity are hopelessly mingled: "[O]n the point, again and again, of desperately stopping him in the street to ask him, I recoil as often in terror. He may be only plotting to *make* me do it—so that he may give me away in his paper!" (173). There is a distinctly playful quality in what James writes about Temple—one senses that he may be teasing his old friend Howells—but the implication that the newspaperman is an ominous and potentially intrusive force nevertheless remains.

For Howells, the intermixture of private life and print was a biographical fact. He grew up in the newspaper business—reportedly he began setting type in his father's printing office at the age of six—and he was a public figure whose activities were reported in the press for most of his life. He felt it necessary to include in a 1905 letter to his sister, in which he mentions that he had met two Russian diplomats who knew and admired his work, a warning that his brother should not use the information in his newspaper: "This flattering fact is of course entirely for home consumption, tell Joe" (*Life* 213). These are presumably the enabling conditions for Howells's lifelong pondering over the relation of public and private—but he reveals it, throughout his work, as a puzzle none of us can escape. In his divorce novel *A Modern Instance*, for example, Howells had already portrayed the threat of the family's unmaking as intertwined with print culture's undoing of the division between spheres. As Amy Kaplan has observed, the failure of Bartley Hubbard's marriage is paralleled by his progress into more and more dubious journalistic practices; and "the newspaper contributes to the breakdown of social order usually attributed to the scandal of divorce, for both equally violate the boundary between private and public realms. Throughout the novel, characters complain about the exposure of private domestic life in the public arena of representation" (*Social Construction* 32–33). The violation of boundaries is dangerous for everyone—Bartley Hubbard is killed by a man whose personal life he has revealed in his newspaper. Temple, as an upright editor, presumably has more in common with Ricker, the novel's example of a journalist with integrity, but his scrupulous slipperiness about his motives for wanting to print the announcement links him with Hubbard's exploitative commercialism. And in fact Temple's conversation with Talbert is distinctly reminiscent of Hubbard's interview with Lapham in a second novel in which he appears briefly, *The Rise of Silas Lapham* (1885).

Kaplan argues that Howells's theory and practice of realism constituted a debate not only with the obsolete (he believed) literary conventions of romance and sentiment, but also with popular forms that alarmed him. It was vital to distinguish realism from its disturbingly similar competitor journalism, which also represented the actual, convened a public, and defined a social role for the writer—Kaplan calls Hubbard a "demonic realist" (27). James evokes a wariness of several professions that claim to anatomize reality in his reference to Temple's sinister "sociological" interest in Talbert. And we may find further evidence that others perceived art and journalism as uncomfortably equivalent in the humor pages of the *Bazar*—composed by *Whole Family* contributor John Kendrick Bangs. "In Jocund Vein" made the same joke about first reporters, then painters, in two successive months (in fact, in the issues that ran the first and second installments of the collaborative novel; see figs. 34 and 35). When the reporter says to the man whose foot has gone through the ice, "Stay where you are, can't you? Don't you know a chance for a thrilling rescue when you see it?" he is presumably betraying his readers, intending to write a misleadingly melodramatic story. The artist is betraying the drowning man himself when he says, "One minute, when I get this effect!" But the cartoons humorously suggest that both are untrustworthy because

THE REPORTER: Hi there! Stay where you are, can't you? Don't you know a chance for a thrilling rescue when you see it?

34. *(above)* Detail from
"In Jocund Vein." *Harper's Bazar*
41.12 (December 1907): 1250.

35. *(right)* Detail from
"In Jocund Vein." *Harper's Bazar*
42.1 (January 1908): 94.

DROWNING PERSON: Help! Help!
ARTIST: One minute, when I get this effect!

both care more about the success of their representations than about live human beings.

Jordan carries on the theme of the dangerous entanglement of intimacy and publicity, writing in "The School-Girl" that the son-in-law Tom Price (Bangs's character) calls the youngest daughter, Alice, "*The Eastridge Animated and Undaunted Daily Bugle and Clarion Call.* He calls me that because I know so much about what is going on; and he says if Mr. Temple could get me on his paper as a regular contributor there wouldn't be a domestic hearth-stone left in Eastridge" (102). A reporter inside the home seems even more dangerous than a sociologist across the fence. This is an image that has subsequently been elaborated; we might think, for example, of the infiltration of a high-society wedding by representatives of *Spy* magazine in the film *The Philadelphia Story* (1940). Such intrusions can also, of course, be understood as a flattering attention. Celebrities complain about violations of their privacy, but their status as celebrities is confirmed and maintained by the paparazzi and the rest of the machinery of modern publicity. The apotheosis of this image is *The Truman Show* (1998), in which the hero's family and hometown are the creations of a media corporation, and his entire life is lived inside an immense set. It is the ultimate nightmare of media intrusion and the exposure of intimacy: every moment of his life, including the most intimate, is being broadcast to the world on television. It is also, of course, a narcissistic fantasy: the world is interested.

Jordan's image of Alice as "Clarry" (Tom's short version—for everyday use—of *Clarion* [120]) is a humorous one. The tone of her chapter is more like Howells's than it is like Freeman's, Vorse's, or Cutting's; one could believe, reading it, that nothing very serious is wrong with the Talbert family. Yet when the image is read alongside other documents, it connects with powerful and pervasive anxieties about privacy and the family. At the end of Cutting's chapter Lorraine is upset about a confrontation between Cyrus and Charles Edward. Alice— entering without ringing the bell and leaving without being seen— glimpses her sister-in-law crying with a photograph of Lyman Wilde nearby and misinterprets this scene in the light of her recent reading of *Lady Hermione's Secret*. She decides that Lorraine "had learned to love Mr. Wilde with a love that was her doom" (108), and proceeds to inform the rest of the family. Jordan shows Alice/"Clarry" creating problems by spreading false reports, as society journalists were accused of doing. More, her surveillance reminds us that there is no privacy for individuals in the family from others in the family, and thus suggests the fundamental tension between individualism and the family. It links as well to one of the oldest critiques of print culture—in being drawn into error by reading, Alice joins a distinguished literary tradition. She has something in common with Dante's Paolo and Francesca, but much more with Catherine Morland of *Northanger Abbey*, who also expected to find the people around her behaving like characters in a romance.

The continuing relevance of this tradition is confirmed by its presence in the materials immediately surrounding the composite novel. We can find a close relation of Alice and Catherine's in a short story by Daisy Rinehart that appeared in the *Bazar* in January 1908 (immediately following Freeman's chapter of *The Whole Family*). The title character of "The Exceeding Wiliness of Mrs. Mimms" is a farm wife who is a faithful reader of the *Female Fireside Friend*. She has asked her husband if she may buy a new dress and been told "no"—with insult added to injury when he tells her that she is "getting too old and gray to care about such tomfoolery" (27). (He has unfortunately just been stung by a wasp.) She draws the conclusion that he no longer loves her. But the coincidential delivery of a new issue of the magazine with a lead article on "The Wiles of the French Wife" leads Mrs. Mimms to try to recapture his attention by changing her hairstyle and flirting with him. Her foolish maneuverings lead her husband to worry that she is losing her mind. Mrs. Mimms makes the classic mistake of the romance reader, uncritically conflating the world of print with the world around her. In the process Rinehart satirizes women's magazines' propensity for giving intimate advice and tendency to invite the mass of readers into doomed imitations of elite behavior.

Mr. Mimms's rusticity and Mrs. Mimms's naïveté are treated as comic, and the story can be read as reinforcing regional and class hierarchy by implicitly contrasting its characters with the sophisticated readers of the *Bazar*. Yet Mrs. Mimms is also the reader's double; by depicting her poring over a woman's magazine, the story collapses the distance between character and reader (as Howells does in the last line of his chapter of *The Whole Family*). The story arrives at its happy ending by expanding the magazine's audience to include Mr. Mimms—he reads it only to ensure getting his money's worth out of the subscription his wife shares with a neighbor, but is so relieved to find the explanation for his wife's strange behavior that he changes his mind about the dress. In fact, he is amused and touched enough to imitate the French husband and bring her "bonbons." Through the mediation of the magazine Mr. Mimms, who was in danger of becoming the "close man," begins to empathize with his wife; the revelation of her vulnerability awakens his latent tenderness for her, and as he offers her the bag of candy he has "something more of indulgence in his face than it had worn for twenty years" (33). The story simultaneously shows that such intimate practices are penetrated by print culture and renders that recognition innocuous by locating it in a household conspicuously remote; then it offers a happy ending that suggests the ideals of companionate marriage may trickle down, after all.

In *The Truman Show*, the hero's family and friends are constantly prompted by a voice in their ears—the show's director transmits instructions telling them what to say and do. Truman alone is spontaneous and undirected. He claims his status as hero by deducing that he is nevertheless the victim of the ultimate media manipulation and escaping. When Truman waves good-bye to his audience (including us) and walks out through a door in the sky marked Exit, he achieves a privacy that is guaranteed because it is the antithesis of the public life he led before. Only by such negations can we forget the voices in our ears. The domestic ideology of the nineteenth century made a specific place for reading in the heart of the family; current family ideals are carried by multiple media. By the standards of individualism and privacy, the presence of "society" in every part of the self and the home is an intrusion, a violation of the true man. Yet from *The Whole Family* to *The Truman Show*, the discourses that purge the public from the private, and make the family whole, wrap us in self-referential reminders that their project can never be concluded. Is the family an intimate necessity or a social fiction? The only possible answer is: both.

Truman Show... why here? why make such a sweeping generalization?

❧ The Sometimes-New Woman ❧

The term *New Woman* has meant many things to many people. From the 1890s well into the twentieth century it invoked a vibrant dialogue over changes in woman's position and women's aspirations. Polemics for and against the New Woman circulated on both sides of the Atlantic; the expanding print media offered thousands of charged, competing images of women; and (surely) millions of private conversations negotiated the nature and valence of this explicitly modern gender identity. Whether she attracted or repelled, the defining feature of the New Woman was that she had *choices*. She might marry, or not; she might have a career, or not; she might support reform and suffrage, or not—but in each case, she was understood to make up her own mind.

The story of *The Whole Family* (by which, here as elsewhere, I mean both the history of the novel's production and the tale conveyed by the text) repeatedly intersects the discourses scholars have analyzed to reconstruct the New Woman, although none of the contributors uses that phrase. When Howells offers coeducation as a topic for the collaboration, he engages a rich, long-lasting, and well-documented debate over women's education.[1] New York women who participated in radical movements have been the focus of several studies; they are evoked both by the novel's references to Bohemian artistic life—including a (fictional) "Crafts Settlement" called "At the Sign of the Three-Legged Stool" (231) and the (historical) Art Students' League—and by the participation of Mary Heaton Vorse, who was one of them.[2] Other studies have anatomized the significance of the Gibson Girl and multitudes of other images circulating in the national magazines, enriching our understanding of the complex visual world of *Harper's Bazar*.[3] And the

New Woman's ability, indeed responsibility, to decide her own direction links her to the problem of individualism posed in chapter 3. She was not automatically inimical to the family, but she unsettled it; the very prospect that she might walk out the door altered a woman's footing inside her home.

The characterization of the New Woman in terms of her choices implies, and scholarship often specifies, her racial identity and class position: it was primarily white, privileged women who seemed to face a future defined by opportunity rather than constraint. That image, of course, elides many obstacles, and it neglects even more profoundly the mass of women who left home to labor—who had few economic options. I note this to direct attention to the social location of the discourses I examine and the limits of my topic. The point can be turned, as well, to suggest the polymorphic portability of figures of social change. At the turn into the twentieth century young urban working women were embracing freedom in their free time, experimenting in a new world of heterosocial, commercialized leisure. They forged a style that Kathy Peiss calls a working-class version of the New Woman. She does not tell us—it may be impossible to know—whether or not her subjects would have used the term themselves. I argue in this chapter that the New Woman should be understood not only as discrete entity but as a fluid notion constantly combined with other images. Explicit references are merely a bright thread running through the tangled braid of discourse, useful as beginning points for tracing how images of continuity and innovation are woven together.

The narratives of *The Whole Family* are consistently and complexly concerned with the problem of female modernity. I begin this chapter by recovering the historical circumstances that made Howells's interest in coeducation topical. It is Freeman, however, who directly poses the problem of the self-directed woman; and I suggest that we can grasp the weight of her challenge only by revising the received accounts of her career. Similarly, Elizabeth Jordan's contribution to the project assumes new significance when her life and works are seen as a whole. (One of the reasons to read *The Whole Family*, I believe, is that it affords an opportunity to encounter this forgotten New Woman.) I conclude by considering the prospects the magazine world mapped out for women. *Harper's Bazar* and *The Whole Family* represent those choices only very partially; but they effectively suggest the syncretism through which successive generations create themselves as sometimes-new women.

Sex and Education

Microhistorical analysis, although focused on a moment, often requires turning back in time to trace a particular development. In the case of the debate over coeducation, we do not have to go far to find voices that still echoed in 1908. The loudest nineteenth-century critic of women's education was Dr. Edward Clarke. His 1873 book *Sex in Education* argues that women who endeavor to pursue academic programs similar to those of men draw blood to their brains and away from their reproductive systems, endangering their health and their ability to bear healthy children. Even women who seem robust and happy at graduation might, as a consequence of that distorted development, be overtaken at any moment by invalidism, insanity, and death. Clarke claims to support appropriate education rather than opposing female education altogether—but he sets such stringent limits to what women might safely do, and his grim clinical accounts describe such high penalties, that the distinction seems moot. Coeducation, of course, is anathema— "a crime before God and humanity, that physiology protests against, and that experience weeps over" (127).

Sex in Education was widely read and debated; it went through seventeen printings, and three books refuting Clarke's claims appeared in 1874 alone.[4] The period of intense controversy was brief, but its consequences were lasting. Looking back in a speech to college alumnae delivered in 1907, Carey Thomas commented that she and others working in women's colleges had been "haunted" by the "gloomy little spectre" (69) of the book. Fears persisted even into the era of *The Whole Family*. Alice Bartlett Stimson, for example, writes in "When the College Girl Comes Home," published in *Harper's Bazar* in 1908, that the woman student's life is filled with activity "to a degree which has made us tremble for her health, until we remembered, with a sigh of thanks to recent investigators, that to the adolescent girl wholesome excitement is as necessary as wholesome food" (798). Thirty-five years later, the same gloomy ghost was still being exorcised.

Meanwhile, the struggle to open higher education to women made rapid progress. It helps to explain Clarke's alarm, and his success in creating alarm, to know that between 1870 and 1880 the number of women enrolled in college went from 11,000 to 40,000, from 21 percent of the student population to more than 33 percent. Female enrollments continued to rise more slowly in succeeding decades—to 56,000 and almost 36 percent in 1890; 85,000 and almost 37 percent in 1900; and 140,000 and almost 40 percent in 1910. After 1880, the majority of these female students were in coeducational rather than women's colleges; by 1900 two-thirds of them were in institutions open to both sexes. How, then, does Howells, in the first chapter of *The Whole Family*, come to show the Talberts' decision to send Peggy to a coeducational college as even slightly daring? If we cut the statistical pie in a different way, we see that the answer is not only—although it is partly—that they are old-fashioned. A broader group of Americans was attending college in the early 1900s than in previous eras, but their numbers were still small in relation to the population as a whole. Thus in the period immediately after the turn of the century, only about 3 percent of women between eighteen and twenty-one years of age were enrolled in institutions of higher education.[5] College women no longer risked open social disapproval, but they remained a relative rarity.

In the first decade of the twentieth century, coeducation was not new and controversial. But it became renewedly controversial. Contemporary observer W. A. Curtis wrote in *The Outlook* in 1902:

A decade ago we believed that opposition to co-education would soon entirely fade away. To be sure, we were far from believing that all colleges would open their doors to women, but the attitude of even the colleges that steadfastly proclaimed their intention to remain exclusively male colleges was not one of condemnation of co-education. Rather was it the wish for the preservation of local customs, the adherence to old traditions. . . . But within the past few years there has been a change in the attitude toward co-education, a strong change in the attitude of the male students everywhere, and here and there a reflection and response to this attitude on the part of faculties and trustees. (887)

The Sometimes-New Woman 161

The debate over whether or not women ought to be educated was not revived—that point had been decisively conceded—but the question of the distinctiveness of women's needs was. There is a haunting familiarity to G. Stanley Hall's assertion in *Munsey's Magazine* in 1906 that he has "never met or read a physician, if he is not a feminist, who does not hold that at times girls should metaphorically be turned out to grass, and lie fallow, so far as strenuous intellectual effort goes" (590). He argues not only that the divergence of the sexes is biologically inevitable, but that it constitutes progress—"differentiation and civilization are practically synonymous." Therefore, "education should push sex distinctions to their uttermost, make boys more manly and girls more womanly" (589). Clearly, coeducation was incompatible with this principle.

Like Curtis, historian Barbara Solomon attributes much of the reaction against coeducation to the disgruntlement of male students, who were sometimes actually outnumbered and outachieved by female students. It was widely charged that the presence of women in one way or another interfered with men's education—as Solomon puts it, women "simply could not win. They either drove men out of the classroom, or they attracted them into it and then distracted them." She suggests that women students may have been scapegoated during a difficult period of curricular change as the elective system was put in place (60–61). Curtis too comments that the claim made by faculty at the University of Chicago that "the young men neglect their studies because of the girls . . . sounds rather strange in view of the complaint of the girls that the boys show them no attention. It sounds strange in view of the fact that no one alleges that the girls neglect their studies because of the boys and are prone to inattention in the class-room because of making sheep's eyes at them" (888). Whatever the merits of the case, some faculty and administrators at coeducational schools believed that "feminization" was threatening male enrollments and male students' education.[6] And for a brief period the amount of public attention focused on the issue was—as William Rainey Harper, president of the University of Chicago, put it in an article in *Harper's Bazar* in 1905—"something extraordinary" (4).

The reaction against coeducation had concrete effects at many institutions, including ones that had formerly welcomed women. Female enrollment at Chicago had risen from one-quarter at its opening in 1892 to slightly more than one-half in 1902, when the administration proposed that freshman and sophomore classes be segregated. The idea was passionately debated and almost unanimously opposed by women students, graduates, and professors. Nevertheless, it was approved by the faculty senate and the trustees and implemented, although on such a small scale that it changed the national climate of discussion more than students' experience (Solomon 58). Stanford, which like Chicago had a charter specifying equality of the sexes, reduced female enrollment, by 1904 limiting it to one-quarter of the student body. It is somewhat startling to learn that the now-vast junior college system in California was established out of concern over the growing number of women enrolling in the University of California (which was expected to grow even faster given Stanford's shift in policy); the hope was that women would be satisfied by education they could obtain living at home and stay away from the university itself. Boston University, a Methodist-sponsored institution that had accepted women since its opening in 1873 (its first president proclaiming that it would welcome women not only as pupils but as professors), publicized an effort to attract more male students, and a bequest from a professor established scholarships "for men only." Such measures were proposed in many places, but they did not succeed everywhere: in 1907 the president of the University of Wisconsin proposed segregated classes similar to those at Chicago, but after a fierce battle the plan was defeated (Solomon 59–60).

The University of Chicago's sex-segregated junior college proved to be costly and cumbersome and had been abandoned by 1907 (Solomon 59). Nationally, the rise in the percentage of institutions admitting both men and women was never reversed, and the percentage of women students continued to rise to peak at just below one-half in 1920.[7] (That figure was finally equaled in the latter 1970s and has now been surpassed—with the result that again some liberal arts administrators fear that the female-dominated campus atmosphere discourages male students [see Lewin].) Rosalind Rosenberg's account of women at the University of Chicago, however, shows that more subtle and consequential gender distinctions were being institutionalized in the same period. In the year she fought unsuccessfully against the junior college, sociologist and activist Marion Talbot also abandoned her hope for a department of "sanitary science," or public health, that would include both social and physical sciences and provide a central focus for the study of urban problems, and proposed instead that a new department should be devoted to the household. In 1904 President Harper created both that department, with Talbot at its head, and a school of social work distinct from the department of sociology. Rosenberg notes that "the trend toward specialization merged with traditional assumptions regarding sex roles to limit women's influence within the university, although Talbot continued to insist, somewhat lamely, that household administration dealt with the same far-flung concerns that she had intended sanitary science to cover." The emergence of social work assured places for women faculty and students but "drove a wedge between women reformers and their academic supporters in the social sciences by establishing an institutional distinction between sociology's more masculine, theoretical side and its more feminine, practical side" (49–50). Establishing gendered realms within the academy at once made a place for women and contained them. Nationally, by 1911, 60 percent of the women teaching at coeducational institutions were in "home economics." We should not yield to the current disdain for this field, which derives all too directly from a reflexive trivialization of women's work; some of its professors offered an interdisciplinary perspective on women's concerns as well as instruction in cooking and sewing (Solomon 86–87). Yet such institutional homes were a constitutively mixed blessing.

For those on campus, the debates and innovations were primarily about the politics of gender in the production of knowledge. When administrators and faculty at coeducational schools worried about their male students, they were also worrying that "feminization" was damaging the quality and prestige of the institution. Not only sociology but other emerging disciplines, such as philological literary studies, were striving to assert their vigorous, rigorous masculinity.[8] For the general public, however, the controversy was most importantly about how changes in women's education affected women's choices outside the classroom—and especially about their consequences for the family. Many, especially parents, worried about the social freedom of the co-educational campus, which gave middle-class daughters an unprecedented degree of opportunity to meet men outside the supervision of the family. This concern is easily visible in *The Whole Family:* Howells shows Talbert struggling not to be embarrassed that Peggy has become engaged to someone he has never met (29). Vorse shows the grandmother questioning the fiancé about his people (fortunately a good family, distantly connected with her own mother) and his religious beliefs (dangerously unformed; 67). Most often, people worried that education, whether in a single-sex or a mixed setting, would discourage women from marrying at all.

In 1904 Frances Abbott introduced her statistical study of three decades of Vassar graduates by writing: "The first question that everybody asks is, Do college women marry?" (350). They do, she found—at a lower rate than that of the female population as a whole, but not a worrisomely low one.[9] Alice Stimson wrote more impressionistically in *Harper's Bazar:* "College girls marry in spite of the predictions to the contrary of a generation ago. They not only marry, but they marry well; indeed, as a class, they carry off the real prizes in the matrimonial market: the young professional men—doctors, lawyers, college instructors—and men engaged in running the big machinery of the industrial world. The college girl marries discriminatingly, and she marries late. Perhaps these are the reasons why the college women so seldom figure in the divorce court" (799). Howells's chapter of *The Whole Family* voices this argument that coeducation helped women to marry wisely: Cyrus Talbert says, "I didn't see how, if a girl was going to get married, she could have a better basis than knowing the fellow through three or four years' hard work together. When you think of the sort of hit-or-miss affairs most marriages are that young people make after a few parties and picnics, coeducation as a preliminary to domestic happiness doesn't seem a bad notion" (6). G. Stanley Hall, on the other hand, warned that "the constant association of the sexes tends to rub off a little of the charm which each normally feels for the other" (591). Curtis, searching for the source of the unchivalrous reaction against coeducation, concluded that the problem was the establishment of a competitive relationship between the sexes. "This is no university matter, this eruption of hostility to woman. . . . It is man, face to face with the fact that woman in this twentieth century is not his ally, his helpmeet, his wife, but his competitor, his rival, and that of all the meeds, the prizes, the rewards that she cheats him out of, it is the supremest prize, herself!" He added, "Once woman doubled our joys and halved our sorrows. She now halves our incomes and doubles those seeking employment" (889). What underlay the fuss over coeducation, according to Curtis, was man's fear that the new woman had so many choices that she no longer needed *him*.

In *The Whole Family* Howells engages with coeducation precisely on the terrain of its effect on the family—indeed, he treats the reform of female education as a possible solution to problems in the marriage relation. Talbert believes that girls "ought to be brought up as nearly like their brothers as can be—that is, if they are to be the wives of other women's brothers. It don't so much matter how an old maid is brought up, but . . . if an old maid could be brought up more like an old bachelor she would be more comfortable to herself, anyway" (23). The idea that women matter mainly as wives and mothers, not as individual human beings, is advanced if not endorsed. Nor does the coeducated Peggy show any signs of New Womanhood—Howells represents her as a shy, pretty, ordinary girl, and the illustrator and other contributors follow his lead. In figure 36, which appeared with the first chapter of the novel and is the most stylized and decorative image Stephens produced for the serial, Peggy is posed holding flowers in a loosely rendered, blossoming landscape, her flowered dress carrying out the motif and eroding the boundary between girl and garden. Later, James foregrounds this aspect of the character, with Charles Edward calling Peggy "a perfect little *decorative* person" (162, emphasis in original). Also, the chief obstacle to improving girls' education turns out to be women: Talbert says, "The difficulty about putting a thing like that in practice is that you have to co-operate in it with women who have been brought up in the old way" (23). This adds up to something very different from advocating choices or self-development for women. It was Mary Wilkins Freeman, speaking in the voice of that unimportant old maid, who forced *The Whole Family* to confront the figure of the woman who makes up her own mind and cannot be contained by the family.

36. Illustration for
The Whole Family, ch. 1, "The Father":
"Peggy." *Harper's Bazar* 41.12
(December 1907): 1163.

From her family's perspective—that is, in eleven of the twelve chapters of *The Whole Family*—the central fact about Elizabeth Talbert is that she is not married. In her own eyes, in her own chapter, what matters is that she has *chosen* not to marry. Freeman commented on her assignment to write "The Old-Maid Aunt" by creating a character who herself comments derisively on the role assigned her by old-fashioned relations who "do not know that today an old-maid aunt is as much of an anomaly as a spinning-wheel, that she has ceased to exist, that she is prehistoric" (33). When Freeman's conception of Lily (as she is called outside Eastridge) was attacked, she defended it to Elizabeth Jordan precisely on the ground that women had changed: "At this minute I can think of a score of women who fifty years ago would have carried out Mr. Howells' idea of the old maid aunt. Today they look as pretty and as up-to-date as their young nieces—and no pretence about it either. They really *are*. Their single state is deliberate choice on their own part, and men are at their feet. Single women have caught up with, and passed, old bachelors in the last half of the century" (266). Freeman claims for her character an explicitly modern identity.

Jordan could scarcely have asked anyone else to contribute this particular chapter. Mary Wilkins Freeman was famous for her portraits of New England spinsters and very closely associated with Harper's. She published fiction focusing on unmarried women in the *Bazar* throughout her career—including her first-accepted story, "Two Old Lovers," in which a suitor finally proposes on his deathbed, and the widely read "A New England Nun," in which a long-engaged woman chooses celibacy over marriage. Freeman's "old maids" are elderly and maidenly, but rarely isolated or pitiable. Lily's spirit of rebellion has many precedents as well—notably in Freeman's most popular story, "The Revolt of 'Mother.'" Her cosmopolitanism is unusual among Freeman's creations, however; she is described as not only emotionally but socially sophisticated, having traveled more widely and acquired better taste and more advanced ideas than most of the other Talberts. Lily's values have not been formed—and her real life is not lived—under her family's mansard roof or even within the village limits of Eastridge. Her independence represents both something old and something new in Freeman's work.

Unsurprisingly, feminists have found Elizabeth Talbert a congenial figure. Leah Blatt Glasser, for example, describes her as "vibrant, dynamic, attractive, energetic, witty, passionate, and wise" (89). Recent Freeman criticism is the one body of work in which *The Whole Family* is considered a serious, substantial item in an author's bibliography and regularly discussed; Mary Reichardt even included "The Old-Maid Aunt" in her *Mary Wilkins Freeman Reader*, published in 1997. Reading Elizabeth in the context of Freeman's other fiction rather than the other chapters of the novel, which portray her as self-centered and (often) self-deluded, helps sustain a celebratory image. Yet Freeman's chapter itself must be read selectively to make Lily a feminist heroine. She has what Glasser chooses to call "regressive thoughts" (91), such as believing that in losing her lover Lyman Wilde and remaining unmarried she has grasped only the "minor sweets of life" and missed "the really big worth-while ones" (33). Moreover, when she wants to discourage Goward's attentions she does not tell him that she is happily unmarried, or simply that she is not interested in him, but pretends instead that she is engaged to another man. She reports in detail the compliments paid her by gentlemen, including even her small nephew Billy, and describes in detail how Eastridge women dress and do their hair—giving special attention to her own wardrobe. Indeed, to judge by the space allocated to them in her narration, the two topics Lily spends most of her time thinking about are men and fashion.

It is difficult to say which is a bigger threat to the family: a woman who is not interested in men or a woman who is interested in all of them and attached to none. Unsubordinated by the marriage relation, and insubordinate in her views, Lily provokes a rhetorical reversal of the power relations between men and women when John Kendrick Bangs, speaking as the son-in-law in the sixth chapter of the novel, observes that she views "all men as her own individual property" (136) and tries to "grab every male being in sight, and attach them to her train" (138). As Glasser points out, Lily also suggests a dangerously free female sexuality (90). Bangs's narrator, Tom Price, blames Lily for the situation with Goward, in a charged although playful vocabulary: "Potential manhood is a difficult force to handle, and none should embark upon the parlous enterprise of arousing it without due regard for the consequences. We may not let loose a young lion from its leash, and, when dire consequences follow, excuse ourselves on the score that we thought the devastating creature was 'only a cub'" (135). He even compares Lily to Eve (131), although he applauds Goward's chivalrous refusal to blame a woman for either his own or Adam's sin. Bangs treats his contribution primarily as an opportunity to make jokes, about the characters and the project itself, yet a serious fear of the spinster as sexual predator underlies the facetious suggestion that the legislature consider "a Bill for the Protection of Boys, and the Suppression of Old Maids Who Don't Mean Anything By It" (135).

Bangs's chapter, like all those after Freeman's, represents Elizabeth as attractive and fashionable. It also credits her with considerable intelligence; Tom Price calls her "chameleonic" (138) in her ability to suit her conversation and demeanor to different men. And Bangs follows the lead of Jordan's immediately preceding chapter in presenting Elizabeth's flirtation with Goward as "thoughtless" (138) rather than malicious; Mary Heaton Vorse and Mary Stewart Cutting (chapters 3 and 4) treat Elizabeth as utterly selfish, but Jordan and Bangs (chapters 5 and 6) make her merely self-absorbed. In chapter 7 Henry James turns the mild pretensions Howells, and all the other contributors except Freeman, attribute to Elizabeth into something more sinister. His "deadly Eliza" (176) is a poseur who has misrepresented her friends to her family, and her family to her friends, in order to claim a spurious social standing. Later, Alice Brown accepts and extends his characterization of the spinster as a maneuvering egotist and finally exiles her from Eastridge and the novel. In Henry Van Dyke's final chapter she is referred to as having "lured off" Goward but does not even make an appearance.

I would not argue that these differences in the contributors' treatment of Elizabeth reflect their opinions on the woman question.[10] There simply is no such correlation with biography; their choices are a complex compound of how Freeman treated their own characters, their plans for the plot, and their reactions to the many elements of the character Freeman created. Even the last is less a matter of how much sympathy they have for aging spinsters than of how they think

Elizabeth reflects on women—Vorse wrote empathetically about the elderly, Elizabeth Stuart Phelps Ward married a younger man, and Brown never married, yet each is resolutely judgmental. I would argue, however, that Elizabeth is so variable because through her the contributors confront the controversial prospect that women with choices will desert the home. Other characters in *The Whole Family* are sometimes more, sometimes less sympathetic depending on who has control of the narrative at a given moment, but nowhere else do the seams of the collaboration strain like this. Jordan's description of the old-maid aunt as a "bomb-shell on our literary hearthstone" (264) is apt not only because Freeman critiques the family, but also because in the world of the New Woman the spinster is a newly explosive figure.

In one of her letters to Jordan during the composition of *The Whole Family*, Alice Brown wonders if Aunt Elizabeth had been intended as a satire. The suggestion was not entirely serious, and Freeman's letters firmly exclude the possibility. Yet what seems to go unacknowledged in the criticism is that "The Old-Maid Aunt" itself opens up this line of interpretation by using first-person narration to delineate Elizabeth's attractions. Freeman wished to contest Howells's image of the spinster, and she followed instructions (as he himself did not) by writing in her character's own voice. How could a narrator who devotes so much time to demonstrating that she is "pretty and . . . up-to-date," and that "men are at [her] feet," not be open to being read as vain and unreliable? The very form of the romance novel is organized by the mandate that a heroine's appeal be unself-conscious, requiring that the story be told in the third person; as Tania Modleski puts it, "We can't say, 'I had no idea how lovely I looked' without implying a 'schizophrenic narrator.' " [11] Elizabeth's instability is overdetermined by charged themes and twisted conventions.

Freeman returns to the sexuality of the aging woman as a topic in "The Amethyst Comb," published in 1914.[12] Viola Longstreet is in many ways a rewriting of Lily Talbert, although she is a widow rather than a spinster. What robbed her of girlhood, as well as the really worthwhile joys of womanhood, was not a failed romance but an early, unhappy marriage to a man old enough to be her father. In recompense she has—she says herself—"held Youth so tight that he has almost choked to death" (218). The third-person narration tells us both that she is beautiful and that the cynical young man she is infatuated with is concealing his amusement at her practice of dressing like a girl: "He considered Viola in corals as too rude a jest to share with her. Had poor Viola once grasped Harold Lind's estimation of her she would have as soon gazed at herself in her coffin" (222). Viola pays a higher price than Lily for her entanglement with a man young enough to be her son, falling from prosperity to poverty and even spending time in hiding to avoid testifying at his embezzlement trial. Yet whether in the midst of her folly or facing her situation after Lind's death, she seems brave and appealing—because we see her through the eyes of her loving friend Jane Carew, supplemented by an omniscient narrator who tells us what Jane does not know or cannot understand.

In fact, "The Amethyst Comb" is Jane's story as much as Viola's. Like her friend she has chosen rather than merely accepted a role, taking to bonnets and dark colors before anyone else thinks she should. Jane embraces age, quiet, and emotional restraint as determinedly as Viola embraces their opposites. Yet she has one moment of passion in the story—when the almost-destitute Viola resists coming to live with her: "[F]or the first time in her life, Viola Longstreet saw Jane Carew's eyes blaze with anger. 'You dare to call it charity coming from me to you?' she said, and Viola gave in" (233). She insists, and Viola acknowledges, that their connection entitles her to the sort of generosity acceptable from a family member. The story ends happily with Viola leaving New York to live with Jane and lead the "sweet, placid life of an older lady in a little village" (234). At first the hair ornament of the story's title indexes Jane's suppressions; she wears her other amethysts but considers the comb too ornate for an older woman, concealing its existence from Viola to avoid being pressed to put it on. After Harold Lind steals it and gives it to Viola, it comes to represent his perversity and—because Jane again does not speak, but simply ends her visit early and feels she may never return—the friends' estrangement. Viola is forced to sell the comb; Jane recovers it; and as the story progresses it becomes laden with still more contradictory meanings. Viola attaches sentimental value to the comb because she believes Lind's gift was his one uncomplicated, generous act of affection; when she finds it in Jane's jewel case she fondles it "as if it had been a baby" (235). Jane's silence at this moment takes on a new meaning: "It was noble of Jane Carew that . . .

although she did not, could not, formulate it to herself, she would no more have deprived the other woman and the dead man of that one little unscathed bond of tender goodness than she would have robbed his grave of flowers" (235–36). Jane gives Viola the comb, and at that final moment of the story it represents above all the steadfast love of one woman for another.

Viola chooses her men badly, and Jane is happily unmarried. Yet in my view the story does not—and Freeman's work as a whole does not—imply that women are necessarily better off as spinsters. Nor are they worse off. Rather, any path a woman might choose has its own rewards, limitations, and dangers.[13] As Elizabeth Meese argues in her influential essay "Signs of Undecidability," Freeman refuses to judge her characters or their decisions. The interpretive debate over "A New England Nun," for example, asks whether Louisa Ellis is retreating into sterility or affirming her autonomy when she breaks her engagement. But the impulse to pose, and the effort to answer, that question—even in terms of ambivalence—simplify Freeman's dramatization of the "irreconcilable and unresolvable oscillations between the positive and negative features of women's lives in the New England villages of the period" (23). The meaning of her texts develops precisely out of the play of alternatives. This resistance to closure is a general characteristic of Freeman's fiction. It is, of course, impossible to achieve in a collaborative text like *The Whole Family*.

Meese demonstrates convincingly that many scholars have judged not only her characters but Freeman herself according to their own opinions about women's roles—and then let those reactions determine their readings (25). As Mary Ellmann writes in *Thinking about Women* (an early and unfairly neglected work of feminist literary criticism), "Books by women are treated as though they themselves are women, and criticism embarks, at its happiest, upon an intellectual measuring of busts and hips" (29). In the 1950s Freeman's biographer Edward Foster used fragmentary evidence and extrapolations from the stories to portray her as a "troubled" woman (143), haunted by memories of an early romance, loving and hating her characters with "partially neurotic ambivalence" (69). In the 1960s Perry Westbrook construed her satire as directed at characters rather than the social order—"The Old-Maid Aunt," for example, is a "depiction of spinsterish vanity and folly"

37. Photograph of Mary Wilkins Freeman by Floride Green (mss 7047), Clifton Waller Barrett Library of American Literature, Special Collections Department, University of Virginia Library.

(161). Both men seem almost embarrassed by Freeman's marriage at the age of forty-nine to a man seven years younger.[14] The difficulties of her later years—Dr. Freeman's alcoholism and drug use, the lawsuit over his will disinheriting his wife and sisters—mesh with negative assessments of her late work to produce a picture of pathetic failure. The feminist recovery of Freeman that began in the 1970s focused instead on Freeman's long, committed relationship with Mary Elizabeth Wales; they lived together for almost twenty years, from Freeman's father's death until her marriage, and remained close afterward. In the 1980s, Brent Kendrick emphasized Freeman's prettiness and femininity, the fact that she was virtually "worshipped" by her audience, and gave a positive picture of her marriage, emphasizing that she and her husband lived together for sixteen years before addictions overwhelmed him and they separated (1). Most recently, Leah Glasser has read Freeman's body and writing together in suggesting that photographs capture her contradictory nature, "the softness in the curls lining her face, the scooped neckline, and the laced border of her dress" contrasting with "the firm determination of her jaw, the set of her mouth, the almost piercing clarity of her eyes" (xvii; see fig. 37).[15] This accumulated biography leaves us with something very much like Meese's "undecidability." We should acknowledge above all the diversity of Freeman's experiences—which included both happiness and unhappiness in various sorts of households, both "Boston marriage" and heterosexual marriage.

Freeman's life and work affirm that sustaining relationships come in many forms. Yet in each social world, some kinds of connections are recognized and valued while others are ignored or forbidden. During the course of Freeman's lifetime, love between women became less and less legitimate. In "The Amethyst Comb," the vocabulary of family relations is repeatedly confused—Viola's husband could be her father, her lover could be her son, the comb is her baby—while Viola and Jane's relation remains essentially unnamed. When Jane asserts her right to help Viola, she does so not by making a statement but by asking a question. When she gives her the comb, she replies to Viola's "this was mine once" with, "It is yours now, dear," as if she were merely confirming Viola in possession of something rightfully hers (235). Viola indeed believes that she has already received the comb as an earnest of love from Harold Lind; she will wear it as a woman crowned by heterosexual romance. In truth, Lind's gesture was destructive—but it misfired, neither humiliating Viola nor permanently dividing the friends, because Jane protects her friend and expresses her devotion by remaining silent. I am not exactly suggesting that this is the love that dare not speak its name; Freeman and Wales would not have told their story in terms of oppositional sexuality, and Freeman did not tell Jane and Viola's that way. Yet in "The Amethyst Comb" she is responding to, and criticizing, the hypervaluation of heterosexuality at the expense of other relations.

Freeman thematizes this subversively open view of human relationships in an apparently slight story that ran in *Harper's Bazar* in the November 1907 issue, one month before the first installment of *The Whole Family*.[16] In "Billy and Susy," two elderly sisters, one a widow whose husband lived only a year after their marriage and one a spinster, live next door to each other—so close that they can talk through their open windows. Their companionship is disrupted when young Mira Holmes gives them yellow kittens whose identities become confused; they quarrel because Mrs. Sarah Drew believes that the kitten Miss Melissa Abbot keeps is Sarah's Billy, while Melissa claims that it is her

38. Illustration for "Billy and Susy," by Mary Wilkins Freeman:
" 'This is Susy; you have got my cat,' insisted Sarah." *Harper's Bazar* 41.11
(November 1907): 1037.

own Susy. Sarah specifically prefers a male cat and dislikes a female — "I
wouldn't have this kind of a cat, anyway. They keep you always drowning kittens" (*Winning Lady* 107). The image of these ladies with their
cats and the tempest-in-a-teapot quality of the conflict certainly draw
on stereotypes of the spinster (see fig. 38). The sisters' estrangement
makes them genuinely miserable, however, and Mira mourns over that
as well as over her own estrangement from the young man who had been
courting her. They independently make up their minds to reconcile at
Thanksgiving (this is one of the holiday stories that were something of
a commercial specialty for Freeman) — but the source of their conflict
has been removed in any case, as *both* cats have had kittens.

This plot turns on the sisters' ladylike reluctance to examine the
question of their kittens' sex too directly, for the two women who help

them with their housework discover the very evening of the quarrel that there is "[n]o Billy at all" (120). The resemblance between the situations of a spinster and a widow, the fuss over the presence or absence of a very small organ, the cats' fecundity despite the lack of Billy (or any tom), seem to add up to a satire on the overvaluation of the male— one might even say, on the doomed hunt for the Lacanian phallus. As Sarah Drew says, "we quarreled over nothing at all" (120). Yet my point is precisely that Freeman is not rejecting men and marriage, but rather protesting the erasure of lives centered elsewhere. Her narrator makes this vision of emotional democracy explicit as the story ends with Mira, her recovered suitor, and her mother sharing supper with the sisters: "Neither she nor her young lover dreamed that the love in the hearts of the two old sisters struck, albeit free from all romance, a note which chorded with their own into a true harmony of thanksgiving" (122; see fig. 39). The heterosexual lovers' insensibility and the need to rule out stigmatized sexuality visible in the phrase "free from all romance" mark the fact that in Freeman's historical moment that vision was a receding, not advancing, possibility. As in "The Amethyst Comb," the fulfilled love that makes the ending happy must remain silent.

When Elizabeth Talbert is juxtaposed with these characters, what is striking about her is not that she is unmarried, or even that she is a spinster by choice, but that she is so isolated. Howells's chapter suggests some possible connections; his narrator implies that friends are important to her, writing that she "passed her life" in visits, and he observes that her brother's wife speaks as if they are close (19). Freeman mentions Lily's friends but leaves them offstage, and she rejects the suggestion of friendship between the sisters-in-law—in refuting Howells's image of the old maid, she makes Lily critical of the Talberts and more or less estranged from all her kin. Thus even in Freeman's own chapter the framework of the collaboration, structured in terms of family relations, does not accommodate her vision of many sorts of sustaining connections; and it is certainly absent from those that follow. Lily's and Viola's trajectories are actually mirror images—Lily ultimately leaves the village to join her friend Mrs. Chataway in New York. But James creates that character as the embodiment and revelation of Lily's pretensions; every detail of his description of the lady and her home, from her powdered face and "extravagant blondness" to the

39. Illustration for
"Billy and Susy," by
Mary Wilkins Freeman:
"Melissa and Sarah."
Harper's Bazar 41.11
(November 1907): 1038.

scrambled smells of the hall in her boardinghouse, announces fakery
(178–81). It is impossible to imagine life with Mrs. Chataway as anything but sordid, particularly when Alice Brown makes her a "Magnetic
Healer and Mediumistic Divulger" who considers Lily well qualified to
work with her (290). Elizabeth is decisively declassed. There is no concrete evidence that the contributors associated Lily Talbert with Lily
Bart, but Wharton's *House of Mirth* had attracted enormous attention
just two years earlier (Hart 199), and some readers, at least, must have
noted the similarity not only in their names and situations but also in
how easily each loses her social footing. On one point, at least, all these
authors agree: solitary women are vulnerable.

Freeman's contribution to *The Whole Family* poses the problem
of modern female identity. Her old-maid aunt is neither the old-
fashioned type of the title nor a programmatically new woman, but
a creatively mixed creature. As Dale Bauer suggests in her essay
on the novel, the spinster challenges the wholeness of the imagined

family. She is disruptive not only thematically but formally—Bauer argues specifically that she "delays the conventional marriage plot and thereby forces us to confront the alternative plots for women offered in *The Whole Family*" (107). Certainly Freeman's disclosure that Peggy's fiancé, Harry Goward, is either in love with her aunt or has done some very indiscreet flirting shapes all the events that follow. Yet Freeman claimed with some justice that Howells's opening had not really initiated a plot (conventional or otherwise); and one could argue that the exposure of Goward's inadequacies and the auditioning of other suitors that ensue *are* in fact the marriage plot. Like Howells, Freeman failed to convey a clear line of development to her successors, and as Bauer demonstrates, they work to contain rather than to develop her challenge. Many of them matchmake for Lily as well as for Peggy. Alice Brown not only exiles her but has her adopt exactly the desexualized clothing and nunlike attitude she has always rejected: Brown's narrator, Peggy, reports that dressed in black, "as I never saw her before," Aunt Elizabeth looks "almost like some sister of charity" (290–91). Alternative plots for women do not materialize in the text of *The Whole Family*; to find them, we must turn to the world that surrounds it, and especially to the lives and works of the contributors.

The Extraordinary Miss Jordan

It is Elizabeth Jordan's life more than her fiction that entitles her to our attention. In her autobiography, *Three Rousing Cheers*, published in 1938 when she was in her early seventies, she describes herself: "I have been pianiste, reporter, newspaper editor, magazine editor, public speaker, playwright, dramatic critic, and novelist, which helps to explain why I have never done any one thing superlatively well. I even took a hand in the moving-picture game. But these different activities have given me an interesting life and a lot of those 'vital human experiences' clubwomen love to discuss" (11; see figs. 40 and 41 for portraits of Jordan). In others' accounts as well she appears as a versatile and talented woman of boundless energy, and unquestionably a New Woman. Yet Jordan never reported finding her independence and self-conscious modernity in conflict with her loyalty to her own family and the idea of the family, with editing a fashion magazine, or with her committed Catholicism. She imagined her life in syncretic terms that made it unnecessary for her to choose between new and old; Jordan is an exponent and exemplar of what I have called the sometimes-new woman.

Jordan begins her autobiography with her schooling at the Convent of Notre Dame in her hometown of Milwaukee, writing lovingly about its community of women. She aspired to join the order herself, although she says her classmates laughed at the idea of such a "high-spirited and irrepressible young person" putting on a religious habit (5–6). Jordan is vague about why becoming a nun appealed to her, beyond her devotion to particular sisters and passionate admiration for the Reverend Mother. But there is no hint of renunciation in her description of the cloistered life. Here and elsewhere, she visualizes life in the convent in terms of intense spirituality and—especially—the companionship of intense personalities. Jordan's volumes of fiction about a convent school, including the May Iverson collections that were probably her most popular work, offer both comic and serious portraits of the girls' crushes and raves, the nuns' loving friendships and dramas of vocation, the power of music in the cloister, and the girls' mischievous adventures and moral choices.[17]

Jordan writes about her family with equal affection, and more ambiguity. She dedicates *Three Rousing Cheers* to the memory of her mother and father, and devotes a great deal of space to fond descriptions and stories of them. She even implies that her self-sufficiency and ambition carry on a family tradition, calling her mother "the most independent woman I have ever known. She had been one of the few college girls of her day—an honor student at Mendota Female College" (23). However, in the first anecdote she tells about her family they appear as an obstacle to her aspirations, an episode that she confesses she remembered for years with "a sinking stomach and a rush of blood to the head" (6). At the age of fourteen Jordan arranged an opportunity to read her first published story to her household without letting them know she had written it: "I would bask in the family's absorption in the tale, and in the adulation that followed the announcement of the author's name" (6). The result, she reports, was disastrous. (I quote at length both to convey the story and to convey a sense of her voice.)

40. Elizabeth Jordan at
seventeen. Uncredited photograph in
Three Rousing Cheers, facing p. 12.

That night, after the family had been soothed by dinner and was assembled in the library, I brought forth my surprise. My grandmother and two of my mother's younger sisters were with us. With my father, mother, and little sister, there would be an audience of six.

When I announced that I wanted them to listen to a story I had just found in the *Evening Wisconsin*, a depressed silence settled over the gathering. My young aunts could think of many things they would rather do than listen to a tale of my selection. My mother and father had plans of their own for the evening. My small sister, Alice, alone was interested. She liked stories, and she hoped the reading would give her an extra half hour before bed-time. It did. After the first shock of the suggestion they all settled down to listen philosophically, and I began the story.

I read it with love and fire. To me it seemed a remarkable tale. But it could not stand that acid test. My young aunts yawned. My grandmother's beautiful old head nodded. "Allie" fell asleep on a rug before the fire, like a young puppy. When I finished the tale and waited for applause, still desperately clutching the newspaper, my aunts started a ruthless dissection of the story.

"What's the use of giving space to a yarn like that?" one of them began. She proceeded, with the other's help, to pick out the story's flaws. There were plenty of them, and she was witty. Enchanted by the interest of her listeners, which was far beyond any aroused by the reading, she developed the theme. The others laughed and agreed with her. They called attention to the faults she had overlooked. A perfect picture of a happy family, united in its interests, was before me. I sat silent and crushed. Then my father spoke.

"What was there about the story that you liked so much, my dear?" he asked. "Why did you want to read it to us?"

The question was the turn of the screw.

"Because I wrote it," I wailed, and burst into loud sobs. (7–8)

Everyone rushed to comfort her and assure her that the story was very good—the tale is thoroughly contained by Jordan's affirmative portrait of her family. Jordan never tried to suggest that such moments could be wholly avoided in well-run homes; she recognized, as she wrote in the *Bazar*'s "With the Editor" column for December 1907, that in "any family, anywhere, any day, there exists the making of a family quarrel."

Nevertheless, this image of "a happy family, united in its interests," engaged in crushing Jordan's belief in herself as a writer, is a powerful and persistent one. All Jordan's optimism cannot exclude traces of the tension between the family and the individual, or, as she puts it in her column, "the social unit and the free lance" (1249).

After her graduation at seventeen, Jordan's parents persuaded her to defer entering the convent while she pursued her other passions—music and literature. Her father helped her obtain her first position with a newspaper, in Milwaukee—she believed that journalism, offering "[h]uman interest in plenty, human contacts, increasing knowledge of life" (23), was the best training for a writer. When Jordan landed a job at the *New York World* two years later, her mother at first resisted the move, wishing her to stay closer to home and concentrate on music, but gave in when reminded of the threat of the veil. Fortunately Jordan was successful, for when her father went bankrupt in the panic of 1893 she became the primary earner for her family. She had already ceased to think of becoming a nun, and her mother abandoned the hope that she would return to music as her primary interest; "it was understood that I would continue my career and earn as much as I could" (105). What had begun as a choice became a necessity—but to judge by *Three Rousing Cheers*, Jordan loved every minute of her long days, and nights, as a reporter and editor.

At Joseph Pulitzer's *World* during the period of its enormous increase in circulation, Jordan was in the center of the "progressive publishing" I discussed in chapter 2. Her choice of that career reflects the relatively recent prestige of the reporter, and her pride in the long hours she worked reflects the ethos of energy that characterized the field. This was—as J. Henry Harper calls it, writing about the changes at Harper's after the turn of the century—"everybody's busy day." Jordan thrived in that atmosphere. In *Ladies of the Press: The Story of Women in Journalism by an Insider*, published in 1936, Ishbel Ross describes her enthusiastically:

> Miss Jordan used to bedazzle the compositors by showing up in immaculate shirt-waists and slinging type with an experienced hand. When everyone else was sweating and in a state of collapse from heat and overwork, Miss Jordan would look completely self-possessed. . . . [She] was

41. Elizabeth Jordan
at thirty. Uncredited
photograph in *Three
Rousing Cheers*, facing
p. 264.

never bothered with minor women's page assignments, but combined the best features of the stunt age with sound writing. She tested the accommodations of jails and asylums, rode an engine cab, interviewed social leaders and covered the news of the town. She traveled through the mountains of Virginia and Tennessee on horseback, fording rivers, climbing gorges, forcing her way through thick forest, her only companion a Negro guide. She visited a lonely mining camp in the mountains, in which no woman had ever set foot. Armed with a Spanish stiletto she explored the camps of the moonshiners and did a series for the *Sunday World* that was copied widely. (177–78)[18]

The sort of writing Jordan did—not merely reporting the news but actively developing stories—is also characteristic of the innovative journalism of the era.

Jordan's tales of her early achievements demonstrate that she was able, and entirely willing, to use her femininity and social privilege as resources in the competitive arena of journalism. Her first "beat," or exclusive story, came when she gained admission to a familial scene from which the *World*'s best reporters had been excluded. President Harrison's grandson, McKee, then about five, was supposed to be the vulnerable spot in Benjamin Harrison's cold make-up. The President was devoted to the youngster and liked to have him around, playing at his feet, even in the presidential offices.

Inevitably, the newspapers of the country had become almost hysterical over that baby. They printed innumerable columns about him. His small interests and activities were described as if they were world news. His photographs smiled from the pages of all the leading journals. There had been nothing quite like it before. (32)

When the family took a seaside holiday in Cape May, New Jersey, near where Jordan was exiled doing promotional pieces about Long Island seashore resorts, "[n]ewspaper men from all over the country battered at the cottage doors in vain" (32). Jordan attributes her own success to luck—she happened to be at the door as Mrs. Harrison and the child emerged and was invited to accompany them to the beach for his first "sea bath"—but it is clear that her compatibility in terms of gender and class, and her dexterity in presenting herself, were also crucial. Jordan makes the interview sound like a social visit and gives a conventional but convincingly particular, even affectionate, description of the child's enjoyment of the beach: "Mrs. Harrison and I seemed alone in the universe as we sat down together and talked for more than an hour, while Baby McKee 'did his stuff' as if his little hour had struck. He intrepidly tackled the ocean. He dropped on the sand and let the waves roll over him. He made short sorties into the water, tentatively at first, then more boldly. He came back at intervals, incoherent with rapture, and dripped on us. We watched him as we talked" (34). Jordan's pleasure in making friends and in getting her story—and, for that matter, in getting to know the president's wife—seem to mingle unself-consciously. Both Mrs. Harrison and the *World*'s editor liked the resulting story, and Jordan's pay and assignments improved from that day forward.

Novelist Gertrude Atherton met Jordan during the 1890s. "Elizabeth Jordan, then the star woman reporter on the *World*, interviewed me shortly after the publication of *The Doomswoman* in book form, and what she and other girl reporters told me of their vicissitudes and mortifications convinced me that this stratum of woman's endeavor was not for me. Miss Jordan had a masterful personality, and a Juno-like beauty that would give any girl confidence—she could hold her own; for that matter she was soon elevated to the editorship of the Woman's Page; but all those other girls who told me their woes disappeared in a few years, worn out, body and soul" (222). Atherton's concise verbal portrait captures vividly the impression Jordan made on those she met. It also suggests that she continued to elide the interview and the visit; the two women formed a lasting friendship (although Jordan dates its origin differently, from Atherton's sojourn at the *World* offices while researching a newspaper novel). *Three Rousing Cheers* does discuss the "mortifications" to which Atherton refers, such as sexual harassment, although it tends to touch on them lightly. Jordan strikes a careful balance between making it clear that she remained utterly respectable and making it understood that she lost enough of her "convent manner" to be liked by her colleagues—even the ones who swore constantly (38). She managed, that is, to be both a lady and a good fellow.

Jordan's autobiography seamlessly combines the narrative of her career with a narrative of her friendships. Together, inseparably, they constituted her life. She explains in the foreword that she has written not because she believes she individually is important but to reminisce about the extraordinary people she has known. The title *Three Rousing Cheers* expresses her own "mental attitude toward life" and also "in a much greater degree, my devotion to the memory of the friends who, for a quarter of a century, used the refrain so constantly and so gaily that it became the rallying cry of our clan" (vii). This is the same language of kinship that Jordan uses about *The Whole Family*, and about Harper's in general (see chapter 2); and in fact, the collaborative Family, the Harper's family, and Jordan's "clan" are thoroughly intertwined. Jordan writes that "during the ten years I edited *Harper's Bazar* I passed more week-ends at Jorjalma [the country home of George Harvey, president of Harper's, and his wife, Alma] than at home. Many authors and editors had the same happy experience, and dozens of life-long friendships began there. We injected our slogan into the speech of most of our fellow-guests—even into those of William Dean Howells, Henry Mills Alden, and Henry James. Those three looked rather startled when they caught themselves bringing it out. They were not natural cheerers, as the rest of us were" (viii). (This comic image might have helped the reviewer who wondered how James had been induced to contribute to *The Whole Family.*) One senses a division between a public and a private Jordan only in the last chapter of the book, in which she recounts her struggle with depression over her failing vision; even then she writes that she tells the story because its happy ending offers encouragement to other victims of cataracts, and ends with "Three rousing cheers!" (394).

Jordan never defends or even discusses the fact that she did not marry. (She does say that she sometimes wondered why she did not fall in love with the brilliant and handsome Arthur Brisbane, editor of the Sunday *World* when she was assistant editor and "the most interesting of the thousands of human beings I have known," as she thinks "[m]ost girls in their twenties" would have, but concludes that the terrific pace of their work and dislike of "sentimental dalliance" in the office prevented it [128].) Around the same time she took over the editorship of the *Bazar* she formed a household with two other women—in naming them she proudly includes their academic credentials and professions: "Harriet Beardslee Prescott, a graduate of Mount Holyoke College and already head of the catalogue department of Columbia University Library, and Martha Hill Cutler, a graduate of Smith College, then studying art in New York" (170). Cutler became part of Jordan's work family as well, contributing many illustrated articles on home decoration and art to *Harper's Bazar.* In describing their arrangement, Jordan emphasizes that each retained her personal liberty. They first tried it for a summer.

> Even for that short interval we protected ourselves by various stipulations. Each of us had her own profession, her own friends, her own interests. It was understood that each would continue to live her life in complete independence of the others. If I wished to give a dinner they would dine out. If they wished to give a dinner I would arrange the meal and the details and also tactfully fade from the picture. If, in the autumn, any or all of us wished to separate the separation would take place with the utmost good feeling on all sides.
>
> Now, in 1937, that association and understanding have existed for almost forty years. My sister Alice says the brilliant success of the experiment is due to the fact that Harriet and Martha have such beautiful

natures. This is true. They have become her sisters, too, and they were daughters to our mother till the time of Mother's death. (170)

The gentle contrast between the teasing sister (who attributes the household's success to its other members) and the adopted sisters is suggestive. All three are mentioned as helping Jordan through the ordeal of her near-blindness and operations, but it is Martha and Harriet of whom she writes, "Nowhere on this earth could there be more devoted friends than those two, whose friendship bore so long and severe a test" (387). Jordan represents herself as having achieved an elective family that provided both individual freedom and loving companionship.

Jordan extends the language of kinship beyond the boundaries of the household and across the boundary of gender as well. She writes of her "best man friend," John à Becket: "During the first year of our acquaintance I had assured him I would be the mother he needed so sorely. He was much older than I but he accepted the relation, and called me 'Mother' to his last day. He always addressed my mother as 'Grandma,' and my 'adopted sisters' . . . as 'Aunt Harriet' and 'Aunt Martha.' He became knight errant to the family" (146). Carroll Smith-Rosenberg has shown that politically radical New Women did not reject the female world of love and the female-guided family, but "wove the traditional ways of their mothers into the heart of their brave new world" (255). Jordan's words remind us that this syncretism not only created new female institutions like the settlement house but also encompassed a multitude of creative daily practices. They also have particular significance for the topic of this book, of course, helping us to see what "The Whole Family" meant to the woman who was the editor and moving spirit of the collaboration.

Jordan belonged to the network of New Women. She took pride in knowing a great many "public women," as she put it—in fact, she writes, "I seem to have known most of them more or less intimately" (330). She did a great deal of public speaking on behalf of the women's suffrage campaign, in particular. In 1916 and 1917 she put her editorial skills to work on its behalf by organizing another composite novel, titled *The Sturdy Oak*, whose action deals with the movement and whose proceeds were devoted to it. Although this collaboration went more smoothly and featured well-known contributors such as Fanny Hurst,

Mary Austin, and—again—Mary Heaton Vorse, it was apparently a less important experience for Jordan; *The Whole Family* occupies an entire chapter of her autobiography but *The Sturdy Oak* is not even mentioned.

The collaboration Jordan remembered most happily took place within the sphere of the women's movement as well. She greatly admired suffrage leader Anna Howard Shaw and was attempting to persuade her to undertake an autobiography when Dr. Shaw's busy schedule was suddenly interrupted by a broken leg. Jordan writes with characteristic humor, "I hardly gave her time to have the bones of her ankle set before I hurried up to the McAlpin Hotel, where she was stopping, to take up again the matter of that book" (330). Every morning for three weeks Jordan and her secretary, Charlotte Lambrecht, went to the hotel; Jordan asked questions, Lambrecht took the reminiscences down in shorthand, Shaw talked, and they "laughed and cried with her; we were tense with interest during every hour" (333). Later Lambrecht typed up her notes and rearranged them in something like chronological order for Jordan, who created an outline, wrote the narrative, and read it, chapter by chapter, to Shaw for her approval. It was published serially in *Metropolitan Magazine* and then in book form in 1915, by Harper's, as *The Story of a Pioneer.* Shaw is listed as the author, although "with the collaboration of Elizabeth Jordan" also appears on the title page.

One name for this sort of collaboration, of course, is ghostwriting, a practice that tends to be seen as primarily commercial and even slightly disreputable; it violates our reverence for individual authorship (discussed in chapter 1). Yet, as described by Jordan, the production of the volume seems a remarkable exercise of recollection and candor on the one side, and of empathy and writerly craft on the other. Jordan considered Shaw "a born talker and probably the best woman speaker America ever had," but both knew she wrote badly (332); she needed help if her experiences—as a pioneer in western Michigan in the 1860s, as a pioneer for women in both the ministry and medicine and in the suffrage movement (she was at this time president of the National Women's Suffrage Association)—were to be recorded. Jordan wanted, too, to convey her friend's spirit—and to keep herself out of the book, which she knew was no easy matter when she was listening so passionately that she felt "as if I had lived her life with her" (333). Jordan praises the other two collaborators while making it clear that she herself deserves considerable credit for the book's success. Shaw, she writes, was "wonderful during her own telling of the tale—extraordinarily open-minded, always willing to follow leads and suggestions," but she "was even more wonderful" during the reading: "she never interrupted it; and at the end she never suggested a change except a correction of some name or date. This seems too good to be true; but it is true, and it forms a unique record in collaboration" (334). On the commercial side of the arrangement, she frankly reports that both she and Shaw were paid generously for the serial, but that she "voluntarily and unnecessarily" (331) made over all the book royalties to Shaw. As so often, Jordan manages here to mesh two apparently contradictory positions: she is a self-supporting writer and earns something from the project, but it also altruistically serves Shaw, the women's movement, and the reading public at large.

Jordan's narrative emphasizes her intimacy with Shaw, and she reports with pleasure that Shaw used the language of kinship to talk about their collaboration, always referring to the book as "our child" (336). Yet the very basis of their connection is that they are "public women." Jordan takes on the role of loving friend, almost a daughter, inducing the hard-working Shaw to attend the theater, concerts, even the occasional vaudeville performance with her; again mixing the vocabularies of public and private, she describes it as making herself "a committee of one" to bring new pleasures into Shaw's life. And alongside her constant use of familial rhetoric she takes pride in a degree of personal freedom—not only from a conventional family but from the political obligations that enmeshed Shaw—that even this "pioneer" for women's rights admires and implicitly compares with a man's: "One evening when we had seen a good play, and were sailing airily into the dressing-room of its distinguished woman star, Dr. Shaw said to me smilingly but almost enviously, 'What an independent cuss you are!' " (335). Whether it is in a vision of nuns as independent women, of her family as the source of her career, of the workplace as a family, or of *The Whole Family* succeeding both as literature and as stunt journalism, Jordan's thinking is constantly syncretic, constantly combines public and private, old and new.

Much of Jordan's early fiction is autobiographical and offers information and insights—not so much into what really happened or what she really thought as into the range and shape of her experience and imagination. For example, one of the stories in her first published volume, a collection of related stories about journalism titled *Tales of the City Room*, shows that Jordan at least contemplated the situation of a woman reporter who is afraid to go home alone late at night and finds it hard to walk the line between the lady and the good fellow. Her Miss Van Dyke does find her work putting her respectability at risk, and at the story's conclusion decides to abandon it and marry—although the words she uses to accept her coworker's proposal are, "I think I'll take the assignment" (231). Similarly, *May Iverson's Career*, a book that brings the heroine of the convent series into journalism, gives a considerably fuller and franker account of sexual harassment than *Three Rousing Cheers*.

Jordan's frequent use of children as characters in her early fiction points up how often her autobiography includes them. Although Jordan had no literal sons or daughters, she would not have thought of herself as a "childless" woman in the late twentieth-century sense, which assumes that all relations except the parental are peripheral. (The same thing might be said of Freeman.) The structure of these works is also revealing; they are not novels but collections that construct "narratives of community" (to use Sandra Zagarell's term). But the common ground that links the stories is not a neighborhood or village (as in Cutting's work, discussed in chapter 3, and Freeman's), but a school or a workplace. (One might argue that many television series, from *Taxi* and *Saved by the Bell* to *NYPD Blue*, extend this form.) The characters' domestic interiors, whether May Iverson's room or reporter Ruth Herrick's apartment, remain important, but they convene communities constituted in public institutions. Jordan's communities also tend to be composed of age peers, marking the growing power of age consciousness, norms, and stratification from the late nineteenth century on. Indeed, both "school-girl" fiction and "childlessness" are themselves elements of that shift (see Chudacoff).

Later Jordan turned to writing mystery novels and other light fiction. These are unambitious works, rarely meriting a mention in *Three Rousing Cheers*, and competent at best, but they refract her characteristic concerns in interesting and occasionally bizarre ways—sometimes very revealingly, as in *The Devil and the Deep Sea*, published in 1929. The novel begins like a genteel English mystery, with the lawyer of a rich old spinster about to read her predictable will to her family. But Catherine Chandler, it quickly appears, wrote a subsequent, very different will, one that includes elaborate arrangements to keep the lawyer himself, her sister, and all her nieces and nephews on a kind of probation in her home for six months, for purposes no one quite understands. Miss Webb, the trained nurse who attended the spinster's death and seems to suspect that her patient was murdered, has also been asked to remain. Various surprising and distressing facts about members of the family emerge as the plot unravels, but the real interest of the book is not in the resolution of a mystery but in personalities and the reconstruction of family.

The most powerful character in the novel (and the best candidate for an autobiographical one) is the spinster, even though she never takes the stage alive. Catherine Chandler was not only rich and beautiful, but also strong-willed, intelligent, and sophisticated. The nurse—herself an attractive, forceful person, a college graduate who also runs the household perfectly—was fascinated by her, as another nurse tells the lawyer: "[A]fter a few months Miss Webb was fairly obsessed by her. It was like a school-girl 'crush' on an older teacher. . . . Miss Chandler had traveled over the world and she'd had wonderful experiences and adventures. She could make one see them all. Even the little she talked to me at night showed me that. She used to make Miss Webb's eyes stick out and her head swim" (207–8). Most of the events of the novel have been planned by this formidable woman; she has even left a message in her own voice, recorded on a phonograph record, for each of her relatives.

Yet Catherine Chandler's aim is to undo the effects of having been an individualist. She writes in her posthumous letter to the lawyer, Nicholas Long, that she has failed her nieces and nephews: "[T]hey all have bitter need of the thing they've never had since they were children, the companionship and affection of decent elders. It's the irony of fate that I, the one human being who could and should have given them this, whose duty it was to give it to them, failed them at every turn. I was gadding around the world in the years when they most needed me.

I was absorbed in my own useless life and trivial interests" (319). Even Miss Webb says, "[S]he was afraid to die after the selfish life she lived; for I suppose there's no doubt that it was one of the most selfish lives a woman ever lived. I loved her, but I felt that she never did anything for anybody" (252). Having seen the error of her ways while in the grip of a terminal illness, Catherine Chandler scripts a scenario to show her relations the error of theirs, and commissions others to carry it out after her death. Notwithstanding the text's direct assertions that she made the wrong choices, she comes off quite well. She has managed both to live her entire life as an independent woman untroubled by family responsibilities and to sacrifice herself for her family—since her diligent planning exhausts her and hastens her death. Once she begins paying attention to her family, she is able to exert control over their lives even posthumously; her schemes for inducing self-reflection are wholly successful, leading all the characters to remake their lives according to her wishes. By the end of her experiment they are not only bowing to the empty chair at the dinner table that (according to the will's instructions) symbolizes her presence, they sing a window-rattling chorus of "For She's a Jolly Good Fellow" for her (325).

The lawyer Nicholas Long, an "ease-loving" (3) bachelor of fifty-eight, proves surprisingly willing to have his life rearranged (although Catherine's eccentric instructions do cause him to congratulate himself on his decision not to propose to her). By the end of six months he has decided to move in permanently and keep all the nieces and nephews with him. (An involuntary "cure" for her drug addiction has killed off the sole surviving member of the older generation of Chandlers.) He tells them, " 'I'll stand back of you like a father. And,' his smile flashed out at them, 'it's going to be a labor of love. I find I rather like being a family man' " (323). It is impossible to recognize the original character in this exchange:

"How does it feel to be so suddenly made the father of six?" she [Miss Webb] smilingly asked him as they followed the others downstairs.

"It feels fine," Long complacently assured her. "I've always suspected that I had a hidden gift that way! But you'll soon know all about how it feels. You've got to be a parent, too." (325)

Long and Miss Webb conveniently fall in love, despite the great difference in their ages, and the family is provided with a mother as well as a father. In the last chapter of the book they both constantly refer to the other characters, all in their twenties and all happily remaining "at home," as "the children." Long sounds virtually parodic in his pride over his belated brood: "I'll offer a large and handsome prize to any one who can show me anywhere a better-looking, clearer-eyed, nicer-mannered family than mine" (329).[19] Many narratives create closure by creating a nuclear family—but this is surely a unique route to that resolution.

Only a trace of the syncretic imagination that makes Jordan so interesting is visible in the text of *The Whole Family*. Certainly it was her authorship of the May Iverson series that determined her chapter would be "The School-Girl," and May and Alice Talbert are similar in personality as well as age. (May begins narrating her convent stories at fourteen; Alice is fifteen [see fig. 42]. Comparing the image of Jordan at seventeen in figure 40, I wonder if illustrator Alice Barber Stephens saw an autobiographical component in Jordan's school-girls, as I do.) Both are enthusiastic and naive, avid readers who tend to think and talk in terms borrowed from books. These well-intentioned but unreliable narrators are victimized by clichés; May writes about one of her friends, for example, that "each day revealed hitherto unsuspected beauties of character and temperament, as real writers say. She was the most generous girl I ever knew, and the soul of truth and honor" (*May Iverson* 11). Alice writes, "I dismissed him with a haughty bow, the way they do on the stage" (110), and "I 'planned my course of action,' as they say in books" (111). May reads a book about motion study, introduces it into the convent, and produces comic disaster, as the girls try so hard to be efficient that they can accomplish nothing but looking outlandish (*May Iverson Tackles Life* ch. 8). In the same literal-minded fashion, as we have seen, Alice interprets Lorraine's behavior according to the sensational novel she has just read and circulates a rumor that her sister-in-law has been weeping over Lyman Wilde's photograph because she is hopelessly in love with him. May starts a newspaper called *The Voice of Truth*, and the first issue's contents are so indiscreet that a sister asks in horror, "Have any copies of this gone out of the building?" (*May Iverson* 234). (This story was published in the *Bazar* in July

1904.) Alice is so curious—"I don't rest until I know what there is to know" (103), she says—and so communicative that her brother-in-law has nicknamed her "Clarry," short for the *Eastridge Animated and Undaunted Daily Bugle and Clarion Call.* These are, of course, the moments whose resonance I emphasized at the conclusion of chapter 3. In the light of Jordan's life and work, it is clear that Alice's intimate identification with print culture and confounding of the public and private—although no doubt calculated for comic rather than thematic effect—are central to Jordan's construction of female modernity.

Jordan follows one of Cutting's suggestions (in the chapter immediately preceding hers) for advancing the plot by having Alice relay to Elizabeth the news that Lorraine knows Lyman Wilde. But she ignores Cutting's concluding references to a scene the next day at the Talbert breakfast table (apparently between Cyrus and Elizabeth, causing Peggy to be taken ill) and another at the factory between Cyrus and Charles Edward (although that is presumably what Jordan expects us to think Lorraine is really crying about). This last suggestion, like much of the material in the chapters by Freeman, Vorse, and Cutting, directs attention away from courtship and toward tensions within the family; but Jordan generally returns the focus to the marriage plot. The fit between the end of Cutting's chapter and the beginning of Jordan's is actually rather loose. Cutting had Lorraine get Wilde's picture and put it on the mantel because she is thinking of him, while Jordan writes that it is usually there—making it difficult to see how Elizabeth could be unaware of the acquaintance and her lost lover's whereabouts. And it is not exactly clear how the scene of Lorraine weeping with her head, and the photograph, among the crumbs on the tea table derives from what Cutting wrote. In fact, I cannot help wondering if it might have been suggested less by "The Daughter-in-law" than by another story by Cutting that appeared in the *Bazar* in December 1907 in which the plot turns on someone being observed weeping over a photograph (see fig. 43).[20] It is impossible to know. But it would certainly be appropriate for Jordan to be reacting out of context to something else she had encountered in print and intertwining the story of *The Whole Family* still more closely into the multiple narratives circulating in the *Bazar.*

42. Illustration for *The Whole Family*, ch. 5,
"The School-Girl": "I found Lorraine with
her head down among the little cakes."
Harper's Bazar 42.4 (April 1908): 359.

43. Illustration for "Oil of Gladness," by Mary Stewart Cutting: "Lying there with Evan's picture, crying—crying!" *Harper's Bazar* 41.12 (December 1907): 1155.

Female Modernity and the Magazine

The image on the cover of the December 1907 issue of *Harper's Bazar,* in which the first installment of *The Whole Family* appears, is an updated madonna (see pl. 2). Against a green background, a woman swathed in a red shawl gazes tenderly at a baby. The simple picture implies a virtually timeless tradition, combining the "natural" bond between mother and infant with a generalized Christianity. Yet of course everything about it, from the colors (of both design elements and skin) to the composition, is culturally coded. This Mary is a version of the American Girl, a figure whose variations during this period Martha Banta has analyzed in detail.[21] The appeal of the image is not its timelessness but its canny, historically specific combination of an old image and current ideals of beauty. The same model could have posed for this madonna and for the "decorative" Peggy (see fig. 36).

Both the subjects and the styles of *Bazar* covers during Jordan's editorship are highly varied, ranging from an elaborate historical scene of two Roman women to a simple image of yellow butterflies against a blue sky.[22] Many in the period leading up to the publication of *The Whole Family* look something like the stylized fashion plate of April 1905 (pl. 3). The covers of the issues containing the composite novel, however, along with those immediately preceding and following it, are for the most part images of contemporary American women; they offer a sort of gallery of portraits of the narrow range of tradition and innovation acceptable in cover girls. All of them evoke Banta's "Beautiful Charmer": "pretty, independent, candid, spontaneous, willful, spoiled, and 'nice' " (48). The bathing beauty of August 1906 (pl. 4) is almost exotic and almost provocative, in comparison to the musing beauties of July 1906 (pl. 5) and May 1907 (pl. 6). Yet both of the latter images display the red hair that (as Lois Banner tells us [176]) had for a very long time been emblematic of a passionate, troublesome personality and had been in fashion since the 1890s. Thus, like the coeducated Peggy, who also has red hair (5), they imply individualism while remaining passively decorative.

The laughing redheaded girl (in corals) on the deck of a boat on the September 1908 cover (pl. 7) expands the covers' range of reference slightly; her situation evokes Banta's "Outdoors Pal" (46), although her parasol qualifies the suggestion of athleticism. The most striking cover of the period, however, is the unusually domestic scene of July 1908 (pl. 8). Children are only very occasionally depicted on *Bazar* covers, as here and on the Christmas issues, and this female figure's relation to them is somewhat ambiguous—is she their mother, their aunt, their sister? The image is also relatively adventurous stylistically, with the popular Japanese influence visible in its use of light and its flattened foreground with blind, fan, and flowers paralleling the picture plane.[23] The enigmatic gaze of this possibly-new, sometimes-new woman is directed not at the family but at the viewer, emerging out of the private realm behind her into the realm of publication that has produced her— and providing what is for me the most evocative image of the necessary paradox I have called "publishing the family."

The verbal texts of *Harper's Bazar* during Jordan's editorship represent a much wider range of choices for women than do the visuals. Feature articles often include discussions of public issues concerning women; I have already mentioned that perspectives from Charles

William Eliot's on women's education to Charlotte Perkins Gilman's on marriage were represented. Jordan's editorial column often advocated choices for women, but just as constantly appealed to women to choose the home. She ran articles on the woman's movement, the campaign for the vote, and—less often—the antisuffrage movement. George Harvey endorsed woman suffrage in an editorial reprinted from the *North American Review* and also published a long series of ambiguously satiric "Reflections Concerning Women" in both the *Review* and the *Bazar*—provoking many letters when he proposed a tax on spinsters on the grounds that they were unproductive members of society, "mere clogs upon the wheels of progress from the sheer obstinacy that holds them from the performance of their proper tasks in life" (296).

The *Bazar* featured a number of articles about the situation of spinsters from a more subjective perspective as well; Freeman's concern with Howells's treatment of the old-maid aunt was not idiosyncratic but part of an ongoing discussion in the magazine. Even Lilian Bell, who in 1902 in the first of her "Talks to Spinsters" asserted that "matrimony . . . is the only legitimate happiness in the world for a woman" (1057), went on in the next to mock the stereotype of the angular, cat-loving, tea-drinking old maid (3). The lengthiest, and probably the most substantial and thoughtful, contribution to the discussion during the period of *The Whole Family* was a 1907 series of seven articles by Anne O'Hagan.[24] Each is a first-person commentary on the life of an unmarried, thirty-eight-year-old professional woman; the biographical details fit O'Hagan herself, although most of the articles include fictionalized dialogue between the spinster, Hester, and her married sister, Maida (see figs. 44 and 45). Just as Lily Talbert represented herself as missing the really worthwhile joys of life, Hester refers to her "compensations"—but she also makes a vivid case for the pleasures of work and freedom and friendship, in contrast to the narrow horizons and harried existence of the wife and mother. Maida pities any spinster, no matter how happy, accomplished, and productive; she sighs, after lunching with an old friend who has just returned from missionary work in China, "Poor Estella! . . . What a pity she never married." Hester replies indignantly, "It seems to me that her life has been wonderful—rich in every sort of experience. Think of the lands and seas

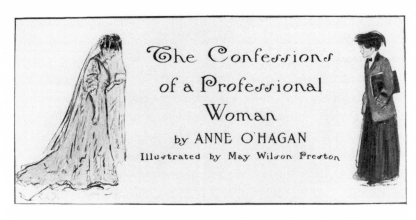

44. Title decoration for "The Confessions of a Professional Woman," by Anne O'Hagan. *Harper's Bazar* 41.9 (September 1907): 848.

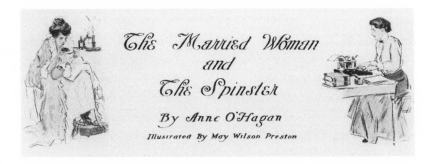

45. Title decoration for "The Married Woman and the Spinster," by Anne O'Hagan. *Harper's Bazar* 41.7 (July 1907): 630.

she knows and all the adventure of travel she has had—the excitement of it. Think of her work, her belief in it, her pride in it, the dignity of helpfulness she feels—the delight she showed in the love that she has won for herself by her own gifts. Oh, it seems wonderful to me—almost as wonderful . . . as if she had doctored Frederick's throat and been a patroness of the Glee Club concerts for eight years" (631). Taken together, the essays offer a vehement defense of the legitimacy of the choice not to marry.

The effort to update the image of the spinster had been under way for some time when Freeman and O'Hagan took it on. In 1869, for example, Fanny Fern wrote a newspaper column titled "The Modern

Old Maid," which ends, "She carries a dainty parasol, and a natty little umbrella, and wears killing bonnets, and has live poets and sages and philosophers in her train, and knows how to use her eyes, and don't care if she never sees a cat, and couldn't tell a snuff-box from a patent reaper, and has a bank-book and dividends, yes, sir! and her name is Phoebe or Alice; and Woman's Rights has done it" (361). From her fashion sense to the men in her train (the expression is the same one used about Lily Talbert) to the need to disrupt a false stereotype, the issues O'Hagan addresses are the same. Hester, too, enjoys the company of men—O'Hagan devotes an entire essay to an explanation and defense of such friendships (including a young poet who reads her his ironically named *Arethusa* [227]).[25] Almost forty years later in the ebb and flow of struggles over women's rights, Freeman and O'Hagan had a well-established claim to choices but also faced new standards. Provoked by Maida "parroting 'wifehood and motherhood'" as the only way of achieving true womanhood, Hester puts "the ultimate question": "[W]hen you married women read the reports of the Magdalene homes, the foundling asylums, and such institutions, are you willing to base your claim to a unique fulness of life upon the grounds that make the ugly tragedy of those records?" (633). Maida of course does not say, "Yes, it's about sex"—erotic fulfillment had not yet emerged as a legitimate value in mass-circulation discourses. Yet after admitting that spinsters can have homes, and love, and everything else that Hester can suggest, she still insists that they are missing a vital "experience" (635); heterosexuality for her is so obviously compulsory that logic cannot undermine her conviction. O'Hagan's series plays out many variations on the debate over voluntary celibacy, and in the process epitomizes the problem of periodization that is one of my topics throughout these chapters: the attitudes of 1869 had not disappeared, and the attitudes of the 1920s had already begun to emerge, in 1907.

In the last article of the series, "The Neurotic Spinster in Literature," O'Hagan skewers recent fiction showing spinsters as victims of "thwarted instinct" who behave absurdly. One exemplary protagonist becomes obsessed with the infant of her lost love and his wife. Another feels a compulsion to acquire a man and a child and marries someone she barely knows. Another "libel" resonates with the story of *The Whole Family*:

I recalled a heroine, well stricken in years according to the old-fashioned computation, who had passed a summer very pleasantly playing with a nice youth just out of college. The heroine had had, as I remember, rather a hard life, devoting herself to an invalid relative or something conventionally drab and dreary of that sort, and this summer was her first holiday in many years. Instead of being bored by the college boy as, with all possible deference to our collegiate system, might not have been unnatural, the old maid falls rather wildly in love with him; [when he] appears with a suitable young person to whom he has become engaged . . . the spinster, figuratively tearing her hair and literally rending her traditions, proclaims to the reader of her story that if she had her life to live again, not duty, not dignity, not honor, should rule her actions, should be her ideals, but love, legitimate or illicit, love, righteous or disgraceful, love and its fulfilment." (972)

O'Hagan exclaims in comic dismay, "It is dizzying to contemplate! Has all the spinster world gone mad together? Or is it merely a few writers? And is my sister Maida right when she chooses to regard these hysterical outbursts as truthful representations of our actual feelings, and when she thus denounces our calm, cheerful, busy, day-by-day existences as mere smiling falsehood covering our tempestuous emotions—the fair verdure of the Vesuvius slopes beneath which boil unimaginable possibilities of wrack and ruin?" (973) This is psychoanalytic language two years before the Clark University conference that announced Freud to the United States.

As much to the point, for my purposes, is the fact that the narrative of the unconscious is carried by, and O'Hagan's series ends with, an essay on fiction. Hester complains to Maida, "[I]f only you would take your ideas of the spinster class from an observation of life instead of from current literature—! Heaven knows you number a sufficient supply of old maids on your list of acquaintances, and you have intimate opportunities for study. Why on earth should you deny the evidence of your senses and resort to the banalities of the printed page—" (971). From the name Hester to the young poet's *Arethusa* to the sisters' discussion of *Hedda Gabler*, literary references weave through the essays as O'Hagan thematizes and comments on the powerful influence of print culture in shaping narratives about women's choices. This intimate narration is in some sense, I have been suggesting, the topic of *The Whole Family*, and my topic throughout this book. In the next chapter we will see why it is that Maida's sympathy—whether for Estella or for Hester—offends. In this chapter and the previous one we have seen the tension between the family and the individual, and the constant crossing of boundaries between spheres, that makes it fitting for the spinster's sister to be the voice of normativity. And in chapter 2 we saw that the mass magazine from the beginning located itself in, drew its power from, that circuit. Henry Mills Alden himself insists on the correspondence of privacy and publicity in his description of the unique role of *Harper's Monthly* in American life:

> The intimate blending of a magazine with the thought and life of a whole people, whose intellectual and emotional sensibility was so quickly responsive to its imaginative literature, and whose curiosity was so fully met by its articles of travel and exploration and by others of an informing character, making it for them a Real Encyclopaedia of the living world, was never so fully realized as in the career of the periodical which was the first example of its type—that of a popular illustrated magazine. It had the exclusive advantage of this intimacy for fully twenty years before others of the same type and class entered the field, amicably sharing its popularity. (51–52)

National culture in its modern form can hardly be imagined without such interpellations.

Magazines are only part of the cultural system that writes the self, of course. In her examination of how one late nineteenth-century family —the Hamiltons of Fort Wayne, Indiana—used books in ordering and understanding their lives, Barbara Sicherman discusses many sorts of reading (although she mentions that *Harper's Magazine* was a "special favorite" [205]). Jane Hunter has shown that diary writing was crucial to the self-narration of late Victorian girls—and also that the practice had a profoundly ambiguous relation to the family, functioning both as a form of discipline and as a zone of privacy. These studies focus on women's reading, leaving comparative claims about men mostly implicit; on the one hand, men certainly read and wrote and surely sometimes incorporated those activities into their core self-understandings; on the other, the privileged relation between women and culture is well established. I want to be explicit about the limit of my claims: the evidence assembled here does not allow me to delineate the exact role played by print culture in constituting American selves—either in various gendered, classed, racialized locations or in relation to other daily practices. It is not precise or ample enough, and my hermeneutic method is not well suited to generating such claims. Indeed, I am not sure that the evidence and method for doing so in a genuinely rigorous way are available yet. We do know that reading and writing played a significant role in self-definition at least for the white middle class—as Sicherman points out, the influence of print culture was probably at its peak in this period, after the radical expansion in the volume of newspapers, magazines, and books in circulation, and before the rise of other mass media. And I do want to argue that the New Woman is a charged figure not only because she evokes the politics of gender—as she certainly does—but also because she challenges the boundary between public and private. The female individualist, the woman who steps out of the home into the working world, the woman whose inner life is manifestly shaped by her reading, may or may not be stigmatized, but she inevitably provokes attention to, and potentially unsettles, the separation of individual from social, male from female, home from marketplace.

A woman reading a magazine represents a moment when the permeability of boundaries can become visible. Let me illustrate the point by tracing the career of an anecdote. In *I Remember*, Harry Harper writes that as the immensely popular serial *Trilby* drew to a close, *Harper's Monthly* received "a pathetic letter from an afflicted mother" (209) asking if the last installments could be made available in advance to her daughter, who was not likely to live long enough to read them in the magazine. They complied, and according to Harper the girl was "much pleased with our courtesy" (210) and indeed died before the conclusion was published. This is a simple story of Harper's corporate benevolence, but it is also about mass fantasy penetrating an urgently personal scene. In *Three Rousing Cheers*, Jordan tells a similar story about Katherine Cecil Thurston's *The Masquerader*, serialized in the *Bazar*. In this case, however, the dying woman wrote to Jordan herself, and although she got the advance proofs, there was an additional complication. Jordan reports that she sent the letter to Frederick Duneka (general manager of Harper's), "knowing he would be interested in it both as a tribute to our fiction and as a human document." However, he was away from the office and "a bright young man on his staff read the letter and was stirred by the advertising possibilities in it. Without consulting anybody else he had it put into print and broadcast throughout the country as a special literary bulletin" (196). Although only initials were used, the woman herself, Jordan, and Duneka were all horrified by this public exposure. For all Jordan's eagerness to disassociate herself and Duneka from any intention to exploit the situation, this development followed from its logic. Without the mediating mother, the transaction was less stably contained in the family circle. And just as Harper's stories are incorporated into the story of the self, the intimate drama of the deathbed fascinates the public and markets the magazine. Note, too, that these are gendered images of passionate reading—a boy or man so deeply engaged with fiction would not be appealing, just as a novel in which a male character suffered the hypnotic penetration of self that turns Trilby into a public performer would be a very unlikely best-seller.

We know these private stories, of course, precisely because Harry Harper and Elizabeth Jordan published them. But long before their anecdotes appeared as nonfiction, Howells—who would certainly have heard them at Franklin Square—had used the situation, with more complications, in his 1908 novel *Fennel and Rue*. He constructs his narrative from the point of view of the author of the serial, Philip Verrian, who is moved—and flattered—by an intelligent letter from a girl intensely interested in the work that is his first notable success. She fears she may not live to see the end in print and hopes he will send it to her in advance. Verrian refers the question to his editor, who is favorably inclined although he wants to do some checking to make sure that she isn't "a woman journalist trying to work us for a 'story' in her Sunday edition" because it is "astonishing what women will do when they take to newspaper work" (6). (Jordan, remember, had been an editor on the Sunday *World*.) Meanwhile, just as in Jordan's anecdote, a publicist for the house has already placed a paragraph about the request in the papers to promote the serial—which Verrian regrets on behalf of the girl and the editor soon regrets on behalf of the house when the letter turns out to be a hoax.

The Sometimes-New Woman   205

Here is Howells's innovation: the persistent theme of *Fennel and Rue* is female inauthenticity, which he represents as virtually inevitable in the modern world. The identity of the working woman, in particular, is disturbingly complex. Verrian considers "all the undertakings of women . . . piteous, not only because women were unequal to the struggle at the best, but because they were hampered always with themselves, with their sex, their femininity," tempted always to tempt men into loving them and returning them to the role of wife and mother (75). When Jordan has a journalist accept a marriage proposal in the words, "I'll take the assignment," the conflation of vocabularies is a resolution; when Howells has Verrian reflect, "[W]hen did a woman ever mean business, except in the one great business?" (63), it indicates a dangerous erosion of boundaries. Indeed, the world of self-interested performance seems to be swallowing everyone, including Verrian, who is persistently mistaken for an actor of the same name (his "dreadful double" [124]), and whose fascination with the complex girl prevents him from marrying an innocent one.

By 1908 several generations of women, and men, had been wrestling with the problem of female modernity. Howells's late works, such as *Fennel and Rue*, seem more engaged with the problems than with the opportunities of the new social arrangements. Yet he had always been a social critic; subtle treatments of the enabling pretenses of gender relations and class cultures, and of the uncomfortable ubiquity of the market, characterize his work throughout his career. Howells, at seventy, had—as Freeman (fifty-five in 1908) and Jordan (forty) had—mixed allegiances to tradition and progress. What I have called the sometimes-new woman is assembled out of this process of synthesis.

The story of the New Woman extends not only back to Fanny Fern in 1869, but forward to my own generation formed in the long 1960s and to the present. As, decade after decade, women invent their own relations to female modernity, the term *new woman* has continued to carry a powerful charge—whether those using it are aware of its history or not. In the midst of the feminist activism of the early 1970s, the phrase was even chosen as the name of a magazine. The "Publisher's Platform" in the first issue explicitly affirms a female individualism framed in the terms discussed in chapter 3: "We at NEW WOMAN stress the importance of the female self—not selflessness and subservience. We believe that life can be a greater experience when one searches out one's own identity, explores one's own individuality, believes in one's own abilities, discovers who or what one is or might be and takes real pleasure in being that person. This kind of thinking—and doing—constitutes the essence of living that many men (but only a few women) have heretofore known" (1971: 3). That first issue also reprinted a cartoon about a housewife from the *New Yorker*, but added another panel by the same artist suggesting how differently a "new" woman might narrate herself (see fig. 46). The first, "traditional" woman, slumped at a table in robe and curlers, writes, "Dear Diary: Took Lisa to the dentist this P.M."— and so on, from children's needs through housework to "Harvey fell asleep watching TV." The "new woman," draped glamorously over a loveseat, dictates into a recorder: "Dear Diary: Got delivery on new Porsche. . . ." She not only drives a powerful car and condescends to her (male) secretary, but puts her self at the center of her story: "Attended lecture on Pyschology and Philosophy of Zen. Must concentrate on free flow of inner energies. Rewrote chapter nine of autobiography." The humor of each image, and of the contrast, derives from exaggeration; yet in the context of *New Woman* the cartoon career girl seems less ironic than optimistic.

Although this affirmation of women's choices became possible through the resurgence of women's movements, *New Woman* was by no means a political publication. Rather, it was a syncretic project, a glossy magazine that asserted female modernity and ran advertisements exactly like, and departments that played variations on, those of other women's magazines. The invitation to subscribe contained in the first issue is perhaps the most striking example of the magazine's blend of feminism and merchandising (fig. 47). The text, printed over the image of a model with heavily made-up eyes and headed "New Woman," reads:

> She's no typical female.
> It's no typical magazine.
> It's the only magazine dedicated to the elevation of the status and image of the thinking woman.
> No need for verbosity.
> We know you know what NEW WOMAN is.

DIARY
OF A TRADITIONAL WOMAN

"Dear Diary: Took Lisa to the dentist this P.M. No cavities, thank goodness. Peter has a sore throat. No temperature. Waxed the kitchen floor. Looks nice. Tried a new recipe for meat loaf. Not bad. Harvey fell asleep watching TV."

Drawing by Frascino: © 1971
The New Yorker Magazine, Inc.

DIARY
OF A NEW WOMAN

"Dear Diary: Got delivery on new Porsche. Runs like a dream. Attended lecture on Psychology and Philosophy of Zen. Must concentrate on free flow of inner energies. Rewrote chapter nine of autobiography. Hired new secretary. Wonder why he smiled such a funny little smile when I asked him how long he planned to work after he got married."

46. "Diary of a Traditional Woman/Diary of a New Woman," by Ed Frascino. *New Woman* June 1971: 27. Reproduced from a copy in the Labadie Collection, *University of Michigan Special Collections Library.* Partially reprinted from the *New Yorker,* © The New Yorker Collection 1971 Ed Frascino from cartoonbank.com. All rights reserved.

47. Advertisement. *New Woman* June 1971: 106. Reproduced from a copy in the Labadie Collection, *University of Michigan Special Collections Library.*

We know you know whether you are one.
New Woman
a woman with a mind for something special . . .
a magazine with something special for the woman with a mind.

Its flattering description of potential readers does not prevent this intimate address—"We know you know"—from repeating the "pointedly personal" tone deplored by the anonymous author of "The Melancholy of Women's Pages" in 1906. That is the effect, I think, not only of the continuity in the industry but of the paradoxical position of the women's magazine: so inescapably dependent on the entanglement of publication and interiority, so visibly between public and private, that the fiction of their separation is unsettled.

The images illustrating the 1970s version of the *New Woman* are clearly Beautiful Charmers—although rendered in the visual vocabulary of a different decade, with a more direct and provocative gaze and the sharp outlines of latter twentieth-century photography rather than the soft ones of early twentieth-century illustration. So, too, were

48. Cover.
New Woman
January 1999.

49. Advertisement.
New Woman
January 1999: 117.

those to be found on the cover of the magazine on the newsstands in the late 1990s (see fig. 48 for an example). In the hands of various owners and editors, *New Woman* continued to market itself as a magazine for "the modern American woman"—the 1999 "Editorial Mission" statement adds, "smart, sexy, open and real"—although its content became even more like that of other women's magazines, with horoscopes and weight loss figuring prominently.[26] It continued to address the reader intimately in such appeals as an "Editor's Letter" headlined "I'm a New Woman" and beginning, "And I bet you are too," with a picture of the new editor smiling straight at the camera and a text discussing her own efforts to come to terms with getting older and the demands of career and family—a situation assumed to be similar to the reader's, or at least to match the reader's aspirations.[27] An advertisement for the magazine's website even offers a kiss to the reader (fig. 49). The headline ("Me & New Woman / We Just Click") adds another twist to the play of solicitation and identification, implying that the model—rather thinner than the editor, dressed for and placed at the beach rather than the office—in fact *is* the reader, eager to embrace the magazine in either print or electronic form. But the magazine's vision of the modern woman—cautiously assertive, enthusiastically consumerist—no longer established a distinctive niche; or, at any rate, it did not achieve a sizable enough market share for Rodale Press, which acquired the magazine in 1997 and closed it with the January 2000 issue.

Neither the 1970s version of *New Woman* nor the 1990s version manifested an awareness of the historical resonance of the magazine's title; yet they continued to create the sometimes-new woman.[28] My point here is not that the past and the present are the same, but that they are different, and linked. In common sense the term *modern* designates the recent and implies a narrative of progressive change—*modernization* understood as a unified process. It carries an evaluative charge, with the act of separating from the past understood as positive (or, occasionally, negative). More analytically, however, we can see modernity as the product of a complex array of processes of transformation working on different time scales and interacting unevenly to produce varied and contingent results. The sense that being up-to-date, forward looking, in the vanguard—being, for example, a "new" woman—is inherently admirable is itself characteristic of modern societies. Yet the experience of change is often ambivalent; certainly women's relation to modernity has been vexed and contradictory (see Felski and other sections of this book). What we encounter in these women's magazines are the traces of historical actors creatively composing their relation to those processes. The next chapter takes a still more extended view of the relays between the bounding of domains of social life, gender, and culture over a long period of transformation.

blah!

⤙ What Is Sentimentality? ⤚

When William Dean Howells and Elizabeth Jordan organized the collaboration that produced *The Whole Family*, they articulated themes and assigned characters, but their expectations about the form of the fiction were left implicit. The process resulted in two major controversies among the contributors, both conducted in terms of literary quality. As we have already seen, the first dispute—over Mary Wilkins Freeman's chapter—was centrally about gender politics. The second—over Edith Wyatt's—was about genre.

In her autobiography Jordan writes that "the mother's chapter caused almost as great a convulsion among the authors as the old maid's did" (273). The surviving correspondence reveals that Wyatt first submitted a chapter composed of letters by various characters, suggesting that the self-forgetful perspective of a mother was better expressed in epistolary form than in first-person narration. No one had questioned Howells's decision to cast his contribution in the form of a dialogue rather than a monologue, but the proofs of Wyatt's chapter (which Jordan apparently mailed out before she had read them) provoked severe criticism. It may, of course, have been very badly written as well as formally different—it was this material that Frederick Duneka called "cruelly incompetent drivel." The manuscript cannot be located, so we do not know. In any case, Jordan was ready to reject the chapter but allow Wyatt to keep her fee. She told Henry James that he should pick up the tale where John Kendrick Bangs had left it, as his contribution would now appear seventh rather than eighth, and she invited Alice French to assume the mother's role in the family. In the end, however, Wyatt persuaded Jordan to let her rewrite and produced the narrative—

undistinguished but certainly not incompetent—that was published as the ninth chapter of the novel. Howells, who had pushed from the first for Wyatt's inclusion, liked it very much.[1] Henry James did not. His letter to Jordan condenses the topics of literary quality, gender, and genre into a question that led me to the investigation whose results follow: "Does your public *want* that so completely lack-lustre domestic sentimentality?" (Edel and Powers 52).

People talk about sentimentality quite a lot, both outside and inside the academy, and they seem to know what they are talking about. Jordan did not write back to ask what James meant by his question. Saying in casual conversation that something is sentimental never provokes puzzlement or gets one accused of using jargon. The category is used, and occasionally examined, in a wide range of academic fields. It has had a long-standing role in American literary history, and has been especially conspicuous in recent years. Unsurprisingly, as cultural studies has foregrounded the way we *live* social relations, the inextricable entanglements of subjectivity and power, sentiment's articulations of feeling and form have seemed more and more interesting. The word and its derivatives crop up so often and so variously in current criticism that it has become difficult to know how various comments and contributions fit together—or, more often, why they don't. For quite a long time, as I followed the scholarly discussions and tried out ways of thinking about *The Whole Family* in relation to them, it seemed that (unlike the rest of the world) I did not know what sentimentality was—and the more I read, the less I knew.

In a way this chapter begins there: it is designed to disrupt the term's apparent transparency. It does not reproduce my own process of discovery, which was much less organized than what follows.[2] Nor does it survey existing or emerging perspectives; rather, it is selective and tendentious. It does undertake to reconstruct sentimentality from the ground up, in the sense that it tries to take nothing for granted; what we most confidently know, as participants in culture or practitioners of a discipline, can be exactly what forecloses analytic knowledge. The term is so plastic and pervasive, and so charged, precisely because our reactions to sentimentality are so deeply rooted in our ways of organizing the relation of self and world. (Thus this chapter provides a particularly salient example of the microhistorical method, connecting

immense social transformations with minute textual details.) I believe
that scholarly usages of this important category are more closely intertwined with everyday meanings of the term than we usually recognize.
They often rely on unexamined and untenable assumptions about the
nature of emotion, and intermittent slides into condemnation or celebration undermine their analytic value. They rarely compare the various meanings of the term in various fields. We need to move on from
arguments for and against sentimentality, and even from interpretations of sentimentality, to the task of conceptualizing it as a transdisci-
plinary object of study. This chapter aims to outline an understanding
of sentimentality that is broad, critical, and coherent.

Although it has become clear that it is time to vacate the discourse of
judgment that has characterized so much work on sentimentality, that
has not proved easy to do—in any field, but particularly in the one from
which I begin, American literary history. The terms of what Laura
Wexler calls the "Douglas-Tompkins debate" (9) are familiar there,
but perhaps not to readers from other disciplines. To put it briefly, do
the popular novels published by women in the mid-nineteenth century represent, as argued by Ann Douglas in *The Feminization of American Culture*, a fall from tough-minded, community-oriented Calvin-
ism into "rancid," individualistic emotionalism—the beginnings of a
debased mass consumer culture that has swallowed up what was most
valuable in American literature and thought (256)? Or do they constitute, as argued by Jane Tompkins in *Sensational Designs*, a complex
and effective affirmation of women's power, a grassroots antipatriar-
chal politics? Douglas and Tompkins do much more than take sides, of
course; both of them pay serious and sustained attention to sentimental fiction, treating it as culturally powerful and historically resonant.
So do other contributions to the discussion.[3] Richard Brodhead adds
a new dimension with his reading of the now-classic novels of Stowe
and Warner as key documents of a middle-class regime of socialization through coercive love that he calls "disciplinary intimacy." Wexler
goes on from her discussion of the critical tradition to analysis of the
cultural work of domestic fiction in terms of race as well as gender and
class. Karen Sánchez-Eppler places women's antislavery fiction in rhetorical and political context and produces a striking account of its phenomenology that I draw on later in this chapter. "Reading sentimental

fiction is," she writes, "a bodily act," and the way words produce "pulse beats and sobs . . . radically contracts the distance between narrated events and the moment of their reading, as the feelings in the story are made tangibly present in the flesh of the reader. . . . [T]ears designate a border realm between the story and its reading, since the tears shed by characters initiate an answering moistness in the reader's eye" (26–27).

Shirley Samuels's 1992 collection *The Culture of Sentiment*, in which Wexler's and Sánchez-Eppler's essays appear, embodies the richness of the work produced by the contest of interpretations over sentimentality. The volume's profusion of uncollated claims also, however, demonstrates the difficulty of the field. And its contributors, particularly the literary critics, relapse with some regularity into the terms of the Douglas-Tompkins debate. Here and elsewhere, essays still argue the question of whether sentimentality is complicit with or subversive of dominant ideology; even the plausible suggestion that it might be both is a maneuver within received perspectives. The authors sometimes seem embarrassed by or defensive about their object of study, engaged in either disavowal or identification. Judith Fetterley's 1994 warning that the historicizing turn may be another way of marginalizing nineteenth-century women's writing at once observes and demonstrates the persistence of the debate: "I am struck by what I see as an asymmetry in certain recent work, the disproportionately negative as opposed to positive assessment of these writers. *The Culture of Sentiment*, for example, . . . noteworthy for the seriousness of attention and engagement it represents, includes a number of essays that seek to present 'sentimentalism' as a complex mixture of positive and negative qualities and effects, but it does not balance essentially negative assessments such as Laura Wexler's . . . with essentially positive assessments." In Fetterley's view the volume includes "a position similar to that articulated by Douglas in *The Feminization of American Culture*" but excludes Tompkins's; and Brodhead's inclusion of women writers in his influential renarration of American literary history merely "serves as the occasion for orchestrating their redismissal" (607–8). Subsequent work has drawn on new perspectives, but often without a decisive break from the old. It has been peculiarly difficult to transform the terms of the discussion.

To resist positions "for" and "against" sentimentality, affirming with Lora Romero that "the politics of culture reside in local formulations . . . rather than in some essential and ineluctable political tendency inhering within them" (7–8), is not to say that the form has no specifiable social meanings. Indeed, it is so full of meanings that we cannot escape the debate simply by recognizing it as a closed circle and announcing its end; we need (as Romero suggests) to study its persistence, investigate its terms, and lift ourselves by the bootstraps into a different discussion. Similarly, it would not clarify much if I were to advocate some purification of terminology—in effect entering yet another version of sentimentality into the field of competition. Rather, what I am after is a description, at a fairly high level of abstraction, of what we are doing when we call something sentimental. Any tidy, prescriptive definition would obscure the way usages of the term bundle heterogeneous elements together and manifest its deep roots and ramified connections. In what follows I refer to vernacular as well as expert understandings in order to show what they have in common as well as what divides them; and I move recursively between theoretical and historical arguments because disaggregating the elements of sentimentality entails both sorting out the logic of claims and tracing changes over time. Complex, culturally powerful categories of this sort are inevitably conglomerates; just what sort of mixed bag is sentimentality?

Answering this question entails my most extended movement away from the historical moment of *The Whole Family*, and from the disciplinary reference point of literary history. I discuss investigations of emotions and social life by scholars working separately in fields ranging from neurobiology to anthropology to history, to revise our perspective on emotion itself; I suggest that the link between sentiment and eighteenth-century notions of sympathy and sensibility should be reclaimed; and I argue that we should make a systematic distinction between sentiment and nineteenth-century domestic ideology, and reconstruct the history of their imbrication. The topic of sentimentality proves to refract, in terms of form, many of the same issues that have concerned me so far; and when I return at the end of the chapter to the collaborative novel, the results of my investigation prove to make a considerable difference in reading it, both helping us to link the authors

and their choices to literary history and alerting us to the significance
of textual details.

Embodied Thoughts

One element never missing from the combinations that constitute
sentimentality is an association with emotion. In stigmatizing usages,
whether vernacular or expert, the emotion involved is characterized as
either affected and shallow or as excessive. In Douglas's account it is
both—a suggestion less contradictory than it seems because counter-
feit emotion may be feigned but is more commonly exaggerated. What
is at stake is authenticity: the spontaneity, the sincerity, and the legitimacy of an emotion are understood to be the same. This equivalence
underpins commentary by defenders as well; Joanne Dobson, for example, argues that sentimental literature can be "an authentic mode of
expressing valid human experience" (175). And it is striking how often
one encounters, in the midst of a critical essay that takes a generally
favorable view of women's literature, a sentence in which sentimentality is implicitly contrasted with raw, real emotion.

Habits of mind based on an opposition between manipulated sentiment and genuine emotion are, in fact, deeply inconsistent with the
social constructionism currently prevailing in the humanities. Yet each
of us is a layperson as well as an expert, and according to the common sense of the modern world, feelings well up naturally inside individuals—tropes of interiority and self-expression are difficult to resist.
Everyday language also has neutral ways of indicating shaped emotion,
of course. When speaking out on a public controversy or making a toast
at a retirement dinner, one can acknowledge that one's "sentiments"
about the topic or occasion are organized in advance, and combine
thinking and feeling, without necessarily being considered insincere or
incapable of rigorous reasoning. One can respectably admit that an object is treasured because it reflexively provokes memory and emotion;
it has "sentimental value." However, admitting such a sensation always
carries the possibility of embarrassment, just as critics who find sentimentality appealing are haunted by its vulnerability to accusations of
banality and inauthenticity. What we see in these usages taken together

is that *sentiment* and its derivatives indicate a moment when emotion is *recognized* as socially constructed.

A definition offered by Steven Gordon in a volume endeavoring to bring together sociology and psychology makes an unpejorative distinction between them that resembles the vernacular usages described above: "I define a sentiment as a socially constructed pattern of sensations, expressive gestures, and cultural meanings organized around a relationship to a social object, usually another person. . . . Most of a culture's vocabulary of named affective states are sentiments rather than emotions" (566). This formulation does not raise questions of authenticity; in fact, the processes by which culture crafts feelings are precisely what interest Gordon and others in the relatively new field of the sociology of emotions. But the opposition between sentiment and emotion is still correlated with an opposition between the social and the natural. Once again, the argument depends on a category—emotion—that is left outside the analysis, taken for granted as a fundamental attribute of human beings.

Many anthropologists and psychologists have seen emotion as a natural phenomenon and have worked from that assumption whether or not they tried to explain the mechanisms through which nature works. But over the past fifteen years an impressive body of work in those fields and various interdisciplines has challenged that view, sometimes in terms closely related to cultural studies. One of the most thought-provoking texts is Michelle Rosaldo's early, influential call for "an anthropology of self and feeling," in which she argues that "feeling is forever given shape through thought and . . . thought is laden with emotional meaning. . . . [W]hat distinguishes thought and affect, differentiating a 'cold' cognition from a 'hot,' is fundamentally a sense of the engagement of the actor's self. Emotions are thoughts somehow 'felt' in flushes, pulses, 'movements' of our livers, minds, hearts, stomachs, skin. They are *embodied* thoughts, thoughts seeped with the apprehension that 'I am involved'" (143). This statement is so powerful because it persuasively addresses not only anthropology, not only social science broadly conceived, but also commonsense understandings of emotion. It meshes intricately with literary critics' emphasis on tears as part of sentimental reading as well (see Sánchez-Eppler; Warhol). In Rosaldo's account, however, both the social and the bodily nature of sentimentality characterize emotion in general.

In their introduction to *Language and the Politics of Emotion*, a collection that demonstrates how quickly anthropologists have moved in the direction Rosaldo suggested, Catherine Lutz and Lila Abu-Lughod characterize most anthropological work before 1980 as essentializing, treating emotions as "things internal, irrational, natural." They advocate abandoning the search for "psychobiological" constants underlying locally variable particulars and functionalist explanations of how different social systems manage emotions in favor of "contextualizing": analyzing specific social situations to demonstrate how "emotion gets its meaning and force from its location and performance in public discourse," and how social life is affected by emotion discourse. Their approach not only challenges naturalizing assumptions and construes emotion as social rather than individual and internal but also brings them very close to the concerns of literary studies. The notion of "discourse," explicated with references to Saussure and Foucault, is at its center.[4]

In the field of psychology as well a strong interest in "the cultural factors that contribute to the shaping and the working of human emotions" has emerged, with categories such as narrative and "emotion scripts" that point toward the realm of literature figuring prominently (Kitayama and Markus 1). Cultural studies, as an investigation of "the subjective side of social relations," would do well to begin to take heed of such empirical explorations (Johnson 43). Reading (for example) Anna Wierzbicka's account of the affective lexicons of Americans and Poles, learning that in Polish to reply to a compliment by saying "thank you" is potentially offensive (because it treats the remark not as a spontaneous observation but as expressing a desire to please, and therefore might be seen as accusing the speaker of insincerity), can renew one's appreciation of the defamiliarizing power of cross-cultural comparison.

And as social scientists pay more attention to language, humanists may want to reconsider the possibility that components of emotion are "demonstrably hardwired" (Kitayama and Markus 1); Phoebe Ellsworth points out that a comprehensive survey of psychological research yields "abundant evidence for both culturally specific and universal emotional processes" (25). Any experience or examination of the body is mediated by discourse, but that does not mean that literal bodies should be ignored altogether. While anthropologist Arjun Appadurai points out that "emotions have a linguistic life and a public and political status that frequently engender formulaic modes of expression," he also emphasizes that "emotions, unlike other phenomena, appear to have a basis in embodied experience, thus inclining us to see them as rooted in some elementary biophysical repertoire that is both limited and universal. To ignore completely this second aspect of emotion is to run the risk of deconstructing emotion altogether as a distinctive phenomenon to be investigated" (92).

Some current empirical research into the physiology of mental life is extraordinarily suggestive. For example, in *Descartes' Error,* neurologist Antonio Damasio provides a lucid and detailed explanation of how subjectivity can be understood as a "perpetually re-created neurobiological state," with identity depending on the continuous reactivation of two sets of representations: one of memories and one (constantly updated) of body states. He shows the brain as continuously responsive, along multiple channels, to neural and chemical signals from various body systems, a kind of "captive audience" of the body; as he puts it, the "mind is embodied, in the full sense of the term, not just embrained." That self is the ground of all mental activity, and there can be, on Damasio's account, no such thing as selfless or wholly unemotional reason. Feelings, the cognitions most closely linked to body landscapes, are woven into mental activity at every stage. To use Rosaldo's metaphor, some cognitions are cool in comparison to others, but none are at absolute zero. Indeed, Damasio cites clinical and experimental evidence to show that individuals with impaired affect also show impaired decision making; lack of emotion causes people to behave foolishly.[5]

Congenial as the implications of such research might seem to be for feminist epistemology (for example), only extended interdisciplinary collaboration can build a middle ground on which evidence of such different sorts could be melded. And only on such a landscape can we respond appropriately to work like Paul Ekman's on the cross-cultural recognizability of facial expressions, or Robert Zajonc's on how the action of facial muscles that produce expressions may actually create subjective sensations by altering blood temperatures in the brain (see

Ellsworth; Zajonc and McIntosh). Only such collaboration will allow us to avoid either naturalizing by claiming that physiology entails particular experiential or behavioral consequences, or rejecting evidence because it conflicts with our social constructionist convictions, so that we can study how such physiological processes might enter variably into cultural processes. This prospective intellectual landscape is hard to imagine partly because such research is rarely available in expositions as accessible to humanists as *Descartes' Error.* It contributes to the difficulty that literary scholarship has, in Neal Oxenhandler's formulation, "no thoroughgoing affective criticism as such. Although emotive terms serve to locate certain crucially sensitive areas in the reading process, they themselves have never become the locus of a sustained theoretical account" (105). As Oxenhandler notes, however, literary scholars' interest in the topic has increased markedly; and our resources are constantly being increased both by the work in the social and biological sciences I have already mentioned and by the new field of emotion history (see Stearns and Lewis for an overview). The study of emotion offers dauntingly broad, but broadly encouraging, prospects.

What are the consequences of these explorations for understanding sentimentality within the horizon of literary and cultural studies? Definitions that rely on judgments of authenticity or inauthenticity are decisively undermined. Beyond that, neither the socially constructed nor the bodily nature of sentiment can serve to distinguish it from emotion in general. Rather, expert ascriptions of sentimentality—like vernacular remarks—tend to mark moments when the discursive processes that construct emotion become visible. Many usages of the term are of this order, indicating that the conventionalized quality of some affective response has been noted without implying strong or systematic distinctions among artifacts or situations that evoke emotion.

Even this relatively modest clarification has benefits. It moves us out of the terms of the Douglas-Tompkins debate into a less judgmental mode, making it clear that characterizing something as sentimental should open, not close, a conversation. Still, we need to go on to explain why sentimentality should be judged negatively; neither the assumption that emotions are natural nor the generalized cultural prescription of emotional control is sufficient to explain the hostility it provokes.[6] I would suggest further that the social construction of emotion often becomes visible when different attitudes about what sensations are appropriate in a given situation—what sociologist Arlie Hochschild calls "feeling rules"—clash. At such moments affective experience is put into question, and no longer seems inevitable, as one chooses whether to yield to an emotion or to resist it. Sentimentality is condemned so vehemently in part because its critics feel implicated in it (as Douglas indeed avows she does). So, too, sentimentality, although not always stigmatized, is always suspect, always questionable; the appearance of the term marks a site where values are contested. We need now to examine the nature of that contest and consider why a particular range of emotions calls up the term when others do not: no use of horror-movie conventions, however stylized, is ever described as sentimental. We are left with the task of analyzing a particular set of emotion scripts, in the midst of ever-widening conversations about the history of emotions and social life.

Feeling Right

A comprehensive view of sentiment cannot begin later than the eighteenth century. Critics of earlier generations routinely nodded to the British origins of sentimentalism. More recently most Americanists have neglected the transatlantic and philosophical antecedents of the form. I want to argue, against the prevailing assumptions of the Douglas-Tompkins debate and subsequent scholarship, that there is a strong relationship between Enlightenment notions of moral sentiments and sympathy, and nineteenth- and twentieth-century sentimentalism. Recognizing that link both recovers an important history and helps us to understand the significance of contemporary usages.

Philosophers such as Lord Shaftesbury, Francis Hutcheson, Adam Smith, and Jean-Jacques Rousseau derive benevolence and, ultimately, morality in general from human faculties that dispose us to sympathize with others. For these thinkers, emotions, whether themselves innate or produced by Lockean psychology, assume a central place in moral thought—they both lead to and manifest virtue. Contemporary philosopher Charles Taylor explains that on this view sentiment matters "because it is in a certain way the touchstone of the morally good. Not because feeling that something is good makes it so . . . but rather because undistorted, normal feeling is my way of access into the design of things, which is the real constitutive good, determining good and bad" (284). The natural goodness of humanity (affirmed with varying degrees of conviction) is visible most directly in our sensations of compassion; and the goodness of God is visible in the implanting of such faculties in humanity.

Taylor's work provides an expansive and thought-provoking framework for assessing the significance of these developments. In *Sources of the Self* he proposes an intellectual history—ranging from Plato and Augustine through Nietzsche and Lyotard—of the sense of deeply resonant interiority that is fundamental to modern identity and of how selves are (in his view) inescapably oriented by the moral sources they acknowledge. The eighteenth-century moral philosophers occupy an important place in the process by which moral sources are relocated inward and by which ordinary life comes to be affirmed as profoundly valuable. The latter view, Taylor points out, is as obvious as we tend to assume—the record of ancient and medieval thought more often shows some sphere of activity, whether that of the warrior or the philosopher, as intrinsically higher than the everyday. The affirmation of everyday life sustains what is virtually a moral consensus in the modern world on the values of justice and benevolence: we may not agree about why it is so or what it would mean to live up to this standard, but we believe that inflicting suffering is wrong and that relieving suffering is good, perhaps even imperative.

The notion of "sentiment" as used in eighteenth-century texts is a crucial element of this modern moral identity. It coordinates complex recognitions of the power of bodily sensations (including emotions), the possibilities of feeling distant from or connected with other human beings, and benevolence as a defining human virtue. A memorable passage from the opening of Adam Smith's *Theory of Moral Sentiments* binds these elements together to conjure a resolution of the dilemma posed by the increasingly individualist topography of the self:

> As we have no immediate experience of what other men feel, we can form
> no idea of the manner in which they are affected, but by conceiving what
> we ourselves should feel in the like situation. Though our brother is upon

the rack, as long as we ourselves are at our ease, our senses will never inform us of what he suffers. They never did, and never can, carry us beyond our own person, and it is by the imagination only that we can form any conception of what are his sensations. Neither can that faculty help us to this any other way, than by representing to us what would be our own, if we were in his case. It is the impressions of our own senses only, not those of his, which our imaginations copy. By the imagination we place ourselves in his situation, we conceive ourselves enduring all the same torments, we enter as it were into his body, and become in some measure the same person with him, and thence form some idea of his sensations, and even feel something which, though weaker in degree, is not altogether unlike them. (9)

Smith both recognizes the social and relational character of emotions and focuses on discrete subjectivity—so closely and productively that he is virtually producing the deep interior self.[7] The vicariousness so often criticized in sentimentality is here seen more neutrally as one of its structural elements. The emotion in question is precisely one felt as an identification with another.

The imagination plays a central role in Smith's scenario for sympathy. So it is not surprising that reading was seen as a way to cultivate improving, morally legitimizing emotions. Indeed, the extensive English literature of sensibility—Mackenzie's *The Man of Feeling* (1771) is the most programmatic example, but the works of Richardson and Sterne are better known—complements the moral philosophers' expositions. Again, it is not surprising that the wide circulation of these narratives provoked the deflating impulse visible in such works as Fielding's *Shamela* and (more complexly) Austen's *Sense and Sensibility. Sentimentality* itself originates in the reaction against the elevation of emotional sensitivity to the status of a moral touchstone. Janet Todd tells us that it "came in as a pejorative term in the 1770's when the idea of sensibility was losing ground"; and that although the adjective "sentimental" has been used more variously, "by 1800 its use was commonly pejorative" (8, 9). The celebratory and the stigmatizing views of sentiment thus arose together.

The trope of the moral sentiment has exerted substantial, although never uncontested, influence in both vernacular thought and literary practice from its moment of origin through the nineteenth century to the present day. Two hundred years later, seemingly casual references may still rely in some detail on the tradition linking sympathy and virtue. Take, for example, the usages of the word *sentimental* in the 1995 movie *Outbreak*. The main plot of the movie concerns the fight of a dedicated military doctor, Col. Sam Daniels (played by Dustin Hoffman), against a strain of hemorrhagic fever with a mortality rate of 100 percent. His efforts to stop an outbreak in the United States are impeded by the powerful General McClintock (Donald Sutherland), who is protecting the secret that this virus is part of an illegal American arsenal of biological weapons. The outcome and the moral drama of the film pivot on the dilemma faced by Daniels's immediate commander, Gen. Billy Ford (Morgan Freeman). For Daniels, relieving suffering is an absolute moral imperative; saving lives threatened by this gruesome and apocalyptic disease justifies any form of insubordination up to and including defying direct orders. His insistence on traveling to the site of the outbreak himself and his reproach to Ford—"Why aren't you *there*, Billy?"—demonstrate his reliance on a psychology of sympathy in which benevolence derives from actually *seeing* others endure the torments of the disease. (My echo of Smith's language here is deliberate.) McClintock, on the other hand, asks Ford to think about long-term risks and benefits for national security, to keep his distance and use instrumental logic rather than follow his heart. When Ford is swayed by his friendship for Daniels and his spontaneous sympathy for the suffering citizens of Cabin Creek, California, what McClintock does is, precisely, to call him sentimental—at no fewer than three key moments. "More of your sentimental bullshit, Billy?" is, despite appearances to the contrary, a highly resonant remark.[8] And although McClintock invokes the pejorative sense the term has had throughout its history, for such an obviously evil character to use *sentimental* as an accusation implicitly aligns the category with the more sympathetic characters who save the day. What the evidence of *Outbreak* shows is not only that these ideas have entered our common sense, but that they have entered as a group.

Antisentimentalism has sometimes occluded recognition of the tradition's influence in literature. Yet, as Fred Kaplan has shown, the English Victorians continued to draw directly and deeply on moral philosophy; Dickens is sentimental in a much more precise sense than usually acknowledged. Across the Atlantic, Herbert Ross Brown's once-definitive study *The Sentimental Novel in America 1789–1850* clearly marks the form's philosophical and British roots but treats the connection as dismissively as the novels.[9] Intellectual historians have delineated the immense influence in antebellum America of Adam Smith's inheritors, the Scottish Common Sense philosophers, and Gregg Camfield has extended that work to show the direct influence of that body of thought on Harriet Beecher Stowe, and its usefulness in understanding Mark Twain. *Uncle Tom's Cabin*'s famous injunction to the reader to "feel right" marks a moment when the relationship between those ideas and antebellum American sentimental fiction was close to the surface. Yet most contemporary critics make no reference to the link. For example, Joanne Dobson's fine 1997 analysis of the specifically literary qualities of sentimental writing defines the form in terms of "human connectedness" (268) without ever mentioning moral philosophy.[10]

Philip Fisher is one critic who both links American sentimental fiction to eighteenth-century European thought—specifically, to Rousseau—and suggests that it changes our common sense. He argues that *Uncle Tom's Cabin* helps to install "new habits of moral perception" in which children and slaves are human and their fate matters—so effectively that "it accomplishes, as a last step, the forgetting of its own strenuous work so that what are newly learned habits are only remembered as facts" (4). Although Fisher makes no reference to the Douglas-Tompkins debate, he shares its evaluative framework, endorsing sentimentalism's democratizing and deploring its pacifying tendencies. An awareness of feminist scholarship indeed might have qualified Fisher's thoroughly celebratory view of sympathy for "the weak and the helpless" (95) and his uncritical view of the family as "throughout human history . . . the only social model for the relations between non-equal members of a society" (102). Compare the essay by Laura Wexler already cited, "Tender Violence," which links sentimental family values to nineteenth-century interracial boarding schools' drastic intervention into Native American kinship and household systems. The same common sense made it obvious that "savage" emotions and "barbaric" domestic arrangements were in need of reform; thus sentimentalism, on Wexler's account, "supplied the rationale for raw intolerance to be packaged as education" (17).

Recovering the connections between sentiment and eighteenth-century sympathy and sensibility allows us to read Wexler's essay less as a continuation of Douglas's hostility to the form than as a contribution to the broad project of historicizing benevolence. The growing power of the view that slavery is obviously evil was part of what Thomas Haskell calls the "unprecedented wave of humanitarian reform [that] swept through the societies of Western Europe, England, and North America in the hundred years following 1750." As he points out, "twentieth-century historians have not been satisfied to attribute those reforms . . . to an advance in man's moral sense or . . . a random outburst of altruism," but rather have linked them to "the growth of capitalism and the beginnings of industrialization. . . . We know now that the reformers were motivated by far more than an unselfish desire to help the downtrodden, and we see more clearly now why their reforms went no farther and took the particular form they did" (339–40). One line of analysis has examined how reforms served the interest of the bourgeoisie. Haskell chooses another (which I consider complementary, not contradictory), examining changes "in *perception* or *cognitive style*" (342). Participation in the market entailed attending to the remote consequences of one's actions; thus it "expanded the range of causal perception and inspired people's confidence in their power to intervene in the course of events" (556)—necessary presuppositions to the humanitarian view that failing to aid a suffering stranger is a wrongful act.

Haskell argues that the lived experience of capitalist social relations led to new habits of causal attribution. Jean-Cristophe Agnew also suggests that it produced a preoccupation with sympathy—but as a way of affirming connectedness in the face of anxiety over the potentially antagonistic reciprocity of commercial transactions and the dangerous fluidity of identity in a world of commodities. In his study of the intimate intertwining of Anglo-American understandings of markets and theaters in the fifteenth through the eighteenth centuries, Agnew argues that for Adam Smith (who was, after all, the author of *The Wealth of Nations* as well as *The Theory of Moral Sentiments*), "fellow-feeling was . . . a mark of the immense distance that separated individual minds rather than a sign of their commonality" (178). Thus not only the vicariousness of sympathy but its implication in a system of production for profit can be identified in this early moment; feelings are, precisely, exchanged. And we can turn to other scholars who, although working on quite disparate materials, have arrived at strikingly congruent accounts of the theater of self and other emerging in this long transition. For example, Jay Fliegelman's contextual reading of the American Declaration of Independence finds "a dialectical relation between the authority of impersonality rooted in the discourse of descriptive science and the authority of sincerity rooted in the discourse of affective experience" (129). Mary Louise Pratt argues in her study of English and European travel literature from 1750 that "science and sentiment" are the "clashing and complementary languages of bourgeois subjectivity" (39). In each case sentimentality plays a key role in suturing the self into new social relations. Fliegelman is describing a world in which particular persons no longer have automatic claims to authority, in which "the claim that sentimental readers constituted (or should constitute) a new moral elite" (62) is being advanced. Pratt shows late eighteenth-century sentimentality as a mode of living colonial relations: "In both travel writing and imaginative literature, the domestic subject of empire found itself enjoined to share new passions, to identify with expansion in a new way, through empathy with individual victim-heroes and heroines" (87). These are influential scholars, yet Americanists writing about sentimentality rarely cite them (nor, for that matter, do they cite each other).

Only a long, broad view of sentimentality makes it possible to see how many scholars' work contributes to the construction of this object of study, for we are investigating the development of modern subjectivities in their intricate imbrication with belief systems and social structures. Our horizon ought to include not only Taylor's sources of the self but also Norbert Elias's "civilizing process." The salience of race not only in "Tender Violence" and *The Culture of Sentiment* but also in a high proportion of recent criticism of sentimentality meshes smoothly into this perspective, as increasingly colonialism is taken to be not merely contemporary with, but integral to the emergence of modernity. An extraordinary efflorescence of work pivoting on reconceptualizations of race and nation undoes the misrecognition of racism as a premodern prejudice, an individual or institutional survival soon to be meliorated by the progress of liberal thought. Rather, we see Enlightenment reason as itself racialized (as in the work of David Theo Goldberg) and the European bourgeois self as articulated on an imperial landscape (as in the work of Ann Stoler). The articulated themes of this work are exclusion, distinction, and the fear of contagion as often as they are benevolence and empathy; but the common object of study is the drama of charged connection. In Peter Hulme's memorable formulation, "Sentimental sympathy began to flow out along the arteries of European commerce in search of its victims" (229).

On this large landscape, a debate over whether a genre (let alone a novel) is conservative or progressive sounds thin and reductive indeed. The critical edge of the conversation is not lost but redirected to defamiliarize contemporary values as the ritual disavowal of sentimentality never could. Empathy is valorized as predictably as sentimentality is stigmatized; Gloria Steinem has even referred in the *New York Times Book Review* to a novel's challenging "men to turn toward women that most revolutionary of all emotions, empathy" (47). Compare Stephen Greenblatt's comment that modernization theorist Daniel Lerner may be right to consider empathy as characteristically (not exclusively) Western but errs in seeing it as "an act of imaginative generosity, a sympathetic appreciation of the situation of the other fellow. For when he speaks confidently of the 'spread of empathy around the world,' we must understand that he is speaking of the exercise of Western power, power that is creative as well as destructive, but that is scarcely ever wholly disinterested or benign" (61). I do not claim that empathy is intrinsically inauthentic or automatically iniquitous any more than I would agree that it is invariably admirable or provides uniformly reliable knowledge of the other.[11] Rather, empathy and sympathy have different politics at different moments, and at any given moment are likely to have mixed and complicated politics; they constitute specific, historical relationships.

One more consequence of this long view remains to be articulated. So far in this account, sentimentality has been at least as strongly linked with men as with women. Indeed, I have avoided foregrounding gender in these two sections of the chapter in the hope of evoking at this point a vivid sense of how novel and remarkable it is that by the mid-nineteenth century sentimentality was seen as feminine. By the late twentieth century, Steinem does not need to specify that men in particular need to be challenged to exercise empathy; everyone "knows" that women are the more sympathetic and emotional sex. How did this happen? The scholarship to which one turns for an answer requires us to come to terms with the category of domesticity, which historians and literary scholars alike use in close association with—often more prominently than—sentimentality.

Home Sweet Home

An unremarked elision between *sentimental* and *domestic* is the source of much confusion in contemporary criticism. We have paid little attention to the slippage from Jane Tompkins's "sentimental power" to Mary Kelley's "literary domestics," from Laura Wexler's account of the debate over sentimentality to her subtitle's reference to "domestic fiction." Domesticity is the category foregrounded in feminist research that has achieved a rich reconstruction of American women's lives in past eras and of gender ideologies. And women's history is certainly indispensable for any understanding of sentimentality. Yet too many literary critics writing about women authors rely on a static and dated conception of "separate spheres."[12] The correlation of the binaries masculine/feminine and public/private is precisely what we need to explain; taking it as an answer rather than a question leaves us only the choice between celebrating and protesting the arrangement, and thus directs us back into the closed circle of the debate. This shift has begun, as evidenced in Cathy Davidson's 1998 special issue of *American Literature* titled "No More Separate Spheres!", but it is by no means firmly established. We need a close, critical engagement with scholarship that examines how subjective life and social life are remapped into the modern configuration. And we cannot understand how sentimentality and domestic ideology figure in the process, and become so thoroughly intertwined, unless we distinguish between them.

One of the most radical arguments for the constitutive status of gendered identity in modernity, and the constitutive role of fiction in creating that identity, has been made by literary critic Nancy Armstrong. Drawing her evidence from conduct books and novels of the eighteenth-century English milieu, she writes in *Desire and Domestic Fiction* (1987) that "a modern, gendered form of subjectivity developed first as a feminine discourse in certain literature for women. . . . The gendering of human identity provided the metaphysical girders of modern culture — its reigning mythology" (14). The rise of the domestic woman is "a major event in political history" (3) because it was (in Armstrong's view) middle-class women who, by redefining virtue and desirability, first seized power from the aristocracy. For Armstrong the whole modern order — including class and state hegemonies — depends on the socializing practices of the home and school, and the naturalized division of social life into the spheres of domestic woman and economic man that they originate. Her claims are (she says in so many words [26]) overstated, but they were an effective riposte to the neglect of women, gender, and culture in then-prevailing accounts of modernization.

Social historians of the United States run the lines of causality in the other direction, although work published in the 1980s and after shows the gathering effect of the cultural turn. Their story begins with the shift away from household production, which separated the daily and generational work of reproducing human life from waged work and profit-oriented production outside the home. Yet here as well the rise of the middle class, the elaboration of domestic ideology, and the re-mapping of a world formerly organized by kinship relations into separate public and private realms are inextricably connected. Mary Ryan's original and influential community study *Cradle of the Middle Class* (1981) argues through close examination of a single county in New York state between 1790 and 1865 that "the American middle class molded its distinctive identity around domestic values and family practices" (15). Stuart Blumin's subsequent study of American urban experience over a longer period, *The Emergence of the Middle Class* (1989), also makes the ideal of domesticity central in the self-definition of a class formed both by the convergence of daily experience and by emerging lines of distinction between the respectable middle and (on one side) elites and (on the other) manual laborers. In each case print culture is assigned an important role in the process; and Ryan's description of the internal dynamics of the Victorian family, in which "love had vanquished force and authority, the female had replaced the male, in the social relations of child-rearing" (159), is in turn an important source for Richard Brodhead's account of "disciplinary intimacy."

It has long been common for literary scholars to invoke this history by referring to the nineteenth-century "cult of domesticity" or "Cult of True Womanhood." The 1966 article by Barbara Welter that proposed the latter category distills a prescriptive ideal of piety, purity, submissiveness, and domesticity from images of women in magazine fiction and conduct books. The essay was original and valuable in its moment, and those virtues undoubtedly figured in the thinking and practice of the period; but it was never a comprehensive account of attitudes, let alone of behavior, and the accuracy of Welter's description even on its own terms has since been challenged.[13] Its persisting influence marks literary critics' proclivity to use historical claims in isolation from their contested and rapidly changing contexts in scholarship. Lines of analysis that stress the positive or negative consequences of domesticity for women, and parallel the Douglas-Tompkins debate, can be traced in women's history. Yet more than ten years ago Linda Kerber was treating the dominance of the separate spheres model as a thing of the past, writing in a review essay that its language "was vulnerable to sloppy use. . . . When they used the metaphor of separate spheres, historians referred, often interchangeably, to an ideology *imposed on* women, a culture *created by* women, a set of boundaries *expected to be observed* by women" (17); they also, she points out, focused primarily on white middle-class women and neglected questions of race and class. The field has since moved on to show how the "separate" sphere of women is inextricably and dynamically part of social life as a whole.

Karen Halttunen's cultural history *Confidence Men and Painted Women* (1982) is neither very recent nor wholly ignored by critics, but its contribution to clarifying the relation of sentiment and domesticity is still substantially unrecognized.[14] Using some materials similar to Welter's but also including attention to such practices as funerals and parlor theatricals, Halttunen describes American middle-class culture in the mid-nineteenth century specifically as a sentimental culture. An expanding market economy in an urbanizing nation created a "world of strangers" in which social identity seemed dangerously fluid (a world

that seems a quite logical development of the consequences of commodification that Agnew describes for an earlier period). Yet by showing that they sincerely felt right, "the socially ambitious could demonstrate that they were not mere confidence men and painted women
'passing' as genteel, but were true ladies and gentlemen deserving of
the higher social place to which they aspired" (xvi–xvii). Halttunen's
analysis gives shape and texture to social practices based on a "sentimental typology of conduct, the belief that every aspect of social
behavior should transparently display the contents of the heart." The
theory of moral sentiments and the scripts of sensibility were trans-
lated into a set of rules for demonstrating sincerity, rules that pre-
scribed matters as specific as "what kind of bonnet a woman should
wear, when a man should remove his glove to shake hands, and how
men and women should shed tears over their dead" (60).

Once these forms of emotional expression are codified, they para-
doxically become a performance. Halttunen shows that by the 1850s
this theatricality had been accepted; the irony of her story is that
through the demand for sincerity, adherence to a set of forms becomes
in itself a sufficient marker of class distinction. Yet the home remains
a site of legitimized emotion and the focus of an intensely emotional
valorization. Both as a place and as an image, the domestic realm is
saturated with feelings. It is easy to observe in the contemporary print
media, in fact, that reprinted snapshots of people in their homes, and
especially with their families, evoke an imaginative leap of connectedness more easily than formal portraits or pictures in official settings
do. The identification takes place *through* the ideology of the family: to
see that the victims of a disaster are mourned by spouses and children,
to realize that even the perpetrator of a horrifying crime was once a
child and has a mother, is to be interpellated in a common humanity.
Judith Williamson comments, "Queen Victoria was the first monarch
to realize the marvelous ideological opportunities offered by photography and insisted on always being photographed as a wife and mother,
rather than a ruler. Photography . . . [provided] a form of representation which cut across classes, disguised social differences, and produced
a sympathy of the exploited with their exploiters. It could make all families look more or less alike" (238). The confluence of associations binds
sentiment and domesticity untidily but powerfully together.

Ironically, sentimentality—first framed as a mode of embodied thought that enabled connection and entailed humanitarian concern for others—was enlisted in the service of an ideology that still affirmed the value of ordinary life but tended to concentrate caring into the relatively narrow confines of middle-class families. By the end of the nineteenth century the sacralization of domesticity had helped to erode commitment to friendship and civic responsibilities so much that those seemed like secondary virtues at best. One might argue that it legitimized and even glorified indifference to the welfare of the wider community at the same time that the home was beginning to appear less as a site of spiritual education and more as a site of consumption and display (see Coontz, *The Way We Never Were* 101–15). Yet the impulse to extend the benefits of the civilized hearth also demonstrates how recursively sentiment and domesticity are filiated; what Wexler's "Tender Violence" shows in the boarding schools that trained African American and Indian children for service in middle-class homes is precisely the convergence of coercive sympathy and domestic ideology.

Women had a special role in sentimental culture; they were the keepers of the intimate and trusting realm of domesticity, and the parlor, which constituted the middle ground between the family circle and the dangerous, impersonal public world, was defined as theirs too (Halttunen 56–59). Yet in Halttunen's—as in Ryan's and Blumin's—accounts of this system, there were clearly defined expectations of men as well. That is often forgotten as we read the twentieth century's overwhelming identification of women and domesticity back into earlier periods. Armstrong, for example, critiques the notion of separate spheres for obscuring the importance of the domestic woman in social life as a whole, but simply defines the discourses that produce that formation as feminine and then describes the men who contribute to them as feminized—tautologically assuming the very naturalized classification by gender whose origins she is excavating (16). Similarly, it is no easy matter to avoid showing the system as either "imposed upon" or "created by" women, either constraining or enabling for them. Despite its historical sophistication Brodhead's work falters here; focusing on the power that disciplinary intimacy assigns to the mother, he leaves the distinct impression that middle-class women are its architects, enforcers, and beneficiaries. To avoid dropping back into the debate we must recognize not only that social life as a whole is shaped by the opposition between public and private, but also that the gendering of social spaces has important, particular consequences for *both* men and women, and that men constantly circulate through "women's" sphere. Ronald Zboray's study of the charge records of the New York Society Library in the 1840s and 1850s confirms that men and women did not read wholly different bodies of literature; Laura McCall's content analysis leads to the same conclusion. In short, when we speak of "separate spheres" we are not describing a fact of social life but invoking an organizing pressure within it.

In the history I have been tracing, domesticity appears not just as a middle-class value but as constitutive of the middle class. That does not, of course, mean that members of other groups did or do not love their families and value their homes. The historical actors emerging as the middle class, however, incorporate such sentiments as part of their sense of self-worth and social belonging. An account of the ways middle-class status is maintained against those above and below as an *embodied* respectability could continue into other realms; it entails not only "feeling right" but also chastity and a healthful home. George Mosse has delineated the way in which "decency," from table manners to sexual virtue, defines middle-class morality and comes to be woven into the hegemonic nationalism of modern European nations, and Lynn Wardley suggests that discourses of hygiene and heredity link the physiological subjects of the eighteenth and late nineteenth centuries. The definition of claims to class standing and social authority in essentially moral terms that has recurred throughout this discussion is bound up with the constitutive paradoxes of bourgeois society. By that I mean not so much a society dominated by the bourgeoisie (old elites retain considerable power) as one in which state authority is understood as impersonal and the public and private are understood as separate. On this landscape, kinship in fact progressively declines as an organizing principle of social life, although (as I have said before) neither hereditary rulers nor household production have entirely vanished even in the industrialized West. Claims to membership in the body politic are both universalizing and inescapably particular, and the family takes its modern form as an institution proclaimed as private but of urgent public concern.

In my view, as I have indicated already, the binary opposition of public and private can no longer be an analytic tool. Rather, the distinction is itself an important object of analysis. The current interest in Jürgen Habermas's early work on the public sphere has resulted in a considerably increased circulation for the category "public," often in terms that position the "private" as a sort of remainder category. Yet Habermas's own usage is more distant from the vernacular and more critical. For him the bourgeois public sphere, as an arena in which citizens come together in reasoned discourse about matters of common concern, is defined not against a generalized private sphere but against the state, on the one hand, and the economic marketplace (private, in the sense of "private property"), on the other. Habermas calls the family form that came into existence with the decline of household production "the intimate sphere" and gives it, as "the wellspring of a specific subjectivity," a more prominent place in his account than is usually recognized (43). He writes that the understandings of the utility of reason on which the public sphere depended were "guided specifically by such private experiences as grew out of the audience-oriented [*publikumsbezogen*] subjectivity of the conjugal family's intimate domain [*Intimsphäre*]. Historically, the latter was the source of privateness in the modern sense of a saturated and free interiority" (28). Habermas's image of subjectivity as "originating" in the home, his treatment of the family as the "wellspring" for the selves who populate other spheres, may be seen and criticized as naturalizing. Yet I would argue, following the implication of "*publikumsbezogen*," that *The Structural Transformation of the Public Sphere* may also be read as acknowledging the reciprocity of realms. A subjectivity that "as the innermost core of the private, was always already oriented to an audience" (49) is already in some sense relational and performative. And far from showing a society divided into two spheres, Habermas shows the developing institutions of modernity—especially the family—complexly combining attributes of publicness, privatization, and intimacy.

The tradition of sentimental fiction is an integral part of this history as Habermas tells it. The self-narration of letters, diaries (which he sees as letters "addressed to the sender" [49]), and epistolary novels had developed, by the end of the eighteenth century, "a terrain of subjectivity barely known at its beginning":

The relations between author, work, and public changed. They became intimate mutual relationships between privatized individuals who were psychologically interested in what was "human," in self-knowledge, and in empathy. Richardson wept over the actors in his novels as much as his readers did; author and reader themselves became actors who "talked heart to heart." . . . On the one hand, the empathetic reader repeated within himself the private relationships displayed before him in literature; from his experience of real familiarity [*Intimität*], he gave life to the fictional one, and in the latter he prepared himself for the former. On the other hand, from the outset the familiarity [*Intimität*] whose vehicle was the written word, the subjectivity that had become fit to print, had in fact become the literature appealing to a wide public of readers. The privatized individuals coming together to form a public also reflected critically and in public on what they had read, thus contributing to the process of enlightenment which they together promoted. . . . In an age in which the sale of monthly and weekly journals doubled within a quarter century, as happened in England after 1750, they made it possible for the reading of novels to become customary in the bourgeois strata. (50–51)

Habermas treats literature as a pedagogy of subjectivity, a curriculum of emotion rules, and positions it as a key causal factor in the emergence of modernity. This claim, like the prominence of "print capitalism" in Benedict Anderson's influential account of the origins of nationalism, indexes how thoroughly social theory has incorporated the cultural turn and points toward the paradoxes that at once make sentimentality so central to modern culture, and create the constant urge to dismiss it.

Here we have rejoined Richard Brodhead's account of the domestic culture of letters and Harper's corporate project as I represented it in chapter 2—both place reading at the heart of family life (see fig. 23). That necessarily, uncomfortably, places "print capitalism" and the commodity there too. The intimate sphere is imagined as (in Habermas's phrase) a "domain of pure humanity" (46) sealed off not only from the state but from the marketplace as well. Yet it is, of course, constituted by its relation to that realm and constitutively penetrated by it at every turn. The domestic sphere is also the new world of goods, the very home of consumer culture.[15] And from the earliest examples, sentimental fiction both represented and generated a trade in emotionally laden objects. The intimate address of publicity has only proliferated and amplified since the days of Richardson and Stowe. (One might argue that the television occupies a more central place on more family hearths than the bookshelf ever did—and it certainly advertises even more intensely and extensively.) The stigma on sentimentality, as we have seen, derives in part from the way that recognizably "packaged" feelings remind us of the socially constructed nature of emotion; evidence that emotion is not only conventionalized but circulates through the commodity system on a vast scale can be downright distasteful.[16]

Attitudes toward greeting cards might stand as a metonym for this embarrassment. As a journalist examining the industry writes, "Never mind that we trust Hallmark with our passions, grand and small, at the rate of eight million cards a day; that Americans will buy nearly seven and a half billion cards of all brands this year; that we send more prepackaged sentiment per person than any society on earth save the decorous Brits"—greeting cards and their makers are treated with a sort of "gleeful derision."[17] It is certainly possible to send a sympathy or Mother's Day card without genuine emotion; but imputing inauthenticity to the conventionalized format actually guards against the troubling recognition that such sentimental expressions can also be deeply sincere. Commodity culture circulates right through home and heart.

Both men and women produce and inhabit this world of meanings, but it is divided into gendered realms. These have fuzzy boundaries (women buy 85 percent of greeting cards, according to the article I quote above [27], which casts some new light on that "derision") but strong centers (print commodities like romance novels and women's magazines are clearly specifically addressed to women). Lauren Berlant has written that "popular discourse on women in the second half of the nineteenth century used the expanding cultural resources of industrial capitalism to make women into a 'new' consumer group circulating around a subject addressed, and newly empowered, by a female culture industry" ("Female Woman" 267). Like Armstrong, Berlant sees this foregrounding of gender identity as effacing other contradictions. She recognizes the "rich archive" of testimony about oppression contained in sentimental culture but suggests that its characteristic gesture is a "female complaint" that depends on the marking of women's discourse as not fully serious and public: it "allows the woman who wants to maintain her privileged alignment with heterosexual culture to speak fearlessly, because the vernacular mode of her discourse assumes the intractability of the conditions of the complaint's production" (268). I would resist any implication that such containment is somehow the bottom line for sentimentality. Yet Berlant directs our attention to what is indeed an inescapable paradox in this knotting together of emotion, domestic ideology, and commodification: the female culture industry invites women to individuate by becoming generic. Sentimental discourses offer personal pleasures through a common practice while constructing all women as "domestically atomized" (270) selves. As Mary Kelley's *Private Woman, Public Stage* also shows, in different accents, we are interpellated into a collective separateness.

Generic woman is, as Berlant and others have pointed out, in fact racialized and class specific. This obfuscating abstraction links her not only to the appropriating circuits of sympathy (as seen in the previous section) but to the very nature of liberal citizenship. Feminist critiques of legal discourses of equality have shown that, as Sánchez-Eppler puts it, the "juridical 'person' has always implicitly occupied a white male body, . . . [and] that success in masking this fact has secured and legitimized the power that accrues to that body" (3). This point has been the focus of much valuable commentary on Habermas's account of the public sphere (one might find a version of it in Marx's critique of liberalism as masking class power, for that matter).[18] As I have already said of the relation of reason and racism: such exclusions are not contingent survivals from a less enlightened era but the very basis of national fraternity. As sentiment is linked to colonialism, domesticity is linked to imperialism; Amy Kaplan's recent work has demonstrated their mutual dependency, letting us hear the full resonance of the nineteenth-century phrase "the empire of the mother" (see Ryan, *Empire*). Let us remember, however, that abstraction also has a liberatory dimension. Once principles of equality and open access have been affirmed, exclusions can be—have been—contested. No one interested in the prospects for democracy in heterogeneous societies can afford to overlook the way the conviction that citizens have a common ground itself performatively establishes a shared although uneven terrain of political debate and struggle. And the abstraction of *woman* is, of course, one of the founding gestures and problems of feminism itself.

Investigating how gender and genre become linked has entangled us in the constitutive conundrums of bourgeois society. Sentimentality is mapped onto a sweeping array of binaries, correlated with woman as opposed to man, the private as opposed to the public, emotion as opposed to reason. Yet each gesture of partition—between gendered realms, between economic necessity and the intimacies of family life, between the morality and the class privilege of an elite—endeavors to forget that separate spheres can never be divided. Neither can the corporeal person be divided from the citizen or the feeling self from the thinking self; our exploration of the physiological basis of cognition indeed suggests that the Habermasian ideal of pure, "rational-critical" debate is as much a chimera as the notion of purely spontaneous emotions. That is not to say that reason has no distinctive power (such an implication in the midst of a book like this would be absurdly self-forgetful). It is, however, to remind us that physical bodies and historical situations are not obstacles to knowledge and agency but their very grounds; they constitute both possibility and limits. Sentimentality is such an elusive, provocative, indispensable category because it beckons us into these paradoxes. Celebrations and critiques occupy the same circuit, and we can end the relay between them only by historicizing the oppositions themselves.

Feeling and Form

How, then, on this broad terrain, are we to think about sentimentality in literature, and particularly in American literary history? I noted earlier that the deployment of sympathy in literature provoked some eighteenth-century writers to critique emotionalism in literature. Its embedding in the practice of domestic reading similarly produced an antisentimental reaction. Nina Baym has shown that the protagonists of the best-known American women's novels of the mid-nineteenth century, such as *The Wide, Wide World* and *The Lamplighter,* try to extricate themselves from human connectedness in order to pursue individual self-development. In postbellum America, literature itself was often defined *against* sentimentality and the domestic culture of letters.[19] Prestigious writing gradually and unevenly became less openly emotional and more ambitiously intellectual, less directly didactic and more conspicuously masculine. Antisentimentalism is an important part of this story, especially for literary studies.

Forty years before he criticized Edith Wyatt's contribution to *The Whole Family*, Henry James was an articulate spokesman for the reaction against sentiment. He writes in an 1867 review, for example, that Rebecca Harding Davis has made herself "the poet of poor people," but her material cannot justify her manner:

> She drenches the whole field beforehand with a flood of lachrymose sentimentalism, and riots in the murky vapors which rise in consequence of the act. . . . Nothing is more respectable on the part of a writer— a novelist—than the intelligent sadness which forces itself upon him on the completion of a dramatic scheme which is in strict accordance with human life and its manifold miseries. But nothing is more trivial than that intellectual temper which, for ever dissolved in the melting mood, goes dripping and trickling over the face of humanity, and washing its honest lineaments out of all recognition. . . . Spontaneous pity is an excellent emotion, but there is nothing so hardening as to have your pity for ever tickled and stimulated, and nothing so debasing as to become an agent between the supply and demand of the commodity.[20]

We see in this review not only James's youthful vehemence, even arrogance, but his sharp recognition of key elements of sentimentality as well: its association with tears, with humanitarian reform, with convention and commodification.

This attack did not in any sense defeat sentimentality (any more than Fielding's or Austen's did); the form pervasively persisted, past that moment and into the present. In the late nineteenth century its legitimizing conventions and capacity for engendering solidarities were particularly important for writers with minimal print access, such as early African American and Native American novelists.[21] Complex transformations of those conventions continue; Charles Chesnutt's use of sentimentality in the frame narrative for *The Conjure Woman*, for example, constitutes a critique as well as a deployment of the form. Sentimentality remains a powerful element of popular literature, and one can scarcely find a canonical author—including James—who is not drawing on or in dialogue with the tradition. That continues to be so even when modernism, with its hostility toward received forms and middle-class culture in general, intensifies the animus against sentimentality.[22]

Meanwhile the emerging profession of literary scholarship also defined literature against the domestic and popular, and progressively masculinized it—although, given the profound identification of interiority and literature with the feminine, that masculinization seems always in need of reassertion. This was not only a matter of excluding women writers (although, as Paul Lauter has shown, it certainly was that). The whole conceptual landscape of criticism, particularly the system of genres, was organized according to gender-inflected values. James wrote against "all those persons, whether men or women, who pursue literature under the sole guidance of sentimentalism" (222), and the target of Cleanth Brooks and Robert Penn Warren's 1946 anthology *Understanding Fiction* (a classic although now neglected site of New Critical antisentimentalism) is not domestic fiction—those writers have already been excluded from the table of contents—but the regionalist Bret Harte.

Brooks and Warren's glossary gives a definition of sentimentality very close to the one with which I began: it is "emotional response in excess of the occasion; emotional response which has not been prepared for in the story in question" (608). It seems likely that this is not just an example but a source of the view that sentimental feelings are simultaneously unreal and overdone; even those who have never seen *Understanding Fiction* may have had English teachers—or English teachers taught by English teachers—influenced by its magisterial pronouncements. Brooks and Warren raise respectful questions about emotion in Dickens ("Is 'The Poor Relation's Story' sentimental? . . . Does not our acceptance of the story as unsentimental depend, to some extent at least, on its being grounded firmly in the character?" [241]), and Joyce (the story they discuss is "Araby"). Harte, on the other hand, is treated in the vocabulary of pathology used later by Douglas; about "Tennessee's Partner" the authors write, "this straining for an emotional effect is one of the surest symptoms that one is dealing with a case of *sentimentality* (see Glossary)." A sentimental person "weeps at some trivial occurrence," "lacks a sense of proportion and gets a morbid enjoyment from an emotional debauch for its own sake" (219). This distaste is in part mapped onto style, in thoroughly gendered and embodied language (other symptoms are a tendency to "prettify" language and editorializing, "nudging the reader to respond" [219]), and in part mapped onto characterization.

Brooks and Warren are most offended not by Harte's domestic ideology, however, but by the story's *failure* to defend family values when it allows the Partner's loyalty to survive Tennessee's elopement with his wife. Why, they ask, "does Tennessee's Partner forgive Tennessee so easily for the wife-stealing? The matter is never explained, and we learn nothing of the state of mind which led the partner to the decision. In other words, Bret Harte has dodged the real psychological issue of his story" (215). On this masculine literary landscape, the story that provokes their most vehement condemnation focuses on love between men and fails to confine emotion to its proper sphere. The Partner displays the suffering, sentimental male body Eve Sedgwick considers "the exemplary instance of the sentimental" in late nineteenth- and early twentieth-century literature, a character that, by her account, "dramatizes, *embodies* for an audience that both desires and cathartically identifies with him, a struggle of masculine identity with emotions or physical stigmata stereotyped as feminine" (146).[23] Our twentieth-century usages of sentimentality are routed through not only the paradoxes of public/private but also the double bind of homo/heterosexual identity. Both the inseparability of binaries I have already noted and the observable nature of such polemics show that Sedgwick is right in proposing that "there isn't a differentiation to be *made* between sentimentality and its denunciation" (153).

Various tropes have focused sentimental discourses in various periods; Sedgwick's discussion of the sentimental man is complemented by Ann Cvetkovich's study of the suffering woman in Victorian fiction, and I would suggest that the equivalent for our own moment may be the figure of the endangered child. Again, my task here is not developing such specific analyses but rather delineating a productive conceptual landscape for them.

The view of the form that I am proposing does not generate definitive answers to the question of whether something is sentimental or not—

an inquiry that is in principle unanswerable. As soon as the question has been asked, the link has been established. Rather, the process by which one creates and evaluates possible responses is what generates the social meaning of the category. Neither this nor any other account of the form could end discussion and produce a consensus for a single definition of sentimentality. But I am, I suppose, appealing here for a change in usage, in the sense that I hope to produce more self-consciousness about the term's necessary range of meanings and the relation of arguments to the range of relevant scholarship.

We can organize answers to the question "What is sentimentality?" like this. Most broadly, when we call an artifact or gesture sentimental, we are pointing to its use of some established convention to evoke emotion; we mark a moment when the discursive processes that construct emotion become visible. Most commonly, we are recognizing that a trope from the immense repertory of sympathy and domesticity has been deployed; we recognize the presence of at least some fragmentary element of an intellectual and literary tradition. Most narrowly, we are asserting that literary works belong to a genre in which those conventions and tropes are central. I am skeptical about claims that fall into this last category when they neglect works' formal heterogeneity to generate classifications.[24] Yet that qualification does not undermine the substance of the recognition that sentimental works consistently engage us in the intricate impasse of the public and private, proclaiming their separation and at the same time demonstrating their inseparability. As emotion, embodied thought that animates cognition with the recognition of the self's engagement; as sympathy, firmly based in the observer's body and imaginatively linking it to another's; as domestic culture, in the peculiar intimacy of the print commodity; sentimentality at once locates us in our embodied and particular selves, and takes us out of them.

Sentimentality in Circulation, circa 1908

How do we read *The Whole Family* differently, given these claims about sentimentality?

The first consequence is that we can appreciate the literary-historical irony of Henry James's chapter being followed by Elizabeth Stuart

Phelps's. The two were long-standing, if mostly implicit, adversaries. Phelps's publishing career began with a short story in *Harper's Magazine* in 1862, when she was twenty, and six years later the best-selling *Gates Ajar* made her famous. That book, with its deployment of sympathy, its vision of heaven as a homelike place, and its instigation of commodity production (there were "Gates Ajar" collars, tippets, cigars, patent medicines, music, and funeral wreaths [Coultrap-McQuin 173]), stands squarely in the sentimental tradition. And while Phelps's voluminous subsequent fiction is highly varied both in topic and in quality, she was never embarrassed to be didactic and emotional. James's early criticism pairs her with Rebecca Harding Davis as a writer who represents the impoverishment of popular fiction.[25] Alfred Habegger speculates that Phelps was the author of a hostile review of *Portrait of a Lady*, and reports that Constance Woolson calls her, in a letter to James, "your poor serious soul-to-soul enemy" (255 n.5). The prestige of Phelps's style of serious fiction had eroded markedly by 1881, when Howells offended her by asking that she abridge a contribution to the *Atlantic Monthly*—to make more room for a piece by James (Coultrap-McQuin 187). She struggled with the changing marketplace but continued to publish frequently until her death in 1911. Indeed, the fact that she was invited to contribute to *The Whole Family* marks the continuing power of sentimentality.

By the time Phelps began to write "The Married Daughter," the eighth chapter of the collaborative novel, her character had been portrayed by every contributor except John Kendrick Bangs (in the role of her husband) as a bossy, thoroughly unpleasant young woman. She therefore adopts much the same stance as that taken by Vorse and Cutting (as described in chapter 3): she is giving a misunderstood member of the family the chance to tell her side of the story. Maria begins with, "We start in life with the most preposterous of all human claims—that one should be understood. We get bravely over that after awhile; but not until the idea has been knocked out of us" (185). The perspective was congenial to Phelps, in fact. Her novel *Walled In*, which ran serially in the *Bazar* during 1907, is a study of the experience of invalidism, which she believed it was difficult for healthy people to understand. The conscientiousness appropriate to a "managing girl" (from

Howells's chapter, 13) trying to look after a disorderly family seems congenial as well. And she must have enjoyed making James's Charles Edward appear utterly ineffectual. Yet much of the chapter seems routinely written and it makes no effort to introduce new themes. Phelps is even inattentive to the material preceding her contribution when she has Maria say that her husband does not have much of a sense of humor (207), unless she is being deliberately insulting—Bangs, a career humorist, certainly tried to make his character funny.

Phelps's chapter of *The Whole Family* is not likely to bring a tear to the eye of the late twentieth-century reader. Yet she tries to evoke the power of sympathy, even including a moment of the sort discussed by Sánchez-Eppler when Maria's own eyes blur with tears as Harry Goward reaffirms his commitment to Peggy (213). She invokes the empire of the mother by sending Maria to a ladies-only hotel called "The Sphinx," a name that recalls the central image of female power in her novel *The Story of Avis*. But Maria's husband soon arrives in New York and takes her away—to a hotel they variously remember as "The Holy Family" and "The Whole Family," but which proves to be "The Happy Family" (208). The value "The Married Daughter" most fervently and persistently affirms is marriage. Maria is no longer troubled by her family's lack of empathy because "Tom understood me from the very first eye-beam" (185). She is happy to be "whirled away" from the ladies' hotel on her "husband's big forgiving arm" (208).

As the quoted phrases suggest, the chapter's language constantly tends toward the formulaic—and never more so than when gender difference is in question. Gestures and behaviors are described as "manful" (213) or "womanish" (209), and Tom follows Maria to New York because they have such different ideas about where to leave a note that he never gets the one she left explaining her trip: " '*Pin-cushion!*' exploded Tom. 'A message—an important message—to a *man*—on a *pin-cushion!*' " (207). The chapter is most sentimental in the broadest sense of the term: its style and the emotions it portrays and invites are highly conventionalized. Inevitably, James disliked it. He never lost his interest in the discourse of domesticity—indeed, his *Bazar* publications are evidence of his desire to win a hearing within it—but as Habegger puts it, "again and again the literary female captured James's attention, only to be haughtily dismissed" (12). James received the proofs of "The Married Daughter" in Paris and wrote to Jordan that when he began to read it, he realized that he ought not subject it to the "searching artistic light" of that city and "laid it away" until he could "surround my perusal of it with more precautions" (Edel and Powers 50). But he does not return to the topic; his next letter laments the ending of the novel as a whole and skewers Wyatt's "The Mother" in particular as a "small convulsion of debility" (52).

The story of Edith Wyatt's contribution to *The Whole Family* is full of ironies. The first is that an author who so often satirized bookish pretense and bad taste should be criticized as sentimental. Wyatt's notable publications in the early years of the century, which brought her to Howells's attention, were Chicago local color stories and the novel *True Love: A Comedy of the Affections*, set in Chicago and rural Illinois. Both sorts of fiction feature villains who affect elevated emotions to cloak their self-dramatizing, self-righteous egotism. *True Love* is critical of courtship conventions and romantic notions of marriage, and—as its contemporary editor put it—begins to "wrestle with the issue of women's desire for independence and originality" (xlviii). Wyatt's work certainly does not lack moments one might discuss in terms of sentimentality, but it is also forcefully antisentimental. Her characteristic themes are muted but visible in "The Mother"—her characters' reports of the aesthete Lyman Wilde demonstrate a satiric touch, and her narrator firmly advocates sense rather than sensibility in thinking about marriage. The chapter is not, in the context of the others, particularly formulaic or emotional, and Howells—also an antisentimentalist—was (in Jordan's words) "as enthusiastic over the mother's chapter as Mr. James was critical" (273). It seems to have been Wyatt's assigned role rather than her style that led James to single it out—"The Mother" names a sentimental topic.

It is ironic, too, that an invitation to collaborate with such a distinguished group of authors—which Howells must have intended, and Wyatt must have received, as an honor—should have turned into such a humiliation for the young writer. The combination of her relatively small reputation and her complete lack of connection with Harper's made Wyatt uniquely vulnerable among the contributors. None of the others was subjected to the sort of insistent criticism that Jordan gave her, nor to the threat of rejection and replacement. It is thus not surprising that the rewritten chapter is scrupulously attentive to previous contributors' characterizations and hints for developing the plot. Several intervening chapters had ignored the opening Cutting had created for Elizabeth to learn of Lyman Wilde's whereabouts; Wyatt has Alice pass on the information very much in the voice Jordan had created for her. She brings back Howells's character Ned Temple and the *Banner*. She tries to reproduce the elaborate diction James had given the married son and spends many paragraphs developing the special relationship that he had suggested between Charles Edward and his mother. It is another irony—this time a predictable one—that James did not feel that she had caught his tone or followed up his preparations effectively (as his letter tells Jordan in emphatic detail).

Wyatt continued to write fiction, but much of her later work was investigative journalism; she wrote about a coal mine disaster and a ferry accident, urban working women and rural women, suffrage and strikes, always in the spirit of Progressive activism. She also published verse, served on the board of Harriet Monroe's *Poetry*, and wrote reviews and literary criticism. Wyatt's career is documented in great detail in her papers at the Newberry Library, which include everything from correspondence to typescripts of her work to contracts. There are five scrapbooks containing her newspaper articles, unpublished lectures, and other minor works. What is missing, however, is any mention whatever of *The Whole Family*.[26] Wyatt preserved her literary records with great care, saving letters from Howells dated both before and after the collaborative novel. And she included admiring essays about Howells's and James's work in *Great Companions*, her collection of criticism, without ever mentioning that she once collaborated with them. It is disappointing not to find the rejected chapter among Wyatt's papers, and extraordinary, surely, to find none of the correspondence about the project—no reminiscence of her participation in such a notable and unusual episode of literary history, not even an indication that she ever published "The Mother." It does not seem too speculative to suggest that Wyatt was trying to erase a painful memory.

"The Mother" was followed by Mary Raymond Shipman Andrews's "The School-Boy." (James pairs Wyatt's "domestic sentimentality" and Andrews's contribution in his letter to Jordan, writing that he cannot trust himself to speak about either [Edel and Powers 51].) Andrews had no doubt come to Jordan's notice in 1906 when "The Perfect Tribute," a story about Abraham Lincoln that she published in *Scribner's*, became so popular that it was reprinted as a small book and ended up selling more than 600,000 copies.[27] She was an apt choice for this particular chapter because she was also known for her stories about boys — *Bob and the Guides*, a collection in a variety of voices but centered on a mischievous, athletic thirteen-year-old inspired by her son, was published the same year. The inclusion of a boy in *The Whole Family*'s roster of characters may seem — and may have been — a lightly taken decision based on symmetry. Yet the chapter connects the novel to the project of creating healthy men that was understood as one of the most important, and difficult, tasks of the family. Anthony Rotundo describes nineteenth-century boys as inhabiting a "distinct cultural world . . . outside the rules of the home and the marketplace" (31). By the end of the century perceptions of that world, and in some complex fashion no doubt the world itself, were shaped by a literature celebrating it written and widely read between the Civil War and the First World War. Marcia Jacobson and Richard Lowry have demonstrated the cultural power of the "boy book," which imagined a space of barefoot freedom that was at once the antithesis and the origin of responsible middle-class masculinity. From the perspective of discourses about the family, that space had to be at once outside the home, connecting the boy with the wide world of nature, and safely created and protected inside it. Then it was to be encapsulated as an interior self in the adult man.

Howells made clear the direction he expected this contribution to take in his opening when he mentioned that Peggy's small brother was suspicious of his prospective brother-in-law because he thought any fellow who would attend a coeducational school was probably a sissy. Howells had himself participated in the creation of the boy book, applauding Thomas Bailey Aldrich's *Story of a Bad Boy* in 1869 and subsequent examples, and by 1906 publishing two such volumes himself. And he had hoped that the most powerful architect of this imagined world, his friend Mark Twain, would write this chapter of *The Whole Family*. When Twain declined the invitation, Jordan substituted one of the few women contributors to the genre.

Andrews's text follows the formulas of the boy book almost to the point of parody, managing to mention a puppy and Billy's desire for a new fishing reel immediately, and beginning two of the first few paragraphs with "Golly" (240–41). Billy keeps a toad behind the washbasin and a snake among his collars, stuffs himself with cookies, puts a worm down one sister's neck and a beetle in the other's hair, is dedicated to sport and fascinated by automobiles, admires "Jack" Denbigh because he is "six feet-two, and strong as an ox" (243) and because he played football at West Point and fought at San Juan—and so on (see fig. 50). In general Andrews's boy fiction—focusing on fishing, hunting, and boyish pranks—might almost have been written to provide moderate, reassuring illustrations of psychologist G. Stanley Hall's theory that boys should be allowed to be little savages so that they would grow up to be vigorous men, not overcivilized neurasthenics. In Gail Bederman's interpretation, "By fully reliving their ancestors' vibrant passions, Hall suggested, little boys could incorporate a primitive's emotional strength into their adult personalities" (95). The biology on which he had based his claims was obsolete by 1906, but this image of the boy and his development, and the idea that men's energies could be renewed by boyish behavior and contact with boys, continued to circulate.

Both the previous sections of this chapter and recent scholarship on masculinity and affect (Ellison; Chapman and Hendler) have prepared us to see that Andrews's stories of boys and men are sentimental in offering highly conventionalized invitations to emotional response and being deeply concerned with human connectedness—usually between different generations or classes. The latter topic is dimly seen in "The School-Boy," in Billy's feeling for Dr. Denbigh, but it pervades *Bob and the Guides* and its sequel, *The Eternal Masculine* (1913). For example, in one story a captain of industry is befriended by a group of Yale students.

> They were out in the street now, marching together, arm linked in arm. Dick Elliott's big hand was on the older man's shoulder, and the touch was pleasant to him—so pleasant that his voice stopped in the middle of a line once, and the phalanx burst into a roar of young laughter.
>
> "Did it swallow a fly?" Jimmy Selden inquired impudently. They were all boys together now for sure.
>
> So, singing and laughing, the five went down the dark street to the sta-

50. Illustration for *The Whole Family*, ch. 10,
"The School-Boy": "I glanced up at him lovingly and
murmured, 'Jack,' just like Peggy did." *Harper's Bazar* 42.9
(September 1908): 818.

tion, Trefethen in the midst, the guest, the hero, quite dazed, and happy as he thought he had forgotten how to be happy. (*Eternal Masculine* 383)

The encounter leads the older man to reclaim the knowledge that fairness and community are more important than profit, and changes all their lives by transforming his future business decisions. The revitalizing power of such a bond is also seen in "The Perfect Tribute," in which Lincoln at Gettysburg, discouraged by the reception of the heartfelt address he has just given, talks with a dying Confederate soldier who appreciates its greatness — thus these protagonists are divided by section as well as generation but, again, are united by shared values.

Andrews sets her story of the bond that develops between a weary president and a suffering youth in a period when tenderness between men was less anxiously regarded than it is now (see Yacovone). By 1906, when she published it, the gradual, uneven shift from the Victorian celebration of fraternal communion to the latter twentieth-century fear of queerness had begun, but "The Perfect Tribute" still found a large and enthusiastic audience. On the other hand, some subsequent reader at the University of Michigan felt the same unease about the story that Brooks and Warren felt reading Bret Harte. He — or less probably she — took a homophobic and antisentimental pencil to the library book that I checked out years later, changing (among other things) the wounded southerner's "sweet, brilliant smile" to a "brilliant smile" (34), and "caressed the boy's shoulder" to "patted the boy's shoulder" (36). It is this kind of aversive reaction that has made twentieth-century sentimental masculinity — despite its ubiquity, from the boy book to the buddy movie — less visible than feminine sentimentality.

The mediating role assigned to women characters in many of Andrews's fictions may work to counter such unease, implying heterosexuality and invoking the family. The central characters of "The Perfect Tribute" are Lincoln, the soldier, and the soldier's young brother, but his absent sister and sweetheart are frequently mentioned (in fact, it is because the former has left town just at the moment when the soldier's condition worsens and he decides to make a will leaving his property to the latter that the unrecognized president is asked for help). When Billy leans toward Dr. Denbigh and, with mocking tenderness,

What Is Sentimentality? 253

murmurs, "Jack," he is imitating his sister. "The Sabine Maiden," a story of masculine hijinks at a camp in the Canadian woods that appears in *The Eternal Masculine*, is elaborately plotted to culminate in the protagonist being chased down the river by his friends wearing only a skirt, and eventually selling nude and cross-dressed photographs of himself as part of a fraternity hazing—and is narrated by his sister-in-law. Yet as my last example shows vividly, such stories evoke the instability of gender performances at the same time they strive to dispel it. We have only begun to explore the complex connections of sentimental masculinity and the history of sexuality.

Those connections are inflected, as well, by class. Andrews's protagonists are mainly privileged boys with egalitarian instincts—which makes them appealing to the common men they deal with, and thus natural leaders. In "Bill the Trapper," when a boy enlists a drifter to help him construct an elaborate trap in Central Park, he even has an uplifting influence on the "drink-hardened" brute (*Bob and the Guides* 198). "He put up his slender, brown little hand and patted Slaggin on his shoulder, and never knew that a thrill shook the dirty, greenish-black old coat. Then he slid his fingers into the great fist with a happy indifference as to cleanness and started back down the path, and the man followed on like a dog" (199–200). Later, Slaggin does "not want to lose the feeling of that friendly little arm against his side; he wanted to keep it close, to clutch it tightly, so that he might through it draw near to decency and cleanliness" (201). Slaggin is not the center of the story; but every word devoted to him, including his name, puts him in his place. Working men are also sometimes innately noble in Andrews's fiction: in "The Perfect Tribute," Lincoln's "labor-knotted" hands (5) do not keep the "aristocratic" (26) southern boys from recognizing him as a kindred spirit. The dying soldier's last words affirm that the Gettysburg Address has shown him that on both sides of the Civil War, "the best of us" are fighting for the love of country (45). Sentimental fraternal communion elides the tension between democracy and elitism, and emerges as patriotism itself.

In briefly identifying Andrews's conservative politics I am not saying, of course, that sentimentality as a genre is conservative. As Gail Bederman has shown, this discourse of manliness and civilization accommodates the project of Ida B. Wells as well as G. Stanley Hall, of

The Very Little
Person

BY

Mary Heaton Vorse

With Illustrations by
Rose O'Neill

51. Frontispiece and title page
for *The Very Little Person,*
by Mary Heaton Vorse (1911).
By Rose Cecil O'Neill.

BOSTON AND NEW YORK
HOUGHTON MIFFLIN COMPANY
The Riverside Press Cambridge
1911

Charlotte Perkins Gilman as well as Theodore Roosevelt. Sentimental masculinity is variously tendentious; these sets of linked concepts open a limited range of possibilities without imposing a single set of values or opinions, just as domestic sentimentality is full of social meaning yet has no single politics.

I will emphasize that fluidity by turning, before closing, to an author treated in an earlier chapter. Mary Heaton Vorse is remembered not as the author of *The Autobiography of an Elderly Woman,* but as the author of *Strike!* She herself made a sharp division between her fiction on domestic topics and her works on social conditions and social movements. Her fictional account of a baby's first year of life, *The Very Little Person* (1911), for example, has no apparent political content and was illustrated by the most famously sentimental of illustrators, Rose O'Neill (inventor of the kewpie; see fig. 51).[28] Biographer Dee Garrison tells us that after about 1912 (when the Lawrence strike solidified her political radicalization) Vorse wrote fiction for the women's magazines primarily to support herself and her family, and referred to the stories as "lollypops" (75). Yet Vorse's work on the family can be substantial and powerful, as we have seen, and in her 1935 volume of reminiscences,

A Footnote to Folly, she writes that reviewing her life has made her see that the division is false.

> Indeed, my book is the record of a woman who in early life got angry because many children lived miserably and died needlessly.
>
> My book was almost finished before I realized that while I thought I was writing about the labor movement, about imperialism, or of war, all the time I was in reality writing about children.
>
> For when you come down to it, the labor movement is about children and about homes. In the last analysis civilization itself is measured by the way in which children will live and what chance they will have in the world. (404)

Here the key sentimental trope of the endangered child is mobilized in the service of the radical left, and linked to the discourse of civilization as well. Of course, my point is also not that sentimentality is progressive, but that its politics reside (to echo Lora Romero) in more local formulations.

These readings of how sentiments circulate in *The Whole Family* do not, cannot, add up to a unified interpretation of sentimentality; there is no single key to be turned. They do depend directly on the previous sections of this chapter. This is not only a matter of avoiding categories such as "authenticity" and "subversion." We begin to grasp the politics of sympathy and empathy only by mapping the "private" and "public" onto a more articulated and analytical map of social life. The importance of the tears in Maria's eyes in Phelps's chapter, the irony of Wyatt's position as author of "The Mother," and the cultural purchase of Andrews's formulaic boy fiction emerge only as we trace the long history of sentimentality. These authors' accumulated works suggest wide horizons of inquiry, and I have only suggested directions for exploration; this chapter has already traveled far enough—in several directions—from the story of the collaborative novel. There is more, however, to be said about form—in particular about how sentimentality and realism shape the novel as a whole. The next chapter examines the novel's final variations on its themes and the strategies deployed to close the story.

❦ Closing the Book ❦

Books end. At some point there are no more pages to turn—a fact that is not only a constitutive condition but a resource of print narrative. Readers often elide the difference between completeness and coherence, usually at the invitation of the text (as critics of the novel have amply demonstrated).[1] The limit of the narrative, like the boundary drawn around the family, projects wholeness. Courtship plots rely on both sorts of cohesion, ending the narrative by renewing the institution of the family with a marriage—as Jane Austen writes playfully in the conclusion of *Northanger Abbey*, "readers . . . see, in the tell-tale compression of the pages before them, that we are all hastening together to perfect felicity" (250). Yet not every novel succeeds in making that resolution persuasive. And although every novel must conjure closure from heterogeneity, as a composite novel *The Whole Family* faces a particularly pronounced challenge. How, then, do the contributors charged with the last chapters consolidate themes, reconcile jarring conventions, resolve the plot, and create closure—if indeed they do?

In the novel's first, serial publication in *Harper's Bazar* there were in fact more pages to turn after the conspicuous announcement of "The End" of *The Whole Family* (see fig. 52). The overleaf offered one of the *Bazar*'s frequent invitations to empathy, Myra Kelly's "The Teacher's Side of It," followed by Helen Van Valkenburgh's poem "The Woman of Public Deeds," and then by Octave Thanet's essay "Men as Lovers." And the issue went on—and the next issue of the *Bazar* went on to another serialized novel. How did the contributors, and how should we, understand the relations of these various texts and the place of literature in the magazine? As I look back over the novel as a whole, I see a

The End

52. End decoration for *The Whole Family*, ch. 12, "The Friend of the Family." *Harper's Bazar* 42.11 (November 1908): 1063.

third controversy that never erupted into an open debate like those over the old maid's and the mother's chapters: a dialogue about how publishing shapes writing. Closing my own narrative entails returning to the concerns of the early pages of this study and examining how the contributors thematize the relation of culture and commerce. I will take up that topic first and let it lead us back to the question of the novel's form. Then we will see what words the final contributors could write to allow the story to end, and allow me to write the phrase "the novel as a whole."

Culture and Commerce

The question of culture was part of the composite novel's portrait of American family life from the first. In the father's chapter Howells broaches the topic by showing literature and art as appurtenances of the privileged classes, but also as sites of debate over values and even of risk. As part of his civic leadership Cyrus Talbert has given the town "a library building, and a soldier's monument" (11)—mentioned together, each simultaneously indexing local pride and a connection to national culture. Later, in the mother's chapter, Edith Wyatt follows his lead and shows Ada Talbert carrying out her appropriate role by chairing the library board (227). Howells's narrator, Ned Temple, a newspaperman and publisher, positions himself as one of the "folk who have to do more constantly with reading and writing"—in contrast to Cyrus, who is one of those concerned with "making and marketing"—but immediately insists that both sorts of work require "intellectual force"

(11). He refers to the Talberts' elder son's artistic aspirations in slighting terms; wanting not only to patronize culture but also to produce it makes Charles Edward ineffective as a manager at the family factory. Temple writes that Charles Edward "putters over the aesthetic details in the business, the new designs for the plated ware, and the illustrated catalogues which the house publishes every year" and adds—bringing the commercial side of his position very much to the fore—"I am in hopes that we shall get the printing" (13). Differences in architectural taste are reviewed (as I discussed in chapter 3), and the spinster aunt's travels in Europe and particular interest in Italian art are mentioned—with a note of ambivalence in Mrs. Temple's observation that Elizabeth's manner is not "uncomfortably cultured" (19).

Mary Wilkins Freeman develops this theme only slightly in the aunt's chapter. She emphasizes her character's good taste and continues to show Charles Edward as weak, focusing on his failure as an artist rather than as a businessman. She takes one important step, however: she turns Elizabeth's vague romantic disappointment into her estrangement from one Lyman Wilde. Although it is balanced by an old-fashioned New England given name, the family name inevitably evokes Oscar Wilde and establishes another link to the aesthetic.

Then, in one of the project's many ironies, Mary Heaton Vorse's chapter, the third, leaves the topic entirely alone. Vorse as a young woman had aspired to be a painter and actually studied at the Art Students' League in New York, where Howells had placed Lorraine, and in Paris; from the fall of 1906 through the spring of 1908 she was living at the A Club, a cooperative housing experiment in Greenwich Village that served as a social center for liberal and radical intellectuals. She was, in other words, the collaboration's only practicing Bohemian. But Vorse had been cast as the grandmother, and she confined herself to business and wrote about domestic topics.

The suburban Mary Stewart Cutting embraces the character of the artistic, unconventional daughter-in-law (as we have seen), filling it out with specific references not only to differences of taste in furniture and painting but, appropriately for *Harper's Bazar*, in fashion. Lorraine shocks her in-laws by wearing aesthetic dress—a flowing yellow gown with a high waist, presumably worn without a corset—to dinner at their house. (In fact, the elder Talberts do not even recognize the style, but confuse it with a "Mother Hubbard," a square-yoked, waistless "wrapper" worn informally around the house for chores or in hot weather or pregnancy.)[2] She emphasizes the conflict between economic practicality and art, reporting that her father gave up painting in order to support his family. Cutting also has Lorraine place her conversations with Lyman Wilde at "the Settlement" (99), creating a still closer link to the nexus of art and reform that characterized the aesthetic movement and its inheritors. None of this was new—or even recent—in the first decade of the twentieth century, of course. Wilde toured America promoting aesthetic dress (among other things) in 1882, and it was in the 1880s that concern first arose over women wearing Mother Hubbards in public. Toynbee Hall had been founded in London in 1884, and the first American settlement houses in New York and Chicago in 1886 and 1889. By the publication of *The Whole Family* in 1907 and 1908, the successive sensations over Wilde had receded into the past, the Arts and Crafts movement was well established, and there were hundreds of settlement houses across the country. There was little danger that the *Bazar*'s readers would share the elder Talberts' ignorance; the novel's allusions were common currency among the American middle class.

Indeed, as Mary Warner Blanchard points out in *Oscar Wilde's America: Counterculture in the Gilded Age*, in 1893 Howells could publish a novel titled *The Coast of Bohemia* and expect his public to understand the reference. This little-known work represents the Art Students' League as the "Synthesis of Art Studies" and links the question of culture to the problems of female modernity discussed in chapter 5. In *The Coast of Bohemia*, as in *Fennel and Rue*, Howells is both attracted and repelled by the complex identity of the New Woman. His character Charmian Maybough is a chameleon who carries off both the "authority" of her fashionable gown and the "originality" of her aesthetic one (117), but prefers the latter. Every element of his description of her studio, tucked upstairs in her mother's elegant flat, proclaims it a stage setting—from the tiger skin to the pipes she does not smoke to the false ceiling that makes it look like an artist's garret. Howells surely ironizes his own past pronouncements, as well as the self-dramatizing girl, when he has her describe it in terms of both realism and dress: "You can imagine what a relief it is to steal away here from all that unreality of mamma's, down there, and give yourself up to the truth of art; I just draw a long breath when I get in here, and leave the world behind. Why, when I get off here alone, for a minute, I unlace!" (129). Art is both an antidote to and an example of the culture of performance. Elizabeth Stuart Phelps clearly expected the *Bazar*'s readers to recognize both the reference and the theme when she wrote in her chapter of *The Whole Family* (in the voice of Maria), "I cannot say that I have ever caught Aunt Elizabeth in a real fib. She may be a 'charmian,' but I don't think she is a liar" (201). Yet the charmer who cannot distinguish performance from self is scarcely less worrisome than the deliberate deceiver.[3]

Henry James gives the opposition of culture and commerce its most explicit and fullest development. This is the late James, who actively cultivated an image as a refined, misunderstood artist; and that is certainly Charles Edward's story. The chapter slowly progresses through a discussion of the characters and their various relations, demonstrating its narrator's supersubtle sensitivity and describing the banality that surrounds him. James makes Charles Edward contemptuous of commercial success in any form: "[W]e've never yet designed a single type of ice-pitcher—since that's the damnable form Father's production more and more runs to . . . that has 'taken' with their awful public. We've tried again and again to strike off something hideous enough, but it has always in these cases appeared to us quite beautiful compared to the object finally turned out, on their improved lines, for the unspeakable market; so that we've only been able to be publicly rueful and depressed about it, and to plead practically, in extenuation of all the extra trouble we saddle them with, that such things are, alas, the worst we can do" (149). The solution the chapter proposes—not only to the quagmire of Peggy's engagement but to the desolation of Charles Edward and Lorraine's existence in Eastridge—seems inevitable: the younger Talberts will take Peggy off to Europe "for a year's true culture" (176).

"The Married Son" is written in what Sergio Perosa calls James's "experimental" style. It is modern (as he suggests) in its dramatization of a limited point of view, intense concern with perception and motive, and involuted language. James even gives Charles Edward a version of one of his most evocative late pronouncements about life and art. In the 1907 preface to *Roderick Hudson* James writes, "Really, universally, relations stop nowhere, and the exquisite problem of the artist is eternally but to draw, by a geometry of his own, the circle within which they shall happily *appear* to do so" (*Literary Criticism: Prefaces* 1041). Compare this passage from *The Whole Family:* "[O]ne has only to look at any human thing very straight . . . to see it shine out in as many aspects as the hues of the prism; or place itself, in other words, in relations that positively stop nowhere. . . . Of course, as Lorraine says, 'Stopping, that's art'" (167). In this text James is more concerned with connecting than with stopping—or, rather, is willing to dwell on points without considering how his sense of an ending meshes with those of the other contributors. Perosa acknowledges that the chapter "is a perfect example of his latter style and technique, but seen from another angle it did prove a stumbling block for anyone else having to start from there. James's contribution froze the action, stopped all movement, and brought the novel to a standstill" (117). The correspondence makes it clear that James did not realize how unassimilable his virtually modernist text would be. Nevertheless the form of his chapter is, in some sense, his most important comment on the relation of commerce and culture.

James communicates his vision of the artist in the ivory tower powerfully, and many readers and critics have accepted it. Another perspective on his attitude toward the market is available, however. The fact that James yearned for success as a dramatist is familiar, and Michael Anesko, Anne Margolis, and others have shown that he was both intensely aware of his potential and actual audiences and a persistent and careful negotiator with publishers.[4] This does not so much supplant as supplement the first perspective, showing us the aesthete enmeshed in complex relations and articulating, and enacting, complex responses to the material situation of the artist. In 1898, for example, he wrote with qualified optimism about the prospects of American literature: "It is assuredly true that literature for the billion will not be literature as we have hitherto known it at its best. But if the billion give the pitch of production and circulation, they do something else besides; they hang before us a wide picture of opportunities—opportunities that would be opportunities still even if, reduced to the *minimum*, they should be only those offered by the vastness of the implied habitat and the complexity of the implied history. It is impossible not to entertain with patience and curiosity the presumption that life so colossal must break into expression at points of proportionate frequency" (*Literary Criticism: Essays* 653).[5] Yet James also sometimes expressed in his own voice the haughty attitudes he gave to Charles Edward and to characters like the narrator of "The Next Time," who writes of "the age of trash triumphant" (*Tales* 187). For example, his comments about Edith Wyatt's chapter include the remark that her version of the mother "does injustice even to *her* public" (Edel and Powers 52). (Elizabeth Jordan chose to omit that particular passage when she published the letter in her autobiography.)

Wyatt, despite James's scorn, perceptively developed the connection to aesthetics and reform established by previous contributors. Chicago was a center of Arts and Crafts activity, and Wyatt demonstrates her familiarity with the movement when she has Ada Talbert describe a visit to Lorraine's sisters' workshop by writing, "They seem to be carpenters, as nearly as I can tell. They wear fillets and bright, loose clothes; and they make very rough-hewn burnt-wood footstools and odd settees with pieces of glass set about in them. It is all very puzzling" (220). Both Ada's lack of sophistication and her hostesses' self-dramatization are gently satirized. Her précis of Lyman Wilde's convictions bears directly on the irony of the Arts and Crafts movement in the United States. Alice reports, "Lorraine says that, though not the most *prominent*, Lyman Wilde is the most *radical* and *temperamental* leader in the great handicraft development in this country. Even most of the persons in favor of it consider that he goes too far. She says, for instance, he is so opposed to machines of all sorts that he thinks it would be better to abolish printing and return to script. He has started what they call a little movement of the kind now, and is training two young scriveners" (221). Yet in fact the styles succeeded because they adapted well to industrial production. Their simple lines and striving for good design, together with the publicity that promoted them, made Arts and Crafts wares attractive to the middle class. (*Bazar* readers had recently learned a great deal about the style when Jordan's companion Martha Cutler published an essay on it as part of her 1906 series "Periods in Household Decoration.") Furniture like the Gustav Stickley sideboard in figure 53—which Lorraine would certainly have liked to see replace the black walnut one in the older Talberts' dining room (see ch. 3)—

53. Oak and mahogany sideboard with iron hardware, 1912–16. Design introduced in 1901 by Gustav Stickley (Craftsman Workshops, Eastwood and New York, New York). *Los Angeles County Museum of Art, gift of Max Palevsky.*

sold widely. Wyatt's oblique, canny comment on the relation of culture and commerce makes the point that print publication, too, is industrial.

Criticism in recent years has increasingly reckoned with that truth and has recognized that when the cultural field is separated into commercial and anticommercial practices, they are constitutively interdependent. James himself comments, in the text quoted above, on the connection of expansion and diversification I discussed in chapter 2, imagining literature to be "as subdivided as a chessboard" (653) and suggesting that "we may get individual publics positively more sifted and evolved than anywhere else, shoals of fish rising to more delicate bait" (654). As I argued (following Richard Brodhead), the very invention of a category of prestigious American literature helped to secure an audience for it, just as the aesthetic claims of Arts and Crafts productions enhanced their desirability. High culture and mass culture also depend on each other because they constantly rework each other's materials. In the latter twentieth century both the incorporation of commercial imagery in elite art practices and the function of the avant-garde as "a kind of research and development arm of the culture industry" (Crow 257) are more visible than ever. Aestheticism, as Jonathan Freedman has shown, is complexly entangled with "the development of a cultural apparatus at once thoroughly professionalized and wholly commodified." After all, he asks,

> what is the aesthete but the consummate professional: the possessor of a "monopoly of knowledge" about the provenance and extent of this mysterious entity, "the aesthetic"—the man (and sometimes the woman) who responds to the demands of a rapidly professionalizing world by forging a career for himself out of the imparting of knowledge about this new "field" to an awed and appreciative public? That the notion of the aesthete strikes us as anomalous may actually be the surest sign of its success. For like all true professionals, the aesthete claims that the purity of his vocation—in this case, the disinterestedness of his dedication to the ideal realm of art—places him beyond the demands of grubbier occupations, lesser trades. (*Professions of Taste* xix)

A critical tradition following Adorno has pointed out that it is in market economies that literature, detached from other relations of artistic production, can be commodified. James's work over his long career analyzes this situation from many perspectives, and not only enacts and thematizes but critiques aestheticism as a response. The full complexity of James's commentary on culture and commerce is not present in any single work, and certainly not in "The Married Son." Yet the combination of his participation in the collaboration and his text is amply suggestive.

Howells apparently did not think James an appropriate contributor to the composite novel, and explicitly discouraged Jordan from asking him. Yet James published regularly in *Harper's Bazar* in the period following his trip to the United States in 1904 and 1905; he addressed the Harper's "million" (see ch. 2) if not his own prospective "billion." Beginning with the lead article in the November 1906 issue, Jordan ran "The Speech of American Women," a four-part series by James;

another series, "The Manners of American Women," began in April 1907. Serious pieces by distinguished authors were a regular feature of the magazine, but James's essays—again, in the late style—do not fit any more smoothly into the discourse of the magazine in general than his chapter does into *The Whole Family*. Despite the palpable sincerity of his desire to win a hearing among American women, he writes not just as an authority but as a judge, rebuking both their speech and their manners. As each essay progresses he expresses his disapproval of their taste more and more openly. James writes, for example, in the second installment of "Manners":

> What *would* be the civilization, what in other words would be the manners, of a lady who, surrounded at breakfast, at luncheon, at dinner, by a couple of dozen or so of small saucers of the most violently heterogeneous food, should proceed to exhaust the contents by a process of incoherent and indiscriminate spooning? Of what elementary power or disposition to discriminate, of what confused invocation of the light of taste, would her practice of slobbering up a dab of hot and a dab of cold, a dab of sweet and a dab of sour, of mixing salads with ices, fish with flesh, hot cakes with mutton chops, pickles with pastry, and maple syrup with everything, appear to be, in general, the symptom and pledge? (455–56)

Most of his examples of bad taste are less literal, and less vividly strange, but he finds this lack of discrimination everywhere. In *The Whole Family*, Mrs. Chataway's "voluminous and tense" wrapper, "flowing like a cataract in some places, yet in others exposing, or at least defining, the ample bed of the stream" and reminding him of "the big cloth spread in a room when any mess is to be made" (178), suggests a similarly repellent collapse of structure. James's countenance in the photograph that accompanied the last article of this series (fig. 54) is appropriately severe; he personifies the censorious Master.

Yet when the *Bazar* illustrates James's work with his own image, presenting him as a literary celebrity, he also participates in the culture of publicity. James takes up this topic most centrally and famously in "The Death of the Lion," which was published in the first issue of the notoriously aesthetic *Yellow Book* in 1894, and in which (if the narrator is to be trusted) a great author is hounded to death by celebrity seekers. But some reference can be found in virtually every extended work—

54. Photograph of Henry James by Alice Broughton, illustrating the last installment of "The Manners of American Women." *Harper's Bazar* 41.7 (July 1907): 649.

Thomas Strychacz has offered an acute reading of *The Sacred Fount* in terms of its passing reference to "the newspaper-man kicked out" (157), for example—and in Charles Edward's suspicions of Temple, discussed in chapter 3, as well. And as Richard Salmon has noted, James was concerned not only with the invasion of authorial privacy and the growing power of the mass media, but also with the saturation of modern societies by publicity—no longer confined to distinct institutions like journalism and advertising, but woven throughout modern experience (2–3). He begins his first *Bazar* article, for example, with the point that it is "one of the commonplaces of journalism . . . that the American woman more and more presents herself as a great success in the world. . . . She has had at her service an unequalled system of publicity," which publicity itself "attests her success, for what is success, at this time of day and in the conditions I refer to, but to be as public as possible? It is the most universal state, then, of the American woman, who enjoys it with fewer restrictions, fewer discriminations, . . . than her sisters elsewhere under the sun; and it has ended as with a practical invitation to us to swell the appreciative chorus" (979–80). (By the end of the series, however, we have learned that the American woman is only the "pretended heiress of all the ages" (115), pitiable because she does not even suspect how badly she speaks and how important a deficiency that is.) James both testifies to the constitutive nature of publicity and acknowledges his own recursive incorporation into the system.

In this vision publicity and publication do not mediate between private and public—they consume and destroy the private while at the same time contaminating the public. Both personal decency and public decorum disappear in the collapse of boundaries. It is a particularly anxious version of the intricate impasse of private and public that has recurred in each chapter of this study of *The Whole Family*. Salmon writes that "publicity, particularly in James's later fiction, is a phantasmagorical condition which disorientates the process of perception and undermines the stability of perspectives. Within this spectacular world, such binary oppositions as 'subject' and 'object,' and 'surface' and 'depth' undergo the same collapse as the separation between 'private' and 'public' space." Yet, as he also notes, James writes from within this disruption; his radical aesthetic and epistemological achievements, his representation of the "liberating mutability of the modern self" (11), are inseparable from the reconfiguration of social space. The connection of culture and commerce—like the family business, the intimate fiction of domestic privacy, the fluid identity of the modern woman, and the paradoxical nature of sentimentality—depends on the simultaneous, precarious establishment and undoing of the boundary between private and public.

Perfect Felicity (with Professional Help)

In the course of this book I have discussed *The Whole Family* in terms of many different forms. The first chapter framed a tradition for the "composite novel" and suggested that Howells may have believed that the collaboration would produce a realist novel. The fifth chapter and this one have connected the novel with sentimentality and modernism, respectively. I have suggested that Bangs's chapter is linked to his work as a humorist, and that Andrews's evokes the boy book. Wyatt's affiliation with the local color movement is less visible, but her chapter is staged as the mother's musings while she drives her buggy—a point that becomes significant when juxtaposed with the prominence of buggy rides in her other works, and of travel in regional fiction in general (see

Howard, "Unraveling"). It helps make sense of her chapter's ending with a train derailment to know that travel delays and accidents figure frequently in realist and regionalist works of the period (see Palmer)—although this connection does not come alive in the text and the effect is actually rather melodramatic.

Such heterogeneity is not surprising in a work by twelve hands. Yet I would argue—and I have argued elsewhere, following Fredric Jameson—that generic discontinuity characterizes the novel in general. Most modern novels are "loose baggy monsters," in James's phrase (*Literary Criticism: Prefaces* 1107), and what we see in *The Whole Family* is a heightened, not an idiosyncratic, negotiation among conventions deriving from various settings and moments. Genre criticism is properly an enterprise of interpretation rather than classification.

This perspective relies on an understanding of genres as themselves baggy monsters which cannot be captured by prescriptive definitions. They are better described in terms of what Wittgenstein calls "family resemblances": "you will not see something that is common to *all*, but similarities, relationships, and a whole series of them at that" (31). Forms are described at many levels—realism, humor, and the boy book (for example) might all be used in relation to the same text because they are asymmetrical categories. And the relations of various elements affect how we see each of them, producing a virtually infinite number of possible combinations. Wittgenstein writes that "the various resemblances between members of a family: build, features, colour of eyes, gait, temperament, etc. etc. overlap and criss-cross" (32). His use of the family as a figure here points out how thoroughly that institution and our desire to establish boundaries are wedded and interwoven. As my imitative form demonstrates, reach for an image of integral connection and "wedded" or one of its kin is likely to appear. Yet I do not want to overstate the connection: the process Wittgenstein is describing can be identified in every sort of category making.

Realism, in particular, is a category as complex as sentimentality—equally charged and contested, similarly active in both vernacular and academic discourses. It has been powerfully argued that realism is cognitively superior to other forms of narrative, and progressive; and just as powerfully, that it deceptively defends the existing order and naturalizes bourgeois subjectivity. Here again the genre is full of social meaning without having a single, unified politics; we need to resist the temptation to be for or against it. Understanding its significance requires not only long historical and transatlantic perspectives, but a detailed engagement with particular reading practices inculcated in particular national literatures.[6]

Like sentimentality, realism is inextricably part of broad social transformations, yet in any given instance it is local and multivalent. It has been linked to the emergence of abstracted clock time and Cartesian space, to secularization and empiricism, to the need to represent new urban and industrial conditions, and so on—one might say, to modernity. It seems to me that, as Christopher Prendergast puts it in his introduction to a collection of essays on French realism, "the deep ambiguity of the project of realism, [is] predicated on a desire for stable knowledge while encountering the conditions of its impossibility" (7). On this view, its project certainly cannot be contained within the remaking of literary form. Indeed it might be said to include an enterprise like my own microhistorical cultural analysis, mobilizing abstractions and empirical details in a quest for historical explanation. Realism is a genre constitutively in dialogue with other projects of knowledge making, and especially with the emerging social sciences—as we saw most vividly in chapter 3's investigation of family talk, and will see again in examining Henry Van Dyke's conclusion to *The Whole Family*.

And certainly, in the United States, literary realism emerges in dialogue with conventions grounded in systems incompatible with the antifoundational thinking associated with modernity. In practice the secular and the sacred, the mimetic and the didactic—like the public and the private, the traditional and the New Woman—often mingle. Authors producing frank narratives of everyday life frequently imbricated them with religious discourse, and some of the antebellum writers who now appear as early realists, such as Rebecca Harding Davis (see Harris), were precisely those cast as antagonists by the self-declared realists of the postbellum period. Increasingly critics are recognizing how thoroughly the genre includes sentimentality, its intimate other.[7]

However, the debates over the definition and relative value of genres that filled literary magazines in the latter nineteenth century had died down by the first decade of the twentieth, according to Nancy Glazener. Neither Howells nor any of the other authors articulates a view of

The Whole Family's relation to realism. Alfred Bendixen writes that Howells planned a "realistic" work because he described the family as "middling" and "average" (xii). The father's chapter, focused on details of everyday life and written in plain language, sustains that assessment. Subsequent contributions—with the striking exception of James's—remain within that framework. Yet their affiliation is not so much a specific enlistment in realism as a diffuse acceptance of its narrative techniques. What James calls "the air of reality" or "solidity of specification" (*Literary Criticism: Essays* 53) characterizes most fiction written in the United States at this period; an extraordinarily baggy version of realism, incorporating many contrasting conventions, is the dominant discourse in *Harper's Bazar* and *Harper's Monthly* alike. Indeed, those narrative techniques arguably remain dominant today in the work of novelists from Michael Crichton to Barbara Kingsolver—and for that matter, many nonfiction writers—yet saying so tells us little of consequence about those authors. I would argue, in fact, that the moment of *The Whole Family* marks both the triumph of realism as a cognitive project and its disappearance as a usably distinctive form.

Perhaps the most mixed, vexed aspect of the mixed form of realist fiction in any period is its plotting. Advocates of the form have consistently campaigned against the happy ending as violating the sprawling nature of reality. Yet virtually all the many versions of the tradition are constructed by works that rely on the marriage plot, or at least on its reversal. The chapters in the first half of *The Whole Family* turn around issues of character and theme, with action dealing with Peggy's marriage to Goward remaining central but not so much advancing as being constantly complicated and deferred—essentially blockaded by conflicts among the other characters. Cutting even moved to shift attention to the relation between father and son, although the suggestion was ignored. In the second half of *The Whole Family*, as the end of the novel approaches and the pressure for narrative closure increases, the authors' contributions to the plot increasingly seem their most salient choices. They are shaping both the fate of the family and the key final elements of the novel's generic positioning.

James's choice, however, is to open the second half with a chapter that virtually ignores plot. "The Married Son" is concerned with perception and taste and even (briefly) the urban atmosphere James had just treated in *The American Scene*. As we have seen, he was interested in portraying the companionate marriage, and he gives Charles Edward a strong opinion about coeducation. Her brother disapproves of Peggy's engagement for exactly the reason many conservatives opposed educating men and women together—it meant taking a daughter of the privileged classes out of the circle of family connections: "Her turning up in such a fashion with the whole thing settled before Father or Mother or Maria or any of us had so much as heard of the young man, much less seen the tip of his nose, had too much in common, for my taste, with the rude betrothals of the people, with some maid-servant's announcement to her employer that she has exchanged vows with the butcher-boy" (174). But James has no visible interest in the marriage plot. His chapter is by a considerable margin the longest in the novel (long enough that he felt obliged to convey a halfhearted permission to Jordan to cut the last section if she wished). Yet it does not move toward narrative resolution, except for generating an arrangement for getting the redeemable members of the family off to Europe.

Elizabeth Stuart Phelps, on the other hand, immediately focuses on the marriage plot and tries to save the engagement. She sends Maria to talk to Peggy, and has Peggy send Maria to New York to talk to Goward—with a characteristic hope for a weak man's reform, she tries to redeem the fickle Goward (on terms of redemption very different from James's). Then Edith Wyatt takes an equally characteristic view and opposes any notion of "true love" that entails a strong woman being loyal to a weak man. She implicitly administers a rebuke to Phelps and her endorsement of the marriage plot when she has the mother get angry at Maria: "I must confess I fail to understand why your sister should wish so patronizingly for you a fortune she would never have accepted for herself. How can she possibly like for you such a mawkish and a morbid thing as the prospect of a marriage with a man in whom neither you nor any other person feels the presence of one single absolute and manly quality?" (230). Wyatt does not attempt to propose a resolution—only to avert one.

Following Wyatt, Mary Raymond Shipman Andrews is at least equally concerned with the problem of Goward's lack of masculinity, but more concerned with arriving at a resolution through marriage. She abandons Goward—in Howells's chapter Billy already suspected him of being a sissy, after all—and proposes a new hero. Cutting had suggested that Eastridge's local physician loves Peggy (Lorraine writes that he smiles affectionately at Alice, but "not the way he used to smile at Peggy. I really thought he cared for Peggy once, though he's so much older" [82]). In Andrews's chapter Dr. Denbigh—"Jack"—is an athlete and a soldier brimming with manliness. Following Freeman's precedent she maneuvers a bit with the characters' relative ages; Denbigh had been introduced as a widower "of long standing" (23) and a crony of Cyrus Talbert's, but she makes him forty (only twice Peggy's age rather than three times). She does not attempt to explain why, if he is in love with Peggy, Denbigh would travel to New York with Maria and flirt with Aunt Elizabeth to help separate her from Goward. And she is willing to introduce a scenario of misunderstanding worthy of a later serial genre, the soap opera: Denbigh chivalrously refuses to allow Peggy to commit to an engagement until she has seen more of the world, so she is vulnerable to being misled by Aunt Elizabeth into thinking there is a romance between the two older people, and in her disappointment becomes engaged to Goward. With Billy's connivance, Denbigh gets Peggy alone and assures her of his unswerving devotion—and Andrews has cleared the way for narrative closure in the form of a wedding.

The next chapter, the eleventh of the novel's twelve and the only one titled with a name rather than a role, is Alice Brown's "Peggy." Brown was first known, and remains best known, for her New England stories, but she wrote well-crafted fiction on many topics and published regularly in the *Bazar*. She too is ready to dismiss Goward, but she rejects Dr. Denbigh as a replacement. Andrews had invented an odd device to explain why the school-boy would be discoursing about Peggy's engagement—Billy reports that Lorraine promised him cookies if he would write down what he knows. Brown uses that to turn Andrews's chapter into a hoax, opening with Peggy's younger sister, Alice, apologizing to her for having collaborated with her brother to produce a truthless tale. Nothing in his chapter really happened. It turns out to be not Peggy but Alice who is infatuated with the doctor: " 'I've adored him for years,' said Alice. 'I could trust him with my whole future. I could trust him with yours' " (266). This revelation puts to work Jordan's characterization of Alice as circulating false reports because of her overactive imagination, overinvestment in love stories, and desire to be the center of attention; both matchmaking and fiction writing fit exactly into Jordan's picture of the school-girl.[8] For that matter, it is consistent with Andrews's portrait of Billy—it is easy to imagine him handing off the repugnant task of writing about a romance to his sister, although of course that portrait itself is now called into question because it is Alice's. The process is confusing, but the result is definite. Brown manages to return the plot to the point at which Wyatt left it—Ada has agreed that Charles Edward and Lorraine ought to take Peggy to Europe, and Goward has just been in a train accident—and then moves decisively to settle the outcome of the story.

Brown's chapter does an extraordinary job of weaving together the threads she has been handed. Jordan writes in *Three Rousing Cheers* that *all* the other authors liked it (277). (Even James, dissatisfied with the project as a whole, acknowledged her achievement by adding a postscript to one of his letters to Jordan: "Yet I do justice to Miss Brown!" [Edel and Powers 52].) Her skillful incorporation of Jordan's Alice and Andrews's Billy is characteristic; she also catches the slangy way of talking Cutting gave Lorraine and the gentle determination to protect Peggy and Charles Edward that Wyatt made central to Ada's character. She offers a completely new hero—Stillman Dane, a psychology professor at Peggy's college who is also a good friend of Charles Edward's (they were in college together). Thus she retrieves and resolves the co-education theme: Peggy will marry a man she met at school, but he has a connection to her family. She gives the first and only accounts of Peggy's college experience, which helps to weave that strand of the novel back into its conclusion. She even offers a fairly plausible explanation of how a nice girl like Peggy got involved with a feckless fellow like Goward in the first place—he told her at a dance how "he had been betrayed over and over by the vain and the worldly, and how his heart was dead and nobody could bring it to life but me" (275), and so on— and in her innocence she believed him.

Brown locates the solution to Peggy's problems with Charles Edward and Lorraine—not only are her conversations with them clarifying, but when she walks into their house she finds that Stillman Dane has arrived there on an unexpected visit. Brown's positioning of Dane, in particular, draws the younger Talberts back toward a less marginal status; he is clearly both a solid citizen and very close to them. Brown portrays the moment when it becomes clear that Peggy and Dane are going to reach an understanding, and friendship will merge into family as he becomes a brother-in-law, as a highly emotional one. As Peggy and Dane return from a walk in the garden Lorraine asks maternally, " 'Well, children?' She turned her bright eyes on us as if she liked us very much, and we two stood facing them two, and it all seemed quite solemn. Suddenly Charles Edward put out his hand and shook Mr. Dane's, and they both looked very much moved, as grandmother would say. I hadn't known they liked each other so well" (286). The dangers of homosocial attachment and proximity to an aesthete like Charles Edward are immediately managed not only by the intensely familial nature of the scene but also by an affirmation of Dane's masculinity. He realizes how late it is: " 'Gee whiz!' said Mr. Dane. I'd never heard him say things like that. It sounded like Billy, and I liked it. 'I've got to catch that midnight train' " (287). As each of these quotations shows, Brown weaves in constant references to the other members of the family.

One of Brown's most interesting decisions, from the perspective of cultural history, was to make Stillman Dane the college "psychology man" (275). Academic psychology had been in a period of expansion since the 1890s—in 1878 no American university had granted a doctoral degree in psychology; by 1904 more than one hundred had been awarded. This was, of course, generally a period of disciplinary formation and professionalization, but Jill Morawski makes clear in an essay in the collection *Inventing the Psychological* that the emergence of a modern science of the self was particularly rapid and effectual. Peggy's class might have used any of the thirty-eight undergraduate textbooks published in the first decade of the century; according to Morawski, any would have conveyed two contradictory but inextricably entangled concepts of the field. One (internally complex in ways I will not try to recount here) emphasized the scientific project of experimental psychology, tending toward determinism and biomechanical explanation. The other, in various ways, spoke the language of individualism and self-control, and undertook what Morawski calls "educating the emotions" (228): "The centrality of scientific determinism in psychological theories provided the discipline with authority and legitimacy, while attention to the desires and interests of middle-class individuals helped to make psychology a commercial success—a sought-after commodity that apparently served their personal and occupational aspirations" (219). Dane's masculine power implicitly relies on the first aspect of his discipline. Peggy's naïveté allows her to voice the hopes placed on the second: "If Stillman Dane had been here all these dreadful things would not have happened, because he is a psychologist, and he would have understood everybody at once and influenced them before they had time to do wrong" (278).

Brown's references to psychology, like Anne O'Hagan's to neurosis (cited in ch. 4), index the interpenetration of expert, educated, and popular discourses of the self. This is also a period in which, David Lubin argues in a study of the realistic portraiture of Thomas Eakins (also in *Inventing the Psychological*), "middle-class Americans came increasingly to see themselves as complex and multi-faceted creatures of ultimately unfathomable psychological depth." The institutionalization of psychology and the development of that particular discourse of interiority are—as we have already seen—aspects of the extended and enormous history in which modern self-making practices are produced and constantly transformed. The connection returns us once again to the confrontation of intimacy and publicity, the intricate impasse of public and private, that is the recurrent theme not only of *The Whole Family* but of this book as well. Harper's composite novel now imagines not only a sociologist across the fence and a reporter in the house, but a psychologist in the bedroom.

Peggy considers becoming a psychologist herself—she tells Stillman Dane that she could never stand to be "pointed at, like Aunt Elizabeth, and have people whisper and say I've had a disappointment. . . . I must have a profession. Do you think I could teach? Do you think I could learn to teach—psychology?" (283). Since Brown has already implied that the origin of Peggy's interest in the field was her crush on Dane, this only adds another involution to the chains of narrative causality that tell us Peggy will be a wife and mother. (Dane hedges—he is sure she could teach something. Meanwhile she studies the ring he wears on his little finger, which he once told her was his mother's engagement ring.) Yet Brown is also working within the characterization and situation she has been given to create some narrative room for Peggy to grow up. Her hero, far from sweeping the heroine off her feet, courts her gently, implying that marriage is not her only destiny; psychological maturity also matters.

Brown, as I have noted, also deals firmly with the problem posed by Aunt Elizabeth. Peggy's comments about her and the scenes between them that Brown crafts project a plausible account of the spinster's psychology: Elizabeth is beautiful but overdresses because she is vain and insecure; she is self-centered and unhappy, and therefore manipulative. Brown develops previous contributors' skepticism about Lyman Wilde's sincerity—or at least his discrimination (231)—into a confirmation that Elizabeth has deluded herself about him and his feeling for her. (He writes her a beautiful letter—on beautiful paper, in beautiful handwriting, expressing beautiful sentiments—which tells her that, exhausted by the intensities of the opera season, he will be leading a cloistered life for some time, but that she has always been his inspiration and still has his undying devotion. As Brown's masculinized Charles Edward puts it in the scene just discussed, "he's had the spirit to make off" [286].) Brown puts Aunt Elizabeth in her place by sending her to work with Mrs. Chataway, creating a symmetry in which her class pretensions are punished by downward mobility. Yet she also implies that the contrasting images of the old maid can be reconciled when Peggy shifts from saying "Aunt Elizabeth" to saying "Aunt Lily" (292). When Peggy tells her aunt that she too is planning a career, even if we do not believe her it seems to suggest that as a legitimate choice for women; and Brown ends the narrative with Peggy embracing her aunt: "I put my arms around her and kissed her on her soft, pink cheeks, and we both cried a little. Then she went away" (292).

Brown seems to make a special effort to honor Henry James, including an allusion to his then-recent and now-famous story "The Beast in the Jungle" (1903). Lorraine tells Stillman Dane that she wants Charles Edward to take this chance to assert himself in the family and take Peggy to Europe: "Don't you remember the Great Magician's story of the man who was always afraid he should miss his opportunity? And the opportunity came, and, sure enough, the man didn't know it, and it slipped by" (278). In her positive portrait of the younger Talberts, and in making Peggy's acquisition of a more cosmopolitan culture central to her resolution, Brown implicitly endorses James's perspective on the family—although her treatment of the characters is characteristically more sympathetic, her resolution characteristically happy. Brown's 1920 collection *Vanishing Points* makes it clear how deeply she admired James. One story, "The Master," is clearly about him: a group of writers begins talking about another, absent author who is generally considered incomprehensible and unsuccessful, and finds that his influence is so pervasive that they send him the laurel wreath they ordinarily burn at the end of their meetings. Other stories explore the theme of publicity discussed in the previous section. In "The Discovery" two reporters find the love letters of a writer they admire and burn them so that no one can invade his posthumous privacy by printing them. "The Hands of the Faithful" is an optimistic reversal of "The Death of the Lion": when an author falls ill, admirers who have been too tactful to approach write to him, and that sense of human connection enables him to recover his health and continue to write. Alice Brown's fiction assures us that the boundary between public and private remains stable, just as "Peggy" assures us that the coeducated girl is not lost to the family, and that culture and manliness are not incompatible. Here and elsewhere, Brown had a genius for the happy ending. (That is both a strength and a limit of her work—which deserves more attention than it is currently receiving.) From any point of view that values closure, Jordan made a fortunate choice in asking her to write the penultimate chapter of *The Whole Family*.

It seems, in fact, that Brown has left little for Henry Van Dyke, chosen to write the last chapter of the novel from the point of view of the friend of the family, to do. He creates the character Gerrit Wendell, a former publisher of the *Eastridge Banner* who is now a globe-trotting writer but still a close friend of Cyrus Talbert. Wendell appears on the scene because the two men promised always to help each other at need, and Cyrus (who once went to Panama to get him when he was "knocked out with the fever" [298]) has summoned him. Van Dyke's first gesture is to invoke exotic landscapes as background, for his narrator and the novel at large; when Wendell receives Cyrus's telegram he has just returned to New York to see a new book through the publishing process and is "trying to find myself at home again in the democratic simplicity of the United States. For two years I had been traveling in the effete, luxurious Orient as a peace correspondent for a famous newspaper;

sleeping under canvas in Syria, in mud houses in Persia, in paper cottages in Japan; riding on camel-hump through Arabia, on horseback through Afghanistan, in palankeen through China, and faring on such food as it pleased Providence to send" (293). He soon makes the contrast explicit: "At supper we had the usual tokens of festivity: broiled chickens and pop-overs and cool, sliced tomatoes and ice-cream with real strawberries in it (how good and clean it tasted after Ispahan and Bagdad!) and the usual family arguing and joking (how natural and wholesome it sounded after Vienna and Paris!)" (301). Such racialized stereotypes have been invoked in passing already; Freeman has Elizabeth imagine Wilde "in the Far East, with a harem" (47), and James makes an allusion to Africa and the "heart of darkness" (see Tintner, "*Roderick Hudson*"). Van Dyke makes them central to his chapter, not only staking out distinctive ground for his character but also insisting on the distinction of Americanness—creating closure by directing the reader's attention away from the family differences that have occupied the novel and toward an asserted difference between the American family and others.

Van Dyke's presence in the text is another small irony of literary history. As a minister, a Princeton English professor, and a highly moral— as well as voluminous and popular—writer, he enhanced the collaboration's authority. He may also have been easy to enlist because Jordan already had a working relationship with him—he had published in the *Bazar* several times during her editorship, including a flowery, formulaic essay on "The Way to Womanhood" in 1905. Van Dyke is most often remembered now for speaking out against the award of the Nobel Prize to Sinclair Lewis in 1930, and provoking Lewis's famous attack on the genteel tradition. The focus of the controversy was precisely their different attitudes toward America and its institutions. Lewis makes Van Dyke's protest emblematic of "the fact that in America most of us—not readers alone but even writers—are still afraid of any literature which is not a glorification of everything American, a glorification of our faults as well as our virtues" (11). He much less justifiably includes Howells in this accusation, saying—in an often-quoted sentence—that he "had the code of a pious old maid whose greatest delight was to have tea at the vicarage" (21). Lewis uses the same image of the old maid that Mary Wilkins Freeman thought was obsolete, and criticized Howells for using, more than twenty years before; he needs it as a contrast that confirms his own modernity and manhood. Thirty years before that, of course, Howells had been the standard-bearer for realism, confirming its up-to-date toughness by opposing effeminate romanticism and sentimentality. Van Dyke's membership in the Family reminds us that cultural ground is defined by repeated polarizations and that the masculinization of American literature always needs doing over again. Yet it can also remind us that the participants in this history are constantly engaged in creative compromise. Sinclair Lewis's first book was turned down by several publishers but accepted at Harper's by an editor who admired it and was willing to work with him on revisions: Elizabeth Jordan. His friendship with her kept him with the firm until her own departure in 1917.

In *The Whole Family*, Van Dyke also seems to be demonstrating that the writer can be masculine. Gerrit Wendell banters with Cyrus Talbert about business, combining the vocabularies of exotic travel and advertising (few of the other contributors seemed to remember that Howells gave the father a sense of humor). Cyrus asks jokingly, "How did you leave my friend the Shah of Persia?" and Wendell replies, "Better . . . since he got on the water-wagon—uses nothing but Eastridge silver-plated ice-pitchers now" (299).[9] He also lends support to Alice Brown's new hero, testifying to his character and strengthening his connection to the family: "'What Dane is that?' I interrupted. 'Is his first name Stillman—nephew of my old friend Harvey Dane, the publisher? Because, if that's so, I know him; about twenty-eight years old; good family, good head, good manners, good principles; just the right age and the right kind for Peggy—a very fine fellow indeed'" (304). He confirms that coeducation has not led Peggy to a romance with a man outside her class. Van Dyke also has Wendell stage an encounter in which Peggy and a repentant Goward bow to each other, formally acknowledging the end of their connection. "That clears up one of my troubles!" says Cyrus when he hears about it (312); propriety has been satisfied. It seems fitting that the link runs through a publisher, and not impossible that Van Dyke was nodding to the family institution Harper & Brothers.

Van Dyke then arranges for a different sort of convention to be observed. The illustrator Howard Chandler Christy writes in the last chapter of his 1906 book *The American Girl* (a striking example of what James called the "system of publicity" on behalf of American women) that a girl always reads the end of a book first. Why? Because "if she can not ascertain whether the wedding-bells are to ring in the last pages— then so much the worse for the unhappy and the unread novelist. She 'doesn't think she'd care to read that book, anyway,' and tosses it aside in favor of the work of a more capable novelist who places on the last page, convenient to her prying eyes, an assurance that the love-affair ends as all should end" (136). (He suggests magazine editors consider placing a frontispiece of a wedding at the beginning of serials; and in fact, Stephens's picture of Peggy [fig. 36] at least guaranteed a marriageable heroine as the center of the novel much more obviously than Howells's first chapter did.) However, Brown had arranged for Peggy to sail for Europe still unmarried—on a ship also carrying her suitor, chaperoned only by her unconventional brother and sister-in-law. Van Dyke has her father put his foot down against such an improper expedition. Ostensibly Cyrus is affirming the importance of women's choices—he says, "Peggy positively shall not be pushed, or inveigled, or dragooned, or personally conducted into marrying anybody at all!"—but he does not go so far as to ask her what she wants. By paradoxical paternal decree, Peggy will "stay at home and be free" (304–5). Van Dyke's preliminary refusal of the marriage plot proves to be a feint, however, to enhance the effect when closure is achieved; he sends Peggy to Europe and still satisfies convention, in both relevant senses. Wendell has mysteriously insisted that Cyrus retain Peggy's stateroom, and he leaves her alone with Stillman Dane at a strategic moment, so the couple turns up on the ship—married.

The action then moves so quickly to a close that it does not give the reader time to reflect on the haste of this resolution, or wonder if the elder Talberts regret missing their daughter's wedding. Our final image of Peggy is informed by Van Dyke's inflection of the narrative toward nationalism. Alice Barber Stephens illustrated his detailed description exactly (pl. 9): "Dane had given her his walking-stick, and she had tied her handkerchief to the handle. She was standing up on a chair, with one of his hands to steady her. Her hat had slipped back on her head. The last thing that we could distinguish on the ship was that brave little girl, her red hair like an aureole, waving her flag of victory and peace"

(316). This is the only one of the novel's illustrations printed in color; its rosy tone is emphasized by the red and white stripes of Peggy's flag, ensuring that it proffers closure and claims coherence not only for *The Whole Family* but for the American family as well.

The visual image lingers, but the moment in the text passes quickly. The paragraph ends, and in the next Van Dyke drops back into familiar resentments. Maria the manager tells everyone how they will spend the afternoon—Wendell rejects her plan in favor of taking just Cyrus and Ada to lunch at Delmonico's—and the novel ends with the words, "we don't want the whole family" (316). Glorified love is juxtaposed with quotidian family jars, and self-referentiality also supplies a sensation of closure.

The image that stands for closure for me is a different one: the figure of the reader turning the page *after* "The End"—to read the next article in the magazine or, in the reprint edition of the novel, the appended author's biographies. Relations really do stop nowhere, so far as I know. Gestures creating the sense that they do necessarily project the prospect of disruption, which can be folded back into the narrative only so long as one does not stop narrating. The endeavor to grasp the dynamic of unity and disunity that shapes *The Whole Family* has constantly led me back to the recognition that each successive interiority—of the self, the family, the nation—faces invasion because it can never flee far enough from the boundary that defines it. I hope I have shown that this paradox is not merely a poststructuralist truism, but an interpretive device that enables us to apprehend the stories, and the story-telling efforts, of historical human beings. To bind a book is also to establish a boundary. My reading has constantly erased that apparent limit by interweaving the story of the novel with other stories of many sorts. Whatever we wish or believe, they are all collaborations. My own exposition and endeavors have no firmer boundary; to finish what I want to say is just—indeed it is too late for me to say anything but—turn the page.

✤ Appendix 1 ✤

Contents and Characters of
The Whole Family, a Novel by Twelve Authors

1. "The Father"
Cyrus Talbert; narrated by Ned Temple / William Dean Howells

2. "The Old-Maid Aunt"
Elizabeth Talbert, also known as Lily / Mary Wilkins Freeman

3. "The Grandmother"
Mrs. Evarts / Mary Heaton Vorse

4. "The Daughter-in-Law"
Lorraine Talbert / Mary Stewart Cutting

5. "The School-Girl"
Alice Talbert / Elizabeth Jordan

6. "The Son-in-Law"
Tom Price / John Kendrick Bangs

7. "The Married Son"
Charles Edward Talbert, also known as Peter and Charley Ned / Henry James

8. "The Married Daughter"
Maria Talbert Price / Elizabeth Stuart Phelps

9. "The Mother"
Ada Evarts Talbert / Edith Wyatt

10. "The School-Boy"
Billy Talbert / Mary Raymond Shipman Andrews

11. "Peggy"
Peggy Talbert / Alice Brown

12. "The Friend of the Family"
Gerrit Wendell / Henry Van Dyke

❧ Appendix 2 ❧

The Generations of the "Family"

Author	Age in 1907	Character	Life Span
Howells	70	Father	1837–1920
Freeman	55	Aunt	1852–1930
Vorse	33	Grandmother	1874–1966
Cutting	56	Daughter-in-Law	1851–1924
Jordan	42	School-Girl	1865–1947
Bangs	45	Son-in-Law	1862–1922
James	64	Married Son	1843–1916
Phelps	65	Married Daughter	1844–1911
Wyatt	34	Mother	1873–1958
Andrews	47	School-Boy	1860–1936
Brown	50	Daughter	1857–1948
Van Dyke	55	Friend of the Family	1852–1933

⇥ Notes ⇤

1. "A Strangely Exciting Story"

1 Elizabeth Jordan, *Three Rousing Cheers* (New York: D. Appleton-Century, 1938) 258. Throughout, quotations from Jordan not otherwise identified are from this book. Although Jordan's autobiography is an indispensable source, it is not a wholly reliable one. In comparing the extant letters with the versions printed in *Three Rousing Cheers*, Leon Edel and Lyall Powers (editors of *Henry James and the Bazar Letters* [New York: New York Public Library, 1958]) and Alfred Bendixen (in his introduction to the reprint of the novel [New York: Ungar, 1986]) found that Jordan had made a number of alterations. I rely on their work as well as my own examination of her papers at the New York Public Library.

   A further note: according to Eugene Exman, Jordan "insisted that her name be pronounced with the stress on the last syllable" (*The House of Harper* [New York: Harper & Row, 1967] 126).

2 The letters quoted in this and the subsequent paragraph are in the Jordan papers and are also published in Howells, *Life in Letters*, ed. Mildred Howells (Garden City, N.Y.: Doubleday, Doran, 1928) 2: 223–25.

3 Howells's scorching letter is not in Jordan's papers. She seems to have been uncharacteristically cautious and destroyed it—unless she was exaggerating the vehemence of the note dated July 31 (one week after Freeman submitted her chapter), in which he suggests placing "The Old-Maid Aunt" late in the book (as first planned) and not sending it to the other contributors. Howells had volunteered to modify his chapter to mesh with subsequent ones, but that possibility is not mentioned after this point.

4 Howells, *Criticism and Fiction* (1891), rpt. in *Selected Literary Criticism,*

vol. 2, ed. Donald Pizer and others (Bloomington: Indiana UP, 1993), quotations from 323 and 302, respectively.

5 See the introduction by D. C. Greetham to the 1992 paperback edition of McGann's *Critique of Modern Textual Criticism* (1983; rpt. Charlottesville: UP of Virginia, 1992) x.

6 "Literature and Culture," in *Columbia Literary History of the United States*, ed. Emory Elliott (New York: Columbia UP, 1988) 468. The classic text here is William Charvat, *The Profession of Authorship in America, 1800–1870* (1968; rpt. New York: Columbia UP, 1992).

7 For that reconstruction, see especially their discussion of the Bellagio declaration in "The Ethical Reaches of Authorship," *South Atlantic Quarterly* 95 (1996): 947–77. For the recovery of collectivity, see their separate introductions to *The Construction of Authorship* (Durham: Duke UP, 1994).

8 My thanks to my research partner Gina Hausknecht, on whose work I rely on in this paragraph and the next. She discovered that the New York Public Library at one time used composite authorship as a classification, but it was applied to only five books and is no longer in use.

9 My thanks to Susanna Ashton for sharing her work in progress on collaborative novels. She has located (counting works by pairs of writers as well as groups) eight collaborations by American authors that appeared between 1800 and 1880, thirty-nine in the period 1880–1910, and sixteen (excluding mysteries and science fiction) since 1910.

10 See the introduction to *Murasaki* (New York: Bantam-Spectra, 1992) and "Shared Worlds," by John Clute, in the *Encyclopedia of Science Fiction* for more information. The first volume of the Thieves' World series (New York: Ace Books, 1979) includes a brief essay by coauthor Robert Asprin titled "The Making of Thieves' World."

11 See Camille Bacon-Smith's *Science Fiction Culture* (Philadelphia: U of Pennsylvania P, 2000) for more information on the science fiction community and a strong argument for the genre's prototypical ability to reveal the developing relations of social production and postmodern culture.

12 See Mike McGrady, *Stranger Than Naked, or, How to Write Dirty Books for Fun and Profit* (New York: Peter H. Wyden, 1970), for a detailed account of the composition, publication, promotion, and reception of this book, which was meant to make not only a profit but a comment on the state of American letters.

13 For the articles on editors and women short story writers, see Flora Mai Holly, "Notes on Some American Magazine Editors," *Bookman* 12

(December 1900): 357–68; and Mary K. Ford, "Some Recent Women Short Story Writers," *Bookman* 27 (April 1908): 152–61. The *Bookman* was published by Dodd & Mead and publicized literary affairs generally (see Christopher Wilson, *The Labor of Words* [Athens: U of Georgia P, 1985] 79). Frank Luther Mott writes that "there seems to have been a minimum of log-rolling in clique-claques. Such prejudice as is discernible seems to have been intelligent prejudice" (*A History of American Magazines*, vol. 4 [Cambridge: Harvard UP, 1957] 434).

14   See the entries on Stephens in *The National Cyclopedia* and *Notable American Women;* for a contemporary view, see North.

15   This point is made very effectively in Karen Kilcup's essay "The Conversation of 'The Whole Family': Gender, Politics, and Aesthetics in Literary Tradition," which introduces a volume of essays she edited on American women writers and masculine literary tradition (*Soft Canons* [Iowa City: U of Iowa P, 1999] 1–24).

16   The phrase is quoted, in the present tense, in J. Henry Harper, *The House of Harper* (Harper & Brothers, 1912) 325.

17   In 1900, during the period when he was actively working at Franklin Square as a literary adviser, Howells read Wyatt's fiction in *McClure's* and wrote to her inviting her to submit a novel to Harper's. He clearly had a genuine, strong liking for Wyatt and her work, writing to T. S. Perry in 1905 that her two novels were "beautifully simple and true fables, as slyly told as Jane Austen's. . . . I'm sure you and Mrs. Perry would like her books and her." She sat next to him at the dinner at Delmonico's for Twain's seventieth birthday, and Howells told Perry she "was the best of the literary crowd" there (*Life in Letters* 2, 214–15). In 1906 Alden declined two stories she had submitted to the *Monthly;* a regretful letter from Howells conveying the news is among her papers at the Newberry Library.

18   The forum on the afterlife was another of Jordan's composite projects, with a number of distinguished authors contributing; its topic was the same as that of Phelps's famous novel *The Gates Ajar.*

19   These appeared in June ("As to 'The Whole Family'" 613), November ("The Whole Family and a Reminiscence" n.p.) and December ("Concerning 'The Whole Family'" n.p.) 1908. The December article listed the authors of the chapters, ending the guessing game. In fact, a list was published, although incomplete and in some cases inaccurate, in the December 1906 issue in which the composite novel was first advertised (see fig. 1). Its appearance seems to have escaped the notice of those participating in the guessing game.

2. The Hearthstone at Harper's

1 John Tebbel, *A History of Book Publishing in the United States*, vol. 1 (New York: R. R. Bowker, 1972) 269–70. This is the standard general history. The fact that Tebbel tends to rely uncritically on his sources (my own observation on this point is confirmed by Harner's *Literary Research Guide*) makes it important to compare the information he supplies with other scholars' work (cited below), but makes him if anything more useful as an index to received opinion in the publishing industry and publishing history.

2 Madison, *Book Publishing in America* (New York: McGraw-Hill, 1966) 25–26. Tebbel writes that at the time of the 1853 fire Harper's "was the largest publisher in the world, with 1,549 books in print, in 2,028 volumes" (1: 279) and that in 1865 Harper's "had been the leading house in America and the world for some time" (1: 283).

3 The essential histories of Harper's from within are J[oseph] Henry Harper, *The House of Harper*; and Eugene Exman, *The Brothers Harper* (New York: Harper & Row, 1965) and *The House of Harper*. Joseph Henry Harper was the grandson of Fletcher Harper and a member of the firm for many years; he will appear frequently in the pages below. Exman was the head of the religious department at Harper's (see Madison, *Book Publishing* 173; and Exman, *House* 235). But see also Madison for a perspective from outside (although not necessarily a disinterested one, as Madison was associated with Henry Holt for many years), and see especially Tebbel. Frank Luther Mott's *History of American Magazines* (4 vols.) provides vital information on the periodicals published by Harper's.

    I should note here that my practice of referring to the corporate entity Harper & Brothers as "Harper's" follows a precedent established in the title of *Harper's Monthly Magazine* and continued by almost everyone who writes about the firm. The information in the paragraphs that follow is drawn from these sources. Thoreau voices his worry in the chapter "Reading" in *Walden*.

4 Fire was, of course, a hazard of the era, but it seemed to have a particular affinity for the Harpers—there were four fires before the famous one of December 10, 1853. For me, the forgotten tragic hero of the 1853 fire is Prof. Henry Drisler, whose almost-completed edition of Yonge's *English-Greek Lexicon* was entirely destroyed; it took him eighteen years to reconstruct his work (J. Henry Harper, *The House of Harper* 96–97). In every other case mentioned in the histories either proofs or plates were saved.

5 Wilson makes this point (xii) and also criticizes (as I do below) the assumption that industry growth is necessarily benevolent and democratizing.

6 The importance of this image of the brothers' working relationship is indicated by the fact that Harper repeats it almost verbatim twenty-odd years later in his memoir *I Remember* (New York: Harper & Brothers, 1934) (8–9).

7 Double-entry bookkeeping was instituted in 1857 (Exman 47), separate accounts in 1869 (Harper, *House* 23). J. Henry Harper phrases his description of the latter innovation in an oddly convoluted way: "As their various families increased, however, individual accounts became necessary; but it was not until ten years before the death of James Harper, in 1869, that they were kept distinct" (23). In other words, he dates the end of the old informal partnership in relation to the passing of the eldest brother, the head of the household.

8 They are quoting W. Holdsworth, *A History of English Law* (1966).

9 Exman's house history is not heavily documented, and he does not cite a source for the anecdote or explain why his version differs from J. Henry Harper's; he is likely relying on oral tradition at Harper's. Has he changed the meaning of the statement? Perhaps not, as at least one instance of the use of "either" to mean "one among several" exists (the *Oxford English Dictionary*'s modern example is from Howells's *Italian Journeys*). On the other hand, it also seems possible that in the earlier versions the "either" refers to the two original founding brothers and not to all equally. Derby's version (107) is intermediate—he says "sometimes" and "Either one." Madison's version (*Book Publishing* 21) approximates Derby's; Tebbel's (1: 275) approximates Exman's.

10 Exman, *The Brothers Harper* 350. This volume appeared some years before Tebbel's and Madison's repetitions of the Bremer story.

11 I should perhaps say that I can cite no direct testimony on such a point because none of the Harper brothers kept a journal or wrote a memoir, and their policy was to refrain from any public statements (there is apparently only one instance of any of them writing for publication). See Exman, *The Brothers Harper* x–xi.

12 According to Madison, this sentence appears in the first issue of the *Monthly*, and although I have been unable to locate it, the assertion is certainly compatible with those of "A Word at the Start," which ends with the publisher's hope that the magazine will "make its way into the hands or the family circle of every intelligent citizen of the United States" (2).

13　The information about *Harper's Young People* and the phrase "family newspaper" are from Exman, *House*, 139 and 80; "the family paper for women" is from Harper, *House* 248.

14　Harper, *House* 8. I am omitting a great deal of interesting biographical information, such as James's term as mayor of New York and his anti-Catholicism, because it is (unfortunately) not directly relevant to my focus in this essay.

15　See Harper, *House* 10, and *I Remember* 13–14. For a relatively recent repetition of the apocryphal story, see Ronald J. Zboray, "Antebellum Reading and the Ironies of Technological Innovation," *American Quarterly* 40 (March 1988): 69.

16　For the policy, see Madison, *Book Publishing in America* 70, as well as the Harper materials themselves. It appears that only two sons of the second generation did not enter the business—Wesley's sons Jack Fletcher, who was killed in battle in 1863, and Charles Wesley, who appears only as the father of "Joe Madison." Fletcher's son "Joe 22nd Street" (J. Henry Harper's father) spent only a few years at Franklin Square before entering the U.S. Foreign Service. J. Henry Harper writes in *The House of Harper* that five men of the second generation entered the firm (he is apparently not counting his father and counting his uncle James Thorne —who was James Harper's son by his second wife, and younger than J. Henry himself—in the third generation), and that eleven men of the third generation did. Assuming that the eight deaths and retirements he mentions include those of the four original founders, that leaves twelve Harpers associated with the firm in 1899 (650). Only ten appear on the genealogical chart Exman includes in *The Brothers Harper*, but it seems likely that a couple of younger Harpers were employed at the firm without becoming members.

17　*I Remember* 39. The author of these words is Rev. van Tassel Sutphen (12); Harper embeds lengthy passages from Sutphen's manuscripts in this memoir and makes no very great effort to make it clear whose voice the reader is hearing at any given moment. In effect, he endorses what Sutphen writes; therefore I write "according to J. Henry Harper."

18　J. Henry (Harry) Harper discusses this volume with amusement in *I Remember* (66–75), somewhat inflating the centrality of Harper's—Ford takes aim at many prominent magazines, editors, and publishers. Harper quotes with many inaccuracies but apparent enjoyment the passage in which the poet who proposes the compromise tells Joseph Harper that he is loyal because "last summer, sir, when I got my fingers frostbitten by being permitted to shake hands with Mr. Harry Harper, you not only allowed me half-pay, but gave my poor idiot sister a job in the factory as a reader of manuscript" (190).

19   The phrase is from the editors' introduction to Dirks, Eley, and Ortner's collection *Culture/Power/History* (Princeton: Princeton UP, 1994) 30.

20   The quoted phrases appear in Alden's *Magazine Writing and the New Literature* (New York: Harper & Brothers, 1908) 193; Ohmann cites them in *Selling Culture* (New York: Verso, 1996) 222.

21   Nancy Glazener discusses the specifically Bostonian cultural authority constructed by the *Atlantic* in chapter 1 of *Reading for Realism* (Durham: Duke UP, 1997). See also Paul DiMaggio, "Social Structure, Institutions, and Cultural Goods: The Case of the United States" (1991), rpt. in *The Politics of Culture*, ed. Gigi Bradford, Michael Gary, and Glenn Wallach (Washington, D.C.: Center for Arts and Culture; and New York: New P, 2000) 38–62.

22   On *Trilby*, see chapter 3 of Jonathan Freedman's *Temple of Culture* (New York: Oxford UP, 2000).

23   Harper, *House* 324. Both quotations from Howells in this paragraph are from a long account of his relations with the firm that he wrote for J. Henry Harper.

24   See Exman, *House* 171–83, for a fuller account.

25   Exman 188. Another member of the third generation, Sleeper Harper, later joined the board of directors.

26   The journal was abruptly transformed some years after Thomas Bucklin Wells took over from Alden. In September 1925 it appeared with different content, becoming a liberal journal of "diversified opinion" without illustration. See Mott 2: 404.

27   For the promotional dimension of distinction, see Brodhead on James Fields's institutionalization of American literature in chapter 3 of *The School of Hawthorne* (New York: Oxford UP, 1986). For the Atlantic dinners, see Mott 2: 509–10. The Howells dinner is presented as the emblem of the 1912 establishment in the opening of Henry May's *End of American Innocence* (1959; rpt. New York: Oxford UP, 1979) and the phrase "custodians of culture" alludes to his work. Wilson, in *The Labor of Words*, points out his neglect of Harvey's role (76).

28   I rely primarily on Exman 205–11. Different sources give rather different accounts of Harvey's role at Harper's; I have been provided with several salutary reminders of the fallibility of scholarship. Madison, for example, writes that Harvey got the firm out of debt (*Book Publishing* 72); Michael

Anesko, in *Letters, Fictions, Lives* (New York: Oxford UP, 1997), writes that Harvey's deep pockets helped salvage Harper's (329) without mentioning J. P. Morgan.

29 "Murdoch Wins Collins, Promises Autonomy," *Publishers Weekly* 234.3 (January 20, 1989): 16. Murdoch had owned approximately 41 percent of Collins since 1981, when a takeover attempt failed. Murdoch bought Harper's in March 1987 and in September sold a 50 percent interest to Collins.

30 Jordan Papers, file 10. This letter is dated February 27 without a year indicated, but its contents indicate that it was written during the composition of *The Whole Family*; the handwriting is consistent with this date.

3. Making the Family Whole

1 See Jean-Louis Flandrin, *Families in Former Times*, trans. Richard Southern (Cambridge: Cambridge UP, 1979), 1–10; and in general the works cited in note 2 below. Raymond Williams's entry in *Keywords* (New York: Oxford UP, 1976) on the topic is, as always, very helpful (108–11).

2 I rely on Stephanie Coontz, *The Social Origins of Private Life* (New York: Verso, 1988) and *The Way We Never Were* (New York: Basic Books-HarperCollins, 1992); Mark Poster, *Critical Theory of the Family* (London: Pluto P, 1978); and Helena M. Wall *Fierce Communion* (Cambridge: Harvard UP, 1990). Steven Mintz and Susan Kellogg, *Domestic Revolutions* (New York: Free P-Macmillan, 1988), is also useful despite its tendency to overvalue middle-class ideals of the family.

3 I cite the first two works from the bibliography in William L. O'Neill, *Divorce in the Progressive Era* (New Haven: Yale UP, 1967); I have examined the third, which was drawn to my attention by Phyllis Eileen Steele, "Hungry Hearts, Idle Wives, and New Women: The American Novel Re-examines Nineteenth-Century Domestic Ideology, 1890–1917" (Ph.D. diss., U of Iowa, 1993).

4 See Steele 217–18. Howells's letters to Herrick appear in *Life in Letters* 2: 229–30, 262. Howells's essay on Herrick's novels is reprinted in *Selected Literary Criticism*, vol. 3, ed. Ronald Gottesman and others (Bloomington: Indiana UP, 1993); the quotation is from 133.

5 See chapter 4 for a fuller discussion of Richard Brodhead's concept "disciplinary intimacy."

6 Copyright citations for the illustrations indicate that this work was serialized in the *Women's Home Companion*.

7   Virginia McAlester and Lee McAlester, *A Field Guide to American Houses* (New York: Knopf, 1984) 241–42, 488. In the 1960s there was a revival of the mansard roof in houses, also shopping centers, apartment houses, and commercial buildings. "Builders . . . learned that a relatively inexpensive way to get a dramatic decorative effect was to construct slightly sloping upper wall surfaces to be covered with shingles or other decorative roofing materials. This technique was apparently first used in apartment projects in Florida and the southwest and then spread rapidly to houses. The style was particularly favored in the late 1960s and early '70s but has persisted into the '80s with modifications" (487–88).

8   There is even an allusion to collaboration, as they enjoy a witticism of which they are "joint authors" (22).

9   See Brent L. Kendrick's "General Introduction" to his collection of Freeman's letters, *The Infant Sphinx* (Metuchen, N.J.: Scarecrow P, 1985), for specifics about Warren Edward Wilkins's activities as a builder and comments on those of his architectural plans that survive; he is described as "an accomplished professional with a fine eye for detail" (42). See also Leah Blatt Glasser's biography of Freeman, *In a Closet Hidden* (Amherst: U of Massachusetts P, 1996) 3 and n, on Freeman's father's influence, and on architecture and her fiction. See Glasser 175 on Freewarren, the Freemans' home in Metuchen.

10 Those who wrote about the home, Wright reports, shared a "common aesthetic position . . . that called for a radical simplification of the dwelling" (*Moralism and the Model Home* [Chicago: U of Chicago P, 1980] 231). Clifford Clark Jr. generalizes more broadly and speculatively, in a way consistent with the critique launched by Freeman and extended by Mary Stewart Cutting: "Social values were changing and certain features of the Victorian house appeared out of date. In particular, they [architects, feminists, builders, and homeowners] questioned the more formalistic emphasis on decorum and display that underlay the design of front entrance halls and parlors. The Victorian house seemed overly ornate and overly specialized; it had too many rooms crammed with too much clutter. The family ideal, similarly, seemed artificial and awkward" (*The American Family Home, 1800–1960* [Chapel Hill: U of North Carolina P, 1986] 131).

11 When Lily sends Goward a telegram "to the effect that if he did not keep his promise with regard to writing F. L. [fond letters] to P. [Peggy] her A. [aunt] would never speak to him again," and so forth, she comments to herself, "It looked like the most melodramatic Sunday personal ever invented" (58–59).

12 It requires some careful calculation to come up with plausible ages for everyone based on Freeman's assertions, but it can be done. Elizabeth says that her sister-in-law is ten years older than she is, which makes Ada forty-four. If Charles Edward is twenty-four, as Cutting says in the next chapter (85), that would mean Ada was twenty when her first child was born—a good fit, and one that also establishes plausible ages for the other children: Maria is close in age to Charles Edward, Peggy is twenty, Alice appears about fourteen and Billy about ten. Cyrus appears older than Ada, however, and it seems unlikely that such a rising young man would have married and had children early. If we guess that he was twenty-four when he married and twenty-five when his son was born, he is fifty—sixteen years older than his sister.

13 "Confessions of a Young Wife" appeared in the May and August issues of 1907. The first installment of the other series was titled "Confessions of a Young Mother" and appeared in March 1907; the others, titled "Some Experiences of a Mother," appeared in May and September 1908. "Joe's Side of It, by a Mere Man" appeared in December 1907, and "The Confessions of an Older Wife" in July 1908. "A Plea for the Small Boy," by Annie Hamilton Donnell, was published in November 1906, and "The Teacher's Side of It," by Myra Kelly, in November 1908. The story about the new baby is "The Introduction," by Annie Hamilton Donnell, which appeared in April 1906, and the one about the thirteen-year-old is "While Mothers Live," by Emily Calvin Blake, November 1908 (see also "The Trying Age," October 1907, by Annie Hamilton Donnell).

14 Howells had also published a *Bazar* essay, "Our Daily Speech," appealing to women to take more care in speaking, in October 1906.

15 See Sara Blair, *Henry James and the Writing of Race and Nation* (New York: Cambridge UP, 1996), on James's dialogue with popular forms. I do not mean to imply that James is in some thorough way a supporter of the ideology of companionate marriage. Rather, I believe, he is interested in its intersection with his own fascination with densely meaningful human interaction both inside and outside conventionalized relations.

16 There is a limit to Lorraine's unconventionality, however—although she reports with approval that at dawn Peter and Harry "took bath-towels and went down to the river and had a swim" (92), she does not accompany them.

17 See Kenneth Cmiel, *Democratic Eloquence* (New York: William Morrow, 1990) 251; Lewis A. Erenberg, *Steppin' Out* (Chicago: U of Chicago P, 1981); and Beth L. Bailey, *From Front Porch to Back Seat* (Baltimore: Johns Hopkins UP, 1988).

18 Jordan also comments on economic issues in marriage, in general advocating for women. For example, in "The Family and the Quarrel," a section of the editor's column that ran with the first chapter of *The Whole Family*, she comments that a "family quarrel in a home where an imperious husband and father holds the power of the purse is a thing of peculiar bitterness and revolt" (1249). In a comment on divorce in her December 1908 column she takes a quite radical position on the value of domestic labor: "For adjusting the allowance of a wife . . . *[e]stimate the cost of replacing by paid labor the work which she does in the home*" (1267).

19 On society journalism, see Maureen E. Montgomery, *Displaying Women* (New York: Routledge, 1998) 141-62. However, on 145-47 she discusses a highly publicized 1906 lawsuit that made the abuses of the institution front-page news; Howells's treating it as controversial thus seems both archaic and topical.

4. The Sometimes-New Woman

1 Barbara Miller Solomon, *In the Company of Educated Women* (New Haven: Yale UP, 1985), provides a general history of women and higher education; Lynn D. Gordon, *Gender and Higher Education in the Progressive Era* (New Haven: Yale UP, 1990), focuses specifically on this period.

2 I have relied on Lois Rudnick, "The New Woman," in *1915, The Cultural Moment*, ed. Adele Heller and Lois Rudnick (New Brunswick, N.J.: Rutgers UP, 1991) 69-81; and Ellen Wiley Todd, *The "New Woman" Revised* (Berkeley: U of California P, 1993). Sandra Adickes, *To Be Young Was Very Heaven* (New York: St. Martin's P, 1997), provides a still more detailed account of women activists in New York during this period along with citations for other sources. Also, since this chapter was finished, Christine Stansell's *American Moderns: Bohemian New York and the Creation of a New Century* (New York: Metropolitan Books-Henry Holt, 2000), which includes women in its broad analysis of Bohemian New York, has appeared.

3 Martha Banta, *Imaging American Women* (New York: Columbia UP, 1987), provides a thorough inventory of visual images of women in the United States; Lois Banner, *American Beauty* (Chicago: U of Chicago P, 1983), a history of ideals of beauty. Patricia Marks includes some visual materials in her study of images of New Women in British and American popular humor magazines, *Bicycles, Bangs, and Bloomers* (Lexington: U of Kentucky P, 1990).

4 On the reaction to Clarke, see Solomon 56–57 and Gordon, *Gender* 18–19.

5 These are widely cited statistics. For female enrollments 1870–80 see Solomon 2 and Gordon, *Gender* 63; for 1880–1910, see Solomon 58 n. 224. For the percentage in coeducational institutions, see Solomon 58, and for the percentage of the female population enrolled, see Solomon 64.

6 May Estelle Cook used this term in 1902 ("Co-Education in Colleges," *Outlook* 72: 890–91); Solomon cites it without giving a specific source (80–81); and Rosalind Rosenberg uses it in *Beyond Separate Spheres* (New Haven: Yale UP) in 1982.

7 Solomon, tables on 63 and 44, respectively. Solomon gives decade figures, which are sufficiently precise for my purpose.

8 See Gerald Graff, *Professing Literature* (U of Chicago P, 1987), esp. 38 and 87; and A. G. Canfield, "Coeducation and Literature," *PMLA* 25 (1910): lxvi–lxxxiii.

9 Her various extrapolations give a rate of about 60 percent.

10 Politics does seem to shape critics' interpretations of Elizabeth, however; literary historian of regionalism Perry Westbrook considers her a "depiction of spinsterish vanity and folly" (*Mary Wilkins Freeman* [New York: Twayne, 1967] 161), while feminist critics tend to view her positively.

11 *Loving with a Vengeance* (Hamden, Conn.: Archon-Shoe String, 1982) 55–56. John Berger's *Ways of Seeing* (New York: Viking, 1973) is the basis of her observations here. Howells did indicate to Jordan that she could call his chapter "The Next-Door Neighbor" if she wished.

12 "The Amethyst Comb" was published in *Harper's Magazine* in February 1914 and collected in *The Copy-Cat* later in the same year.

13 Freeman similarly refuses to judge between spinsterhood and marriage in another story of the same stage in her career as *The Whole Family*, "The Secret," collected in the 1907 volume *The Fair Lavinia*. A woman who has forcibly expressed the view that remaining single is the best choice for many women looks out over the snow and reflects on a proposal: "She realized dimly that if she were to say 'No' to her lover, that in spite of her radiant beauty, which was of a kind to endure, in spite of her triumphant philosophy of obtaining whatever she could from the minor joys of existence, and not allowing her body or soul to become lean through deprivation of the larger ones, she would, in reality, live her life and die her death, as it were, in that cold glitter outside her window. It would be peaceful and beautiful and good, but she would miss the best and sweetest of food for her heart. There was nothing of the nun about her. She was religious, but she was not ascetic. It would have been different if she had

never loved any man at all. Then she might have been satisfied and quite content, but the aspect of that cold and virgin radiance outside seemed terrible to her with the leaping flame in her heart" (225–26).

14 I rely on Kendrick's edition of Freeman's letters (201) for Dr. Freeman's age, which is given differently in various sources.

    After her marriage, the former Mary E. Wilkins adopted her husband's name for both public and private use; for simplicity's sake I have used "Freeman" even for earlier periods.

15 This photograph of Freeman was used on the cover of Glasser's book, and it offers a convincing illustration of her point. The metaphorical treatment of an author's appearance risks the equation of body and work that Ellman criticizes, of course. What I want to convey here is both my appreciation of Glasser's insight and its embedding in a biographical tradition that must be regarded critically, even warily.

16 Mary E. Wilkins Freeman, "Billy and Susy: A Thanksiving Story," *Harper's Bazar* 41 (1907): 1033–39, collected in *The Winning Lady and Others* (1909).

17 See *Tales of the Cloister* (1901; Freeport, N.Y.: Books for Libraries P, 1970) as well as *May Iverson—Her Book* (1904; Freeport, N.Y.: Books for Libraries P, 1969) and *May Iverson Tackles Life* (New York: Harper & Brothers, 1912).

18 In her autobiography Jordan generally endorses the information in Ross's account, correcting some minor details not relevant here.

19 Many of Jordan's novels create elective families of one sort or another; see *The Trap* (New York: D. Appleton-Century, 1937) and *Faraway Island* (New York: D. Appleton-Century, 1941), for example.

20 The story is "Oil of Gladness." The woman in the illustration is a poor relative visiting the family on whom the story centers, and she is crying over her son's photograph because she misses him. The daughters of the family spend money they had intended to use to buy a much-needed new rug to bring him for a visit, because they realize that what truly makes their mother happy is to give to others.

21 See also, on ideals of beauty in the period, Banner, chs. 8–10.

22 The Roman women appear in October 1902 and September 1903, the butterflies in November 1908.

23 This cover is by Ethel Penniwell Brown (1871–1959), a formally trained artist from Delaware who worked primarily as an illustrator during the first decade of the century and went on to a long career as a painter. See the biographical entry on AskArt.com; my thanks to Jonathan Director for locating this information.

24 I include in the group an anonymous article titled "Reflections of an Un-married Daughter," which is about the difficulty of living an independent life with an old-fashioned mother in the house. The tone and perspective of the article are very much like O'Hagan's in subsequent issues, and the illustrator is the same used in the first few. It seems likely that this particular article was published without attribution to avoid distressing O'Hagan's mother. (It brings the same perspective into the pages of the *Bazar* even if it was not written by O'Hagan, of course.)

O'Hagan in fact married in 1908, and continued to write and do political work after becoming Mrs. Francis Shinn. See her obituary, *New York Times* 25 June 1933. She was one of the contributors to *The Sturdy Oak*.

25 In Greek mythology Arethusa is a nymph who flees persistently from a lover and is changed into a spring by Artemis; the story was retold by Ovid and then by Shelley. It is also the name of a New England orchid that grows in swamps. Mary Wilkins Freeman combines the literary and botanical associations in her story "Arethusa," about a girl's fundamental maidenliness (preserved even after her marriage).

26 The "Editorial Mission" is contained in the magazine's media kit for 1999, a copy of which is in my possession. The market research materials show that the magazine portrayed its readers to advertisers as "innovators" who (for example) prefer products that offer the latest in technology.

27 Judith Coyne, "Editor's Letter," *New Woman* March 1999: 16.

28 To extend this analysis, one might want to examine *Lilac*, a glossy magazine recently founded by two young, Western-educated Israeli Arab women. The editor comments, "We decided this is going to be a magazine for modern women. . . . And I have a feeling it's going to be a magazine for not-so-modern women either. We sold many, many issues in a religous Muslim town" (Deborah Sontag, "A Magazine Is Unveiled, in More Ways Than One," *New York Times* 28 April 2000, natl. ed.: A4).

5. What Is Sentimentality?

1 This narrative is based on Alfred Bendixen's discussion of the sequence of events in his introduction to the novel, as well as my own examination of the letters in the New York Public Library. As he indicates, one can deduce from James's letters to Jordan that she sent out Wyatt's first version without reading it. The form of James's question in the sentence

that ends this paragraph is that of the document itself rather than the slightly altered version Jordan quotes in *Three Rousing Cheers*.

2 My thanks to the participants in the San Antonio American Literature Association Conference on Women Writers in 1993, whose enthusiastic response to a very early version of this material encouraged me to pursue the investigation.

3 My account is, of course, radically compressed and neglects many valuable contributions; I am synthesizing to make particular points rather than undertaking a review of the literature. See Mary Chapman and Glenn Hendler, eds., *Sentimental Men* (Berkeley: U of California P, 1999), for a fuller review. Note, too, that such critics as Nina Baym who (in *Woman's Fiction* [Ithaca: Cornell UP, 1978]) avoided the impasse of the debate sometimes found that very choice marginalizing their work.

4 *Language and the Politics of Emotion* (New York: Cambridge UP, 1990) 1-2, 7. Each editor is separately the author of an important book contributing to the new anthropology of emotion. Their claim that this anthropological work accepts the "psychological orthodoxy" that emotions are "psychobiological processes that respond to cross-cultural environmental differences but retain a robust essence untouched by the social or cultural" (2) should be regarded with some skepticism. Compare Phoebe C. Ellsworth's account of psychology in the 1960s as dominated by cultural relativism, an orthodoxy that was successfully challenged by the research into universals that is currently being challenged by social constructionism ("Sense, Culture and Sensibility," in *Emotion and Culture*, ed. Shinobu Kitayama and Hazel Rose Markus [Washington, D.C.: American Psychological Association, 1994] 24-25).

5 Antonio R. Damasio, *Descartes' Error* (New York: G. P. Putnam's Sons, Grosset/Putnam, 1994), quotations from 100, xv, and 118, respectively. For the point made in the last sentence of the paragraph, see p. 53. I should note that the patients Damasio discusses show impaired decision making only in some areas, and that testing the phenomenon requires considerable ingenuity. Also, although Damasio deals wonderfully with questions of individual variation and with the debate over innate versus acquired characteristics, there is little place for culture, class, race, or gender in his analysis.

6 See Anna Wierzbicka, "Emotion, Language, and Cultural Scripts," in Kitayama and Markus 133-96; and Lutz and Abu-Lughod's introduction to *Language and the Politics of Emotion*.

7 The theatricality of the relations of sympathy in French and English lit-

erature of this period has also been anatomized by David Marshall in *The Surprising Effects of Sympathy* (Chicago: U of Chicago P, 1988). My thinking here owes much to conversations with Adela Pinch, whose perspective is available in *Strange Fits of Passion* (Stanford: Stanford UP, 1996).

8 This account, of course, leaves much unsaid; Daniels's subordinates also face moral dilemmas, and the racial and national issues engaged are complex. My thanks to my son Nicholas Dean, who persuaded me to take him to see this movie and later helped track down the quotations on the videotape.

9 Making this connection, of course, constitutes only a small part of the analysis needed to place any given sentimental fiction in the moment of its production. For example, the fine historical work of Cathy Davidson (see *Revolution and the Word* [New York: Oxford UP, 1986]); the essays in *The Culture of Sentiment* (New York: Oxford UP, 1992); and Elizabeth Barnes's *States of Sympathy* (New York: Columbia UP, 1997) offer many other frameworks for the early American novel.

10 Dobson writes that we can recognize sentimental literature "by its concern with subject matter that privileges affectional ties, and by conventions and tropes designed to convey the primary vision of human connection in a dehumanized world" ("Reclaiming Sentimental Literature," *American Literature* 69 [1997]: 268).

11 See Candace Clark's *Misery and Company* (U of Chicago P, 1997) for an empirical account of how sympathy works in the contemporary United States.

12 The disciplinary distinction made here is not, I know, a stable or simple one; many of the contributors to the extended interdisciplinary exchange on these topics are best understood as working in American studies, women's studies, and cultural studies, and their sources and claims cross any conventional boundaries one might draw between historical and literary scholarship. But intellectual differences between those trained and employed in different institutional settings remain observable and important, and many publications are interdisciplinary only in the limited sense that they cite material from another field.

13 See Laura McCall, "Symmetrical Minds: Literary Men and Women in Antebellum America" (Ph.D. diss., U of Michigan, 1988). Since writing this critique I have been pleased to learn that Mary Kelley, in a comment on the historical importance of Welter's essay, also considers it no longer usable; see her "Commentary on Barbara Welter, 'The Cult of True Womanhood: 1820–1860' (1966)," in *Locating American Studies*, ed. Lucy Maddox (Baltimore: Johns Hopkins UP, 1999) 67–70.

Literary scholarship's reliance on the "cult of true womanhood" is virtually a monument to the dangers of interdisciplinary work. A literary critic working with the same texts Welter examines might be more wary of the notions that characters in fiction can be extracted from the narratives in which they move, and that they correspond to women in history. But once those "images of women" have been extracted—that is, produced—by Welter and entered into historical discourse, literary scholars cite them as "historical background." Some readers may feel that my critique of the use of Welter is itself dated, and over the past ten years I have occasionally hoped it was so. But the reference regularly recurs; not very long ago I read a manuscript forthcoming from a good university press that was virtually uncritical in its use of the Cult of True Womanhood (complete with capital letters) as a foil for the work of Kate Chopin. It therefore seems worth making the point explicitly and emphatically.

14 I should note that Halttunen in *Confidence Men and Painted Women* (New Haven: Yale UP, 1982) does use the construction "cult of domesticity" that I criticize above, although with a specific and limited historical reference that entails less difficulty than some usages do.

15 See, for example, John Brewer and Roy Porter's introduction to their anthology *Consumption and the World of Goods* (New York: Routledge, 1993): "The new accent in the eighteenth century upon domesticity, and the emotional intensification of the nuclear family, clearly derive in part from growing opportunities for the cherishing of household 'decencies,' comforts and luxuries" (5). See Lori Merish, "Sentimental Consumption: Harriet Beecher Stowe and the Aesthetics of Middle-Class Ownership," *American Literary History* 8 (1996): 1–33, for a reading of the work of Harriet Beecher Stowe in terms of consumption.

16 See Arlie Russell Hochschild, *The Managed Heart* (Berkeley: U of California P, 1983), for a study of this reaction.

17 Gerri Hirshey, "Happy [   ] Day to You," *New York Times Magazine* 2 July 1995: 20. The "we" here is misleading as the group that purchases greeting cards and the group that feels derision are probably overlapping rather than identical, but ambivalence is widespread enough to make the observation worth repeating.

18 See Craig Calhoun, ed., *Habermas and the Public Sphere* (Cambridge: MIT P, 1992). I would agree with Calhoun's comment in the introduction that Habermas judges "the eighteenth century by Locke and Kant, the nineteenth century by Marx and Mill, and the twentieth century by the typical suburban television viewer" (33), but would also point out that

he is more critical in his account of the earlier periods than might appear from the norm he uses to denounce the present state of democracy.

19 See Richard Brodhead, *Cultures of Letters* (Chicago: U of Chicago P, 1993), and, for an incisive overview, Brodhead's entry ("Culture and Consciousness") in *The Columbia Literary History of the United States.*

20 Henry James, *Literary Criticism*, ed. Leon Edel (New York: Library of America, 1984) 221–22; the review (of *Waiting for the Verdict*) was originally published in the *Nation* November 21, 1867. The quotation in the next paragraph is from the same source.

21 See, for example, Richard Yarborough's introduction to *Contending Forces* (1900), by Pauline E. Hopkins (New York: Oxford UP, 1988). I have adopted the phrase "minimal print access" from Susan Bernardin, "On the Meeting Grounds of Sentiment: Alice Callahan's *Wynema* and Foundational Native American Women's Literature," a talk delivered at the Conference "19th-Century American Women Writers in the 21st Century," Hartford, Connecticut, June 1, 1996.

22 Suzanne Clark tells this story insightfully and traces the return of the repressed in *Sentimental Modernism* (Bloomington: Indiana UP, 1991).

23 I would, of course, argue that masculine- and feminine-inflected versions of sentiment coexisted for much longer than Sedgwick indicates, but would agree that the formation she describes takes on a particularly vexed power in this period.

24 See chapter 6, "Perfect Felicity (with Professional Help)," for a brief discussion of genre criticism as an enterprise.

25 Both references were made in passing in the course of negative reviews of other works, one in 1870, the other in 1875. The fluidity of generic ascriptions in these reviews demonstrates the evaluative, rather than analytical, function of the categories—in the first James uses them to exemplify "dreary realism" (862); in the second, unwholesome, feminine pathos (279).

I refer to Elizabeth Stuart Phelps because the author published under that name even after her marriage in 1888 to Herbert Dickenson Ward. It was also her mother's name, taken after her mother's death, and as her mother was also a published author, care needs to be taken to distinguish them.

26 The single mention of *The Whole Family* I found in the collection is a typed slip with information about an essay on the novel by Earl Walbridge in *The Colophon*, in which Wyatt's contribution is praised. It is in a folder marked "Biographical and critical material concerning," which

contains no work by Wyatt herself; some of the contents are clearly from a cutting service. (The Jordan papers include a detailed record of her participation, of course.)

27 The information about sales of *The Perfect Tribute* is from Bendixen's biographical note in his edition of *The Whole Family* (336). I derive the point about the basis of *Bob and Guides* (New York: Charles Scribner's Sons, 1906) from its dedication, which reads "This book is dedicated / to / my inspiration, collaborator / and property / the real Bob / Paul Shipman Andrews."

28 On O'Neill, a fascinating example of the sometimes-new woman, see Shelly Armitage, *Kewpies and Beyond* (Jackson: UP of Mississippi, 1994). *The Very Little Person* (Cambridge: Riverside-Houghton Mifflin, 1911) is interesting both in itself and as a point of contact between Vorse and O'Neill.

6. Closing the Book

1 Frank Kermode, *The Sense of an Ending* (1966; rpt. New York: Oxford UP, 1975), stands at the beginning of this body of work. Other classics are D. A. Miller, *Narrative and Its Discontents* (Princeton: Princeton UP, 1981); Marianna Torgovnick, *Closure in the Novel* (Princeton: Princeton UP, 1981); and Peter Brooks, *Reading for the Plot* (1984; rpt. New York: Vintage-Random House, 1985). Judith Roof, *Come as You Are* (New York: Columbia UP, 1996), is a more recent contribution.

2 See Mary Warner Blanchard, *Oscar Wilde's America* (New Haven: Yale UP, 1998) 137–77, on aesthetic dress. Lorraine's dress is described as "a sweet little yellow Empire gown"; see Joan L. Severa, *Dressed for the Photographer* (Kent, Ohio: Kent State UP, 1995), on that style (195, 463) and on Mother Hubbards (381, 487, 534–35).

3 See Blanchard on cultural resonances of *The Coast of Bohemia*. I would argue, however, that she misses the humor in Howells's treatment of Charmian.

4 See Daniel Mark Fogel, *A Companion to Henry James Studies* (Westport, Conn.: Greenwood P, 1993), on the connections and contrasts among the many strands of James criticism.

5 This is one of the "American Letters" published in *Literature*, a British periodical being reprinted in New York during this period (Mott 4: 229n).

6 The work of Georg Lukács is, for me, the classic moment in arguments for realism; the arguments against it are most strongly stated by the work of the *Screen* group in the 1970s (such as Colin MacCabe's). For powerful views of realism as a cultural revolution, see Ian Watt's classic *Rise of the Novel* (Berkeley: U of California P, 1957); Fredric Jameson's "Realist Floor Plan," in *On Signs*, ed. Marshall Blonsky (Baltimore: Johns Hopkins UP, 1985); and Jonathan Crary, *Techniques of the Observer* (Cambridge: October-MIT P, 1990). I would stand by most of what I wrote about realism in *Form and History in American Literary Naturalism*, but subsequent work has, of course, changed the salient questions. On American realism, I have been most influenced by Amy Kaplan, *The Social Construction of American Realism* (Chicago: U of Chicago P, 1988); and Kenneth W. Warren, *Black and White Strangers* (Chicago: U of Chicago P, 1993). Also, for the literary discourses in which it took shape, see Michael Davitt Bell, *The Problem of American Realism* (Chicago: U of Chicago P, 1993); and Nancy Glazener, *Reading for Realism* (Durham: Duke UP, 1997). For recent, thought-provoking contributions to the reconstruction of the social meanings of American realism, see Brook Thomas, *American Literary Realism and the Failed Promise of Contract* (Berkeley: U of California P, 1997); Joyce W. Warren, "Performativity and the Positioning of American Literary Realism," in *Challenging Boundaries*, ed. Joyce W. Warren and Margaret Dickie (Athens: U of Georgia P, 2000), 3–25; and—especially for what follows—Susan Mizruchi, *The Science of Sacrifice* (Princeton: Princeton UP, 1998).

7 See, for example, William M. Morgan, "Public Engagements: Humanitarianism and Complicity in U.S. Literary Realism" (Ph.D. diss., Brandeis U, 2000).

8 Brown is presumably nodding to Jordan offstage when she has Peggy quote Alice's teacher as saying "before many years she'll be in all the magazines" (273).

9 This is a parade of familiarity rather than the display of actual knowledge; since the Koran forbids the consumption of alcohol, the ruler of an Islamic nation is an unlikely candidate for such an Americanized conversion to temperance—but that does not seem to be part of the joke.

❖ References ❖

Abbott, Frances M. "Three Decades of College Women." *Popular Science Monthly* 65 (August 1904): 350–59.

Abbott, Jacob. *The Harper Establishment; or, How the Story Books Are Made.* 1855. Rpt. Waltham, Mass.: Mark Press, 1955.

Abu-Lughod, Lila. *Veiled Sentiments: Honor and Poetry in a Bedouin Society.* Berkeley: U of California P, 1986.

Adickes, Sandra. *To Be Young Was Very Heaven: Women in New York before the First World War.* New York: St. Martin's, 1997.

Advertisement for *The Whole Family. Harper's Bazar* 42 (December 1908), advt. suppl. 2.

Advertisement for *The Whole Family. Harper's Monthly Magazine* 117 (November 1908) n.p.

Advertisement for *The Whole Family. Harper's Monthly Magazine* 118 (May 1909) n.p.

Advertisement for *The Whole Family. Harper's Weekly* 52 (5 December 1908): 34.

Agnew, Jean-Cristophe. *Worlds Apart: The Market and the Theater in Anglo-American Thought, 1550–1750.* New York: Cambridge UP, 1986.

Alden, Henry Mills. "Editor's Study." *Harper's Monthly Magazine* 105 (September 1902): 646–48.

———. *Magazine Writing and the New Literature.* New York: Harper & Brothers, 1908.

American Sociological Society. *Papers and Proceedings*, vol. 3. Third Annual Meeting. General Topic: The Family. Held at Atlantic City, N.J., December 28–30, 1908. Published for the ASS by the University of Chicago Press, 1909.

Ames, Kenneth L. *Death in the Dining Room and Other Tales of Victorian Culture.* Philadelphia: Temple UP, 1992.

Anderson, Benedict. *Imagined Communities: Reflections on the Origin and*

Spread of Nationalism. 1983. Rev. ed. New York: Verso-New Left Books, 1991.

Anderson, Perry. *Considerations on Western Marxism*. London: New Left Books, 1976.

———. *The Origins of Postmodernity*. New York: Verso, 1998.

Andrews, Mary Raymond Shipman. *Bob and the Guides*. New York: Charles Scribner's Sons, 1906.

———. *The Eternal Masculine: Stories of Men and Boys*. New York: Charles Scribner's Sons, 1913.

———. *The Perfect Tribute*. 1906. New York: Charles Scribner's Sons, 1910.

Anesko, Michael. *"Friction with the Market": Henry James and the Profession of Authorship*. New York: Oxford UP, 1986.

———. *Letters, Fictions, Lives: Henry James and William Dean Howells*. New York: Oxford UP, 1997.

Anon. "The Melancholy of Woman's Pages." *Atlantic Monthly* 97 (April 1906): 574–75.

Anon. ["R. G."] "The Pros and Cons of Co-education." Letter. *Nation* 76 (April 2, 1903): 267–68.

Anon. [Anne O'Hagan?] "Some Reflections of an Unmarried Daughter," by Herself. *Harper's Bazar* 41 (January 1907): 11–16.

Appadurai, Arjun. "Topographies of the Self: Praise and Emotion in Hindu India." In Lutz and Abu-Lughod 92–112.

Appleton, C. E. "American Efforts after International Copyright." *Fortnightly Review* 27, n.s., 21 (1 February 1877): 237–56.

Armitage, Shelley. *Kewpies and Beyond: The World of Rose O'Neill*. Jackson: UP of Mississippi, 1994.

Armstrong, Nancy. *Desire and Domestic Fiction: A Political History of the Novel*. New York: Oxford UP, 1987.

Arnold, Martin. "Making Books—Common Sense: No Offense." *New York Times* 5 March 1998, natl. ed.: B3.

"As to 'The Whole Family,'" *Harper's Bazar* 42 (June 1908): 613.

Ashe, Penelope [pseud.]. See *Naked Came the Stranger*.

Ashton, Susanna. Personal communication. June 8, 2001.

———. "Veribly a Purple Cow: *The Whole Family* and the Collaborative Search for Coherence." *Studies in the Novel* 33.1 (spring 2001): 51–79.

Asprin, Robert Lynn, and Lynn Abbey. *Thieves' World*. New York: Ace Books, 1979.

Atherton, Gertrude. *Adventures of a Novelist*. New York: Liveright, 1932.

Austen, Jane. *The Novels of Jane Austen*. 2d ed. Ed. R. W. Chapman. Vol. 5: *Northanger Abbey and Persuasion*. Oxford: Clarendon-Oxford UP, 1926.

Bacon-Smith, Camille. *Science Fiction Culture*. Feminist Cultural Studies, the Media, and Political Culture series. Philadelphia: U of Pennsylvania P, 2000.

Bailey, Beth L. *From Front Porch to Back Seat: Courtship in Twentieth-Century America*. Baltimore: Johns Hopkins UP, 1988.

Balibar, Etienne, and Immanuel Wallerstein. *Race, Nation, Class: Ambiguous Identities*. Trans. (of Balibar) Chris Turner. New York: Verso, 1991.

Bangs, Francis Hyde. *John Kendrick Bangs: Humorist of the Nineties*. New York: Knopf, 1941.

Banner, Lois W. *American Beauty*. Chicago: U of Chicago P, 1983.

Banta, Martha. *Imaging American Women: Idea and Ideals in Cultural History*. New York: Columbia UP, 1987.

Barnes, Elizabeth. *States of Sympathy: Seduction and Democracy in the American Novel*. New York: Columbia UP, 1997.

Barrett, Michèle. *Imagination in Theory: Culture, Writing, Words, and Things*. New York: New York UP, 1999.

Barrett, Michèle, and Mary McIntosh. *The Anti-social Family*. London: Verso-New Left Books, 1982.

Bauer, Dale. "The Politics of Collaboration in *The Whole Family*." In *Old Maids to Radical Spinsters: Unmarried Women in the Twentieth-Century Novel*, ed. Laura L. Doan. Chicago: U of Ilinois P, 1991. 107-22.

Baym, Nina. *Woman's Fiction: A Guide to Novels by and about Women in America, 1820-1870*. Ithaca: Cornell UP, 1978.

———. "Women's Novels and Women's Minds: An Unsentimental View of Nineteenth-Century American Women's Fiction." *Novel* 31 (1998): 335-50.

Bederman, Gail. *Manliness and Civilization: A Cultural History of Gender and Race in the United States, 1880-1917*. Chicago: U of Chicago P, 1995.

Bell, Lilian. "Talks to Spinsters, I: The Loneliness of the Unloved." *Harper's Bazar* 36 (December 1902): 1054-59.

———. "Talks to Spinsters, II: On the Tendency to Crabbedness." *Harper's Bazar* 37 (January 1903): 3-8.

Bell, Michael Davitt. *The Problem of American Realism: Studies in the Cultural History of a Literary Idea*. Chicago: U of Chicago P, 1993.

Bendixen, Alfred. "Introduction: The Whole Story behind *The Whole Family*" and Appendix. In *The Whole Family: A Novel by Twelve Authors*. Ed. Alfred Bendixen. New York: Ungar, 1986. xi-li; 317-41.

Berger, John, with Sven Blomberg, Chris Fox, Michael Dibb, and Richard Hollis. *Ways of Seeing*. New York: Richard Seaver-Viking, 1973.

Berlant, Lauren. "The Female Complaint." *Social Text* 19-20 (1988): 237-59.

———. "The Female Woman: Fanny Fern and the Form of Sentiment." In Samuels. 265-81, 335-40.

Bernardin, Susan. "On the Meeting Grounds of Sentiment: Alice Callahan's *Wynema* and Foundational Native American Women's Literature." Talk delivered at the conference "19th-Century American Women Writers in the 21st Century." Hartford, Conn., June 1, 1996.

Blair, Sara. *Henry James and the Writing of Race and Nation.* New York: Cambridge UP, 1996.

Blair, Walter, and Hamlin Hill. *America's Humor: From Poor Richard to Doonesbury.* New York: Oxford UP, 1978.

Blanchard, Mary Warner. *Oscar Wilde's America: Counterculture in the Gilded Age.* New Haven: Yale UP, 1998.

Blumin, Stuart M. *The Emergence of the Middle Class: Social Experience in the American City, 1760–1900.* Cambridge: Cambridge UP, 1989.

"Books and Writers." Review of *The Whole Family. Harper's Bazar* 42 (December 1908): n.p.

Bowman, Leslie Greene. *American Arts and Crafts: Virtue in Design. A Catalogue of the Palevsky Collection and Related Works at the Los Angeles County Museum of Art.* Boston: Los Angeles Museum of Art in association with Bulfinch Press-Little, Brown, 1992.

Brady, Laura Ann. "Collaborative Literary Writing: Issues of Authorship and Authority." Diss. U of Minnesota, 1988.

"The Brave New World of Publishing: Fathers and Sons." *Economist* (London) 310 (14 January 1989): 83–84.

Brewer, John, and Roy Porter, eds. *Consumption and the World of Goods.* New York: Routledge, 1993.

Brodhead, Richard H. *Cultures of Letters: Scenes of Reading and Writing in Nineteenth-Century America.* Chicago: U of Chicago P, 1993.

———. "Literature and Culture." *Columbia Literary History of the United States.* Ed. Emory Elliott. New York: Columbia UP. 1988. 467–81.

———. *The School of Hawthorne.* New York: Oxford UP, 1986.

Brooks, Cleanth Jr., and Robert Penn Warren. *Understanding Fiction.* New York: F. S. Crofts, 1946.

Brooks, Geraldine. "Murdoch." *New York Times Magazine* 19 July 1998: 20–23.

Brooks, Peter. 1984. *Reading for the Plot: Design and Intention in Narrative.* New York: Vintage-Random House, 1985.

Brown, Herbert Ross. *The Sentimental Novel in America 1789–1860.* 1940. Rpt. New York: Pageant Books, 1959.

Calhoun, Craig, ed. *Habermas and the Public Sphere.* Cambridge: MIT P, 1992.

Camfield, Gregg. "The Moral Aesthetics of Sentimentality: A Missing Key to Uncle Tom's Cabin." *Nineteenth-Century Literature* 43 (1988): 319–45.

———. *Sentimental Twain: Samuel Clemens in the Maze of Moral Philosophy.* Philadelphia: U of Pennsylvania P, 1994.

Canfield, A. G. "Coeducation and Literature." *Publications of the Modern Language Association* 25 (1910): lxvi–lxxxiii.

Chapman, Mary, and Glenn Hendler, eds. *Sentimental Men: Masculinity and the Politics of Affect in American Culture.* Berkeley: U of California P, 1999.

Chartier, Roger. *The Order of Books: Readers, Authors and Libraries in Europe between the Fourteenth and Eighteenth Centuries.* Trans. Lydia G. Cochrane. Stanford: Stanford UP, 1994.

Charvat, William. *The Profession of Authorship in America, 1800–1870.* 1968. Rpt. New York: Columbia UP, 1992.

Christie, Agatha, Dorothy L. Sayers, G. K. Chesterton, and Certain Other Members of the Detection Club. *The Floating Admiral.* 1931. Rpt. New York: Berkley-Jove, 1993.

Christy, Howard Chandler. 1906. *The American Girl.* Rpt. New York: Da Capo-Plenum, 1976.

"Chronicle and Comment: 'The Whole Family.'" *Bookman* 28 (January 1909): 422–24.

Chudacoff, Howard P. *How Old Are You? Age Consciousness in American Culture.* Princeton: Princeton UP, 1989.

Clark, Candace. *Misery and Company: Sympathy in Everyday Life.* Chicago: U of Chicago P, 1997.

Clark, Clifford Edward Jr. *The American Family Home, 1800–1960.* Chapel Hill: U of North Carolina P, 1986.

Clark, Suzanne. *Sentimental Modernism: Women Writers and the Revolution of the Word.* Bloomington: Indiana UP, 1991.

Clarke, Edward H. *Sex in Education; or, A Fair Chance for the Girls.* Boston: James R. Osgood, 1873. Rpt. Medicine and Society in America series. New York: Arno Press and the New York Times, 1972.

Clute, John, and Peter Nicholls, eds. *The Encyclopedia of Science Fiction.* 1993. Rev. ed. New York: St. Martin's-Griffin, 1995.

Cmiel, Kenneth. *Democratic Eloquence: The Fight over Popular Speech in Nineteenth-Century America.* New York: William Morrow, 1990.

"Concerning *The Whole Family.*" *Harper's Bazar* 42 (December 1908): n.p.

Cook, May Estelle. "Co-Education in Colleges. II. A Woman's View." *Outlook* 72.15 (December 13, 1902): 890–91.

Coontz, Stephanie. *The Social Origins of Private Life: A History of American Families, 1600–1900.* New York: Verso, 1988.

———. *The Way We Never Were: American Families and the Nostalgia Trap.* New York: Basic Books-HarperCollins, 1992.

Cott, Nancy F. *The Grounding of Modern Feminism*. New Haven: Yale UP, 1987.

Coultrap-McQuin, Susan. *Doing Literary Business: American Women Writers in the Nineteenth Century*. Chapel Hill: U of North Carolina P, 1990.

Coyne, Judith. "Editor's Letter: I'm a New Woman." *New Woman* March 1999: 16.

Crary, Jonathan. *Techniques of the Observer: On Vision and Modernity in the Nineteenth Century*. Cambridge: October–MIT P, 1990.

Crow, Thomas. "Modernism and Mass Culture in the Visual Arts." In *Pollock and After: The Critical Debate*, ed. Francis Frascina. New York: Icon Editions-Harper & Row, 1985. 233–66.

Crowley, John W. "The Wholefamdamnily." Review of *The Whole Family*, ed. Alfred Bendixen. *New England Quarterly* 60 (1987): 106–13.

Culver, Stuart. "Representing the Author: Henry James, Intellectual Property and the Work of Writing." In *Henry James: Fiction as History*, ed. Ian F. A. Bell. Totowa, N.J.: Vision and Barnes & Noble, 1984. 114–36.

"Current Fiction." Review of *The Whole Family*. *Nation* 87 (3 December 1908): 552–53.

Curtis, W. A. "Co-education in Colleges. I. A Man's View." *Outlook* 72.15 (December 13, 1902): 887–90.

Cutler, Martha. "Periods of Household Decoration. 2. The Arts and Crafts Movement." *Harper's Bazar* 40 (February 1906): 162–66.

Cutting, Mary Stewart. *Little Stories of Courtship*. 1905. Rpt. Garden City, N.Y.: Doubleday, Page, 1920.

———. *Little Stories of Married Life*. 1902. Rpt. Garden City, N.Y.: Doubleday, Page, 1920.

———. *More Stories of Married Life*. Garden City, N.Y.: Doubleday, Page, 1906.

———. "Oil of Gladness." *Harper's Bazar* 41 (December 1907): 1150–57.

———. *Refractory Husbands*. 1913. Garden City, N.Y.: Doubleday, Page, 1920.

———. "Social Life in the Home, III: The Family." *Harper's Bazar* 41 (July 1907): 707–9.

———. *Some of Us Are Married*. Garden City, N.Y.: Doubleday, Page, 1920.

———. *The Suburban Whirl and Other Stories of Married Life*. New York: McClure, 1907.

———. "Talks to Wives, I: To the Wives of 'Close' Men." *Harper's Bazar* 40 (July 1906): 657–59.

———. "Talks to Wives, II: To the Wife Who Is in Danger of Losing her Husband's Affection." *Harper's Bazar* 40 (August 1906): 728–30.

————. "Talks to Wives, V: To the Wife Who Suffers from Incompatibility." *Harper's Bazar* 40 (November 1906): 1044–46.

————. "Talks to Wives, VI: To the Wife Who Seeks Power." *Harper's Bazar* 40 (December 1906): 1173–75.

————. *The Wayfarers.* New York: McClure, 1908.

Cvetkovich, Ann. *Mixed Feelings: Feminism, Mass Culture, and Victorian Sensationalism.* New Brunswick, N.J.: Rutgers UP, 1992.

Damasio, Antonio R. *Descartes' Error: Emotion, Reason and the Human Brain.* New York: G. P. Putnam's Sons, Grosset/Putnam, 1994.

Davidoff, Leonore, and Catherine Hall. *Family Fortunes: Men and Women of the English Middle Class, 1780–1850.* Chicago: U of Chicago P, 1987.

Davidson, Cathy N., ed. "Preface: No More Separate Spheres!" *American Literature* 70 (1998): 443–63.

————. *Reading in America: Literature and Social History.* Baltimore: Johns Hopkins UP, 1989.

————. *Revolution and the Word: The Rise of the Novel in America.* New York: Oxford UP, 1986.

Degler, Carl N. *At Odds: Women and the Family in America from the Revolution to the Present.* New York: Oxford UP, 1980.

Derby, J[ames]. C[ephas]. *Fifty Years among Authors, Books, and Publishers.* New York: G. W. Carleton, 1884.

DiMaggio, Paul. "Cultural Entrepreneurship in Nineteenth-Century Boston: The Creation of an Organizational Base for High Culture in America." 1982. Rpt. in *Rethinking Popular Culture: Contemporary Perspectives in Cultural Studies,* ed. Chandra Mukerji and Michael Schudson. Berkeley: U of California P, 1991. 374–97.

————. "Social Structure, Institutions, and Cultural Goods: The Case of the United States." 1991. Rpt. in *The Politics of Culture: Policy Perspectives for Individuals, Institutions, and Communities,* ed. Gigi Bradford, Michael Gary, and Glenn Wallach. Washington, D.C.: Center for Arts and Culture; and New York: New P, 2000. 38–62.

Dirks, Nicholas B., Geoff Eley, and Sherry B. Ortner, eds. *Culture/ Power/History: A Reader in Contemporary Social Theory.* Princeton: Princeton UP, 1994.

Dobson, Joanne. "The American Renaissance Reenvisioned." In Warren 164–82.

————. "Reclaiming Sentimental Literature." *American Literature* 69 (1997): 263–88.

Douglas, Ann. *The Feminization of American Culture.* 1977. Rpt. New York: Anchor/Doubleday, 1988.

Dworkin, Ronald. "Law as Interpretation." *Critical Inquiry* 9 (1982): 179–200.

Eagleton, Terry. *The Ideology of the Aesthetic.* Cambridge: Basil Blackwell, 1990.

Edel, Leon, and Lyall Powers, eds. *Henry James and the* Bazar *Letters.* In *Howells and James: A Double Billing.* Rpt. New York: New York Public Library, 1958.

Elias, Norbert. *The Civilizing Process: The History of Manners [and] State Formation and Civilization.* Trans. Edmunch Jephcott. 1939. Cambridge: Basil Blackwell, 1994.

Elliott, Emory, ed. *Columbia Literary History of the United States.* New York: Columbia UP, 1988.

Ellison, Julie. *Cato's Tears and the Making of Anglo-American Emotion.* Chicago: U of Chicago P, 1999.

Ellmann, Mary. *Thinking about Women.* New York: Harcourt Brace Jovanovich, 1968.

Ellsworth, Phoebe C. "Sense, Culture and Sensibility." In Kitayama and Markus 23–50.

Erenberg, Lewis A. *Steppin' Out: New York Nightlife and the Transformation of American Culture, 1890–1930.* Chicago: U of Chicago P, 1981.

Exman, Eugene. *The Brothers Harper: A Unique Publishing Partnership and Its Impact upon the Cultural life of America from 1817 to 1853.* New York: Harper & Row, 1965.

———. *The House of Harper: One Hundred and Fifty Years of Publishing.* New York: Harper & Row, 1967.

Fabrikant, Geraldine. "Murdoch Bets Heavily on a Global Vision." *New York Times* 29 July 1996, natl. ed.: C1, C6–C7.

Felski, Rita. *The Gender of Modernity.* Cambridge: Harvard UP, 1995.

Fern, Fanny [Sara Payson Willis Parton]. "The Modern Old Maid." Orig. in *New York Ledger* June 5, 1869. Rpt. in *Ruth Hall & Other Writings,* ed. Joyce W. Warren. American Women Writers series. New Brunswick, N.J.: Rutgers UP, 1986. 360–61.

Fetterley, Judith. "Commentary: Nineteenth-Century American Women Writers and the Politics of Recovery." *American Literary History* 6 (fall 1994): 600–611.

Fisher, Philip. 1985. *Hard Facts: Setting and Form in the American Novel.* Rpt. New York: Oxford UP, 1987.

Flandrin, Jean-Louis. *Families in Former Times: Kinship, Household and Sexuality.* 1976. Trans. Richard Southern. Cambridge: Cambridge UP, 1979.

Fliegelman, Jay. *Declaring Independence: Jefferson, Natural Language, and the Culture of Performance*. Stanford: Stanford UP, 1993.

Fogel, Daniel Mark. *A Companion to Henry James Studies*. Westport, Conn.: Greenwood P, 1993.

Ford, James L. *The Literary Shop and Other Tales*. 1894. 2d ed. New York: Geo. H. Richmond, 1895.

Ford, Mary K. "Some Recent Women Short Story Writers." *Bookman* 27 (April 1908): 152–61.

Foster, Edward. *Mary E. Wilkins Freeman*. New York: Hendricks, 1956.

Foucault, Michel. "What Is an Author?" In *Textual Strategies: Perspectives in Post-structuralist Criticism*, ed. Josué V. Harari. Ithaca: Cornell UP, 1979. 141–60.

Frazier, David L. "Howells' Symbolic Houses: The Plutocrats and Palaces." *American Literary Realism* 11 (1977): 267–79.

Freedman, Jonathan. *Professions of Taste: Henry James, British Aestheticism, and Commodity Culture*. Stanford: Stanford UP, 1990.

———. *The Temple of Culture: Assimilation and Anti-Semitism in Literary Anglo-America*. New York: Oxford UP, 2000.

Freeman, Mary E. Wilkins. *By the Light of the Soul: A Novel*. New York: Harper & Brothers, 1907.

———. *The Copy-Cat and Other Stories*. 1914. Short Story Index Reprint series. Freeport, N.Y.: Books for Libraries P, 1970.

———. *The Fair Lavinia and Others*. New York: Harper & Brothers, 1907.

——— *A Humble Romance and Other Stories*. 1887. Rpt. New York: AMS P, 1970.

———. *The Infant Sphinx: Collected Letters of Mary E. Wilkins Freeman*. Ed. Brent L. Kendrick. Metuchen, N.J.: Scarecrow P, 1985.

———. *A Mary Wilkins Freeman Reader*, ed. Mary R. Reichardt. Lincoln: U of Nebraska P, 1997.

———. *Six Trees*. New York: Harper & Brothers, 1903.

———. *The Winning Lady and Others*. New York: Harper & Brothers, 1909.

Gaines, Clarence H. " 'The Whole Family.' " *North American Review* 188 (December 1908): 928–30.

Gambone, Philip. "Moon over Manatee." Review of *Naked Came the Manatee*. *New York Times Book Review* 2 March 1997: 18.

Garrison, Dee. *Mary Heaton Vorse: The Life of an American Insurgent*. Philadelphia: Temple UP, 1989.

"George T. Tobin, Artist and Illustrator Who Did Portraits of the Noted, Is Dead." *New York Times* 7 May 1956: 27.

Gilman, Charlotte Perkins. *Women and Economics: A Study of the Economic*

Relation between Men and Women as a Factor in Social Evolution. 1898. Ed.
Carl N. Degler. New York: Harper & Row-Harper Torchbooks, 1966.

Ginzburg, Carlo. "Microhistory: Two or Three Things That I Know about
It." Trans. John and Anne C. Tedeschi. *Critical Inquiry* 20 (Autumn
1993): 10–35.

Glasser, Leah Blatt. *In a Closet Hidden: The Life and Works of Mary E.
Wilkins Freeman.* Amherst: U of Massachusetts P, 1996.

Glazener, Nancy. *Reading for Realism: The History of a U.S. Literary
Institution, 1850–1910.* Durham: Duke UP, 1997.

Goldberg, David T. *Racist Culture: Philosophy and the Politics of Meaning.*
Cambridge: Basil Blackwell, 1993.

Gordon, Lynn D. *Gender and Higher Education in the Progressive Era.* New
Haven: Yale UP, 1990.

———. "The Gibson Girl Goes to College: Popular Culture and Women's
Higher Education in the Progressive Era, 1890–1920." *American Quarterly*
39.2 (summer 1987): 211–30.

Gordon, Steven L. "The Sociology of Sentiments and Emotion." In *Social
Psychology: Sociological Perspectives*, ed. Morris Rosenberg and Ralph H.
Turner. New York: Basic Books, 1981. 562–92.

Graff, Gerald. *Professing Literature: An Institutional History.* Chicago: U of
Chicago P, 1987.

Greenblatt, Stephen J. "Improvisation and Power." In *Literature and Society*,
ed. Eward W. Said. Baltimore: Johns Hopkins UP, 1980. 57–99.

Griffin, Robert J. "Anonymity and Authorship." *New Literary History* 30
(1999): 877–95.

Griffin, Susan M. *The Historical Eye: The Texture of the Visual in Late James.*
Boston: Northeastern UP, 1991.

Gussow, Mel. "John Updike, Impresario of Fictional Relay Race." *New York
Times* 2 August 1997, natl. ed.: 11.

———. "Now the Plot Quickens: Whodunit? Who Wunit?" *New York
Times* 13 September 1997, natl. ed.: B18.

Habegger, Afred. *Henry James and the "Woman Business."* New York:
Cambridge UP, 1989.

Habermas, Jürgen. *The Structural Transformation of the Public Sphere: An
Inquiry into a Category of Bourgeois Society.* 1962. Trans. Thomas Burger
with Frederick Lawrence. Cambridge: MIT P, 1989.

Hall, G. Stanley. "The Question of Coeducation." *Munsey's Magazine* 34.5
(February 1906): 588–92.

Hall, Stuart. "The Problem of Ideology: Marxism Without Guarantees."
1983. Rpt. in *Stuart Hall: Critical Dialogues in Cultural Studies*, ed. David
Morley and Kuan-Hsing Chen. New York: Routledge, 1996. 25–46.

Hall, Stuart, David Held, Don Hubert, and Kenneth Thompson. *Modernity: An Introduction to Modern Societies*. Cambridge: Polity P, 1995.

Halttunen, Karen. *Confidence Men and Painted Women: A Study of Middle-Class Culture in America, 1830–1870*. New Haven: Yale UP, 1982.

Harner, James L. *Literary Research Guide: A Guide to Reference Sources for the Study of Literatures in English and Related Topics*. 2d ed. New York: Modern Language Association, 1993.

"Harper's Bazar for 1907." *Harper's Bazar* 40 (December 1906): advt. supplement, 10–11.

Harper, J[oseph]. Henry. *The House of Harper: A Century of Publishing in Franklin Square*. New York: Harper & Brothers, 1912.

———. *I Remember*. New York: Harper & Brothers, 1934.

Harper, William R[ainey]. "On Co-education I: A Stage of Educational Development"; and "On Co-education II: Coeducation Capable of Modification in Adjustment to Special Situations." *Harper's Bazar* 39 (January and March 1905): 1–6, 195–98.

"HarperCollins Cancels Books in Unusual Step for Industry." *New York Times* 27 June 1997, natl. ed.: A1, C3.

Harris, Sharon M. *Rebecca Harding Davis and American Realism*. Philadelphia: U of Pennsylvania P, 1991.

Hart, James D. *The Popular Book: A History of America's Literary Taste*. Berkeley: U of California P, 1963.

Harvey, George. "Reflections Concerning Women." *Harper's Bazar* 41 (March 1907): 296–304.

———. "Reflections Concerning Women." *Harper's Bazar* 41 (May 1907): 518–22.

———. "Reflections Concerning Women." *Harper's Bazar* 41 (June 1907): 618–22.

Haskell, Thomas L. "Capitalism and the Origins of the Humanitarian Sensibility, Parts I and II." *American Historical Review* 90 (1985): 339–61, 547–66.

Hawkins, Chauncey J. *Will the Home Survive: A Study of Tendencies in Modern Literature*. New York: Thomas Whittaker, 1907.

Hayward, Jennifer. *Consuming Pleasures: Active Audiences and Serial Fictions from Dickens to Soap Opera*. Lexington: UP of Kentucky, 1997.

Hirsch, Michael. "Setting Course." [Special report on Rupert Murdoch.] *Newsweek* 127.7 (12 February 1996): 8–15.

Hirshey, Gerri. "Happy [   ] Day to You." *New York Times Magazine* 2 July 1995: 20–27, 34, 43–45.

Hochschild, Arlie Russell. *The Managed Heart: The Commercialization of Human Feeling*. Berkeley: U of California P, 1983.

Hoge, Warren. "Murdoch Blames Staff for Embarrassment over Hong Kong Book." *New York Times* 5 March 1998, natl. ed.: A4.

———. "Murdoch Halts a Book Critical of China." *New York Times* 28 February 1998, natl. ed.: A5.

Holloway, Lynette. " 'Star Trek' Book Draws a Lawsuit by Studio." *New York Times* 2 May 1998, natl. ed.: A12.

Holly, Flora Mai. "Notes on Some American Magazine Editors." *Bookman* 12 (December 1900): 357–68.

Howard, June. *Form and History in American Literary Naturalism.* Chapel Hill: U of North Carolina P, 1985.

———. "Unraveling Regions, Unsettling Periods: Sarah Orne Jewett and American Literary History." *American Literature* 68 (June 1996): 365–84.

Howells, William Dean. *The Coast of Bohemia: A Novel.* New York: Harper & Brothers, 1893.

———. *Fennel and Rue.* New York: Harper & Brothers, 1908.

———. *Life in Letters of William Dean Howells.* Ed. Mildred Howells. Vol. 2. Garden City, N.Y.: Doubleday, Doran, 1928.

———. *Literature and Life: Studies.* New York: Harper & Brothers, 1902.

———. *Selected Literary Criticism.* Vol. 2: *1886–1897.* Ed. Donald Pizer and others. Bloomington: Indiana UP, 1993.

———. *Selected Literary Criticism.* Vol. 3: *1898–1920.* Ed. Ronald Gottesman and others. Bloomington: Indiana UP, 1993.

Howells, William Dean, and Henry Mills Alden, eds. *Different Girls.* Harper's Novelettes. New York: Harper & Brothers, 1906.

Hulme, Peter. *Colonial Encounters: Europe and the Native Caribbean, 1492–1797.* New York: Routledge, 1986.

Hunter, Jane H. "Inscribing the Self in the Heart of the Family: Diaries and Girlhood in Late-Victorian America." *American Quarterly* 44 (1992): 51–81.

Inness, Sherrie A. *Intimate Communities: Representation and Social Transformation in Women's College Fiction, 1895–1910.* Bowling Green, Ohio: Bowling Green State U Popular P, 1995.

Jacobson, Marcia. *Being a Boy Again: Autobiography and the American Boy Book.* Tuscaloosa: U of Alabama P, 1994.

———. *Henry James and the Mass Market.* University, Ala.: U of Alabama P, 1983.

James, Henry. *The Complete Tales of Henry James.* Vol. 9: *1892–1898.* Ed. Leon Edel. New York: J. B. Lippincott, 1964.

———. *Literary Criticism: Essays on Literature; American Writers; English Writers.* Ed. Leon Edel. New York: Library of America, 1984.

———. *Literary Criticism: French Writers; Other European Writers; The*

Prefaces to the New York Edition. Ed. Leon Edel. New York: Library of
America, 1984.

———. "The Manners of American Women, Part 2." *Harper's Bazar* 41
(May 1907): 453–58.

———. "The Manners of American Women, Part 4." *Harper's Bazar* 41
(July 1907): 646–51.

———. *The Sacred Fount.* 1901. Rpt. New York: Grove, 1953.

———. "The Speech of American Women, Part 1." *Harper's Bazar* 40
(November 1906): 979–82.

———. "The Speech of American Women, Part 4." *Harper's Bazar* 41
(February 1906): 113–17.

Jameson, Fredric. "Marxism and Historicism." 1979. Rpt. in *The Ideologies of
Theory: Essays 1971–1986.* Vol. 2: *The Syntax of History.* Minneapolis: U of
Minnesota P, 1988. 148–77.

———. *The Political Unconscious: Narrative as a Socially Symbolic Act.* Ithaca:
Cornell UP, 1981.

———. "The Realist Floor Plan." In *On Signs*, ed. Marshall Blonsky.
Baltimore: Johns Hopkins UP, 1985. 373–83.

Jaszi, Peter. "On the Author Effect: Contemporary Copyright and
Collective Creativity." In *The Construction of Authorship: Textual
Appropriation in Law and Literature*, ed. Martha Woodmansee and
Peter Jaszi. Durham: Duke UP, 1994. 29–56.

Johnson, Richard. "What Is Cultural Studies Anyway?" *Social Text* 16
(1987): 38–80.

Jordan, David Starr. "The Question of Coeducation." *Munsey's Magazine*
34.6 (March 1906): 683–88.

Jordan, Elizabeth G[arver]. *Black Butterflies: A Story of Youth.* New York:
Century, 1927.

———. *The Devil and the Deep Sea.* New York: A. L. Burt, 1929.

———. *Faraway Island.* New York: D. Appleton-Century, 1941.

———. *The Four-Flusher: The Story of a Woman of Action.* New York:
Century, 1931.

———. *May Iverson—Her Book.* 1904. Short Story Index Reprint series.
Freeport, N.Y.: Books for Libraries P, 1969.

———. *May Iverson Tackles Life.* New York: Harper & Brothers, 1912.

———. *May Iverson's Career.* New York: Harper & Brothers, 1914.

———. *Page Mr. Pomeroy.* New York: D. Appleton-Century, 1934.

———. Papers. Manuscripts and Archives Division, The New York Public
Library, Astor, Lenox and Tilden Foundations.

———, ed. *The Sturdy Oak: A Composite Novel of American Politics.* 1917.
Intro. Ida H. Washington. Athens: Ohio UP, 1998.

————. *Tales of the City Room.* New York: Charles Scribner's Sons, 1898.

————. *Tales of the Cloister.* 1901. Short Story Index Reprint series. Freeport, N.Y.: Books for Libraries P, 1970.

————. *Three Rousing Cheers.* New York: D. Appleton-Century, 1938.

————. *The Trap.* New York: D. Appleton-Century, 1937.

————. *The Wings of Youth.* New York: Harper & Brothers, 1918.

————. "With the Editor." *Harper's Bazar* 40 (August 1906): 762–64.

————. "With the Editor." *Harper's Bazar* 41 (December 1907): 1248–49.

————. "With the Editor." *Harper's Bazar* 42 (December 1908): 1266–67.

Kaestle, Carl F., Helen Damon-Moore, Lawrence C. Stedman, Katherine Tinsley, and William Vance Trollinger Jr. *Literacy in the United States: Readers and Reading since 1880.* New Haven: Yale UP, 1991.

Kaplan, Amy. "Manifest Domesticity." *American Literature* 70 (1998): 581–606.

————. *The Social Construction of American Realism.* Chicago: U of Chicago P, 1988.

Kaplan, Fred. *Sacred Tears: Sentimentality in Victorian Literature.* Princeton: Princeton UP, 1987.

Kasson, John F. *Rudeness and Civility: Manners in Nineteenth-Century Urban America.* New York: Hill and Wang–Farrar Straus and Giroux, 1990.

Kelley, Mary. "Commentary on Barbara Welter, 'The Cult of True Womanhood: 1820–1860' (1966)." In *Locating American Studies: The Evolution of a Discipline*, ed. Lucy Maddox. Baltimore: Johns Hopkins UP, 1999. 67–70.

————. *Private Woman, Public Stage: Literary Domesticity in Nineteenth-Century America.* New York: Oxford UP, 1984.

Kelly, Florence Finch. " 'The Whole Family' and Its Troubles: Co-operative Novel by Twelve Leading Literary Lights Achieves an Impression of the Comedy of Confussion [*sic*]." *New York Times* 23 October 1908 (first part of two-part book supplement, dated October 23 and 24): 590.

Kelly, Joan. *Women, History, and Theory: The Essays of Joan Kelly.* Chicago: U of Chicago P, 1984.

Kendrick, Brent L. "General Introduction." In *The Infant Sphinx: Collected Letters of Mary E. Wilkins Freeman.* Ed. Brent L. Kendrick. Metuchen, N.J.: Scarecrow P, 1985. 1–31.

Kerber, Linda K. "Separate Spheres, Female Worlds, Woman's Place: The Rhetoric of Women's History." *Journal of American History* 75 (June 1988): 9–39.

Kermode, Frank. 1966. *The Sense of an Ending: Studies in the Theory of Fiction.* New York: Oxford UP, 1975.

Kesey, Ken. Introduction to *Caverns: A Novel*, by O. U. Levon [Robert

Blucher, Ben Bochner, James Finley, Jeff Forester, Bennett Huffman, Lynne Jeffress, Ken Kesey, Neil Lidstrom, H. Highwater Powers, Jane Sather, Charles Varani, Meredith Wadley, Likia Yukman, and Ken Zimmerman]. New York: Penguin, 1990.

Kessler, Carol Farley. *Elizabeth Stuart Phelps*. Boston: Twayne, 1982.

Kilcup, Karen L. "The Conversation of 'The Whole Family': Gender, Politics, and Aesthetics in Literary Tradition." In *Soft Canons: American Women Writers and Masculine Tradition*, ed. Karen L. Kilcup. Iowa City: U of Iowa P, 1999. 1–24.

Kitayama, Shinobu, and Hazel Rose Markus, eds. *Emotion and Culture: Empirical Studies of Mutual Influence*. Washington, D.C.: American Psychological Association, 1994.

Koestenbaum, Wayne. *Double Talk: The Erotics of Male Literary Collaboration*. New York: Routledge, 1989.

Lauter, Paul. *Canons and Contexts*. New York: Oxford UP, 1991.

Levine, Lawrence W. *Highbrow/Lowbrow: The Emergence of Cultural Hierarchy in America*. Cambridge: Harvard UP, 1988.

Lewin, Tamar. "American Colleges Begin to Ask, 'Where Have All the Men Gone?'" *New York Times* 6 December 1998, natl. ed.: 1, 38.

Lewis, Sinclair, and Erik Axel Karlfeldt. *Addresses on the Occasion of the Award of the Nobel Prize, Stockholm, December, 1930*. New York: Harcourt, Brace, n.d.

Little, Carl. *Edward Hopper's New England*. San Francisco: Pomegranate Artbooks–Chameleon, 1993.

Lorde, Audre. *Sister Outsider: Essays and Speeches*. Trumansberg, N.Y.: Crossing P, 1984.

Lowry, Richard S. "Domestic Interiors: Boyhood Nostalgia and Affective Labor in the Gilded Age." In Pfister and Schnog 111–30.

———. *"Littery Man": Mark Twain and Modern Authorship*. New York: Oxford UP, 1996.

Lubin, David M. "Modern Psychological Selfhood in the Art of Thomas Eakins." In Pfister and Schnog 133–66.

Lukács, Georg. *Studies in European Realism*. New York: Universal Library–Grosset & Dunlap, 1964.

Lutz, Catherine A. *Unnatural Emotions: Everyday Sentiments on a Micronesian Atoll and Their Challenge to Western Theory*. Chicago: U of Chicago P, 1988.

Lutz, Catherine A., and Lila Abu-Lughod, eds. *Language and the Politics of Emotion*. New York: Cambridge UP, 1990.

Lyall, Sarah. "Murdoch Apologizes to Ex-Hong Kong Chief for Canceled Book." *New York Times* March 7, 1998, natl. ed.: A3.

MacCabe, Colin. "Realism and the Cinema: Notes on Some Brechtian Theses." *Screen* 15.2 (1974): 7–29.

Maddox, Lucy, ed. *Locating American Studies: The Evolution of a Discipline.* Baltimore: Johns Hopkins UP, 1999.

Madison, Charles A. *Book Publishing in America.* New York: McGraw-Hill, 1966.

———. *Irving to Irving: Author-Publisher Relations 1800–1974.* New York: R. R. Bowker, 1974.

Margolis, Anne T. *Henry James and the Problem of Audience: An International Act.* Studies in Modern Literature 49. Ann Arbor: UMI Research P, 1981.

Marks, Patricia. *Bicycles, Bangs, and Bloomers: The New Woman in the Popular Press.* Lexington: U of Kentucky P, 1990.

Marsh, Margaret. *Suburban Lives.* New Brunswick, N.J.: Rutgers UP, 1990.

———. "Suburban Men and Masculine Domesticity, 1870–1915." *American Quarterly* 40.2 (June 1988): 165–86.

Marshall, David. *The Surprising Effects of Sympathy: Marivaux, Diderot, Rousseau, and Mary Shelley.* Chicago: U of Chicago P, 1988.

Martin, George R. R., ed. *Wild Cards: A Mosaic Novel.* New York: Bantam-Spectra, 1987.

May, Elaine Tyler. *Great Expectations: Marriage and Divorce in Post-Victorian America.* Chicago: U of Chicago P, 1980.

May, Henry F. *The End of American Innocence: A Study of the First Years of Our Own Time, 1912–1917.* 1959. Rpt. New York: Oxford UP, 1979.

McAlester, Virginia, and Lee McAlester. *A Field Guide to American Houses.* New York: Knopf, 1984.

McCall, Laura. " 'Not So Wild a Dream': The Domestic Fantasies of Literary Men and Women, 1820–1860." In *A Shared Experience: Men, Women, and the History of Gender,* ed. Laura McCall and Donald Yacovone. New York: New York UP, 1998. 176–94.

———. "Symmetrical Minds: Literary Men and Women in Antebellum America." Diss. U of Michigan, 1988.

McDowell, Edwin. "HarperCollins Buys 3 Jeffrey Archer Books." *New York Times* 10 July 1990, microfilm ed.: C20.

McGann, Jerome J. 1983. *A Critique of Modern Textual Criticism.* Charlottesville: UP of Virginia, 1992.

McGrady, Mike. *Stranger Than Naked; or, How to Write Dirty Books for Fun and Profit: A Manual.* New York: Peter H. Wyden, 1970.

Meese, Elizabeth A. *Crossing the Double-Cross: The Practice of Feminist Criticism.* Chapel Hill: U of North Carolina P, 1986.

Merish, Lori. "Sentimental Consumption: Harriet Beecher Stowe and the

Aesthetics of Middle-Class Ownership." *American Literary History* 8 (1996): 1–33.

Miller, D. A. *Narrative and Its Discontents: Problems of Closure in the Traditional Novel.* Princeton: Princeton UP, 1981.

Miller, Elise. "The Feminization of American Realist Theory." *American Literary Realism 1870–1910* 23 (1990): 20–41.

Mintz, Steven, and Susan Kellogg. *Domestic Revolutions: A Social History of American Family Life.* New York: Free P-Macmillan, 1988.

Missing in Manhattan. By the Adams Round Table [Mary Higgins Clark, Justin Scott, Lucy Freeman, Judith Kelman, Stanley Cohen, Warren Murphy, Mickey Friedman, Thomas Chastain, Joyce Harrington, and Dorothy Salisbury Davis; created by Bill Adler]. New York: Berkley Prime Crime, 1992.

Mizruchi, Susan L. *The Science of Sacrifice: American Literature and Modern Social Theory.* Princeton: Princeton UP, 1998.

Modleski, Tania. *Loving with a Vengeance: Mass-Produced Fantasies for Women.* Hamden, Conn.: Archon-Shoe String, 1982.

Montgomery, Maureen E. *Displaying Women: Spectacles of Leisure in Edith Wharton's New York.* New York: Routledge, 1998.

Montrose, Louis. "New Historicisms." In *Redrawing the Boundaries: The Transformation of English and American Literary Studies,* ed. Stephen Greenblatt and Giles Ginn. New York: Modern Language Association, 1992. 392–418.

Morawski, Jill G. "Educating the Emotions: Academic Psychology, Textbooks, and the Psychology Industry, 1890-1940." In Pfister and Schnog 217-44.

Morgan, William M. "Public Engagments: Humanitarianism and Complicity in United States Literary Realism." Diss. Brandeis U, 2000.

Morris, Ann R., and Maggie Dunn. *The Composite Novel: The Short Story Cycle in Transition.* Studies in Literary Themes and Genres 6. New York: Twayne, 1995.

Morris, Willie. *New York Days.* New York: Little, Brown, 1993.

Morton, Donald, and Mas'ud Zavarzadeh. "The Cultural Politics of the Fiction Workshop." *Cultural Critique* 11 (winter 1988–89): 155–73.

Mosse, George L. *Nationalism and Sexuality: Middle-Class Morality and Sexual Norms in Modern Europe.* Madison: U of Wisconsin P, 1985.

Mott, Frank Luther. *A History of American Magazines.* 5 vols. Cambridge: Harvard UP, 1930–68.

"Mrs. F. A. Shinn, Writer, Dies at 63." *New York Times* 25 June 1933: 22:1.

Murasaki. A Novel in Six Parts by Poul Anderson, Greg Bear, Gregory

Benford, David Brin, Nancy Kress, and Frederik Pohl. Ed. Robert
　　Silverberg. New York: Bantam-Spectra, 1992.

"Murdoch Wins Collins, Promises Autonomy." *Publishers Weekly* 234.3
　　(20 January 1989): 16, 18.

Naked Came the Stranger. By Mike McGrady and others; Penelope Ashe,
　　pseud. New York: Lyle Stuart, 1969.

North, Elizabeth Lore. "Women Illustrators of Child Life." *Outlook* 78
　　(1 October 1904): 270–80.

O'Hagan, Anne. "The Confessions of a Professional Woman." *Harper's
　　Bazar* 41 (September 1907): 848–54.

———. "The Married Woman and the Spinster." *Harper's Bazar* 41 (July
　　1907): 630–35.

———. "The Neurotic Spinster in Literature." *Harper's Bazar* 41 (October
　　1907): 971–73.

———. "Some Compensations of Spinsterhood." *Harper's Bazar* 41
　　(February 1907): 106–12.

———. "The Spinster's Men Friends." *Harper's Bazar* 41 (March 1907):
　　227–32.

———. "What Becomes of Our Ideals?" *Harper's Bazar* 41 (August 1907):
　　747–51.

Ohmann, Richard. *Selling Culture: Magazines, Markets and Class at the Turn
　　of the Century.* New York: Verso, 1996.

O'Neill, William L. *Divorce in the Progressive Era.* New Haven: Yale UP,
　　1967.

Oxenhandler, Neal. "The Changing Concept of Literary Emotion: A
　　Selective History." *New Literary History* 20 (1988): 105–21.

Palmer, Stephanie. "Thwarted Travelers: Region and Class in Late
　　Nineteenth-Century American Literature." Diss. U of Michigan, 1998.

Panzer, Mary. *Mathew Brady and the Image of History.* Washington, D.C.:
　　Smithsonian Institution P for the National Portrait Gallery, 1997.

Pearce, Roy Harvey. "Historicism Once More." 1958. Rpt. in *Historicism
　　Once More: Problems and Occasions for the American Scholar.* Princeton:
　　Princeton UP, 1969. 3–45.

Peiss, Kathy. *Cheap Amusements: Working Women and Leisure in Turn-of-the-
　　Century New York.* Philadelphia: Temple UP, 1986.

Perkins, David. *Is Literary History Possible?* Baltimore: Johns Hopkins UP,
　　1992.

Perosa, Sergio. *Henry James and the Experimental Novel.* Charlottesville: U
　　of Virginia P, 1978.

Pfister, Joel, and Nancy Schnog, eds. *Inventing the Psychological: Toward a
　　Cultural History of Emotional Life in America.* New Haven: Yale UP, 1997.

Phelps [Ward], Elizabeth Stuart. *The Gates Ajar.* 1869. Rpt. Ed. Helen
Scotin Smith. Cambridge: Belknap–Harvard UP, 1964.
———. *The Story of Avis.* 1877. Rpt. Ed. Carol Farley Kessler. New
Brunswick, N.J.: Rutgers UP, 1985.
———. *Walled In: A Novel.* New York: Harper & Brothers, 1907.
Pinch, Adela. *Strange Fits of Passion: Epistemologies of Emotion, Hume to
Austen.* Stanford: Stanford UP, 1996.
Poovey, Mary. *Uneven Developments: The Ideological Work of Gender in
Mid-Victorian England.* Chicago: U of Chicago P, 1988.
Poster, Mark. *Critical Theory of the Family.* New York: Seabury, 1978.
Pratt, Mary Louise. *Imperial Eyes: Travel Writing and Transculturation.* New
York: Routledge, 1992.
Prendergast, Christopher, and Margaret Cohen, eds. *Spectacles of Realism:
Gender, Body, Genre.* Minneapolis: U of Minnesota P, 1995.
Radway, Janice A. *A Feeling for Books: The Book-of-the-Month Club, Literary
Taste, and Middle-Class Desire.* Chapel Hill: U of North Carolina P, 1997.
Reichardt, Mary R. "Mary Wilkins Freeman: One Hundred Years of
Criticism." *Legacy* 4.2 (1987): 31–44.
Rinehart, Daisy. "The Exceeding Wiliness of Mrs. Mimms." *Harper's Bazar*
42 (January 1908): 27–33.
Romero, Lora. *Home Fronts: Domesticity and Its Critics in the Antebellum
United States.* Durham: Duke UP, 1997.
Roof, Judith. *Come as You Are: Sexuality and Narrative.* New York: Columbia
UP, 1996.
Rosaldo, Michelle Z. "Toward an Anthropology of Self and Feeling." In
Culture Theory: Essays on Mind, Self and Emotion, ed. Richard A. Shweder
and Robert A. LeVine. New York: Cambridge UP, 1984. 137–57.
Rose, Nikolas. *The Psychological Complex: Psychology, Politics and Society in
England, 1869–1939.* Boston: Routledge & Kegan Paul, 1985.
Rosenberg, Rosalind. *Beyond Separate Spheres: Intellectual Roots of Modern
Feminism.* New Haven: Yale UP, 1982.
Ross, Ishbel. *Ladies of the Press: The Story of Women in Journalism by an
Insider.* New York: Harper & Brothers, 1936.
Rotundo, E. Anthony. *American Manhood: Transformations in Masculinity
from the Revolution to the Modern Era.* New York: Basic Books–Harper-
Collins, 1993.
Rubin, Joan Shelley. *The Making of Middlebrow Culture.* Chapel Hill: U of
North Carolina P, 1992.
Rudnick, Lois. "The New Woman." In *1915, The Cultural Moment: The New
Politics, the New Woman, the New Psychology, the New Art and the New*

Theatre in America, ed. Adele Heller and Lois Rudnick. New Brunswick, N.J.: Rutgers UP, 1991. 69–81.

Ryan, Mary P. *Cradle of the Middle Class: The Family in Oneida County, New York, 1790–1865*. Cambridge: Cambridge UP, 1981.

———. *The Empire of the Mother: American Writing about Domesticity 1830–1860*. 1982. Rpt. New York: Harrington Park P, 1985.

Sachs, Julius. "The Intellectual Reactions of Co-education." *Educational Review* 35 (May 1908): 466–75. [Address delivered before the Social Education Conference in Boston, March 6, 1908.]

Salmon, Richard. *Henry James and the Culture of Publicity*. New York: Cambridge UP, 1997.

Samuels, Shirley, ed. *The Culture of Sentiment: Race, Gender and Sentimentality in Nineteenth-Century America*. New York: Oxford UP, 1992.

Sánchez-Eppler, Karen. *Touching Liberty: Abolition, Feminism, and the Politics of the Body*. Berkeley: U of California P, 1993.

Schorer, Mark. *Sinclair Lewis: An American Life*. New York: McGraw-Hill, 1961.

Scobey, David. *Empire City: The Making and Meaning of the New York Cityscape, 1850–1890*. Philadelphia: Temple UP, forthcoming.

Screen Reader I: Cinema/Ideology/Politics. London: SEFT, 1977.

Sedgwick, Eve Kosofsky. *Epistemology of the Closet*. Berkeley: U of California P, 1990.

Severa, Joan L. *Dressed for the Photographer: Ordinary Americans and Fashion, 1840–1900*. Kent, Ohio: Kent State UP, 1995.

Sicherman, Barbara. "Sense and Sensibility: A Case Study of Women's Reading in Late-Victorian America." In Davidson, *Reading in America* 201–25.

Six of One by Half a Dozen of the Other: An Every Day Novel. By Harriet Beecher Stowe, Adeline D. T. Whitney, Lucretia P. Hale, Frederic W. Loring, Frederic B. Perkins, and Edward E. Hale. Boston: Roberts Brothers, 1872. Originally published serially in the magazine *Old and New*.

Smith, Adam. *The Theory of Moral Sentiments*. 1759. Rpt. as vol. 1 of *The Glasgow Edition of the Works and Correspondence of Adam Smith*. Ed. D. D. Raphael and A. L. MacFie. Oxford: Clarendon P, 1976.

Smith-Rosenberg, Carroll. *Disorderly Conduct: Visions of Gender in Victorian America*. New York: Knopf, 1985.

Snyder, Robert W. "Vaudeville and the Transformation of Popular Culture." In *Inventing Times Square: Commerce and Culture at the Crossroads of the World*, ed. William R. Taylor. Baltimore: Johns Hopkins UP, 1991. 133–46.

Solomon, Barbara Miller. *In the Company of Educated Women: A History of Women and Higher Education in America.* New Haven: Yale UP, 1985.

Sontag, Deborah. "A Magazine Is Unveiled, in More Ways Than One." *New York Times* 28 Apr. 2000, natl. ed.: A4.

Spiegelman, Art, and R. Sikoryak, eds. *The Narrative Corpse: A Chain-Story by 69 Artists.* Richmond, Va.: Raw Books and Gates of Heck, 1995.

Stallybrass, Peter. "Shakespeare, the Individual, and the Text." In *Cultural Studies,* ed. Lawrence Grossberg, Cary Nelson, and Paula A. Treichler. New York: Routledge, 1992. 593–610.

Stallybrass, Peter, and Allon White. *The Politics and Poetics of Transgression.* Ithaca: Cornell UP, 1986.

Stearns, Peter N., and Jan Lewis, eds. *An Emotional History of the United States.* History of Emotions series. New York: New York UP, 1998.

Steele, Phyllis Eileen. "Hungry Hearts, Idle Wives, and New Women: The American Novel Re-examines Nineteenth-Century Domestic Ideology, 1890–1917." Diss. U of Iowa, 1993.

Steinem, Gloria. "He Just Doesn't Get It." *New York Times Book Review* 21 May 1995: 47.

"Stephens, Alice Barber." *National Cyclopedia.* 1933 ed.

"Stephens, Alice Barber." *Notable American Women 1607–1950: A Biographical Dictionary.* Vol. 3, ed. Edward T. James and others. Cambridge: Harvard UP, 1971.

Stillinger, Jack. *Multiple Authorship and the Myth of Solitary Genius.* New York: Oxford UP, 1991.

Stimson, Alice Bartlett. "When the College Girl Comes Home." *Harper's Bazar* 42 (August 1908): 797–99.

Stoler, Ann Laura. *Race and the Education of Desire: Foucault's* History of Sexuality *and the Colonial Order of Things.* Durham: Duke UP, 1995.

Strychacz, Thomas. *Modernism, Mass Culture, and Professionalism.* New York: Cambridge UP, 1993.

Tassin, Algernon. *The Magazine in America.* New York: Dodd, Mead, 1916.

Taylor, Charles. *Sources of the Self: The Making of the Modern Identity.* Cambridge: Harvard UP, 1989.

Tebbel, John. *A History of Book Publishing in the United States.* Vol. 1: *The Creation of an Industry, 1630–1865.* New York: R. R. Bowker, 1972.

———. *A History of Book Publishing in the United States.* Vol. 2: *The Expansion of an Industry, 1865–1919.* New York: R. R. Bowker, 1975.

Thomas, Brook. *American Literary Realism and the Failed Promise of Contract.* Berkeley: U of California P, 1997.

Thomas, M. Carey. "Present Tendencies in Women's College and University Education." *Educational Review* 35 (January 1908): 64–85. [Address delivered at the Quarter-Centennial Meeting of the Association of Collegiate Alumnae, Boston, November 6, 1907.]

Thoreau, Henry David. 1854. *Walden, or Life in the Woods*. Ed. J. Lyndon Shanley. Princeton: Princeton UP, 1971.

Tichi, Cecelia. "Women Writers and the New Woman." In *Columbia Literary History of the United States*, ed. Emory Elliott. New York: Columbia UP, 1988. 589–606.

Tintner, Adeline R. "Autobiography as Fiction: 'The Usurping Consciousness' as Hero of James's Memoirs." *Twentieth Century Literature* 23 (1977): 239–60.

———. "*Roderick Hudson*: A Centennial Reading." *Henry James Review* 2 (1980–81): 172–98.

Todd, Ellen Wiley. *The "New Woman" Revised: Painting and Gender Politics on Fourteenth Street*. Berkeley: U of California P, 1993.

Todd, Janet. *Sensibility: An Introduction*. New York: Methuen, 1986.

Tompkins, Jane. *Sensational Designs: The Cultural Work of American Fiction 1790–1860*. New York: Oxford UP, 1985.

Torgovnick, Marianna. *Closure in the Novel*. Princeton: Princeton UP, 1981.

Trachtenberg, Alan. *The Incorporation of America: Culture and Society in the Gilded Age*. New York: Farrar, Straus and Giroux–Hill and Wang, 1982.

Trahey, Jane, ed. *Harper's Bazaar: 100 Years of the American Female*. New York: Random House, 1967.

Triggs, Oscar Lovell. *Chapters in the History of the Arts and Crafts Movement*. Chicago: Bohemia Guild of the Industrial Art League, 1902.

Van Hise, James. *Trek: The Printed Adventures*. Las Vegas: Pioneer Books, 1993.

Van Rensselaer, M. G. "American Country Dwellings. I." *Century* 32 (May 1886): 3–20.

[Vorse, Mary Heaton.] *Autobiography of an Elderly Woman*. 1911. Rpt. New York: Arno–New York Times, 1974.

———. "The Land of Old Age. IV: The Conventions of Age." *Harper's Bazar* 41 (April 1907): 363–68.

Vorse, Mary Heaton. *A Footnote to Folly: Reminiscences of Mary Heaton Vorse*. New York: Farrar & Rinehart, 1935.

———. 1930. *Strike!* Rpt. Chicago: U of Illinois P, 1991.

———. "Tourist Third." *Harper's Monthly Magazine* 158 (March 1929): 508–15.

———. *The Very Little Person*. Cambridge: Riverside-Houghton Mifflin, 1911.

Walbridge, Earle F. "Novels by Several Hands." *The Colophon: A Quarterly for Bookmen*, n.s., 3 (summer 1938): 364–76.

Walker, Dorothea. *Alice Brown*. New York: Twayne, 1974.

Wall, Helena M. *Fierce Communion: Family and Community in Early America*. Cambridge: Harvard UP, 1990.

Wardley, Lynn. "'The Angel at the Grave': Evolution and the Female Naturalist." Talk delivered at the conference "19th-Century American Women Writers in the 21st Century." Hartford, Conn., June 2, 1996.

Warhol, Robyn R. "As You Stand, So You Feel and Are: The Crying Body and the Nineteenth-Century Text." In *Tattoo, Torture, Mutilation, and Adornment: The Denaturalization of the Body in Culture and Text*, ed. Frances E. Mascia-Lees and Patricia Sharpe. Albany: State U of New York P, 1992. 100–125.

Warren, Joyce W., ed. *The (Other) American Traditions: Nineteenth-Century American Women Writers*. New Brunswick, N.J.: Rutgers UP, 1993.

Warren, Joyce W., and Margaret Dickie, eds. *Challenging Boundaries: Gender and Periodization*. Athens: U of Georgia P, 2000.

Warren, Kenneth W. *Black and White Strangers: Race and American Literary Realism*. Chicago: U of Chicago P, 1993.

Watt, Ian. *The Rise of the Novel: Studies in Defoe, Richardson and Fielding*. Berkeley: U of California P, 1957.

Welter, Barbara. "The Cult of True Womanhood, 1820–1860." *American Quarterly* 18 (1966): 151–74. Rpt. in *Dimity Convictions: The American Woman in the Nineteenth Century*. Athens: Ohio UP, 1976.

Westbrook, Matthew David. "Invisible Countries: The Poetics of the American Information Commodity, 1891–1918." Diss. U of Michigan, 1996.

Westbrook, Perry D. *Mary Wilkins Freeman*. New York: Twayne, 1967.

Wexler, Laura. "Tender Violence: Literary Eavesdropping, Domestic Fiction, and Educational Reform." In Samuels 9–38.

[Whitelock, William Wallace.] *The Literary Guillotine*. New York: John Lane, 1903.

The Whole Family: A Novel by Twelve Authors. [William Dean Howells, Mary E. Wilkins Freeman, Mary Heaton Vorse, Mary Stewart Cutting, Elizabeth Jordan, John Kendrick Bangs, Henry James, Elizabeth Stuart Phelps, Edith Wyatt, Mary R. Shipman Andrews, Alice Brown, and Henry Van Dyke. New York: Harper & Brothers, 1908.

"'The Whole Family' and a Reminiscence." *Harper's Bazar* 42 (November 1908): n.p.

Wiebe, Robert H. *Self-Rule: A Cultural History of American Democracy*. Chicago: U of Chicago P, 1995.

Wierzbicka, Anna. "Emotion, Language, and Cultural Scripts." In Kitayama and Markus 133–96.

Williams, Raymond. *Keywords: A Vocabulary of Culture and Society*. New York: Oxford UP, 1976.

———. *Marxism and Literature*. London: Oxford UP, 1977.

Williamson, Judith. "Family, Education, Photography." 1986. Rpt. in *Culture/Power/History: A Reader in Contemporary Social Theory*, ed. Nicholas B. Dirks, Geoff Eley, and Sherry B. Ortner. Princeton: Princeton UP, 1994. 236–44.

Wilson, Christopher P. *The Labor of Words: Literary Professionalism in the Progressive Era*. Athens: U of Georgia P, 1985.

Wittgenstein, Ludwig. *Philosophical Investigations: The English Text of the Third Edition*. Trans. G. E. M. Anscombe. New York: Macmillan, 1958.

Woodmansee, Martha. "On the Author Effect: Recovering Collectivity." In *The Construction of Authorship: Textual Appropriation in Law and Literature*, ed. Woodmansee and Peter Jaszi. Durham: Duke UP, 1994. 15–28.

Woodmansee, Martha, and Peter Jaszi. "The Ethical Reaches of Authorship." *South Atlantic Quarterly* 95 (1996): 947–77.

"A Word at the Start." *Harper's New Monthly Magazine* 1.1 (June 1850): 1–2.

Wright, Gwendolyn. *Building the Dream: A Social History of Housing in America*. Cambridge: MIT P, 1981.

———. *Moralism and the Model Home: Domestic Architecture and Cultural Conflict in Chicago, 1873–1913*. Chicago: U of Chicago P, 1980.

Wyatt, Edith. *Every One His Own Way*. New York: McClure, Phillips, 1901.

———. *Great Companions*. 1917. Essay Index Reprint series. Freeport, N.Y.: Books for Libraries P, 1966.

———. Papers. Newberry Library, Chicago.

———. *True Love: A Comedy of the Affections*. 1903. Rpt. Intro. Babette Inglehart. Chicago: U of Illinois P, 1988.

Yacovone, Donald. " 'Surpassing the Love of Women': Victorian Manhood and the Language of Fraternal Love." In *A Shared Experience: Men, Women, and the History of Gender*, ed. Laura McCall and Donald Yacovone. New York: New York UP, 1998. 195–221.

Yarborough, Richard. Introduction to *Contending Forces: A Romance Illustrative of Negro Life North and South* (1900), by Pauline E. Hopkins. New York: Oxford UP, 1988.

Youmans, William Jay. "Individuality for Woman: Editor's Table." *Popular Science Monthly* September 1891. Rpt. in *Men's Ideas/Women's Realities: Popular Science, 1870–1915*, ed. Louise Michele Newman. New York: Pergamon P, 1985. 305–6.

Zagarell, Sandra A. "Narrative of Community: The Identification of a Genre." *Signs* 13 (1988): 498–527.

————. Introduction to Mary Wilkins Freeman, *A New England Nun and Other Stories*. New York: Penguin, 2000.

Zajonc, R. B., and Daniel N. McIntosh. "Emotions Research: Some Promising Questions and Some Questionable Promises." *Psychological Science* 3 (1992): 70–74.

Zboray, Ronald J. "Antebellum Reading and the Ironies of Technological Innovation." *American Quarterly* 40 (March 1988): 65–82.

————. *A Fictive People: Antebellum Economic Development and the American Reading Public*. New York: Oxford UP, 1993.

→ Index ←

Aging and elderly women, 18 (fig. 2),
   42 (fig. 6), 134–36, 137 (fig. 31), 138,
   171–72
Agnew, Jean-Christophe, 228, 234
Alden, Henry Mills, 19, 63, 85, 95–96,
   203
Aldrich, Thomas Bailey, 250
American Sociological Society, 113–14
Andrews, Mary Raymond Shipman,
   34, 122–23, 250–51, 272–73
Anthropology of emotions, 219–21,
   301 n.4
Architecture: dining rooms, 141–44,
   142 (fig. 32), 263–64, 264 (fig. 53);
   impact on family life, 123–25, 131,
   141–43, 295 n.10; mansard roof,
   125–26, 131
Armstrong, Nancy, 232, 235, 239
Art and aesthetics: commercialism,
   84, 261, 264–65; fashion, 18 (fig. 2),
   42 (fig. 6), 259–61; Henry James on,
   261–62; race and ethnicity, 146
Arts and Crafts movement, 260, 263–
   64
Art Students' League, 259, 260
Atherton, Gertrude, 185–86
Atlantic Monthly, 72, 81, 86–87
Authorship, 21–26, 31–32, 94

Bang, John Kendricks, 27, 33–34, 38,
   103, 153–54, 154 (figs. 34 and 35),
   169–70
Banta, Martha, 197, 198
Bauer, Dale, 26, 178–79
Bederman, Gail, 122, 251, 254
Bendixen, Alfred, 1, 14, 53, 147, 300 n.1
Berlant, Lauren, 239–40
Beveridge, Alfred, 122–23
Bohemianism, 133, 259–60, 263–64
Boy books, 34, 250–54
Brodhead, Richard: cult of domes-
   ticity, 233; high culture v. mass
   culture, 81, 264–65; on the liter-
   ary marketplace, 81, 84, 235–36; on
   sentimentality, 215–16
Brooks, Cleanth, 243–44
Brown, Alice: conclusion of *The Whole
   Family*, 274–75; on Elizabeth Tal-
   bert, 170, 171; and Henry James,
   277–78; on marriage, 273, 277, 281

Capitalism, 228–29, 239
Children, 34, 191–94, 250–55
Christy, Howard Chandler, 280–81
Clarke, Edward, 160–61
Class: in America, 80–85; in boy
   books, 254; family and, 109–10, 122;

Class (*continued*)
  literature, 258–59; sentimentality
  and, 234
Clemens, Samuel. *See* Twain, Mark
Coeducation: Howells on, 8, 106, 166;
  marriage and, 164–65, 272, 274,
  280–81; men and, 140–41, 162–65;
  and the New Woman, 20, 128–
  29, 140–41, 160–66; women in the
  university, 160–65
Collaborative fiction, 21–31, 129–30,
  189–90
Colonialism, 229–30, 240
Commercialism, 24–26, 84, 239, 261,
  264–65
Copyright law, international, 25, 94
Courtship, 138, 144, 169–70, 195, 263,
  271–77, 280–81, 299 n.20
Culture, American: architecture, 123–
  27, 131; commercialism, 24–26, 84,
  239, 261, 264–65; democracy and,
  80–87, 279; fashion, 18 (fig. 2), 42
  (fig. 6), 259–61; race and racism,
  86; women's magazines, 38–53,
  203–11, 208 (fig. 46), 209 (fig. 47),
  300 nn.26 and 27. *See also* Family;
  Harper & Brothers; *Harper's Bazar;*
  Sentimentality
Curtis, W. A., 161–62
Cutler, Martha Hill, 187–88, 263
Cutting, Mary Stewart: articles in
  Harper's Bazar, 115; on eating habits,
  143–44; on Elizabeth Talbert, 138,
  170, 171; on masculine domesticity,
  147; on middle-class culture, 144–
  46; on suburban life and marriage,
  146–50; wives' roles, 140–41, 149–50
Cvetkovich, Ann, 244

Damasio, Antonio, 221, 301 n.5
Dane, Stillman (suitor), 274–77, 281

Davis, Rebecca Harding, 242, 246, 270
Democracy, 80–87, 279
Detective fiction, 28
DiMaggio, Paul, 80, 81, 82, 84, 86
Dobson, Joanne, 218, 227
Domesticity: architecture, 123–26, 131,
  141–44, 142 (fig. 32), 263–64, 264
  (fig. 53), 295 n.10; consumerism and,
  235, 238–39, 303 n.15; men and, 120–
  23, 128, 131, 141; middle-class ideal
  of, 111, 131, 233–36; sentimentality
  and, 233–35; women and, 140–41,
  149–50, 231–33, 302 nn.12 and 13;
  work and leisure in, 147, 231–33, 237,
  302 nn.12 and 13
Douglas, Ann, 215, 218, 227, 243–44
Douglas-Tompkins debate, 215, 222,
  223, 233
Duneka, Frederick, 19, 36, 90, 95, 205

Education: Howells on, 8, 106, 166;
  marriage and, 164–65, 272, 274,
  280–81; men and, 140–41, 162–65;
  and the New Woman, 20, 128–
  29, 140–41, 160–66; women in the
  university, 160–65
Eliot, Charles William, 46 (fig. 10),
  189
Ellsworth, Phoebe, 220–21
Emotions, 217–25, 230–31, 275–76, 301
  n.4
Etiquette and manners: eating habits,
  140–44, 142 (fig. 32), 145 (fig. 33);
  expressions of sentimentality and,
  234; informality, 144–46; "Manners of American Women" (James),
  265–66
Mrs. Evarts (grandmother), 133–36,
  137 (fig. 31), 138
Exman, Eugene, 68, 73, 79, 91

Family: architecture's impact on, 123–

25, 131, 141-43; children, 34, 191-94, 250-55; coeducation's effects on, 166; elderly women and aging, 18 (fig. 2), 42 (fig. 6), 134-36, 137 (fig. 31), 138, 171-72; engagement and marriage, 150, 166, 280; gender roles in, 108-14, 120, 128-29, 141; individualism and, 106, 115-16; intimacy of, 102-4, 132; masculine domesticity, 120-21; relations between spouses, 140-41, 147-48; structures of, 9, 108, 112-13, 188, 191-94. *See also* Marriage; Spinster; *The Whole Family*

Fashion, 18 (fig. 2), 42 (fig. 6), 259-61

Foucault, Michel, 22

Freedman, Jonathan, 85, 265

Freeman, Mary Wilkins: on choice to marry, 168, 170-74, 177, 298 n.13; friendships between women, 175-78, 176 (fig. 38), 178 (fig. 39); future of the family, 150; life of, 173-75, 174 (fig. 37), 299 n.15; spinsters, 2, 8, 15, 19-20, 130-33, 168, 171-73, 201

Friendships, 175-78, 188-90, 251-53, 274-75

Gender: cult of domesticity, 231-33, 302 nn.12 and 13; empathy and sympathy, 230-31; gender roles in family, 108-14, 120, 128-29, 141; and identity, 232-33; kinship and, 188-90; literary criticism and, 243-44; sentimentality and, 215-16, 235, 239-44, 255

Gilman, Charlotte Perkins, 109, 113, 114, 199, 255

Glasser, Leah Blatt, 169, 174, 299 n.15

Goward, Harry (suitor), 144, 169-70, 271, 274, 280

Greeting cards, 239

Habegger, Alfred, 246, 247-48

Habermas, Jürgen, 24, 237-38, 240-41

Hagerty, James, 114, 122

Hall, G. Stanley, 162, 165-66, 251, 254

Hall, Stuart, 4

Halttunen, Karen, 233, 235

Harper, Fletcher, 60, 70, 88

Harper, J. Henry, 64-66, 68, 84, 88, 97, 99

Harper & Brothers: cultural diversity in publications, 86-87; family tradition of, 64-68, 73-80, 98-104, 291 n.6, 292 n.16; Franklin Square plant, 60-63, 61 (fig. 18), 75-77, 76 (figs. 25 and 26), 82-83; George S. Harvey and, 90-95, 97-99, 115, 199; influence on American reading and cultural life, 60-62, 71-73, 82-84; piracy and relations with authors, 69-70; reorganization of, 88-93, 96-101. *See also* Jordan, Elizabeth; *The Whole Family*

Harper's Bazar: articles on changes in the family, 114-15, 121-22, 165; articles on spinsters, 199-201, 200 (figs. 44 and 45); cover illustrations, 197-98; Elizabeth Jordan at, 38, 90-97, 102-3, 186-88; *Family* authors' relationships with, 14, 35-38, 94; Henry James and, 35-36, 265-66; middle class and, 64, 72, 82. *See also* Magazines, women's; *The Whole Family*

Harper's Monthly Magazine, 61-63, 72, 82

Harper's Weekly, 63-64

Harvey, George S., 90-95, 97-99, 115, 199

The House of Harper, 64-68

Howells, William Dean: on authorship, 24-25; on coeducation, 8,

Howells, William Dean (*continued*)
106, 166; *Harper's Bazar* and, 38;
on marriage, 106–7, 116–17, 132–33;
on the New Woman, 205–6, 260–
61; on privacy, 152–53; on realism,
279–80; relationship with Harper &
Brothers, 95; and *The Whole Family*,
13, 15, 19, 104–5, 115–16, 129–31, 171

Individuality, 106, 115–16, 139, 229

James, Henry: and Alice Brown, 277–
78; on the American woman, 140,
265–66; on art and aesthetics, 261–
62; on domesticity, 141, 247–48;
Elizabeth Jordan and, 35–36; Elizabeth Stuart Phelps and, 246, 248;
on Elizabeth Talbert (aunt), 170; on
sentimentality, 8, 242–43
Jordan, Elizabeth: early employment,
182–83; at *Harper's Bazar*, 38, 90–97,
102–3, 186–88; and Henry James,
35–36; individualism and the family,
115–16; on male domesticity, 121;
as New Woman, 96–97, 159–60,
187–90; at *New York World*, 183–
86; *Three Rousing Cheers*, 1, 179–80,
184 (fig. 41), 186, 204–5; working
women in her fiction, 190–92
Journalism, 151–56

Kaplan, Amy, 153, 240
Kaplan, Fred, 226–27
Kasson, John, 80–81
Kelley, Mary, 231, 240
Kellogg, Susan, 109, 112
Kerber, Linda, 110, 233
Kinship, 9, 108, 188

Lewis, Sinclair, 279–80
Literature and literacy: book distribution and, 71–72, 84; boy books,
250–54; commercialism, 264–65;

Harper & Brothers and, 72–73;
masculinization of, 279–80; realism
in, 269–70, 305 n.6; sentimentality
in, 227–28, 242–44; women's magazines, 38–53, 203–11, 208 (fig. 46),
209 (fig. 47), 300 nn.26 and 27. *See
also* Harper & Brothers; *Harper's
Bazar*

Madison, Charles, 71, 79
Magazines, women's, 38–53, 203–
11, 208 (fig. 46), 209 (fig. 47), 300
nn.26 and 27
Marriage: on choice to marry, 168,
170–74, 177, 298 n.13; coeducation,
164–65, 272, 274, 280–81; companionate marriage, 111, 147–48; courtship and family, 150, 195, 274–77,
280–81; Howells on, 106–7, 116–
17, 132–33; privacy in, 111, 140–41,
152–53
Marsh, Margaret, 120, 147
Marxist criticism, 4, 5, 7, 240
McClure, S. S., 89, 90
Men: boy books, 250–54; and coeducation, 140–41, 162–65; domesticity of, 120–23, 128, 141; friendships, 251–53, 252 (fig. 50), 274–75;
and sentimentality, 243–44, 255
Middle class: culture and, 85–86, 144–
46; in Harpers' publications, 64, 72,
82; literacy and, 85, 204–5; male domesticity, 120–23, 128; self-image of,
276; sentimentality and domesticity
in, 111, 131, 233–36
Mintz, Steven, 109, 112
Morgan, J. P., 88–89, 90
Morris, Willie, 99–100
Mosse, George, 236
Mott, Frank Luther, 53, 62, 64
Murdoch, Rupert, 100–101

New Woman: coeducation, 20, 128–29, 140–41, 160–66; fashion, 18 (fig. 2), 42 (fig. 6), 260–61; in *Harper's Bazar* cover illustrations, 197–98; kinship and, 188–90; spinster as, 2, 8, 19–20, 178–79, 199–202

New Woman (magazine), 206–11, 208 (fig. 46), 209 (fig. 47), 300 nn.26 and 27

New York World, 90, 183–86

O'Hagan, Anne, 115, 199–202, 300 n.24

Ohmann, Richard, 84–85, 86, 89

Perosa, Sergio, 32, 261, 262

Phelps, Elizabeth Stuart, 34–35, 171, 246–48, 272

Philosophy, 223–26

Physiology of emotions, 221–22

Prescott, Harriet Beardslee, 187–88

Price, Maria Talbert (daughter), 246–47

Price, Tom (son-in-law), 169–70

Privacy, 111, 140–41, 151–56, 203–4

Psychology, 220–21, 275–76, 301 n.5

Publicity, 151–53, 266–67

Putnam, George Palmer, 69

Race and racism: culture, American, 86; and domestic values, 122, 278–79; sentimentality, 229–30, 235, 242; slavery, 228

Realism, 269–71, 279–80, 305 n.6

Romanticism, 22–24, 280–81

Rosaldo, Michelle, 219–20

Rosenberg, Rosalind, 163–64

Salmon, Richard, 267, 268

Samuels, Shirley, 216

Sánchez-Eppler, Karen, 215–16, 240, 247

Sangster, Margaret, 96

Science fiction, 28–29

Sedgwick, Eve, 244

Sentimentality: American literature, 242–43; in boy books, 250–54; domesticity, 233–35; emotions and, 217–25, 230–31, 275–76, 301 n.4; gender and, 215–26, 235, 239–44, 255; Henry James on, 8, 242–43; moral sentiment, 224–26; race and racism, 229–30, 235, 242

Serial fiction, 21–31, 129–30, 189–90

Settlement houses, 260

Sexuality, 169, 175–77, 201

Shaw, Anna Howard, 189–90

Sicherman, Barbara, 203, 204

Slavery, 228

Small, Albion, 113, 114

Smith, Adam, 224–25, 227

Smith-Rosenberg, Carroll, 188

Spinster: on choice to marry, 168, 170–74, 177–78, 298 n.13; *Harper's Bazar* articles on, 199–201, 200 (figs. 44 and 45); as the New Woman, 2, 8, 19–20, 178–79, 199–202; otherness of, 130–33; role in family, 168–71, 178–79, 192–93

Stallybrass, Peter, 22, 24

Stephens, Alice Barber, 118–19, 135–36, 137 (fig. 31), 166, 167 (fig. 36), 281

Stimson, Alice Bartlett, 160–61, 165

Suffrage, women's, 188–90, 199, 201

Sutphen, van Tassel, 82–83, 97

Talbert, Ada Evarts (mother), 133–36, 137 (fig. 31), 138–39

Talbert, Alice (school girl), 194–95, 196 (fig. 42), 273–74

Talbert, Charles Edward (son), 138, 140–41, 144, 152, 259, 261, 272

Talbert, Cyrus (father), 120, 124–31, 138–39, 165, 281

Talbert, Elizabeth (aunt), 130–33, 138, 168–71

Talbert, Lorraine (daughter-in-law), 138–40, 141–44, 142 (fig. 32), 145 (fig. 33), 195, 263, 299 n.20

Talbert, Peggy (daughter), 161, 166, 167 (fig. 36), 271–74, 280–81

Talbot, Marion, 163–64

Taylor, Charles, 223–24

Tebbel, John, 58, 78, 290 n.1

Temple, Ned, 118, 120, 151–52, 258–59

Thanet, Octave, 257

Tompkins, Jane, 215, 216, 231

Twain, Mark, 15, 25, 95

Understanding Fiction, 243

University: psychology as academic discipline in, 275–76; women in, 162–65

Van Dyke, Henry, 19, 33, 37, 170, 278–82

Vaudeville, 8, 101, 104–5

Vorse, Mary Heaton: Bohemian lifestyle of, 133, 259; on elderly women and aging, 134–36, 137 (fig. 31), 138, 255; on Elizabeth Talbert, 170, 171; fiction writing of, 27, 33, 34, 37, 115, 136–37; future of the family, 150

Wales, Mary Elizabeth, 174–75

Wardley, Lynn, 236

Warren, Robert Penn, 243–44

Westbrook, Perry, 173–74

Wexler, Laura, 215–16, 227–28, 231, 235

The Whole Family: collaborative method in, 26–27, 104–5, 129–30; early twentieth century reflected in, 20–21; illustrations in, 118–19, 135–36, 137 (fig. 31), 166, 167 (fig. 36), 281; motif of family solidarity, 102–4; promotion of, 94–95; realism in, 270–71; reviews of, 53–57, 104; vaudeville, 8, 104–5

Wiebe, Robert, 71, 72, 85–86, 97

Wilde, Lyman (suitor), 138, 169, 195, 263, 277, 299 n.20

Wilson, Christopher, 89, 94, 95–96

Wittgenstein, Ludwig, 269

Women: in boy books, 254; coeducation, 128–29, 140–41, 160–66; domesticity, 140–41, 149–50, 231–36, 302 nn.12 and 13; elderly women and aging, 18 (fig. 2), 42 (fig. 6), 134–36, 137 (fig. 31), 138, 171–72; etiquette and manners, 140, 265–66; friendships between, 175–78, 176 (fig. 38), 178 (fig. 39), 188–90; in Harper's Bazar cover illustrations, 197–98; lifestyle choices and the New Woman, 158–59; and magazines, 38–53, 115, 203–5; New Woman (magazine), 206–11, 208 (fig. 46), 209 (fig. 47), 300 nn.26 and 27; roles as wives, 140–41, 149–50, 232; and sentimentality, 235, 239–40; women's suffrage, 188–90, 199, 201

Woodmansee, Martha, 22, 26

Woolson, Constance, 246

Work and leisure, 147, 231–33, 237, 302 nn.12 and 13

Wright, Gwendolyn, 123, 124, 127

Wyatt, Edith, 33–34, 37, 248–49, 272, 289 n.17

Zagarell, Sandra, 146–47, 191

Zboray, Ronald, 71, 236

June Howard is Professor of English, American Culture, and
Women's Studies at the University of Michigan. She is the author of
Form and History in American Literary Naturalism and the editor
of *New Essays on "Country of the Pointed Firs"*.

Library of Congress Cataloging-in-Publication Data
Howard June.
* Publishing the family / June Howard.
p. cm. — (New Americanists)
Includes bibliographical references and index.
ISBN 0-8223-2762-7 (acid-free paper) —
ISBN 0-8223-2771-6 (pbk. : acid-free paper)
1. Whole family. 2. Literature publishing—United States—History—
20th century. 3. Howells, William Dean, 1837–1920—Criticism and
interpretation. 4. Serialized fiction—United States—History and
criticism. 5. Domestic fiction, American—History and criticism.
6. Harper's bazar. I. Title. II. Series.
PS3545.H96 H69 2001
813'.52—dc21 2001033106